THE LYRE AND THE CROSS:
INCOMPATIBILITY OR SYMBIOSIS OF THE POETIC VEIN AND STRICT MONASTICISM IN THE POETRY OF ALUN IDRIS JONES, A WELSH NOVICE MONK

EVA SCHMID-MÖRWALD

1994
INSTITUT FÜR ANGLISTIK UND AMERIKANISTIK
UNIVERSITÄT SALZBURG
A-5020 SALZBURG
AUSTRIA

Front cover: Great Cloister at the charterhouse of Sélignac
© Huw Jones

ISBN 3-7052-0409-2

TO BERNHARD AND MY PARENTS

CONTENTS

	PREFACE	i
	ACKNOWLEDGEMENTS	ii
1.	**INTRODUCTION**	**1**
1.1.	General Aspects of the Relation Between Religion and Poetry	3
1.2.	Specifying the Sacred	6
1.3.	Sacred and Profane: Religious Poets of the Past	8
1.4.	The Two Vocations: (In-)Compatibility of the Poetic and Religious Existence	10
1.4.1.	The Carthusian Poet-Monk	12
1.4.2.	The Trappist Poet-Monk	15
2.	**THE MAKING OF A MONK**: ALUN IDRIS' CALL TO MONASTICISM	**17**
2.1.	Family Background	17
2.2.	Early Influences - Conversion to Roman Catholicism	18
2.3.	Brother David	20
2.4.	The Welsh Background: Cultural and Literary Heritage	24
2.5.	Literary Influences	29
2.6.	The Two Vocations in Alun Idris Jones	31
3.	**THE LYRE AND THE CROSS**: ALUN IDRIS' POETRY WRITTEN IN CONTEMPLATIVE ORDERS	**33**
3.1.	**THE CARTHUSIAN PERIOD**	**33**
3.1.1.	Poetry as a Mirror of Carthusian Life	34
3.1.1.1.	The Nature of Contemplative Life - the "Daily Routine"	34
3.1.1.2.	Solitude and Silence	48
3.1.1.3.	Retreat	60
3.1.1.4.	Main Feasts	67
3.1.1.5.	The Doubt, Fear and Despair of Carthusian Life: Poetry as an Outlet	81
3.1.1.6.	Recent, Unexpected Events as a Frequent Source of Inspiration	86
3.1.2.	Poetry as a Form of Meditation	94
3.1.2.1.	Grace and Providence	95
3.1.2.2.	Time, Death and Afterlife	102
3.1.2.3.	Memories	110
3.1.2.4.	The Power of the Word	115
3.1.2.5.	A Miscellany of Meditations	118

3.1.3.	Poetry as a Form of Prayer - the Importance of Music	125
3.1.3.1.	Community Prayers	126
3.1.3.2.	Personal Prayers	127
3.1.4.	The Affective Component: Poetry as a Means of Declaration and Celebration	130
3.1.4.1.	Enthusiasm for God	131
3.1.4.2.	The Love for La Trappe	134
3.1.5.	(In-)Compatibility of the Carthusian and the Poetic Vocation	138
3.2.	**THE TRAPPIST PERIOD**	**142**
3.2.1.	Poetry as a Mirror of Trappist Life	142
3.2.1.1.	The "Daily Routine"	142
3.2.1.2.	Fears and Concern about the Future	157
3.2.1.3.	Inner Tension and Despair	161
3.2.1.4.	Recent Events as a Stimulating Source of Poems	167
3.2.2.	Poetry as a Form of Meditation	175
3.2.2.1.	Grace	175
3.2.2.2.	Time, Death and Afterlife	181
3.2.2.3.	The Power of the Word	191
3.2.2.4.	Providence	199
3.2.2.5.	Apparitions	203
3.2.3.	Poetry of Hiraeth	208
3.2.3.1.	The Nature of Hiraeth	208
3.2.3.2.	The Hiraeth for Reclusion	210
3.2.3.3.	Other Poems of Hiraeth	217
3.2.4.	Hymns	223
3.2.5.	Feeling the Union with God: Poetry as a Means of Declaration and Celebration	228
3.2.6.	(In-)Compatibility of the Trappist and the Poetic Vocation	234
3.3.	**THE PERIOD OF RESTLESS SEARCH**	**237**
3.3.1.	Providence	238
3.3.2.	The Charismatic Renewal	240
3.3.3.	Hiraeth for Solitude and Silence, Reclusion	243
3.3.4.	Back to Enclosure - Celebrating the Unity with God	248
3.3.5.	Prayerful Meditations	252
3.3.6.	Memories	259
3.3.7.	Recent Events	261

3.4.	**INTERIM PERIOD OUTSIDE MONASTIC QUARTERS**	269
3.4.1.	Accumulated Feelings of Inner Strain: Poetry as an Outlet	269
3.4.2.	Religious Meditations	275
3.4.3.	Hymns	279
3.4.4.	Hiraeth	283
3.4.5.	Meditations on Time	287
3.4.6.	Celebrating Friendship and Love	291
3.4.7.	The Divine Pull: Celebrating the Love of God	308
3.4.8.	The Two Vocations: Complementary facets of one Person?	317
4.	**CONCLUSION**	**319**

APPENDIX I:	Timetables of a Day in the Life of Strictly Contemplative Monks	322
	1. The Carthusians	322
	2. The Trappists	323
	3. The Camaldolese	324
APPENDIX II:	Photos of Various Contemplative Monasteries	325
APPENDIX III:	A Selection of Unpublished Poems	335

5.	**BIBLIOGRAPHY**	**339**
5.1.	PRIMARY LITERATURE IN ENGLISH	339
5.1.1.	Poetry	339
5.1.2.	Prose	339
5.1.3.	Translations	339
5.1.4.	Unpublished English and French Poems	340
5.2.	SECONDARY LITERATURE IN ENGLISH	340
5.2.1.	Religion and Poetry	340
5.2.2.	Wales	345
5.2.3.	General Reference Books Cited in the Present Study	346
5.3.	PRIMARY LITERATURE IN WELSH	347
5.3.1.	Poetry	347
5.3.2.	Prose	348
5.3.3.	Translations into Welsh	348
5.3.4.	Published Music	348
5.3.5.	Interviews with the Poet	349
5.3.6.	Unpublished Welsh Poems	349
5.4.	SECONDARY LITERATURE IN WELSH	353

PREFACE

For this present study the entire corpus of English, French and Latin poems written by Alun Idris Jones has been considered and researched up to those written in 1991, a period which spans his life both as a Carthusian as well as a Trappist monk, terminating with his final entry to the Norbertine Canons at Kilnacrott, Ireland. His poetry being so firmly interwoven with his call to be a contemplative monk, research has also been made into the poet's personal background, particularly his life in monastic surroundings. Biographical details have either been woven into the text or are supplied in footnotes. Frequent references are made to letters from the poet to the present writer. This unpublished correspondence, a most valuable documentation in itself, has equally been used to shed light upon his poetic catharsis.

As regards theoretical expositions on life in the Carthusian and Trappist Orders, I have limited myself to a short description of a typical day in these monasteries, which can be found in Appendix I of this book. In view of the vast richness of literature about these orders any survey attempted on my part could hardly be more than a superficial outline. Thus, for more details concerning the history and development of these orders I refer the reader to the numerous volumes already written on the subject. However, I reproduce a number of photos taken by Huw Jones at the charterhouse in Sélignac and at La Trappe (Appendix II), which have not been published elsewhere and which might be considered unique, as permission to take photos in these monasteries is only very seldom given.

Alun Idris' English poetry is only one side of the coin: as a Welshman he was brought up bilingually, and a great number of his poems have been written in Welsh. Unfortunately, due to the invincible language barrier, it has been impossible for me to survey and discuss his entire literary output, the Welsh part being regretfully excluded. Nevertheless, impressed by the stirring nature and depth of his English lyrics, I felt the urge to draw attention to the work of this young, powerful poet. However, giving a comprehensive picture embracing all his verse will be, I hope, someone else's task. Nonetheless, the complete bibliography of his Welsh verse as well as secondary literature in Welsh about the poet up to July 1994 has been compiled and is included in chapters 5.3. and 5.4. of the present volume.

Alun Idris' poems have received so far little scholarly attention, his literary renown being limited to Wales. However, this poet, unknown to the world, provides a wealth of material which merits attention.

ACKNOWLEDGEMENTS

I should like to express my sincere thanks to Dozent Dr. James Hogg, whose guidance and advice over the years proved most valuable. I am deeply grateful for his constant encouragement and support during this project, in particular for his comments on the manuscript and for reading the final typescript.

I should equally like to thank Professor Dr. Franz Zaic for having facilitated my research and for his encouragement.

I also wish to acknowledge my sincere indebtedness to Brother David, whose letters have been most enlightening and helpful. The insight gained about the life in a contemplative monastery through this correspondence as well as through a number of interviews has been most informative, representing a reliable source of first hand information for a laywoman.

Furthermore, I am very grateful to: Dom Augustin Devaux of the charterhouse of Sélignac for sending me a summary of his still unpublished work about Carthusian Latin poets; Frater Marianus of Stift Engelszell for providing a detailed description of the horary in the Trappist monastery; Idris and Olwen Jones for the interviews I was allowed to make with them about their son; Huw Jones for allowing me to use the photographs taken at Sélignac; the Reverend Emyr Evans for his most interesting contribution concerning the importance of the Welsh background in the poetry of Alun Idris, an essay which has proved to be most valuable; Mrs. Nest Davies of *Plu'r Gweunydd*, for supplying a copy of an article about *Cri o Gell*; the staff of the University Library at Bangor for their help in the Welsh library section; and Richard Tinkler for his assistance in proof-reading the manuscript.

Finally, I should also like to thank my family, in particular my parents, my sister, and above all my husband for his understanding and assistance in the preparation of the manuscript. They have all given me invaluable moral support.

1. INTRODUCTION

In his preface to *Religious Trends in English Poetry*, H.N. Fairchild (1939, vii) felt obliged to defend the relevance of his study, being fully aware of a possible lack of appreciation, perhaps even opposition that he might be confronted with: "Though this project will hardly arouse much popular enthusiasm ..." This statement, uttered more than half a century ago, is still valid today and may well be applied to the present thesis, too: the general interest in literature is perhaps only latent nowadays, with even less enthusiasm for poetry. Or, as Michael Roberts poignantly wrote: "More often than prose or mathematics, poetry is received in a hostile spirit, as if its publication were an affront to the reader" (Roberts 1982, 21). As regards religious poetry, public or private interest is of an even more restricted extent. Religion is likely to be regarded as something intensely private, which it doubtless is, and people tend to shrink from intruding on another's privacy, at least as far as their religious poetic utterances are concerned.

The modern mind tends to trust logic far more than facts or manifestations which reach beyond his/her understanding, things which - if at all - can only be grasped by feeling and belief. Indifference, negation and scepticism are features of the prevailing attitude amongst modern western minds. Though the existence of religion and belief is not disputed, it is restricted to those who seem naive enough to believe. Religion - especially religion of that emotional and imaginative sort which inspires poetic expression - seems to be at low tide. It is smiled at, confronted with indifference, or even hostility. And yet, religious poetry can be just as startling, or boring, as other types of poetry: that is to say that the religious nature of a poem does not exclude it from being genuine poetry.

When the two vocations meet in one person - the religious to devote one's entire life to God, and the poetic vocation to be a true poet -, the poet-monk has to investigate the possible union of the two, a problem which might be difficult to solve in a strictly contemplative monastery. Alun Idris Jones, alias Brother David, a young Welsh novice monk, is a contemporary example of a poet-monk trying to blend the two vocations. It cannot only be a personal decision, for the monk is part of the monastic community and has to obey his superiors. His decision must be in accordance with the order's attitude. Frequently, the result depends on the question of whether the poet-monk ranks himself amongst the group of "occasional" or "vocational" poets; this will be discussed later.

The contemplative monk aims at being close to God, feeling Him, experiencing Him: if his lyrical abilities allow him to capture such moments of intense love in verse form, he enables his readers to share the bliss experienced, offering glances at a realm of solitude otherwise unknown. Contemplative monks lead the life of semi-hermits. The idea of becoming a hermit, a recluse, has always been tempting to Alun Idris. Jacques Doyon writes about the medieval recluses, who existed in great number:

> Ces héroïnes de l'amour fou sont des personnages de tragédies de Racine. Elles vivent leur passion dévorante et mystique dans une tension effrayante, ainsi qu'un grand amour à l'issue incertaine et dangereuse. Elles ont mené jusqu'à son extrême limite l'acte de pénitence absolue. C'est un cas unique dans l'histoire, dans la mesure où la réclusion s'est étirée sur mille ans. Qui dit mieux? (Doyon 1984, 14f.)

Love is central to the recluse. Doyon admits that "vingt-quatre heures de la vie d'une recluse, au XVe siècle, surprendront plus d'un lecteur moderne" (Doyon 1984, 12). The daily life of a recluse of our century will equally be a surprise to the modern reader. Doyon discusses different ways to concentrate entirely on God. One school of thought states that the greater the solitude, the purer the contemplative life can be. Here, however, the question arises whether poetic activity intensifies or dilutes the pureness of contemplative life, whether it is meant as a form of contemplation or as a way of compensation or escape. This duality summarizes the core of the problem.

Without intending to pass a judgment at this point, there is certainly a strong original link between Alun Idris' call to solitude and his urge to write poetry: "It was in fact solitude that made me write poetry" (letter, 19.11.1989). Apparently, the poems contained in *The Threshold of Paradise* stem from the intensity of his religious experience. In solitude the monks try to find an inner void to be filled with the divine spirit. The closeness to God and the immense love felt in such moments on the one hand, the separation from Him, His absence, thus desperate loneliness on the other are borderline experiences which the human soul wishes to communicate. Poetry, which has always been intensely linked to love, appears to be the perfect medium.

It may be asked what such an investigation into religious poetry really tells us about the actual feelings of the poet who uttered them. The inevitable differences between art and life may deceive the reader, as the poet may be influenced by certain external factors: the pressure of literary tradition and fashion, the desire to imitate more successful writers, the temptation to say what one does not mean in order to be thought witty or edifying or sublime (cf. Fairchild 1939, viii). In the case of Alun Idris' poetry, however, such external influences are of minute importance: he wrote the first 2 volumes of poetry in monastic surroundings, convinced that nobody else would ever be able to share those thoughts with him. Any attempts to pander to the present literary fashion cannot be traced at all, rather the contrary. The only element mentioned above, which has influenced his writings, is his consciousness of tradition, also literary tradition. This does not mean that he favours one particular literary movement; he just has a marked consciousness for tradition in the general sense. His Welsh upbringing is no doubt firmly interrelated with this consciousness. The use of traditional forms of verse and archaisms, to be found frequently in his poetry, clearly reflect this idea.

Monasticism has always been closely linked with literature - the wealth of books to be found in numerous monastic libraries testifies to this long tradition. Literary monks have always existed, in particular in the learned orders, like the Benedictines or the Augustinians. The situation is more complex as regards more contemplative orientated orders, where the monk's prime sense of being is to serve God alone; i.e. to follow *one* vocation. And yet, even in Carthusian monasteries monks have also been poets, as is demonstrated in chapter 1.4.1. Can the two vocations be successfully unified, sustaining each other in perfect symbiosis? Is it possible for the poetic vein to be fostered in a strictly contemplative monastery, without gaining the upper hand, i.e. becoming superior to the call for contemplation and solitude? The question requires careful examination.

Some general aspects of the relation between religion and poetry are given below, before the specific problem of the (in-)compatibility of the poetic and the religious existence is touched upon. A few theoretical considerations and examples of other poet-monks of the past will pave the way to a closer examination of the case of Alun Idris Jones; "Brother David".

1.1. GENERAL ASPECTS OF THE RELATION BETWEEN RELIGION AND POETRY

> Since the expression of man's deepest feelings is always in rhythmic form of some kind, we should expect to find a close connection between the religious and the poetic impulse: some would add the corollary that all poetry is in some sense religious. (Spender and Hall 1963, 273)

Even if it is true that there is a moment of conception, which precedes the discovery of words in which the vision is to be expressed, the process of finding words must modify and shape the original thought (cf. Spender and Hall 1963, 273). And yet, Fairchild states:

> It is generally recognized that there is a large poetic element in religion and a large religious element in poetry. A juxtaposition of the two may shed some light upon each. (Fairchild 1939, vii)

Changing trends in religion have conditioned the poetry of various periods in different ways and to differing degrees.[1] Other critics, however, do not overestimate the connection between religion and poetry, primarily considering poetry as an "exploration of the possibilities of language" (Roberts 1982, 22).

Nevertheless, if we look back to the primitive beginnings of any race, we see that poetry starts with some practical purpose in mind that can be named religious, whether in the form of praise, incantation or propitiation. Early sacred writings are in poetic form, as for instance the hymns contained in the *Three Hundred Songs of China* (eleventh to sixth centuries B.C.), or the hymns to the Sun God of the Egyptian Eighteenth Dynasty (1580 B.C.). Equally, the sayings of the Delphic Oracle, we are told, were always conveyed by the priests in the form of verse - generally hexameters. Apparently, the drama, too, begins as part of a liturgy: Greek Dionysaic mysteries developed into the works of the great tragedians, while elaborations of the

---

[1] One could, for example, analyse the relation between Christianity and Romanticism, or the influence of modern science upon the basically religious art of the poet.

Christian mass evolved into the miracle plays of the Middle Ages (cf. Spender and Hall 1963, 273).

Sir Philip Sidney writes in his *Defence of Poesie:* "Among the *Romanes* a Poet was called *Vates*, which is as much as a diviner, foreseer, or Prophet" (Feuillerat 1968, 6). He refers to the religious origin of any type of literary or artistic activity. Historically speaking, poet and prophet were united, an attitude which was deeply rooted in the Renaissance mind and which, of course, was reflected in the literature of that period. Even in the Middle Ages, poetry was considered to be the servant to theology (cf. Böhler 1971, 51). Sidney spoke of the divine force in the poet (cf. Feuillerat 1968, 8f.) and considered those books, which are inspired by God, to be the best. He held the opinion that God speaks through poets in the same way as through prophets in the Old Testament.

Sidney's contemporary Puttenham writes in the heading to the third chapter of his *Arte of English Poesie* "How the Poets were the first priests, the first prophets, the first legislators and polititians in the world" (Willcock and Walker 1936, 6). 300 years later Carlyle writes:

> *Vates* means both Prophet and Poet: and indeed at all times, Prophet and Poet, well understood, have much kindred of meaning. Fundamentally indeed they are still the same; in this most important respect especially. That they have penetrated both of them into the sacred mystery of the Universe. (Carlyle 1840, 75)

Carlyle's contemporary W.S. Lilly (1904, 36) arrived at the same conclusion: "Poets *are* prophets, in the proper sense of the word." Hugh Thomas Kerr in *The Gospel in Modern Poetry* (New York, c.1926) draws a similar analogy, although tending to be slightly more restrictive: he holds the opinion that the function of the poet, like that of the preacher, is not to prove things, but to make people see. He holds that not all the poets are necessarily Christian, but all are essentially religious, wistfully seeking a "beyond" (cf. Burr 1961, 918).

There is, as the old Greeks used to say, something inspired in all of us; even ordinary virtue is of divine inspiration. To quote Wordsworth (*Prelude*, Book XIII on "Imagination and Taste"):[2]

> Poets, even as prophets, each with each
> Connected in a mighty scheme of truth.
> Have each his own peculiar faculty:
> Heaven's gift.

Santayana arrives at the conclusion that "religion and poetry are identical in essence, and differ merely in the way in which they are attached to practical affairs" (Buckley 1968, 6).

Until the religious "revival" of the 1930s, it was a prevalent opinion that Western literature in general had ceased to be interested in traditional religious values and should be judged by secular and aesthetic standards only. Two world-wars, however, and world-wide economic depression excited doubt regarding the inevitability of automatic material and moral

---

[2] Selincourt 1959, 471.

progress. Both religious and secular critics began to question humanistic, secular and naturalistic standards, and to seek profoundly and essentially religious elements in historic and contemporary literature (cf. Burr 1961, 850f.).

Some critics give testimony to the vitality of customary idealism in poetry and religion[3], whilst others maintain that English poetry and poetic tradition were sidetracked from their richest tradition by scientific rationalism, and so departed from religion, but that T.S. Eliot and others have begun to resume the earlier line of growth.[4] Obviously, over the course of time poetry has become more varied and fulfils other functions, becoming more sharply separated from religion.

> A mystic who is also a poet will be likely to feel a clash between his need to identify himself with created beings for the purpose of his art, and his need to learn detachment from them if he is to follow the way of union with God, the *Via Negativa*. [...] The poet's is the *Via Positiva*, the Way of Affirmation of Images (to use Charles Williams' term), and the union between the two ways implicit in Thomas Traherne's work is hard indeed to attain. (Spender and Hall 1963, 273)

Religious poetry often tends to be didactic rather than merely an expression of revelation, turning into what Eliot termed "Propagandist religious poetry".[5] It is therefore necessary to make a distinction between poetry as the expression of personal religious feeling and that which is designed for public worship. While both express the desire for nearness to God, they differ in tone and imagery. To turn to religious, as distinct from devotional poetry, a further distinction can be made: there is religious poetry in a very general sense, i.e. concerned with some power or order felt to be greater than man himself, and there is also the kind of religious poetry that expresses belief in some generally accepted doctrine, as with the works of Dante or Milton. When thinking of English religious poetry, what first comes to mind is the lyrical expression of love and longing for God in the carols and laments of the Middle Ages, and then the poetry of the "Metaphysicals", with the eighteenth-century hymns of Watts, Cowper and Wesley as a minor third (cf. Spender and Hall 1963, 274). Man expresses his apprehension of the spiritual by physical analogies. Thus, mystical poetry has been accustomed to use the language of erotic love to describe the love between man and his maker.

---

[3] N. Burr mentions *Poetry, Religion and the Spiritual Life* by George Finger Thomas, published in Houston, 1951 (cf. Burr 1961, 909f.).
[4] This view is held in Cleanth Brooks' *Modern Poetry and the Traditions*, Chapel Hill, N.C., 1939. Brooks discusses Archibald MacLeish at length (cf. Burr 1961, 910).
[5] Eliot 1966, 391. See below, p.7.

1.2. SPECIFYING THE SACRED

It is interesting to note that since Blake and Wordsworth there has been a good deal of discussion about the religious nature of poetry, but not about the nature of "religious poetry", for that concept has scarcely been a real issue since the 17th century. T.S. Eliot has justly remarked that to the great majority of people "religious poetry is a variety of *minor* poetry" (Eliot 1966, 390). David Cecil is even more explicit when he writes:

> Religious emotion is the most sublime known to man. But, in Christian Europe at any rate, it has not proved the most fertile soil for poetry. Though the great religious poets have been equal to any, they have been fewer in number than the great secular poets. And a large proportion of religious verse is poor stuff. The average hymn is a by-word for forced feeble sentiment, flat conventional expression. (Cecil 1951, xi)

This is chiefly the fault, one might say, of those who claim the title of "religious poet" for themselves. The very loftiness of the religious sentiment is in part responsible. Furthermore, those in whom the emotion is strong do not always have the faculty to express it (cf. Cecil 1951, xi f.). And yet, some critics demonstrate a strongly affirmative nature and the extraordinary persistence of a hope for "poetry which exists against the tenor of the age" (Buckley 1968, 9). These critics speak as poets, not as observers of poetry, and furthermore not of religion in poetry but of poetry as a religious act (cf. Buckley 1968, 9). The following short selection of modern critics and their ideas about the nature of religious poetry will shed some light upon the question.

Elizabeth Jennings prefers to call religious poetry "poems on religious themes" and holds that these poems "must always be judged by the same critical criteria which we bring to bear on poems concerned with any other subject" (Jennings 1981, 9). To enjoy religious poetry we must,

> without too much strain, make a "willing suspension of disbelief". One does not have to be in love to watch or read *Romeo and Juliet* or Chaucer's *Troilus and Creysede*, one need not have visited Rome to enjoy Browning's *Two in the Campagna*, but it does of course help if one *has* been in love or visited Italy. (Jennings 1981, 9)

She distinguishes religious poems from devotional poems; i.e. the second being substitutes for prayer which teach and seek to convert. Whatever its theme may be, real poetry offers experience, not sermons. In the 20th century it appears difficult to find true religious verse, because this age is not an age of faith. It is a period of fear, anxiety, materialism, although in tangible and material matters, an age of enlightenment.

In his essay on "Religion and Literature" T.S. Eliot (1966, 388-401) distinguishes between three senses in which one can speak of "religious literature": "The first is that of which we say that it is 'religious literature' in the same way that we speak of 'historical literature' or of 'scientific literature'" (389). Such literature was created by writers who, incidental to their religious, historical or philosophic purpose, possessed the gift of poetic language.

"The second kind of relation of religion to literature is that which is found in what is called 'religious' or 'devotional' poetry" (390). The usual attitude of the lover of verse towards this type is that it is poetry with clear limitations:

> For the great majority of people who love poetry, *'religious* poetry' is a variety of *minor* poetry: the religious poet is not a poet who is treating the whole subject matter of poetry in a religious spirit, but a poet who is dealing with a confined part of this subject matter: who is leaving out what men consider their major passions, and thereby confessing his ignorance of them. I think that this is the real attitude of most poetry lovers towards such poets as Vaughan, or Southwell, or Crashaw, or George Herbert, or Gerard Hopkins. (390)

Eliot admits that up to a point these critics are right, for there is a kind of poetry "which is the product of a special religious awareness, which may exist without the general awareness which we expect of the major poet" (391). In some poetical works, this general awareness may have existed; however, the preliminary steps which represent it may have been suppressed. It may be very difficult to discriminate between such writers and those in whom the religious or devotional genius represents a special and limited awareness. Eliot ranks Vaughan, Southwell, and George Herbert amongst writers with this limited awareness, and states that they are not great religious poets in the sense in which Dante, Corneille, or Racine are great Christian religious poets. Since the time of Chaucer, Christian poetry (in the sense in which Eliot means it) has been limited in England almost exclusively to the realms of minor poetry.

The third type of religious poetry could be placed under the heading of propaganda; i.e. literary works of writers who sincerely aim at forwarding the cause of religion (cf. 391). Such writings do not enter into any serious consideration of the relation between religion and literature "because they are conscious operations in a world in which it is assumed that Religion and Literature are not related. It is a conscious and limited relating" (392).

Eliot summarizes his attitude unambiguously in the following statement:

> What I wish to affirm is that the whole of modern literature is corrupted by what I call Secularism, that it is simply unaware of, simply cannot understand the meaning of, the primacy of the supernatural over the natural life: of something which I assume to be our primary concern. (398)

Vincent Buckley holds that the religious impulse persists in a remarkable way in poetry, so that we may say that, even in a desacralised society like our own, there are still some poets who concern themselves with estimating, defining, and recreating manifestations of the sacred (cf. Buckley 1968, 17). Buckley's ideas about the term "religious" are rather general in form, opposing the prevailing tendency of many people to limit "religious" as narrowly as possible (cf. Buckley 1968, 1). Fairchild, for example, uses the term "religious" almost exclusivley as an equivalent for "devout", thus differing fundamentally from Buckley's views.[6] A more general view is also adopted by Peter Levi, who writes in his "Introduction" to *The Penguin Book of English Christian Verse*: "If our definition of Christianity in poems is too severe, we shall be left with an anthology of little more than hymns" (Levi 1988, 19).

Similar to Elizabeth Jennings, Thomas Merton distinguishes "religious poetry" from "devotional poetry". The first springs from a true religious experience, which, he suggests, does not necessarily mean a mystical experience. "Devotional poetry" is verse which deals with religious themes, even on a truly poetic level. Such poetry may be piously inspired; it may be produced for a true religious purpose and can be directed towards the salvation of souls. In *Bread in the Wilderness* Merton writes:

> A truly religious poem is not born merely of a religious purpose. Neither poetry nor contemplation is built out of good intentions. Indeed, a poem that springs from no deeper spiritual need than a devout intention will necessarily appear to be at the same time forced and tame. Art that is simply "willed" is not art, and it tends to have the same disquieting effect upon the reader as forced piety and religious strain in those who are trying hard to be contemplatives, as if infused contemplation were the result of human effort rather than a gift of God [...] The Psalms, on the other hand, are at the same time the simplest and the greatest of all religious poems. (quoted by Woodcock 1978, 54f.)

Merton ranks religious poetry higher than devotional poetry, criticizing the second as of lesser quality, for its origin is not as high as the first.

1.3. SACRED AND PROFANE: RELIGIOUS POETS OF THE PAST[7]

Religious poetry as a genre has existed from the earliest times onwards, spanning most cultures. One may take the psalm or the hymn as its prototype, poems written to celebrate, thank or invoke the adorable forces. However, throughout English poetry we are faced with the difficult task of locating religious imaginative life in poetic form, as the most interesting expressions of religious feeling are seldom found in such predictable poetry. The term "sacred" may, at least, help us to appreciate the variety of religious poetry (cf. Buckley 1968, 22).

Throughout a large part of the 16th century, after Wyatt, there was little demand for religious poetry. Where an interest is discernible, it is an interest in a certain category of feeling, avowedly devout. Thereafter, the category of the 'divine' or 'sacred' poem arose, which then persisted well into the 18th century. Seeking religious poets between Wyatt and Donne, Buckley mentions Fulke Greville, perhaps Spenser and arguably Sir John Davies (cf. Buckley 1968, 29ff.).

---

[6] For instance, when Fairchild deals with "divine poetry" of the 18th century, he actually discusses poems addressed directly to God, most of them hymns, many designated for congregational singing.

[7] This brief survey by no means claims to be complete. It merely aims to indicate the names of a number of English poets who might be classified as religious poets.

With the Metaphysicals it seems that the attempt to relegate sacred poetry to a separate genre was parallelled by the aim to specify the worshipper's confrontation with God as its subject, resulting in marked innovations of poetic form.

> One influential view was that sacred poetry was poetry put to a sacralising use or uses; versifying the things of God, composing the soul before him, reworking psalms and parables, in other words, recreating forms already sacred. (Buckley 1968, 32)

In a sense, much Metaphysical religious poetry is a "churchy poetry" though, not necessarily one carrying much feeling of communal experience. In their concentrated efforts to versify psalms and parables or rework traditional prayers, the Metaphysicals had the paradoxical task of inventing poetic forms in order to reinforce a message already declared. Nevertheless, the venture was surprisingly varied, and a large number of poets participated, such as Southwell, Jonson, Donne, Herbert, Crashaw, Marvell, King, Vaughan, and Traherne for example (cf. Buckley 1968, 32f.). Critics seem to agree on several possible causes of this flowering:

> First, the polemics and schisms of the preceding century had so sharpened the religious issues as to make them dramatically relevant to the daily life of the spirit; second, the very grossness of much of the polemic had led to a paradoxical purifying of devotional habits in at least some talented poets; third, the greater flowering of stage-drama had provided a dramatic habit on which the dialectic of the individual's religious life could rely, if not for models [...], at any rate for stimulus and support; and, fourth, [...] there were available to them techniques of meditation, or of spiritual 'composition', which were themselves of a dramatic as well as a devotional cast. (Buckley 1968, 33f.)

After Herbert and Vaughan, the path taken by religious poetry to its temporary end in the late Restoration period is a regressive one (cf. Buckley 1968, 37).

The second half of the 19th century is the second outstanding epoch of religious poetry in England. It produced no Donne or Milton, nor any writer who expresses the spirit of Anglican Christianity so completely as Herbert, but four poets, Browning, Patmore, Hopkins and Christina Rossetti, were the equals, if not the superiors, of Vaughan and Crashaw (cf. Cecil 1951, xxvii). Actually, Herbert and Hopkins are probably the two most centrally religious poets in the English language, with religious matters and topics forming the essential core and peripheral bounds of their poetic output (cf. Buckley 1968, 1).

Since the beginnings of the Romantic movement, two strains of religious poetry can be seen. Amongst the first that Buckley mentions are Blake, Wordsworth, Coleridge, Whitman, Yeats, Lawrence, Dylan Thomas, and Roethke, whose "motive-power is to re-define God's action in the world in such a way as to create a quite new sense of God and of man's relation with him" (Buckley 1968, 49). The second line would be that which runs through Smart, Hopkins, Eliot, the later Auden, and the earlier Robert Lowell, whose "motive-power" is, generally, to re-define God's action in the world in such a way as to reinforce a sense of its presence and urgency [...] The first seeks to create a tradition, the second to redefine one. The first records the action of God, and its feelings are those of amazement, inadequacy, a need to speak, even to expound; the second practises the presence of God, and its feelings are those of worship, sinfulness, a need to address and be heard. (Buckley 1968, 49)

Buckley arrives at the conclusion that even among the poets he calls religious, professedly Christian poets are now in a minority. Other Christian poets of the present century who should be mentioned are Edwin Muir, Edith Sitwell, Roy Campbell, Thomas Merton, R.S. Thomas, and Elizabeth Jennings.

1.4. THE TWO VOCATIONS: (IN-)COMPATIBILITY OF THE POETIC AND RELIGIOUS EXISTENCE

Can the two concepts - that of the contemplative monk on the one hand, fully orientated towards solitude and silence, and that of the poet, striving for the spread of one's literary output,[8] on the other - be successfully reconciled in one person? Can a contemplative lead an almost heremitic life, while at the same time being driven by a tremendous urge for poetic creativity, a wish to let the poetic vein of his innermost core flow and find an outlet? Opinions diverge considerably in answering this question of whether or not poetic and religious existence can be harmoniously unified in one person.

Kierkegaard for instance considered poetic and religious existence irreconcilable: from the Christian point of view, every poetic existence is sin, the sin to compose instead of to be, to deal with the good and truth in one's fantasy instead of living it to the full. Equally, Schleiermacher held the opinion that as an artist he was entirely unchristian, while as a Christian he was fully unartistic (cf. Kranz 1978, 16). Such statements may suggest personal experience; however, they do not necessarily represent matters of fact.

In an essay on "Poetry and the Contemplative Life", James A. Thielen[9] stresses the centrality of liturgy, theology and mystical experience. He even maintains that Christian poetry is not possible except when the writer is a contemplative. Naturally, Alun Idris' poetry corresponds to such a definition in all its entirety.

Numerous poet-monks or poet-priests display the difficulties of unifying the two vocations satisfactorily. The tension in G.M. Hopkins between his singularity and the discipline of his order, as well as the conflict between the priest and the poet in him was hard to bear, causing enormous sufferings and desolations (cf. Every 1950, 22). The most outstanding examples of more recent times, apart from Hopkins, are probably R.S. Thomas and Thomas Merton.

---

[8] For instance, we know that G.M. Hopkins as a poet suffered from want of a human audience (cf. Every 1950, 24).
[9] Quoted by Burr 1961, 928.

George Woodcock in his critical study on Thomas Merton, makes the following observation:

> Many more ways than one exist of losing one's ordinary, worldly self. Perhaps the simplest, for Merton, was that which he took when he left secular life and became the obedient cenobitic monk who followed a traditional path into the priesthood and was known in his community as Father Louis. Another, and not an incompatible way, was the solitary path of contemplation leading to the sense of mystical encounter with the unknowable God. But - as poets and other artists know - the act of artistic or intellectual creation can be yet another form of self-abnegation. The creative persona is not the self as commonly understood; he is a different being from the man with the same name whom the world encounters in the street or at the bank; his creative powers enter him and manifest themselves as mysteriously as the contemplative's intuitions. Some writers have recognized this fact by assuming different names under which to publish their works, less out of modesty than from the sense of another voice speaking within them.[10]
> (Woodcock 1978, 2)

In the mature Merton one detects a trio of beings, all different but existing without conflict. There was Father Louis, who carried on the monastic and priestly duties; the nameless hermit who had ventured forth into the desert of contemplation; and there was the creative writer whom the wider world knew. "These three Mertons lived in harmony because they sustained each other and were in fact the aspects of a single whole" (Woodcock 1978, 2).

R.S. Thomas, one of the most famous poet-priests of the present century, does not perceive any contradiction between the two vocations, when he openly declares:

> Poetry is religion, religion is poetry. The message of the New Testament is poetry. Christ was a poet, the New Testament is a metaphor, the Resurrection is a metaphor; and I feel perfectly within my rights in approaching my whole vocation as priest and as preacher as one who is to present poetry; and when I preach poetry I am preaching Christianity, and when one discusses Christianity one is discussing poetry in its imaginative aspects. The core of both are imagination as far as I'm concerned, so that I'm not personally worried about this at all. (Ormond 1972, 53)

The question of the possible union between the two vocations leads us to the following reflection: can a saint be a poet, or a poet a saint? Numerous examples in history suggest a positive answer: Paulinus of Noly, Petrus Damiani, Heinrich Seuse, Robert Bellarmine, Alfons of Liguori, Teresa of Avila, Thérèse de Lisieux, for instance. There are many saints who wrote good poems, like Ambrosius, Ephrem, Hrabanus Maurus, Jacopone da Todi, Thomas Aquinas, Raymund Lull, Thomas More, J.H. Newman. Poetic genius and holiness are united in Gregory of Nazianzus, Notker Balbulus, Francis of Assisi, John of the Cross, G.M. Hopkins (cf. Kranz 1978, 17ff.). One should remember though, that probably every one of them would have sacrificed their poetic activities for the Lord's sake. Teresa of Avila was willing to burn her manuscript, had her confessor asked her to do so. Hopkins destroyed his *Juvenilia* and reproduced it only after having been requested to do so by his superior. Many poets, as for

---

[10] A secular example is Eric Blair, who became famous as George Orwell.

instance John Donne, repented and revoked their "profane" literature towards the end of their lives (cf. Kranz 1978, 18). Such behaviour strongly indicates that the creative, poetic impulse cannot easily be combined with a religious vocation.

1.4.1. THE CARTHUSIAN POET-MONK

The severity of the Carthusian way of living has not altered significantly since the days of its founder St. Bruno, who together with his disciples had turned to the ideals of the Egyptian and Eastern hermits and coenobites (cf. Thompson 1930, 6). Bound to a strict rule of silence, the Carthusians spend most of their time in solitary cells in order to maintain the individual seclusion, which is considered the ideal basis for undisturbed contemplation. The striving for perfect renunciation remains at the core of their essence; they have chosen a way of life that is defined by simply being in the presence of God (cf. Heim 1985, xi f.). Their virtual seclusion from the rest of mankind provides the fertile soil for an entire and exclusive orientation towards the Lord, silence and solitude helping to liberate the searching soul from all distractions.

Those who don't understand the call to silence think of it as emptiness; however, it is this emptying of earthly vapidness which creates room for the reality of the spirit to enter; then it is full in abundance (cf. Lockhart 1985, 107f.). In his message to the Carthusians (who "have chosen the better part" - cf. Luke 10:41) on their 900th anniversary, Pope John Paul II writes:

> It must be acknowledged that in these days, when perhaps too much importance is given to activity, the value of your eremitic life is sometimes insufficiently understood, or underestimated - particularly when so many workers are needed in the Lord's vineyard. (John Paul II 1984, 139)

In their life of seclusion and prayer, Carthusian monks have contributed much to religious literature, often at the highest spiritual level. The bulk of Carthusian writings deal largely with mystical experiences and are, of necessity, esoteric. Many of these Carthusian writings are attempts to communicate the incommunicable, knowledge received in contemplation, which cannot be communicated except to others who have also had such mystical experiences. We know of several monks who in their total humility destroyed most of their writings, as e.g. Augustine Guillerand (1877-1945) (cf. Lockhart 1985, 49). Frequently, the identity of Carthusian authors is only revealed posthumously, - and not always then.

In a letter to the present writer dated 5 July 1993, the vicar of the charterhouse of Sélignac, Dom Augustin Devaux, emphasizes that "quoi qu'il en soit des autres ordres monastiques, les chartreux tiennent fortement que leur vocation tient uniquement dans la recherche de Dieu seul dans la solitude; hors de là ils n'ont pas raison d'être". Thus, a poetic vocation in the charterhouse can only be subordinated to this principal aim, as a means to promote the spiritual quest in solitude. Dom Augustin states more precisely:

Et c'est là tout le problème. Comme le dit Jean Guitton en effet "Le plus difficile en ce monde, pour la plupart, ce n'est pas d'avoir une vocation, c'est de n'en avoir qu'une", ou pour parler comme Etienne Gilson de son cas personnel: "L'art et la philosophie exigent chacun le don de toute une vie; il est difficile d'être vraiment aux deux à la fois!"

The primacy of the search for God imposes the first restrictions on a poet in the Carthusian Order: the subject must always be religious. Yet modern poetry regards religious topics as of secondary interest, as they may perhaps be equally well treated in prose. This first restriction minimises the truly poetic effort as regards form for a poet in the Order. Dom Augustin concedes that the poet may regard his creativity as analogue to God's act of creation, comparing his effort to the creativity of Carthusian laybrothers. However, his case is really very different to theirs, as his time is more limited by other religious obligations and the intellectual effort involved in poetic creativity is, in general, more absorbing for the spirit than manual activities. There is a danger in becoming more involved, a danger which lurks in all activities in the charterhouse. In his search for Carthusian Latin poets, Dom Augustin Devaux discovered a monk in the seventeenth century at the charterhouse of Paris who allowed himself to become so absorbed that he noted down his poetic thoughts while celebrating the mass; he was immediately exiled to a small house that was still in course of foundation, where he would not create a scandal. There is thus a problem of equilibrium, which poses itself as regards every secondary activity in the cell.

There is a special paradox involved in poetical activity. Dom Augustin quotes the late General Procurator of the Order, Dom Jean-Baptiste Porion, who elucidated it in a letter dated 10 June 1957 to a young monk, who was a poet: "Les poètes normalement ont besoin d'une audience. Il faut donc dire qu'un poète au désert est un vivant paradoxe." He added further that the poet who is not a Carthusian must purify his desire for glory, his need to be recognised by a special form of asceticism, which is often that proclaimed by Péguy, - to succeed either in one's life or one's work, as it is impossible to chase two hares. And even if the Carthusian poet does purify his intention in exchanging his desire for glory with the aim to edify, the Carthusian vocation is there to remind him that the Carthusian Order is by no means a teaching Order: only in rare and exceptional cases is publication allowed, and then only for special reasons. Thus normally in the charterhouse the monk poet must write essentially for the joy of creating something beautiful for God alone and for the solace of recording his interior life, without any other satisfaction beyond this simple act, - an aim certainly justifiable and maybe even necessary to avoid intellectual stagnation, which may become a danger in the charterhouse, when polarised to activism. Dom Augustin concludes: "Cette actigité d'expression 'pour soi seul' est normalement très crucifiante pour qui compose difficilement par là spirituellement fructueuse."

The output of poetry written in Carthusian monasteries is, however, considerable. The vicar of the charterhouse of Sélignac is presently compiling an anthology of Latin poetry written in the Carthusian Order. The result has not been published yet, but a short summary of his research was included in a letter to the present writer.

Dom Augustin has limited his investigations to those poets who have been published: 65 poets, of whom 17 remain anonymous. The majority of the latter (13) are constituted by collections of Latin hymns copied in the charterhouse in the fifteenth century: these items are generally held to have been composed by Carthusians, and this seems highly probable, as they sometimes deal with specifically Carthusian devotions.

Chronologically, these 65 poets are essentially grouped in three centuries representing the greatest prosperity of the Order; the fifteenth, sixteenth and seventeenth centuries (84%).[11] Nothing extraordinary in that; in the 12th century the Order was born, and for the two centuries of scholasticism - the 13th and 14th - Latin literature was smothered by dialectic. On the contrary, the very uneven geographical distribution of Carthusian poets is instructive: 26 (40%) came from the former Spanish Low Countries, which today form Belgium and the two most northern provinces of France. All these charterhouses without exception were in urban or semi-urban areas, installed in suburbs of often important towns; thus close to a potential public, whereby the diminution of the solitude is obvious. Similarly the 9 poets from the province of the Rhine came also from urban charterhouses, as did 3 of the French Carthusian poets. It is, of course, almost superfluous to note that all the subjects treated were religious ones.

Dom Augustin divides the 65 poets into two groups of very unequal significance: "occasional" and "vocational" poets. The first group contented themselves with the composition of one or two fugitive pieces, inspired by a fortuitous occasion, most frequently the publication of a book by a religious brother or a friend. They are either in the form of compliments to the author or the evocation of the subject treated. Some of these "amateurs" display an extraordinary technical virtuosity, even in the employment of the most difficult lyrical Latin metres and are full of spirit; facts which presuppose very serious studies, imply contacts, but involve no spiritual problem.[12]

Dom Augustin speaks of 15 vocational poets. Before the invention of printing, the dissemination of a literary work involved the gathering together of a sufficient audience, which was only possible by attending some form of court, either professionally like the troubadours or the Minnesänger, etc., or as a courtier, maybe to a great lord or even a university. There was no public for the Carthusian poet and manuscripts of their works are, therefore, very rare.

In some Carthusian poetry he notices an indirect form of religious instruction, as in the work of the priors Hugues de Miramar and Conrad of Hainburg, as well as that of the procurator Albert of Prague. Another driving force for composition can be discovered in Denis

---

[11] 17 in the 15th century, including 13 anonymous poets, 14 in the 16th century, 23 in the 17th century, after which Latin poetry died out everywhere in Europe.

[12] This is true of six Spanish priors, who thus are divided off from their famous colleague, Dom Juan de Padilla, a very famous vernacular poet, who is mentioned in all the historical handbooks of Spanish literature.

the Carthusian,[13] who developed an absolute mania for writing. Spiritual authors hold that he was incapable of being silent and thus turned to authorship as compensation. His poetry shows considerable polish. Similarly, Zachary Ferreri, who was only a novice in the Carthusian Order for a few months, was a real poet, who produced technically very fine verse, full of imagination, colour and vivacity. His life was equally remarkable: he was a Benedictine monk, abbot, curialist, pronotary, prominent participant at the Council of Pisa, Bishop of a small diocese in the Kingdom of Naples and, above all, a prolific poet, who even compiled a collection of hymns for all occasions that was used in the Roman Rite for some years. To quote Dom Augustin: "Mais par quelle aberration un pareil agité s'était-il cru la vocation cartusienne?"

At times the monks use poetic devices unsuitable for the Carthusian Order, as is the case with Lanspergius, whose simple hymns, intended to stimulate piety, do not pose any specific psychological problem, although his total production does seem to. Dom Augustin points out that he uses literary forms that seem most unsuitable for a Carthusian, - such as fictitious sermons that constitute three-fifths of his total works, fictitious letters, short treatises, a dialogue between Christ and a faithful soul.

Theodore Petreius, a historian and man of learning by vocation, was also a poet, but he always remained a historian, always occupied in narrating events.

The English Carthusian Dom Robert Clarke compiled a number of poems, but only one was published. Thus only his "Christiad" survives. Clarke had to face the problem that all poets dealing with the life of Christ are confronted with: "comment lutter en style épique avec les récits sobres, tout simples et très prenants des Evangiles."[14]

For obvious reasons, there are not many poet-monks known outside the monastery today, for the Carthusians shun publicity on principle. In a charterhouse the superiors are quite reserved about writing poetry, at least about publishing it. If monks are interested in literature and poetry, in the majority of cases the monk keeps his interest as a private one, suppressing the urge to share his musings with others.

1.4.2. THE TRAPPIST POET-MONK

The Trappist Order, i.e. the Cistercian Order of the Strict Observance, is the most austere offshoot of the Benedictine Order. While the Carthusians stress solitude, it is the communal element which is much more strongly stressed in a Cistercian monastery. In this respect the two contemplative Orders form a sharp contrast. Alun Idris' desire to lead a more solitary life led to his asking for permission to spend some time at Camaldoli, where the monks

---

[13] Denis the Carthusian (1402-71), called the "Ecstatic Doctor" (following the term "Angelic Doctor" for St. Thomas Aquinas), is probably the most prolific of all sacred writers: 42 stout volumes, 700 pages each, and more than 200 tracts, the most famous one being *De Contemplatione* (cf. Lockhart 1985, 48).
[14] Dom Augustin Devaux, in a letter to the present writer, dated 5.7.1993.

used to be eremitic. The difficulty in a Trappist monastery is that the monks are very rarely alone, for they live together in their "shared loneliness" ("What might have been", *World*, 6). The main difference is that in a Trappist monastery the solitude is interior, the rule of silence being very rigid. The monks are all together, but they do not communicate on that level, there is only an "interior communication" (interview, 13.8.1990). The weekly walk in the charterhouse provides more ground for actual conversation, whereas the Trappist Order is a completely silent one, although a kind of sign language is allowed, which can be used for transmitting necessary information.[15] Both at La Trappe and in the charterhouse it is considered of utmost importance to be solitary, but their means of acquiring that solitude is different. The Trappists are silent but also cenobitic, forming communities dedicated to contemplation, rather than collections of eremitic individuals, such as the Carthusians and the Camaldolese, who follow that course in solitude as well as silence.

The motivating force for writing poetry in the Trappist monastery is certainly similar to the original stimulus for writing in a charterhouse, although the outward situation is rather different. Like the Carthusians, the Trappists shun publicity in general; it must be added, however, that permission to write basically depends on the discretion of the superiors of the various religious houses, who impede or favour the poetic vein.

In his early years at Gethsemani, Thomas Merton, the most famous example of a Trappist poet-monk in the 20th century, saw a conflict arising between his two vocations. Although Merton claims in *The Seven Storey Mountain* that he had always understood that art was contemplation, he felt that when turning to monasticism "writing seemed to him a temptation that might draw a veil between him and the truth". Merton himself was of the opinion that joining the Trappist Order meant that he had to give up everything, most of all writing. However, it was Gethsemani that did not allow him to give up writing and showed him that his two vocations were not incompatible but rather complementary (cf. Woodcock 1978, 18f.).[16] Merton's Cistercian superiors displayed much wisdom, as they realized that his life as a contemplative and his activities as a writer were likely to feed each other, to his benefit and equally to that of the Order and the Church.

Thomas Merton accords the artist a special access to truth, analogous to that of the contemplative, as he writes in *Bread in the Wilderness*. The richness in affective and spiritual

---

[15] However, this does not mean that the vocal cords of the monks remain unused, nor is the natural desire to hear a human voice unsatisfied. The monks in the choir chant every day, all the monks join in the vocal prayer; instruction is given to the scholastics and novices in oral form; speech is allowed when the community meets in chapter to discuss its affairs, and at every meal a monk would be chosen to read passages from some religious book aloud to those who are eating in the refectory. Basically, speech is abandoned for profane purposes, but it can still be used for sacred ones (cf. Woodcock 1978, 48).

[16] "Merton found himself impelled to write poems when he first reached the Abbey, and confessed it to his spiritual director, hoping that he would be forbidden to write and then would have to obey. But the confessor encouraged him to continue. He went to the Abbot, and to his surprise the Abbot not only added his own exhortations to continue but also suggested that Merton's writing might be used for the benefit of the monastery and the faith." (Woodcock 1978, 19).

associations of a poetic line enables the reader to experience the original feeling or mood the poet aimed to capture:

> The words of a poem are not merely the signs of concepts: they are also rich in affective and spiritual associations. The poet uses words not merely to make declarations, statements of fact. That is usually the last thing that concerns him. He seeks above all to put words together in such a way that they exercise a mysterious and vital reactivity among themselves, and so release their secret content of associations to produce in the reader an experience that enriches the depths of his spirit in a manner quite unique. (quoted by Woodcock 1978, 53)

2. THE MAKING OF A MONK: ALUN IDRIS' CALL TO MONASTICISM

2.1. FAMILY BACKGROUND

Alun Idris Jones stems from a Welsh middle-class Baptist background. His father, Idris Jones (1915-1993), was born at Moel Ddiwyd, the farm next to Dolwar Fach (Ann Griffiths' farm) in the old Montgomeryshire (now Powys). He studied German and French at Aberystwyth. Idris Jones spent all his life dealing with literature, teaching German and French at school, sometimes Welsh as well, even Italian for a certain period. He was the head of the Modern Language Department at Croisyceiliog in South Wales. He retired from active teaching in July 1980. Idris Jones showed much interest in poetry, translating a great deal into Welsh himself. He was a leading member of a literary circle in Caernarvon, concentrating on Welsh literature. Idris Jones died on 17 April 1993.

While his father's interest in music was limited, Alun Idris' mother's musical talents are remarkable. Olwen Mair Lloyd Jones, née Edwards, composed the hymn tune which sparked off the poetry of her son. Born on 28 September 1919 in Wrexham, she grew up at Llanfyllin. She studied French and English at Bangor, doing her M.A. thesis on developments in the appreciation of the poetry of Baudelaire, while she was teaching. The parental interest in literature and music provided the fertile soil for the two sons to nourish and develop that interest as well.

Huw Jones, their eldest son, five and a half years older than his brother Alun, is a well-known figure in Wales. The present S4C chief executive founded a pop group when he was in the 6th form[17] and, to a large extent, used to compose his own songs, both music and the lyrics (cf. interview, 13.8.1990). Soon the first contacts with the BBC were established, though not on a professional basis. Still in college he worked as a quiz master for a children's programme.

---
[17] Huw Jenkins, Eluned Evans and Huw Jones called themselves "Huw2 + Eluned", like a mathematical formula (cf. letter, 11.11.1990). The pop group lasted a couple of years.

After having finished studying French at Jesus College, Oxford, he founded a record company called Sain[18] together with Dafydd Iwan and another friend. His concern for the language and plight of Wales is reflected in his songs and his activities for the television company. His first record - Dŵr ("Water") and Gwas Bach y Peiriant Pres - had launched Sain, now the biggest and most successful record company in Wales.[19]

In 1981 he founded Teledu'r Tir Glas,[20] an Independent Television Company, responsible for producing some of Wales' main popular Welsh language entertainment programmes. This company has been hailed as a "pioneering force" (*Caernarfon Herald*, November 5, 1993, 4) in the field of children's television. Apart from running Tir Glas, Huw Jones is the director of a studio on wheels called Barcud ("kite"), a studio available both for Tir Glas and any other Independent Television Company which wish to use it, mostly for Welsh language programmes.[21] In 1989 he introduced the *Eisteddfod*.[22] Since the 1990s he has acted behind the scenes rather than on the TV screen, producing programmes himself. In November 1993 he was made head of Welsh Television.

In view of Huw Jones' career with the Welsh TV, his talent as a businessman and his success as a pop singer, it appears hard to believe that his brother Alun should be completely different in character, aspiring to a silent life, cut off from the public, entirely dedicated to the Lord.

2.2. EARLY INFLUENCES - CONVERSION TO ROMAN CATHOLICISM

Born in Cardiff on 16 November 1953, Alun Idris Jones was brought up as a member of the Baptist Church, just as his brother was. Two influences are worth mentioning: one is Father John Fitzgerald, O.Carm., who was Alun Idris' confessor when he was a student. The other is Father Edwin Regan, a priest who used to celebrate the mass in Welsh. Equally, the Welsh school he went to when he was a child, Bryntaf in Cardiff, a very chapel-orienated, very Welsh school, left its traces (cf. letter, 11.11.1990).

---

[18] "Sain" means "sound". They started in a canteen on a small industrial state, before a proper recording studio, which is a sound studio only, was built in Llandwrog. He began recording his own projects, singing some of his own songs on TV, introducing programmes etc. (cf. letter, 11.11.1990).
[19] Archimandrite Barnabas refers to him as Alun Irdis' "pop-singer brother Hugh Jones" (Burton 1985, 105).
[20] "Glas" means "green", "virgin", "fresh", "tir" means "land". Companies like Tir Glas provide programmes for Channel 4, which in Wales was made available for mainly Welsh language programmes.
[21] Cf. *Caernarfon Herald*, November 5, 1993, 4.
[22] The National *Eisteddfod* is an annual bardic festival, which includes competitions in literature, drama and poetry, choral singing, orchestral works etc. Competitions are carried out all day long and every day during the *eisteddfod* week. The two chief competitions are the Chair, offered for an *awdl* (ode) in the strict traditional metres of Welsh alliterative verse, and the Crown, usually offered for a *pryddest* (poem) in free metres, which allows more scope for experiments than the Chair competition (cf. Fraser 1952, 131). It must be remembered, however, that although the National is the largest *eisteddfod* of the year, and the only one which receives publicity outside Wales, there are innumerable smaller local *eisteddfodau* held every year (cf. Fraser 1952, 134).

For a year and half a term Alun Idris went to the Welsh secondary school Rhydfelen. Due to severe asthma he was forced to move to a school nearer home during the first term in form two, viz. Cae'r Castell. The change of schools brought him into contact with evangelical friends. He underwent an evangelical conversion on Maundy Thursday, 23 March 1967, in the aftermath of a Billy Graham summer campaign. At the age of thirteen, he was baptised in the Baptist chapel at Cardiff on 8 October 1967 and shortly afterwards, on 15 October, admitted as a full member of the community.[23]

In order to do A-levels, he changed to Cardiff High School, a very English school, where his character was really formed. During that period, the Sunday school teacher Justice Dewi Watkin Powell was a strong influence for Alun Idris. He was a very open-minded man who had studied at Jesus College, Oxford, being very keen on monastic life. "He opened my mind to the Christian heritage outside the Baptist frontiers" (letter, 11.11.1990). He exposed his pupils to other influences, visiting many different churches. Serious doubts about the veracity of the Baptist religion started to creep in and later made him stop receiving Baptist communion.

Mainly as a result of private study, he wished to convert to Roman Catholicism at the age of fifteen, but his minister advised him to wait. However, from Christmas 1969 onwards he attended mass rather than the Baptist chapel services. He displayed an interest in the Eastern Orthodox Church as well, which he had got to know through his Sunday school teacher. "Father Laurence Bévenot[24] eventually helped me to see that the Catholic Church was the true church. The fulness was in the Catholic church, not the Eastern Orthodox Church, and certainly not the Anglican Church" (letter, 11.11.1990).

His parents agreed to his reconciliation with the Catholic Church when he had reached the age of seventeen. Dom Laurence Bévenot, his spiritual director, arranged the ceremony in the Crypt of Ampleforth Abbey in St. David's Chapel: the parish which he attended was served by monks of Ampleforth. He was received into the Catholic Church in a private ceremony on Holy Saturday, 10 April 1971, and baptized *sub conditione* between 5 and 6 p.m. in St. David's Chapel, Ampleforth. The baptism was performed by Dom Edmund Hatton, who was novice master at Ampleforth at the time. Alun Idris received Holy Communion at midnight mass from Abbot Basil Hume, the future cardinal and present archbishop of Westminster[25] (cf. letter, 11.11.1990). Doubtless, the Benedictine parish at Ampleforth exercised an influence on the young adolescent.

Still a teenager, the poet was deeply impressed by the spiritual legacy of Thérèse de Lisieux and the Curé d'Ars, but also by Thomas à Kempis, the author of the "Imitation of Christ"; these writers still maintain their attraction for the poet.

---

[23] "I received my first protestant communion then" (letter, 11.11.1990).
[24] Dom Laurence died in November 1990. His influence on Alun Idris was outstanding.
[25] The poems "(5 p.m. as I write)" (*Threshold*, 48) and "Evening of same day (10/4/82)" (*Threshold*, 47) refer to this occasion.

The first time Alun Idris heard of La Trappe was after having been received into the church in 1971, when his parents sent him to France to master the language, where he lived as an exchange student in a French family. He happened to go to church one Saturday evening and incidentally he heard a sermon on La Grande Trappe at l'église de Sainte Jeanne d'Arc in Rouen, which was not too far away from the monastery. This was his first encounter with La Trappe (cf. letter, 11.11.1990), an encounter with important consequences.

After taking A-levels in 1972, Alun Idris stayed on at school till Easter 1973 to learn Greek from scratch, and nearly entered Prinknash Abbey near Gloucester, a community of Benedictines of the Primitive Observance. However, having been granted a scholarship, he was advised to pursue a course of university studies first at the University College of Wales at Aberystwyth, taking Latin, Greek and Philosophy, reading his philosophy in Welsh (cf. letter, 19.10.1990). During the long vacation of 1974 Alun Idris first visited La Grande Trappe.

2.3. BROTHER DAVID

After graduating with joint honours in Latin and Greek in 1976, Alun Idris made a retreat with a strictly contemplative community near Bourg-en-Bresse in France, the Carthusian monastery at Sélignac. His entry at the English charterhouse was not possible:

> He could not be received by the Charterhouse in Sussex because he had not been a Catholic long enough, but he found admission in the Trappist Order at La Trappe itself. There his original Carthusian longings came to the surface and with his Superiors' consent he moved to the Carthusian Monastery at Sélignac in central France." (Burton 1985, 104f.)

He returned to La Grande Trappe for a prolonged stay before eventually entering the Carthusian monastery in France as Frère David[26] on 20 December 1976, as there was an awareness that "the Lord might be calling me to complete solitude. That was not letting me settle ..." (letter, 11.11.1990).

Huw Jones was allowed to make an interview with his brother at Sélignac in 1981: it was recorded in Welsh and in English. The Welsh version is the longer and far more effective of the two, as it was more natural for them to converse in their mother tongue. On 22 November 1981 the Welsh interview was broadcast on Radio Cymru for the first time. The Prior had given permission,[27] though the Superior General had not been informed. To ask for the latter's explicit permission was redundant, for according to a decision made at the previous general chapter the immediate superior's permission was sufficient. However, the Superior

---

[26] St. David is the patron saint of Wales. Alun Idris always kept the name: Frère David in Sélignac, Dom David at La Trappe, Brother David in Roscrea, and now at Kilnacrott Abbey he is still called Brother David. The only exception was at Farnborough Abbey, where he received the name Brother John.
[27] "Such is the separation from the world and its things that not even the monk's face is to be seen in the cell." This was the condition the Prior imposed as regards taking photographs.

General was decidedly incensed when the news finally reached him, as a Carthusian is not supposed to give interviews if it might be avoided.

"I would not have said some of the things I said on it now. It sounds dreadfully arrogant at times, but I was very enthusiastic about the Cathusian ideal at the time" (letter, 19.11.1989). Certainly the inverview was honest and straight from the heart. The questions were objective, sensible and not emotionally orientated. The interview roused considerable interest amongst the listeners and had to be repeated on the radio. An article was reproduced with *Radio Times*' permission in *Dinesydd* ("Citizen").

In his autobiography Archimandrite Barnabas writes about Alun Idris:

> My memories of Alan [sic], now frère David, are among the happiest of my souvenirs du passé. He used to stay for a few days, join in all the offices, help in the house and garden. When we talked he was amusing, full of life and outgoing. If he is finally professed in the Carthusian order, his lively personality cannot radiate among people, though it will certainly shine in God's presence. I admire his total launching into the deep of God's Mystery and love and wished there were many more like him in Wales. Our people may not be aware of his existence, but for me he is one of our glories and a sign that we can still produce such types as we did in the golden age of the Celtic Church, whose memorials abound in stone throughout the land." (Burton 1985, 105)

Unfortunately, he was unable to make solemn profession after seven years, leaving the Order on 25 March 1984, the day on which his temporary vows expired (cf. Hogg 1988a, v-vi).

Just before this time, he was given permission to make a short retreat with the Benedictines of the Solesmes Congregation at Quarr Abbey on the Isle of Wight, followed by five weeks spent at the English charterhouse of St. Hugh near Horsham. It was not possible, however, to save his vocation and go to Parkminster; the Grande Chartreuse would later refuse him permission (cf. letter, 11.11.1990). During this period of reflection the poet decided to return to La Grande Trappe, that monastery he had always felt strongly attracted to. He officially became a postulant of La Trappe on 25 March 1984, when his vows expired. However, the order regarded his writing of poetry as irreconcilable with a monastic vocation and thus he moved on to Roscrea Abbey, a Trappist foundation in Southern Ireland, nearly two years later.[28] There Alun Idris noticed how truly a "fils de la Trappe" (letter, 27.9.1989) he was, unable to overcome the inner tension caused by the French insistence on perpetual silence, handled less rigorously in Ireland, despite the kind-heartedness of the Irish monks. "There was a pull back to Wales and to the pure solitude" (letter, 11.11.1990). Deterred partially by the presence of a monastic school attached to the abbey, which inevitably lessened the seclusion of the monks, he eventually left the Trappists after long and painful considerations and returned to Wales on 20 June 1986. At Roscrea he had become enthusiastic about the possibility of re-establishing monasticism in North Wales and also fascinated by the dream of becoming a recluse, while at the same time being immersed in the activism of the

---

[28] He left La Trappe on 23 January, 1986, arriving at Roscrea on 25 January, after a long boat and train journey - a reference to this journey can be found in the poem "France, ma France!" (*Beyond*, 102).

Charismatic Renewal he had got to know about in France. He sought to follow his inspiration in this direction after leaving Roscrea and spent one month with the charismatic monastic community "du Lion de Juda", whose mother house is not far from La Trappe. This charismatic community is accomodated in an old Cistercian abbey building, l'Abbaye Blanche in Normandy. There seemed to be the possibility of making a foundation in the British Isles. However, there was some opposition and he thus returned to studies on 8 September 1986, taking instead a graduate diploma in Primary Education in 1986-87 at Normal College, Bangor, which works in conjunction with the University College of North Wales. He obtained his diploma in June 1987.

After visiting several religious houses in Great Britain he made a prolonged stay with the Benedictines of the English Congregation at Ealing Abbey, situated in the suburbs of London. During that period he was directed by Dom Dunstan Watkins, a Welsh Benedictine at Ealing, who was an expert in Ignatian retreats. It was felt by the English Congregation that he was more suited to a purely contemplative life; life in a populous London suburb, with educational obligations to boot, clashing with the ideals of a contemplative orientated soul (cf. Hogg 1993, xvi). After a preliminary month at Farnborough from 15 January to 11 February 1988, retreats at Pluscarden Abbey in Scotland, Prinknash and Ramsgate in England followed. Attracted by the strong musical tradition of the community, he finally entered Prinknash's daughter-house, the Benedictine community of the Subiaco Congregation at Farnborough in Hampshire on 15 January 1988, a Benedictine Abbey of Strict Observance (cf. Hogg 1988b, x-xi). On 7 March 1988 the official postulancy began. He was clothed as a Benedictine on 10 December 1988, the Feast of St. John Roberts, the local Welsh Benedictine martyr, and, named after the saint, was called "Brother John". Alun Idris feels particularly close to this Welsh saint: "I know that St. John Roberts wanted to do what I would like to do myself, i.e. to bring Catholic Christianity back to Wales and make it really Welsh" (letter, 10.12.1989).

Farnborough, too, felt that his contemplative formation was coming out strongly, in particular the novice master saw him as very much more contemplatively orientated than the rest of the community. Farnborough Abbey basically caters for the parish, allowing the monks less time to spend in contemplative prayer. The musical tradition at Farnborough, however, is outstanding and satisfied Alun Idris' own interest in music totally.

The decision to go to Farnborough was a hurried one, taken during a period of unrest. The poet-monk had wanted to settle, and Farnborough was willing to take him. Furthermore, there was a possibility to indulge in academic work there.

Brother John left the abbey early in 1989 and returned to Wales. To enter Prinknash Abbey was not possible at the time due to inner problems in the Order (cf. letter, 29.10.1989). Thus he stayed with the former Prior of Farnborough, Dom Basil Heath-Robinson, at Talacre Abbey from 7 March 1989 to 19 April 1989. During that period they used to chant the entire office in Latin daily in the chapel. Dom Basil took care of the empty abbey until it was sold.[29]

---

[29] Today Talacre Abbey is used as a hotel (cf. letter, 8.4.1990).

Alun Idris had hopes of seeing the monastic life re-established in North Wales: a project in which Dom Gilbert Jones, Abbot of Ramsgate and newly elected Praeses of the Subiaco Congregation, a Welshman himself, was keenly interested. Matthew, another young Welshman, had announced his intention of entering Farnborough at this moment, where he became Br. Benedict, which would have made available at least the nucleus for a community, but the local bishop remained unsympathetic and withheld approval for the project (cf. Hogg 1993, xvi). Thus Alun Idris' hopes to initiate a Benedictine foundation in North Wales were shattered. Dom Basil advised him to return to his studies; - a providential decision, as Dom Benedict soon left Farnborough, becoming a Premonstratensian canon at Storrington in Sussex (cf. Hogg 1993, xvi f.).

Fortunately, Dr. Oliver Davies commissioned the poet to participate in translating the Church Fathers from Latin and Greek into modern English, which occupied him from 20 April until the start of the new academic year in autumn 1989, when the poet commenced a three-year Bachelor of Divinity course at the University College, Bangor, whilst reflecting on the future. During that period he joined groups working for the spiritual renewal in Wales:

> I feel that at present the way the spirit can act most powerfully is through the renewal. And that is where I would like to be working. Of course, it is to the Lord who decides. [...] I tend to feel I would like to be involved with the renewal because the need for young clergy who are open to the spirit of these movements is very great and part of the problem in Britain. Not enough priests have been involved. (letter, 11.11.1990)

Alun Idris condensed the three year B.D. course into two in view of his previous studies, graduating in June 1991. During that period he was directed by Dr. John Ryan, O.M.I., a Welsh-speaking priest who celebrates the Welsh masses in the area. It was this priest who established the first contact with Holy Trinity Abbey at Kilnacrott, a Premonstratensian house in County Cavan, Ireland. After spending some time at the Abbey in September 1991, Alun Idris entered the community on the feast of St. Luke, 18 October 1991 and took the habit on the Feast of the Immaculate Conception, the 9th of December that particular year; the vigil of the feast of St. John Roberts. He reverted to his religious name of David. A two year noviciate was imposed on him, but with theological studies in Dublin recommencing after the first, although a "Leaving Cert." in Italian was granted in the first. The cultural, pastoral, and musical activities of the canons are clearly sympathetic to him. On 8 December 1993 Brother David gave himself to the Lord through the bond of sacred profession, kneeling before Fr. Abbot at the Solemn Mass. He was given the rest of the Premonstratensian habit, after placing his vows on the altar.

Only a few weeks later the Order sent him to the Angelicum in Rome in order to study Spirituality, an S.T.L. in Spiritual Theology being useful for eventual counselling work. Brother David left Ireland on 30 January 1994. He has settled very well in the eternal city, - the liturgy is executed with great care and beauty there and much silent adoration goes on in church, which has always been of utmost importance to the poet. He was admitted to second cycle studies and will stay in Rome until summer 1995.

2.4. THE WELSH BACKGROUND: CULTURAL AND LITERARY HERITAGE

Matthew Arnold visited 19th century Llandudno. He summed up that "Wales is where the past still lives, where every place has its tradition, every name is poetry, and where the people, the genuine people, still know this past, this tradition" (quoted by Abse 1983, xii). The sensitive visitor to Wales is still likely to apprehend its vivid past, even at the end of the 20th century.

Alun Idris' poetry is pervaded by the cultural background the author stems from. The real influence on his poetry is not so much from the English side as from the Welsh, which accounts for all the classicism and archaisms, as the author himself observes:

> Welsh has evolved less than English, Welsh poetry has kept to the bardic rules, kept the discipline. That is reflected in the English structure of what I've been writing. There is a certain concern for order in Welsh poetry [...] R.S. Thomas [...] is not at all in the bardic line, at least not from the structural point of view. His thought may have certain echoes of Welsh non-conformity etc. although he is an Anglican himself. The fact is that he writes in quite a revolutionary style which is not at all typically Welsh. (letter, 11.11.1990)

Welsh literature is one of the oldest vernacular literatures: it spans from the sixth century, when the poets Aneirin and Taliesin flourished in the north, to the present day (cf. Stephens 1986, v). The element of the Welsh natural native mystic tradition has been of tremendous importance to Alun Idris, in particular outstanding hymn-writers like Ann Griffiths or William Williams Pantycelyn.[30] Emyr Evans[31] writes about Alun Idris: "It is the Christo-centric nature of Alun's singing which brings the abiding greatness of the Protestant Calvinist Ann Griffiths to mind. Her lyrics are her hymns of praise per Christum Dominum Nostrum." Ann Griffiths' mystical theology in Welsh sets the pattern of expression for Alun Idris. It is the theology of the fullness of the Christian life lived in union with Christ, - and lived in such a way that it is experienced and understood. Emyr Evans continues:

---

[30] Pantycelyn is the name of the farm this famous hymn-writer comes from, a normal way to call people in Wales. Thomas Parry describes as the characteristic of William Williams of Pantycelyn's work: "his immense and profound passion, the impression left on us that this man's experience is seething in him, swelling up like the sea till it possesses him wholly, every limb, every instinct, every impulse in his personality. Here is poetic inspiration in a sense of which the old Welsh poets knew nothing." (Parry 1962, 286).

[31] Emyr Evans in a letter to the present writer, dated 4 January 1991. Emyr Evans spent three years studying philosophy at Oxford and another three years studying theology. His abiding interest in poetry, literature and music is well-rooted. Song, both in the sense of poetry and music, has been the very essence of life from his childhood onwards.

The adoration of Christ crucified and risen was the spring of Ann Griffiths' poetic creativity. For Alun, the same adoration emerges during the years of silence and solitude and beyond. So does the awareness of the transcending cosmic beauty of God in Jesus Christ.

Welsh poets are of more influence than English. "I was reading far more Welsh poetry than English poetry in solitude" (letter, 11.11.1990)[32], as Alun Idris himself points out.

The Welsh poet may employ so-called "free metres" (which include blank verse, quatrains, couplets, sonnets etc.) or some of the 24 "classical" (or "strict") metres of Welsh prosody, the *cywydd metre*, the *englyn* etc. which are based on a counting of syllables per line and which also involve the poet in the use of *cynghanedd* (of which there are numerous different kinds).[33] When looking at some of Alun Idris' Welsh poems, one can detect alliteration, internal rhyme as well as consonantal correspondence at times. As regards his English verse, he seems to employ typically Welsh forms as well. Does the knowledge of classical Welsh metres influence his English poetry? Is it a conscious or an unconscious influence? Doubtless, in his early English poems, the Welsh metres are an influence, because a number of them were written for hymn tunes. Alun Idris often selected a Welsh hymn metre for a poem because he wanted to sing the verse, in order to add a further dimension to it (cf. letter, 10.3.1991). Alun Idris is more interested in the creation of sound effects rather than strict *cynghanedd*:

> As regards *cynghanedd*, I tend to aim for what sounds *cynghaneddol* (consonantal) - or simply harmonious - without being technically so. The Welsh ear is attuned to the fairness of audible order, and it is more an instinctive, almost subconscious use of sound effect that is at work, rather than a deliberate one to be in a definite tradition. The problem with the Welsh bardic laws is that they can at times be oppressive. The Chair at the *Eisteddfod* demands *cynghanedd* - to the full - whereas the Crown gives greater liberty in this respect. (letter, 10.3.1991)

Although he avoids writing in strict *cynghanedd*, he can not avoid being influenced by it. ("One is so used to hearing it in Wales.") He explains:

> I love the sound and sight of *cynghanedd* [...] but I never felt that poetry [...] was that kind of exercise. [...] I always felt that poetry, at least for me, is something very direct, it has always been the way I have expressed my innermost

---

[32] Here the high Anglican priest Gwenallt Jones, who wrote a lot of poetry, can be mentioned as having exerted certain influence on the poet as well.
[33] At school Alun Idris was taught the rules of *cynghanedd*, being especially trained at *cynghanedd draws* and *cynghanedd groes*. The other two main types are even more difficult (*cynghanedd lusg* and *cynghanedd sain*). Thomas Parry mentions these as the four main types to which they all can, basically, be reduced (cf. Parry 1962, 122-124). With *cynghanedd draws* all the principal consonants have to exist in both halves of the lines, but the order is not of capital importance. As regards *cynghanedd groes*, the principal consonants in both halves of the lines also appear in the same order, which makes this type more demanding (cf. letter, 10.3.1991). Of the 24 strict metres, three are the most popular ones: the *cywydd*, the *englyn* and the *hir a thoddaid*. It is for the *cywydd* that the Chair is given at the National *Eisteddfod* (cf. Parry 1962, 125f.). Writing such forms entails a lot of patience: "I always tended to avoid getting into that straight jacket unless I really had to." (letter, 10.3.1991).

thoughts. To do that I felt I needed a certain freedom to operate. The sonnet, for example, does give you a certain form, restrictions, but it is a form within which you can, nevertheless, breathe, whereas *cynghanedd* is so demanding that you cannot let your mind wander. You cannot sigh a poem. You've got to sigh with reservation." (letter, 10.3.1991)

As regards metre, rhyme and diction the poet does not perceive any significant difference between his English and Welsh verse. The only difference worth mentioning would be that the Welsh verse appears less archaic than the English, because both Welsh verse and the Welsh language are fairly conservative by nature and have evolved less. "On the whole the words and word forms used in the Welsh poetry I've written are used in everyday life." Alun Idris is aware of the impression his English verse gives:

It is very archaic but in fact it is, in a sense, wanting to preserve a distance which is automatically there in the Welsh verse in a way, because there is a certain elegance about the Welsh language, especially when you use it in verse. It is very easy to write in a poetic way in Welsh. [...] In English, I sense, in order to get that distance if you like, that idea of dignity and nobility of verse, it is necessary to use words which are, perhaps, a bit more carefully chosen than they would be in conversation." (letter, 10.3.1991)

Concerning metre, he does not see much difference between his English and his Welsh poetic output, whereas as regards rhyme the difference would be the ease with which rhymes are formed. While it is fairly easy to find rhymes in English, it is more difficult to do so in Welsh, according to the poet, for the simple reason that the Welsh language has a more restricted vocabulary. The English language is extremely rich, having many sources: Greek, Latin, Anglo-Saxon, Norman-French, Celtic, even Indian. As a result, one usually finds two words in English for one word in Welsh. In Welsh the diction is not as wide as in English.

Some of Alun Idris' poems exist both in English and in Welsh:

What I did from the beginning was to produce an English one as a self-contained creation. Ideas of the Welsh would tend to come over to the English one, come out in another form, the same theme, the same thoughts perhaps, expressed in a different medium. This happened a lot in the charterhouse, especially in the early stages: for every English one there would be a Welsh one, the Welsh came first in beginning. But the English one would be a unit of its own, it would not be a translation." (letter, 10.3.1991)

Asked whether he preferred to compose in Welsh he negates, explaining that to him it depended on the circumstances, "a poem comes out of the context in which it is written" (letter, 10.3.1991). "In France I liked to compose in French. Again that reflects the context." The habit of writing in French did not stop after leaving the country. The fact that he wrote Latin poems was apparently caused by the fact that in the charterhouse Latin was the language of the day, the monks worshipped in Latin most of the time, the studies also being largely made in Latin, at least as regards the main text books (cf. letter, 10.3.1991).

"I don't really mind whether it's Welsh or English, they both come pretty easily. Actually the English comes out easier for the reasons that have already been given. On the other hand, the Welsh poems - when they come - tend to be slightly more direct, more elegant at times. I don't know what it is, but there is a certain distance in the English ones, which is not there in the Welsh." (letter, 10.3.1991)

Apparently, the bilingual poet considers Welsh to be his mother tongue, which becomes obvious in the last quote. Equally, the Reverend Emyr Evans[34] states about Alun Idris:

> Alun's singing has the fullest immediacy and power when singing in his own native tongue. The Welsh language, ancient in its origin, is his mother tongue. His mystical theology is verbally clothed most impressively in his Welsh verse.

Welsh is a language which has survived the English conquest of Wales in the 13th century. It has even survived its prohibition under the Act of Union of 1536. The 14th century had seen an astonishing flowering of the already centuries old Welsh poetic tradition. Rooted in Taliesin in the 6th century, the poetic tradition of praise was a profound expression of Catholic faith in the 14th century. Emyr Evans continues:

> Alun Idris, as a Catholic, does not sing today in the company of modern Welsh poets through the strict classical metre of ancient tradition. Rather he uses lyrical forms and his lyrics are disciplined usage of words in the construction of illuminating images. They cannot be translated from the Welsh without loss of a distinctive colour, which is incorporated in the Welshness of his vision. In English, similarities remain in the same basic noble conceptions of thought, but the painting is different in its intensity. The basis of his art is Welsh.

Emyr Evans draws parallels to their famous compatriot Dylan Thomas and quotes the Northern Irish poet William Robert Rodgers: "But the first thing about Dylan was that he was Welsh. [...] Words sang for him, and that is the birthmark of a poet. Dylan preferred *sound sense to sound sense*" (Rodgers 1954, 913). In an unsigned review of Dylan Thomas' *Collected Poems 1934-52*, published by Dent, we read in the *Times Literary Supplement* of November 28, 1952:

> In this moving poem ['Do not go gentle into that good night'] with its economy of structure and rhyme-sound is a reminder of Mr. Thomas's debt to the Welsh poetic tradition. It is said that he does not speak Welsh. It is certain that he thinks Welsh. [...] It would be valuable to have a more precise estimate of [...] how much the rhythm and structure of his poems owe to the traditional Welsh forms.

Emyr Evans draws an analogy to Alun Idris:

---

[34] Emyr Evans in a letter to the present writer, dated 4.1.1991.

The first thing about Alun Idris is that he is Welsh. He is at one with Dylan Thomas in his care for words. Words instinctively sing for Alun. It is also his birthmark as a poet. But he does differ from Dylan Thomas in that he prefers sound *sense* to *sound* sense. What sound sense? God's sound sense, - His order, which is also His gracious presence *per christum dominum nostrum*. This is what commands Alun's attention. (letter, 4.1.1991)

The poet's Welsh background is of fundamental importance and basic to his verse, a fact which cannot be doubted. As Emyr Evans points out, words sing for Alun Idris, he uses them to create beauty for God and give Him honour. This commands his attention, much more than the matter of "Wales" as such, which does not necessarily play an essential part:

My poetry tends to be more universal in a sense because dealing with God, dealing with love, solitude and silence is dealing with things which are beyond Wales. [...] I never regarded Wales as an absolute, whereas things like the spiritual life, truth, providence and God, being faithful to one's function, one's role in eternity, whatever that is, is more central than everything Welsh. Wales would come into that insofar as I feel I have a duty towards Wales and a pull towards Wales and a longing to serve Wales, and to keep it Wales." (letter, 10.3.1991)

The principal problem with linguistic minorities is the fact that only a very limited group of people have access to their cultural world. The language is threatened with extinction, hence any form of literary activity equally fights for survival. Accompanied by the disappearance of a language is the vanishing of a particular culture, and history is full of such examples. However, it can be observed that, depending on the social status of a linguistic minority, they often fight tenaciously and untiringly for the survival of their language. Welsh culture belongs to this vast group of small-population cultures throughout the world that "do not fit into the conventional and rather restricted nucleus of mass-cultures" (Jones and Thomas 1986, 5).[35] Welsh culture is still very much alive - the enormous interest in the annual National *Eisteddfod* impressively illustrates its vitality. The existence and flourishing of this competition meeting strikes the non-Welsh visitor as quite exceptional. Maxwell Fraser describes this distinctively Welsh institution:

---

[35] Bobi Jones attempted to summarize the salient features that give Welsh literature its particular character and colour (cf. Jones and Thomas 1986, 5f.):
- Its longevity: the sheer length of unbroken experience of Welsh literature.
- The splendour of the medieval prose tales, and, in particular, the influential charm of the Arthurian legend.
- Dafydd ap Gwilym as one of the most remarkable poets in the Middle Ages: both form and content in his poetry are profound and varied.
- The polished classicisms of the aristocratic poets of the 14th and 15th centuries.
- *Cynghanedd*: this method of patterning verse is probably unequalled in any other literature as regards its complexity.
- After the Act of Annexation: versifying was not limited merely to the middle and upper classes.
- In the 18th and 19th centuries, the powerful experiential movement of the Methodist Revival gave rise to a profound and widespread occupation with hymn-writing: the expression of feelings and thoughts dealing with essential things of life became the calling of scores of writers amongst the ordinary folk, as e.g. Ann Griffiths.
- Welsh literature has always been parallelled by a certain social and linguistic crisis. This ever-present danger lends a certain thrill and urgency to Welsh *engagé* literature that is a part of its permanent character.

The Eisteddfod is the final expression of all that is most vital and lovable in Welsh life, and reflects to perfection the Welsh character, with its love of good company, gaiety, music, poetry, oratory, and intellectual rivalry. (Fraser 1952, 125)

Summarizing the influences of the Welsh language and literature, one may say that the instinct is there to observe form and to create beauty through form, sound effects etc. As regards the writing of Welsh poetry, Alun Idris prefers the freer medium, i.e. not using *cynghanedd*. The Welsh language is quite dignified and it can be made to sound beautiful when it is well read. According to the poet, it is easy in a sense to write pleasant sounding Welsh poetry "because of the nature of the language; one has to make a certain effort with English" (letter, 7.4.1991). The use of archaisms in his English verse is an echo of this statement, an effort to find that touch of dignity and "distance" which in Alun Idris' opinion belongs to poetry. The sonnet is very popular in Wales, and apparently it represents a suitable medium for Alun Idris to express his thoughts, both in his Welsh and his English verse. As regards other forms, the Welsh influence is there principally in the form of conservatism with regard to diction, rhyme and metre. In the poet's opinion, most Welsh poets wrote in a Christian ambience, and many contributed, in passing, to the country's rich hymnology. Equally, many of his own poems are meant also to be sung (cf. letter, 10.3.1991). The tunes attached to the poems add another dimension to them.

Religious poetry has a long tradition in Wales. Welsh poetry written by monks is known for certain to have existed in the early period of Welsh literature. Nine *englynion* of praise to the Trinity are preserved, written in the tenth century (cf. Parry 1962, 21). Religion was the theme of many an ode in the Middle Ages.[36]

> If monks and friars were in the habit of writing poetry (and why should they not have been?) it is possible that there were once many poems like this, but that they have gone the same way as so many other things - into oblivion. (Parry 1962, 57)

2.5. LITERARY INFLUENCES

Since his college days, Alun Idris has always been enchanted by the poetry of Shakespeare, "the eternity of his lines, the beauty of his language, the depth of thought behind" (letter, 15.10.1989). At school, an admiration for both Wordsworth and Keats developed, in particular for the latter. The admiration for these poets certainly reinforced Alun Idris' own predilection for the sonnet. However, due to the rigorous, strict conditions in the monasteries

---

[36] We find a great deal of so-called poems to God, which as a rule contained praise to God and the Trinity, a confession of sin, and a plea for mercy. Equally widespread were poems to saints, saints' lives being popular in the Middle Ages (cf. Parry 1962, 55f.).

he had not been able to read much of their poetry since his school days. Among the French he particularly liked Lamartine, Victor Hugo, Alfred Vigny:

> But the poems I was writing were really independent of literary sources. We had no contact with the literature *we* are talking of in the charterhouse. The only source of poetry I would be reading would be hymns. I had my great-grandmother's prayer-book and hymn-book with me. (letter, 11.11.1990)

Those hymns were written in an old English style, which was, however, of some influence.

Another literary figure, who is also an important spiritual guide for Alun Idris, is Cardinal Newman: a Roman Catholic writer himself, yet much of his thought transcends any particular religious tenet. Newman did not write for literary fame, financial reward, or merely for the joy of writing. Duty to truth alone was his motive (cf. Lapati 1972, 7), which relates him to Alun Idris. Furthermore, Newman's versatility in employing diverse modes of expression impressed the novice monk. Although Newman subordinated style to thought, he was painstakingly scrupulous in producing his manuscripts (cf. Lapati 1972, 119). His style and the power of his words and thought are impressive. Newman's sense of providence certainly confirmed Alun Idris' own belief. A faith in providence derived from the life of Newman does not demand any recognition of the miraculous or the magical (cf. Wakefield 1984, 4).

Alun Idris had always been very fond of Welsh poetry. T.H. Parry-Williams, one of the great Welsh poets who died in 1975, while Alun Idris was studying in Aberystwyth, certainly exerts powerful influence. Parry-Williams' cousin, R. Williams Parry, is of equal importance to Alun Idris, - the novice monk was sent some of Williams Parry's work when he was at Sélignac: "I remember being moved by it. In fact that was before I wrote much myself, if at all. [...] I remember being in great admiration that he could write such words." (letter, 8.4.1990). The figure of the monk keeps appearing in "Yr Haf", a famous poem by Williams Parry, reminding the lover that he must think of more lasting joys, and not place his happiness in this life. Parry himself puts his own philosophy into the lover's answers. There is joy here. Why wait for the beyond?[37] When referring to Welsh writers, Alun Idris mentions that "these are all unknown outside Wales, this is one reason why I think it is important that a Welsh person should write in English as well" (letter, 8.4.1990). A sound argument in favour of writing in both languages, in spite of the poet's serious concern about the decline of the Welsh language.

---

[37] Cf. letter, 6.5.1990. "Yr Haf" (Williams Parry 1978, 55-92) is one of the great classics of Welsh literature. It won R. Williams Parry the Chair in the 1910 *Eisteddfod*; he lectured at Bangor and died in 1956.

2.6. THE TWO VOCATIONS IN ALUN IDRIS JONES

Alun Idris wrote little poetry before entering the Carthusian monastery at Sélignac[38] and his poetic activity there did not become intense until three or four years later. The first time he felt the urge to write a poem was on the occasion of his mother's competition for the National *Eisteddfod* in 1978: she had written a hymn tune which Alun Idris liked, and made him compose a poem for it. The Welsh version of "Ash Wednesday" (*Threshold*, 25) did not fit to the tune too well (cf. letter, 29.10.1989), thus he wrote a Welsh poem to St. David. He produced the English version shortly afterwards: "St. David's Day" (*Threshold*, 27).

However, it was not before the winter of 1980 that he started to pay more attention to poems. His interest in poetry increased constantly, and a whole volume of poems was written. In the charterhouse at Sélignac, however, literary pursuits were, to say the least, not encouraged; in particular as regards the publication of his verse. The situation became more tense as the time approached for Br. David to take his final vows after seven years and he was forbidden to read certain books which had been sent to him as presents by his family, and strongly discouraged from writing poetry. His Superiors sensed a certain danger in his creative output, interpreting the desire to communicate his ideas in the form of poetry as hidden pride. A Carthusian's main object is to pray and contemplate, devote one's entire being to the Lord. His father saw no happy future for his son in an Order where any form of literary, creative or artistic activity seemed to be frowned upon, and thus requested a transfer to a more open monastic order, or, failing that, his complete release from monastic life.[39] The conflict terminated in the monk's crisis of frustration at not being allowed to continue; he never considered writing poetry as a sinful offence against a monastic or priestly calling. In 1982 the novice monk was asked to destroy anything else he wrote. He was given to understand that he should have destroyed what he had already written, and that he had no right to show it to people outside; he was asked to obey as regards future creations. This explains the absence of verse between then and 1984.

Despite the growing difficulties, Alun Idris was granted permission to publish a volume of poems written in Welsh, *Cri o Gell*. Daniel Mullins, the auxiliary Bishop of Cardiff from 1968-78, Bishop of Menevia (=St. David's) from 1988, was interested in literature and Welsh culture and felt the need for publishing Alun Idris' poetry. Both he and Dom Laurence Bévenot wanted to see it in print, the Welsh poetry as well as the interview his brother had done with him. Therefore the bishop wrote for permission to the Order, which allowed the publication of the Welsh selection (the publication of any English poem was strictly prohibited) under three conditions (cf. interview in Fraham, 1.7.1990):

---

[38] He wrote some poetry at school, even winning a Chair for one poem on the Feast of St. David in 1965 (cf. interview, 13.8.1990). But according to the author himself poetry is very much a part of Welsh life, just as music is: "It's part of the Welsh blood. All the time being bathed in music and verse. It's probably far more important to Welsh people than to others, it's very deep in Welsh psyche, the Welsh spirit" (letter, 15.10.1989).
[39] Cf. letter of Idris Jones to the present writer, dated 27 September, 1989.

a) it was to be published anonymously
b) there was to be no mention of the Order (which explains the crosses in the poems)
c) it must be considered an exception, there will be no repetition of this favour.

This was the end of publishing any more verse within the Carthusian Order.

The attitude of the superiors at La Trappe towards Alun Idris' literary inclinations did not significantly differ from that held in the charterhouse. Although the novice master allowed him to write poetry, he made it clear that La Trappe was for prayer and not so much for writing poetry. Here again the crucial point was Brother David's wish to publish the verse, while the superiors advised him to keep quiet about it and not let anybody else read it. The Trappist community at Roscrea, Ireland, however, encouraged his writing of poetry, which had come to a complete stop.

Apparently, the poetic vein had started to flow within the novice monk, and a strong tension between his literary inclination and the demands of a religious order were noticeable. There is a certain outward similarity between Alun Idris' position in the various monasteries and the tense situation in which G.M. Hopkins[40] found himself, with the difference, however, that the former has never been tempted to burn his poetry and has never looked upon the writing of poetry as a sinful offence against his monastic or priestly calling (cf. letter of Idris Jones, 27 September 1989). Additionally, whilst the "sprung rhythms" of some of Hopkins' verse were largely inspired by the alliteration, assonance and other features of the 24 strict metres of ancient Welsh poetry, Alun Idris' work shows a predilection for rhymed verse forms, particularly the sonnet. And yet there can be no doubt about the applicability of Hopkins' words to Brother David's situation, namely that it is difficult to be, "a priest true to heaven and a poet true to earth." It must be emphasized, however, that Brother David does not see such a contrast in the two vocations. On the contrary, to him poetry and priesthood or monasticism may form a wonderful symbiosis, namely when poetry is used to praise the Lord, and thus he represents both "a priest true to heaven" equally as "a poet true to earth".[41] To him the poetic vein is a divine grace which should be used to praise God.

---

[40] Incidentally, St. Beuno's, the college where G.M. Hopkins studied for the priesthood during three years and where he wrote some of his best-known poems, is not very far away from Caernarvon, where Alun Idris' parents live (cf. letter, 10.12.1989). Hopkins is said to have virtually killed himself trying to reconcile the functions of priest and poet: "The versifier and the preacher get on together; but real poetry is nonconformist" (Carter 1953, 246).

[41] The latter might need further explanation. Although a monk's thinking and striving is for the "via unitiva" only, he is, nevertheless, as all human beings are, earthbound, having to accept the mundane and transitory part in us. Against the idea of considering the body as prison of the mind and soul, the body is equally a divine gift as the mind and soul are. Thus in combination with being "true to heaven" there can be no objection to the natural connection with the earth. Another important point is that, despite their comtemplative lives and seclusion from the rest of society, the Carthusians, as well as other contemplative Orders, do not neglect the world as such, as might appear on the outside, but they are firmly tied up with it: they pray for our world and thus form a certain part of the entire Christian mystical body, which is just as important as the socially engaged, communitarian, neighbour-oriented section of the church.

3. THE LYRE AND THE CROSS: ALUN IDRIS' POETRY WRITTEN IN CONTEMPLATIVE ORDERS

This chapter, which forms the central part of the investigation, is divided into four parts: the Carthusian period, the Trappist period, the so-called period of restless search and finally the interim period outside monastic quarters. These parts reflect the poet's own spiritual path until autumn 1991. Each of the chapters examines the relationship between the two vocations, in particular as regards the function of poetry for the contemplative monk, as well as monastic or spiritual criteria which serve as stimuli of the poetic vein.

3.1. THE CARTHUSIAN PERIOD

1 General view of the charterhouse at Sélignac

3.1.1. POETRY AS A MIRROR OF CARTHUSIAN LIFE

3.1.1.1. THE NATURE OF CONTEMPLATIVE LIFE - THE "DAILY ROUTINE"

The poems in *The Threshold of Paradise* mirror to a considerable extent Alun Idris' life and spiritual pilgrimage in the charterhouse at Sélignac. They offer insight into a silent and solitary life generally unknown and inaccessible to our society, and invite the reader to share the experience conveyed therein. The poems stem from the intensity of life in the Carthusian Order and represent a vivid testimony illustrating the Carthusian's daily experience. A great deal has been written about life in Carthusian monasteries, offering a detailed description of such a life in solitude and silence;[42] however, the poems contained in *The Threshold of Paradise* were composed "from within" the monastic walls by a person intimately involved, a Carthusian monk, which adds to the degree of authenticity conveyed. The poetic skill used to express his experience turns the poetry into a rare documentation of life in the charterhouse. The poems dealt with in this chapter offer authentic glimpses of the everyday experience of a Carthusian monk, allowing the reader to enter a realm from which he is normally firmly excluded.

In a contemplative monastery life does not offer much variety, the days resemble each other closely, even monotonously. In "Just another day" (*Threshold*, 61f.), Alun Idris describes a complete day in the charterhouse. This rather elaborate poem consists of 23 quatrains written in iambic tetrameter, though the majority of the lines start with inversion. The one-line afterthought attached to the poem at the very end represents the 24th stanza, thereby completing the 24th hour of the day. The verse describes a Sunday, the only day (apart from feast days) which is slightly different from the others (cf. Thompson 1930, 37).

The poem starts in the middle of the night, when the day begins for the Carthusian with the night office. Except at Christmas, on Easter Sunday and at Whitsuntide, the monk is roused by a bell or other signal at about eleven o'clock for matins of the Blessed Virgin. A second bell summons him and the other monks to church, where they celebrate the night office, which, following the Carthusian rite, is fairly long, vigils, with matins and lauds, lasting about four hours in total. This means that they are sometimes scarcely over before three o'clock in the morning. Having finished matins and lauds the monks return to their cells, reciting lauds of the Blessed Virgin before retiring to their beds to repose a second time, awaiting the hour of prime[43] (cf. Thompson 1930, 35f.):

> Matins are sung, and sleep returns
> To heavy eyelids that have kept
> Prayer's silent Lamp, that onward burns,
> Vigilant o'er the Prayer that slept.

---

[42] The number of books, essays and works of vulgarisation is considerable. Suffice to say that the most comprehensive work on the Carthusian Order in England was written by E. Margaret Thompson in 1930.
[43] Until the mid fifteenth century the monks did not retire to bed again after matins and lauds, but the night office started later.

> Now as I dose I hear the sound
> That, far away, doth others rouse.
> For them e'en now begins the Round
> Of sacred duties in thine house.
>
> Onward and onward as I sleep
> The Torch is passed from quire to quire:
> Convent on convent now doth keep
> Each in its turn the Vestal fire.

The medial pauses suggest an idea of balance and peace, reinforcing the prevailing solemn tone. The spondee in "Prayer's silent Lamp" places additional emphasis on the idea of prayer going round the world, when now for others "begins the Round / Of sacred duties in thine house". The capitalized "Round" suggests how the "Torch" of prayer is passed on continuously: the Trappists start their prayers when the Carthusians stop, and when they have finished, they hand the prayer on to the Benedictines. The Carmelites are the first to hold the "silent Lamp", they chant their matins before they go to bed, around ten o'clock in the evening:

> Sleep will have gained my eyes again
> Ere Bennet's sons take up the Light.
> Onward I'll *s*leep a*s P*rayer'*s s*weet *s*train
> From Carmel'*s* pea*c*e *p*ervade*s* the night.

The quatrain describes how the members of the other orders "take up the Light" while the Carthusians are taking their rest: "Bennet's sons" refers, of course, to the followers of St. Benedict. The imagery used in l.4, "Carmel's peace pervades the night", underlines the idea that the Carmelites prefer a quiet, very peaceful form of prayer, using simple chants when they sing. The use of "pervade" beautifully suggests the power of their silent prayer, which fills the night quietly. The alliteration of p's and s's (both voiced and voiceless) suggest the soothing continuity of prayer. The oxymoron in l.3, "Prayer's sweet strain", seeks to imply both the bliss of prayer and the effort linked with it. Every night, the Carthusian's sleep is interrupted for several hours in order to praise the Lord, a penance of somewhat physical and mental severity. "It was, as it were, a lamp being passed from one to the other. When the whole monastic world has finished, people wake up." (interview, 13.8.1990).

At "excitation", which is the monastic word for being woken up, we read:

> ... Yea, so it was! Sleep took my soul!
> Now 'tis my turn to join my voice
> - When I have found my frock, my cowl -
> To this vast Hymn, with lesser noise -
>
> For 'tis in silence that I sing:
> Only my breath doth cross my lips;
> Yet, as I hear this Prime bell ring,
> My prayer into a greater slips:

The exclamatory "Yea, so it was!" firmly implies the idea of awakening, being ready and prepared with new energies for the new day to come. The buoyant "Now 'tis my turn" surprises in its lightness, visualizing a monk sparkling with vitality. There is a strong human touch apparent in these lines, waking up in his cell and getting ready is vividly presented and complemented by that very typical gesture in the early morning, "- When I have found my frock, my cowl -" as though there was much choice in a Carthusian wardrobe! Brother David was in charge of night excitation, i.e. he had to wake up his brethren at night, who would answer by knocking on the floor with a wooden stick to tell him that they were awake. After having completed his task, he then is ready to join in this "vast Hymn" of prayer, "with lesser noise" though, as is explained in the quatrain to follow. Traditionally, the monks whisper their prayers in their cells, which is reflected in these lines. His prayer is part of the "vast Hymn", which suggests the idea of song and adds an affective component to prayer, celebrating in song the love of God. The monks get up at 6.30 ("I hear this Prime bell ring"), at 6.45[44] they start reciting prime, and thus they join the great prayer of the church, "My prayer into a greater slips":

> One in my quire, I'm one with all
> Who at this hour these Psalms recite:
> From sea to sea, in pew and stall,
> Monks, sisters, faithful now unite -
>
> And greet with me the Sabbath dawn,
> Offer with me its firstfruits sweet[45]
> Deep in the calm of waking Morn,
> Laid - ere't be soiled - before Thy feet.

The peace and solemnity conveyed in l.1 is the basis for the growing excitement implied as the stanza progresses, underlined by the enumerations and pauses: it is the thrill of inviting the world to join the prayer. "In pew" (l.3) suggests the prayer in the parish, as this is a Sunday morning, while the "stall" of course refers to the monastery. Asking all the faithful to join in the vast prayer creates a certain tension, which is powerfully suggested by the solemn phrase "now unite", with the pause in between adding to its degree of solemnity.

In a Carthusian monastery Sunday is a day of peace. Only essential work is executed. It is a calm day, devoted to sacred study. And yet after thanksgiving we read in stanza 15:

> And so it is! - The warning bell
> Rings as I trace one last wee line ...
> O! noisy solitary bell!
> How for the peaceful World I pine!

"In a monastery one can be almost more hurried than in the world because one is always called by the bell. Even if you are trying to write a poem it is difficult because the bell is always calling in a very sort of dramatic way." (interview, 13.8.1990). A surprising thought indeed,

---

[44] Times vary slightly from country to country.
[45] "Firstfruit" is spelt as one word in 1 Cor 15:20 (King James Version).

which, however, appears in other poems as well. The bell is presented as the driving force regulating and organizing life in the monastery.

"... And None was sung ... and Faults were said, / As we before the altar lay": the Carthusians hold a weekly chapter of faults in the chapterhouse. The prior makes any comments that have to be made. There is, of course, one fault which is graver than any other in this silent order: to speak without permission. If a monk commits such a sin he is physically disciplined upon his shoulders ("Whipped for the frailty of our clay"). Rather than a painful it is more a humiliating experience, a custom which certainly helps to maintain the observance (cf. interview, 13.8.1990). "... A song was heard ... and sins were washed / In Absolution's sacred stream ...": soliloquies are allowed, however, the monks also have the liberty to sing.[46]

After vespers the monks dedicate themselves to "Lectio Divina": "'Reading Divine' - O Sacred Word! / Here in Night's peace make heard thy power." The interior rhyme in "Word" and "heard" suggests the aim of lectio divina, grasping and being filled with the "Sacred Word", meditating on it, interiorizing the Word.

"Recollection" is the term for the half-hour before compline, which is spent in prayer: "Let me in this last precious prayer / Leave far behind the noise of words." The first half of that period should be spent looking back over the day, the second half on preparing the points of meditation for the next morning. Compline is always recited in the cell. As they begin the Divine Office, so the monks end it with the Lord's prayer (cf. Thompson 1930, 37).

> Each day will pass as this one, God!
> Compline to Compline counts the beat
> Of Life's accelerating plod,
> Time's rhythmic fierce goose-stepping feet.
>
> Soon will the bell close off the day:
> Th'Angelus and "le Grand Silence"
> Will seal in peace its hours for aye
> - And these mine eyes in somnolence.
>
> ... And so it was.

The rhythm of the last but one stanza is characterized by a strong beat: the accumulation of the harsh voiceless plosives /k/, /p/ and /t/ particularly in the second line suggests almost military dictatorship of time in its inexorable march. The sound symbolism in l.4, the dominance of voiceless consonants and sharp fricatives emphasize the idea of brutality, time demanding its inevitable progress. The imagery used in "Time's rhythmic fierce goose-stepping feet" powerfully conveys the sense of inexorability. The closing stanza, however, in particular ll.3 and 4, forms a rhythmical contrast to the previous one, conveying a gentle, soft tone, with long vowels and diphthongs prevailing, thereby creating a peaceful and solemn atmosphere. The short sentence attached to the poem demands attention for various reasons. It echoes the

---

[46] "It was in fact easier to sing there than in a coenobitic monastery when you are always together" (interview, 13.8.1990).

opening line of stanza 15 quoted above, "And so it is", thereby suggesting the fulfilment of the divine plan, transforming it from the present into the past. "And so it was" not only involves retrospection, however, it also reminds one of the "amen" of a prayer. "Amen" actually means "and so be it". The adaptation of this line therefore implies that the deed was done, and God's will observed.

"Just another day" is furnished with music written especially for the poem by Alun Idris himself. This musical accompaniment leads us back to the idea of prayer as a "Vast Hymn", music and song coupled in divine harmony helping to make prayer even more powerful.

In a charterhouse the bell is of special importance as it indicates the progression of the various parts of the day, calling the monks to church, to prayer, to work etc. The almighty voice of the bell organizes the Carthusian day, which can at times be a burden, as is implied in the previous poem. The power of the bell is also apparent in the following lines taken from "Easter Week" (*Threshold*, 52):

> Almighty Bell, voice of my God,
> Rule o'er the Cloister by thy nod:
> Thou art the King of this small band -
> Each sentry waits for thy command.

The opening line of this poem echoes an inscription on one of the bells of the Grande Chartreuse: "vox dilecti" (the voice of the beloved), which refers to the Song of Songs, Canticum Canticorum 5:2, "Ego dormio et cor meum vigilat. Vox dilecti mei pulsantis: 'Aperi mihi, soror mea, amica mea, columba mea,' immaculata mea, quia caput meum plenum est rore, et cincinni mei guttis noctium."[47] The prescription, which is taken from the Rule of St. Benedict, is that the monks should cease everything they are doing when they hear the bell; it functions as a "signal", as is specified in the Rule of St. Benedict, chapter 43, paragraph 1: "Ad horam divini Officii, mox auditus fuerit signus, relictis omnibus quaelibet fuerint in manibus, summa cum festinatione curratur, cum gravitate tamen, ut non scurrilitas inveniat fomitem." (Seidle 1978, 136).[48] The Rule stipulates: One must leave everything that one has in hand and go quickly, with all haste, but with dignity, however, so as not to give any occasion for dissipation. Thus, nothing should be preferred to the divine office, i.e. nothing may enjoy primacy over it. This explains why the bell is so powerful, why it is the "King of this small band": it bends the monk's will.

The poem refers directly to the Rule of St. Benedict's[49] specifications for the canonical hours:

---

[47] "I slept, but my heart lay waking; I dreamed - ah! there is my darling knocking! 'Open to me, my own', he calls, 'my dear, my dove, my paragon.' My head is drenched with dew, my hair with drops of the night." In Carthusian monasteries there are two sets of bells: one is geared to the clock, the other to the church.
[48] St. Benedict established the use of the monastic bell while he was living in a hermitage. The monks first used pieces of wood, later the bell.
[49] In the Rule of St. Benedict 16:1 we read: "Ut ait Propheta: *Septies in die laudem dixi tibi*." (Seidle 1978, 100). - As the prophet says: *seven times a day I praise Thee*. The reference is to Psalm 119 (118):164, where we read: "Septies in die laudem dixi tibi super iudicia iustitiae tuae."

> "Arise! Prepare to meet your God;
> Keep watch! Be girded, vested, shod.
> Seven times a day lift up your hands -
> Lo! calling the muezzin stands.

St. Benedict wished to preserve the scriptural seven. Therefore he legislated for the celebration of this sacred number at matins, prime, terce, sext, none, vespers and compline. He elucidates further in his rule: "Nam de nocturnis Vigiliis idem ipse Propheta ait: *Media nocte surgebam ad confitendium tibi.*" (Seidle 1978, 100). - As regards vigils the same prophet said: *in the middle of the night, I would get up to praise thee.*[50] This passage signalizes the origin of the night office, which is reflected in Alun Idris' poem: "The eighth is in the heart of night, / In silence deep, 'neath sacred light."

In the closing stanza the poet addresses the bell subserviantly, emphasizing his own insignificance in comparison with the power of it:

> Yea, brazen Master sing thy song.
> Gargantua, toy with thy gong:
> Thy slightest wish is my command -
> All little, I before thee stand.

The metaphor "Gargantua" he uses for the bell recalls a giant who figures in children's books in France. Although hardly petrifying, the nod of the bell is "gargantuan" in its effects, regulating the life of the monks. The poet is determined to serve and to listen to the bell's song, "Thy slightest wish is my command".[51] The tune "Iam lucis orto sidere" has been deliberately chosen for this poem to suggest the passage of time: it is a tune for prime, the first hour of the day (cf. interview, 13.8.1990).

Life in the Carthusian monastery is monotonous, any occasion which differs from the usual daily routine appears to be a welcome change. "Some stray lines (begun after the June examination)" (*Threshold*, 77) consists of eight stanzas written in iambic tetrameter (employing embraced rhyme) and deals with the subject of holidays at Sélignac: the end of the exams is followed by a holiday; for a month the monks do not have any official study. Of course, such a vacation is a purely interior break, no travelling is involved (cf. letter, 16.9.1990). And yet, the very thought of a holiday provokes a feeling of joy, most of all as it recalls happy memories, as is apparent in the third stanza:

> Vacation! Holiday! Repose!
> - When I recall what these once meant
> - Nay, what they mean e'en now to those
> Who twelve whole months in toil have spent.

---

[50] Cf. Psalm 119 (118):62.
[51] The power of the bell in the contemplative monastery is also apparent in "'C'est le mois de Marie.'" (*Threshold*, 70) where we read: "The sacred Silence of the night / Is sealed by three metallic chords." The alliteration underlines the definiteness expressed. "From Angelus to Angelus / No sound may cross these fastened lips": the accumulation of fricatives is used as a means of emphasis, furthermore the spondee employed in "No sound" underlines the utter silence dictated by the bell.

> I ruminate o'er what this life
> Contains for those who live it well -
> The sound of Silence after Strife,
> The alternance of heav'n and hell ...

The enumeration in the opening line expresses a certain unrest and excitement concerning what lies ahead. It is the same excitement as was experienced before, as he realizes on second thought; the exclamatory "Nay" in l.3 suggests his own surprise at this insight. The rhythmical unevenness of this stanza perfectly reflects the poet's excitement. A more meditative quatrain follows, which is completely regular in rhythm. The long vowels and diphthongs add to the feeling of balance conveyed, a balance "of Silence after Strife", "of heav'n and hell". Given the nature of these extremes, one can hardly think of such life as monotonous, and yet it seems to be so, for there are but these two options. The equilibrium achieved is indicated by the regularity of the rhythm. The capitalization in l.3 indicates that both "Silence" and "Strife" belong to the monastic world as parts of the creation, producing an alternating experience of "heav'n and hell". These meditative lines are succeeded by the vividness of stanza five, which continues the mood of the third stanza:

> "Variety! Ah! spice of Life!
> Did people but perceive thy worth,
> Did married man but see his wife,
> Did happy souls know of their mirth ...
>
> - Alas! - 'Tis but the celibate
> That knows the value of a ring;
> And he for whom things alternate
> No more, alone finds time to sing.

The "irregularity" of the rhythm of the first line and the spondaic openings of the other lines suggest the nature of variety, this "spice of Life", exciting, unexpected and thrilling, which, of course, does not exist in the charterhouse. The mournful exclamation "Ah!" adds a very human touch to the line. The parallelism employed serves to place emphasis on the basic question, namely, whether people who experience this "spice of Life" every day are still able to appreciate it; i.e. whether they remain conscious of the precious nature of this gift. The repetition of the structure also suggests the weariness of passing the same day, everyday. The succeeding stanza clearly demonstrates the idea that not possessing variety emphasizes the value of diversity all the more. The poet's personal experience is presented with striking honesty, all the pain involved being condensed in the mournful sigh "Alas!". The finality and absoluteness of the truth observed finds sorrowful expression in the enjambement of l.3: the spondee at the beginning of l.4, "No more", adds all the more emphasis to the sorrow of not having variety at his disposal anymore.

In the two closing stanzas the poet once again considers the two possibilities:

> Could I but have my time again
> And know but one more unknown dawn,
> O! dazzled heart! how sweet the strain
> With which thou'dst gather up the morn!

... And yet ...! - Couldst now this whole world see,
How great in fact would be the thrill?
Is't not just this Man's misery,
No more to know how to sit still?

The first of these two stanzas conveys the mood of eager excitement at the very thought of having but "one more unknown dawn", the three stresses at the beginning of that phrase powerfully suggest the thrill. The exclamations that follow complete this idea, while the imagery used ("strain", "gather up") adds an element of activity on a very subtle level, active personal intervention which is opposed to the contemplative life. "... And yet ...!", this introductory exclamation of the closing stanza indicates the change in attitude. The poet tries to find consoling words, words of explanation, but does not really manage to convince the reader. Furthermore, l.3 provides a metrical difficulty: although the elision at the beginning of the line serves to supply the correct number of syllables, it is hard to make it sound as if it has a natural rhythm, thereby additionally weakening the poet's argumentation.

The weariness of passing every day alike is also implied in a poem with the rather unusually long, circumstantial title "One hour before taking the step of prostrating myself in community to beg admission to the ranks of the Fathers" (*Threshold*, 28), reflecting a moment of great importance in the life of a monk, which will influence the rest of his life. The poet meditates on the future that lies ahead, starting his poem on a rather cheerful note:

"What lies ahead?" the oceans sigh.
What lies beyond this blue, blue sky
That melts into the bluer sea
Of far, far, far off Mystery?

The idea of the "vast Unknown" (second stanza) is implied in conventional metaphors. The three-fold repetition in l.4 serves as an additional means of emphasis. The poet's curiosity to know is apparent in the first seven stanzas of a poem which consists of eleven stanzas written in iambic tetrameter rhyming in couplets, with a great number of the lines starting with inversion. The poet's anticipation, his unbounded desire to know what will happen is particularly expressed in the fifth and sixth quatrain:

Discovery! O Grace! O Grace!
Fair Newness! Soon I'll see thy face
Unveiled by Time's receding shade,
Now 'twixt two Nows awhile delayed.

Surprise! How sweet thy sudden name!
Adventure! Men have sung thy fame.
What lurks behind this unturned page,
What plot unstitched, unsolved by age?

The exclamations and apostrophes, the repetition in l.1 of the fifth stanza reinforce his excitement, underlined by the spondaic first foot in ll.2-4. The thrill is continued in stanza six, where again exclamations and short phrases help to place additional emphasis on the sweetness of surprise. The diction employed ("lurks" or "plot unstitched") add to the feeling of pleasurable anticipation conveyed. The "unturned page" hints at the idea of the Book of Life as pre-written scripture, whose pages are gradually turned. In stanza three we find another reference to it, which makes the poet's belief in providence apparent: "Unknown, yet foreknown Mystery, / Thou'rt writ in Future's History." However, the excitement is experienced in vain: after having pondered elaborately about the sweetness of surprise during the previous seven stanzas, we read about the dawns of his future in stanza eight:

> But now each one knows where it goes,
> HORARIUM is all it knows:
> Each like the last reflects the next [corr.][52]
> And duplicates till death one text.

The rhythm in the first line powerfully suggests the monotony; the anapaestic substitution in "each one knows where it goes", reinforced by the interior rhyme, implies the idea of uniformity. "HORARIUM" is the graven word, as is suggested by the orthography in capital letters, it is the horarium which will regulate his future life, "Each like the last reflects the next". The imagery used in l.4 indicates in a rather direct manner the monotony of his life ahead: "And duplicates till death one text". The pattern of d-t-d-t underlines the regular nature of his life to come. Using "text" is another suggestion towards the Book of Life, whose pages resemble each other inexorably in the case of a Carthusian monk. In the closing stanza Alun Idris employs vivid imagery:

> The pregnancy of this dark night
> Doth labour 'neath new bursting light:
> This yesterday that doth arise
> Bears p'haps just one, one small, Surprise?

There is still a gleam of hope apparent in these lines, lending them a very human touch. The imagery he uses to describe the approach of the new day is powerful. Speaking of the "pregnancy of this dark night" firmly suggests the wonder about the new day to come, the hope he has for that day, when he will beg admission to the ranks of the Fathers, as is implied in the title. However, the imagery used also suggests the difficulties and pains involved in letting this new day behold the light of life, having awaited it for so long. The new-born day is a "yesterday" though, which again echoes the idea of providence central to the entire poem. It is a "yesterday" in the sense that everything has already been foreseen by God.

The title "'Vous nettoyerez tous les reliquaires de la Chapelle des Reliques.'" (*Threshold*, 69) suggests the occasion of the poem's origin. It tells of an ordinary incident in the day-to-day life in the monastery. The subtitle of the poem, "Opera Communia", "work in common", refers to that part of the day when the monks are engaged in physical work.

---

[52] Corrected by the poet.

Sometimes they work together, at times also outside the cell, which occurs only rarely though. Such an occasion inspired the sonnet:

> I spent an afternoon among the Saints.
> They did not say a word, yet spoke to me
> Of bygone days: of Martyrs' unheard plaints,
> Of unseen Virgins' sealed virginity,
> Confessors' proven virtue, Pontiffs' faith,
> Of mine own Brethren now gone on before ...

The opening line, a complete sentence, attracts attention due to its conciseness, which underlines the special nature of the occasion. The succeeding lines partly run on and form the units of a longer sentence, a technique which can be called a characteristic feature of Alun Idris' verse. The experience was in a way exceptional, for he had to leave the cell for a while; the poet's amazement is noticeable in the enumerations of the thoughts it provoked. The long vowels and diphthongs produce a slow rhythm, which corresponds to the mood conveyed while pondering over the past. This slow movement forms a contrast to the quicker rhythm clinging to the first two lines, which echo the present.

In "Veilleuse" (*Threshold*, 69) the monk appears in his role as the faithful watcher, keeping vigil all through the night. Alun Idris uses the conventional symbol of the candle to represent the waning life of the human being, employing it in particular as a symbol of the life of a recluse:

> Burn on, burn on, thou faithful light,
> All, all alone, watch through the night;
> Stand by thy Master, stay awake,
> Consume thy life-blood for his sake.
>
> Thou art my teacher, silent flame:
> Night, morn, noon, e'en, thou'rt e'er the same;
> As earth rolls on in blissful sleep,
> Faithful till death, thou'lt vigil keep.

The candle burns day and night beside the Lord, like the recluse, consuming itself in sacrifice, prayer, reparation and love. This ideal, the idea of becoming a recluse had always been tempting to Alun Idris. The attraction he feels to hermits and recluses is iterated in the lines quoted. The poem is dedicated to Julian of Norwich[53] who, as she was a recluse herself, exerts a powerful fascination for the poet. In the Middle Ages, unlike today, solitary life was almost popular, taking on various forms: there were hermits, itinerant male solitaries who wandered from one place to another according to circumstances, and there were the recluses, who were shut off from normal social life (cf. Wolters 1976, 21). Mother Julian was one of the latter. In those days recluses were walled in, sealed into a cell adjoining the sanctuary, frequently off the

---

[53] Julian of Norwich, the author of the *Divine Revelations*, compiled two accounts: the shorter version was written immediately after her visions, while the second, much longer script was written towards the end of her life, "enriched by the fruits of twenty years' brooding" (Wolters 1976, 14). The two manuscript versions bracket a lifetime of meditation.

east end of a church (cf. letter, 28.2.1990). The recluse would be confined there until death: "Faithful till death, thou'lt vigil keep." To burn quietly over the years like a sanctuary lamp. This is the ideal of the poet, the hermit's call.

The repetition used in the opening lines suggests encouragement to continue such self-sacrifice. The imperative, which characterizes the first stanza, can be found throughout the entire poem, at times reinforced by anaphoras, as in stanza three: "Burn as Creation takes its rest, / Burn thou as burning eyes are blest", but most strikingly employed in the fifth stanza:

> Burn while the burning Fever kills,
> Burn as the touch of Moera chills;
> Burn till Life's burning burns no more ...
> Burnt Youth! Press hard thine aging whore.

L.1 powerfully suggests the idea of a life dedicated to self-sacrificing devotion, burning with and for the love of God until "the touch of Moera chills": a metaphor implying the extinction of the flame by the Goddess of Fate. The word play in 1.3, characteristic of Alun Idris, encourages the flame to continue burning for God till death, until the pains and sorrows of life are not felt anymore. This idea is also implied in 1.4, where the poet uses unusually direct and powerful imagery to convey the thought.

The poem closes with a plea addressed to the Lord to burn like such a flame as a recluse:

> Lord, let me burn as this fair light,
> Give, give my body day and night,
> From hour to hour dissolve in love,
> Shine till Aurora shine above.

The urgency of his plea is underlined by the rhythm abounding in stressed syllables in the first line: four stressed syllables in sequence, separated only by a pause after "Lord", and the closing spondaic foot powerfully suggest the urgent and compelling nature of his request. The spondaic repetition in 1.2 continues the notion of the quest: the two closing lines, however, are more balanced, meditating on the presence of Love while burning for God, "dissolve in love" until death, "Shine till Aurora shine above." The beautifully used imagery suggests the melting of the soul in the Love of God, until a new morning arises after death.

In the final seventh year, which was a year of complete solitude and virtual reclusion, the yearning for perfect solitude became very strong, as is reflected in this poem (cf. letter, 28.2.1990).

The presence of both scholastic and mystical theology in the solitary life of a Carthusian monk is captured in the following stanza taken from an early poem called "All Saints' Day" (*Threshold*, 1), where we read about those monks who have trodden that path before:

> Each pointed hood concealed a world of thought,
> Each hidden breast its war with Darkness fought.
> Who shall e'er know the pains, the joys each knew -
> Brother with brother could here share so few. [corr.]

The imagery used in the first two lines suggests that both the intellect ("Each pointed hood") and affection ("Each hidden breast") are working with united effort, a thought that is reinforced by the anaphora used. Both by reason and feeling is the "war with Darkness fought": it is a battle starting every day anew, "Darkness" suggesting weakness and despair, as inherent in divine providence, indicated by the capitalization. "Darkness" forms a part of the Carthusian life as well. "The pains, the joys each knew" shall for ever be unknown, this is the fate each monk has to cope with, for "Brother with brother could here share so few". Although on their weekly recreation the monks are allowed, even encouraged to talk to their brethren, they are no longer accustomed to verbally expressing and sharing their inward experiences; it is a world that remains closed off, isolated.

In "Maundy Thursday" (*Threshold*, 44f.) we explicitly read about the debate between faith and reason concerning their role and respective importance. The traditional unanimity between scholastic and mystical theology is reflected therein: while scholastic theology takes its origin in the intellect, its object being truth, mystical theology has its roots in the affection, in emotion, its object being the good (cf. Kleineidam 1983, 192). The two types employ different methods: the former operates via logic, the latter via feeling.

The poem is an allegory depicting the contrast between the message of the Franciscans, who place more emphasis on love, and the Dominicans who concentrate rather on understanding, with St. Bonaventura and St. Thomas Aquinas as representatives of the two approaches. The question asked in the opening lines triggers off the poem: "Can it be that in this vessel / All the Godhead meekly hides?" Maundy Thursday, the day when the Eucharist was inaugurated, seems to be predetermined for the emergence of such a question, which provokes the following debate:

> "What is Faith?" inquires Reason,
>   "Common maid!" I know her not.
> Break my laws? 'Tis highest treason.
>   Creeds against my kingdom plot."
> Reign, great King; enjoy thy season.
>   Faith would not exchange her lot.
>
> Nay, she sees what thou wilt never
>   See or feel or know at all.
> Unlike thee, nor wise nor clever,
>   She knows nought, her heart is small.
> Nought, all nought, she hungers ever
>   For a word, a thought, a call.

The poem, written in tetrameters, is fundamentally trochaic, which underlines the vivacity of the discussion. In the first stanza, presenting reason's point of view, plosive and sharp consonants dominate, while the second stanza, suggesting the position of faith, is given much more smoothness and gentleness by the long vowels and diphthongs prevailing. In particular the enumeration in l.2 "See or feel or know at all" implies the superiority of faith. "Nought, all nought," suggests the idea of the void, the inner emptiness which is necessary to experience

God. The lines also hint at the message of the gospels, when the Lord says "whoever does not accept the kingdom of God like a Child will never enter it" (Mark 10:15; Luke 18:17). Being completely empty one is ready to experience the Lord, "she hungers ever / For a word, a thought, a call." - the enumeration adds to the feeling of urgency conveyed, to feel God is all that "Faith" is striving for. This longing for a sign echoes the poet's own yearning as we read in the fifth stanza:

> ... Call me, Lord, my heart is broken.
>   Speak! My pride is emptied, crushed.
> From a dream as though awoken,
>   This loud brain is strangely hushed. [...]

Reason cannot give the answer, it is incapable of providing a sign, as is implied in 1.4; as if awoken from a dream the poet realizes that he cannot count on reason, which he had hoped he could ("my pride is emptied, crushed."). He experiences a stage of utter nakedness, with his heart broken, feeling the void, as we read in the closing stanza: "Nothing, utter, utter nothing - / Such I am; the mask I tear." At last he is prepared to trust faith. He lays bare his innermost kernel, peels off the last protecting layers. Only now, trusting his faith, is he able to feel God: "Now I grasp Thee, God in hiding! - / Faith! 'Tis Faith! 'Tis Vision clear!" However, the blend of faith and reason is essential: "one has to bear in mind that the intellect is basic and it was really through an intellectual vision of the fulness of truth that I came to the Catholic faith rather than an emotional one in the first place" (letter, 19.11.1989).

The poem is a meditation on the Real Presence, underlined by the tune which it can be chanted to. "Tantum ergo Sacramentum" is a melody familiar in its association with the Real Presence in the Eucharist. In solitude the Real Presence of the Lord is sensed far more because His presence is the only company the monk has during the whole day. Consequently the eucharist is the only human contact, a contact both human and divine: there is a physical communion.[54]

"After receiving Miss W.'s letter" (*Threshold*, 56) is a meditation on what the world outside thinks of Carthusian monks. It is a poem written in a mood of spiritual unrest, which becomes apparent in the roughness of rhythm employed. This poem presents an outburst of feeling, the poet's own mood of being troubled in mind is firmly conveyed therein: it is strong in its emotional impact, despite its unevenness in rhythm:

> The whole world thinks that we are holy men,
> And some would call us "saints" - not knowing who
> Or what hides in this sacred robbers' den
> Each day to nail the Crucified anew
> By their indifference t'ward the One they touch
> Too often - and no more with that "first love",
> - Nay, with entrenched lukewarmness, and that such
> As would to tears the hardest layman move.
> Whip on! Xxxxxxxxxxx! Fast until your ribs
> Rub 'gainst your itching Cilice-shirts - and pray

---

[54] The Carthusians fast till midday (cf. Blüm 1983b, 30).

At length within yourselves most fragrant fibs
In well-paid idleness, eight hours a day,
Till Grace, abused, your souls to blazes blast ...
While saints that no one knew be first at last.

At the beginning the tone of the poem is gentle, despite the spondee in the second foot, emphasizing the great number suggested. The tone changes abruptly with the spondee in "not knowing" in l.2, followed by an enumeration of all the things not known to "the whole world", the sins which are committed in a Carthusian monastery. "Indifference" is the graven word, by which each day the monks "nail the Crucified anew". Such imagery powerfully conveys the emotions stirred in the poet at the very thought of indifference. "Entrenched lukewarmness" is the fiend, when the thrill of "that 'first love'" is gone. The unevenness of the rhythm in l.7 (inverted first and third foot, pyrrhic followed by a spondee at the end of the line) places additional emphasis on the extent of the abuse: the abuse is so great that it would even "to tears the hardest layman move". After having concluded his reproach in the last line of the second quatrain, the verdict, though not pronounced, is executed: the accusations have been so severe as to not make it necessary to explicitly pass judgment. The order to "Whip on!" is to be taken literally, - it refers to the Carthusian custom of taking the discipline. (The "Xxxxxxxxxxx" stands for the name of the order, which remained anonymous in the publication.) Harder fasting is required, so that the hairy shirt the monk never takes off rubs and itches all the more, "Till Grace, abused, your souls to blazes blast ...". The imagery employed vividly visualizes the punishment required to atone for the sin of having abused grace. The degree of the abuse is reinforced by the hissing sounds abounding in this line. The closing line, which contrasts in its gentle tone with its predecessors, explains the cause for this emotional tirade, in particular when relating it to the title of the poem. Apparently the outburst was triggered off by a letter the poet had received by a lady, whom he considers to be one of those "saints that no one knew", who will be "first at last": she is a simple woman who has not lost that "first love", who in her pure and honest love for God does not abuse divine grace.

Taking "the discipline" is part of the Carthusian life, each Friday the Carthusians (as well as the Trappists) whip themselves. The Carthusians lacerate the upper part of their torso as they must also continually wear their constantly itching shirt (cf. interview in Fraham, 1.7.1990). "Trois heures du matin, un vendredi" (*Threshold*, 57) describes this experience.

"Mais ça fait mal!" dit le novice à son Saint Maître.
"C'est fait pour ça," fit celui-ci, en souriant.
"Pas sérieux," dit à son tour le nouveau prêtre, [corr.]
"Austérité bien sucrée pour les friands!
"Ce n'est pas ça qui réduira mon Purgatoire:
"Ce qui me coûte, c'est le pain qui va avec!"
... C'est vrai, c'est vrai, on cherche trop sa propre gloire.
La Sainteté réside-t-elle en ce pain sec?

The humorous tone of these lines, which could almost be described as a kind of gallows humour, is surprising when bearing in mind the experience they reflect; the conversational note adds to that feeling. Life in a Carthusian monastery is a life lead at the extreme, the shift of emphasis of what is important to the Carthusian monk, which differs considerably to men living outside monastic quarters, is firmly conveyed. These first two quatrains of the sonnet also reflect that the sense of humour is not lost at all, not even in so strict a monastery as a Carthusian one. In the interview with Huw Jones, the poet's brother, Alun Idris explicitly points out the tremendous amount of humour present in the Carthusian monastery, which had surprised the monk himself at the beginning. When asked to give an example, he mentioned "receiving messages over the wall in the form of earthworms and snowballs" (Jones, Elwyn, 2).

The image of the "five course fast" taken from "Taste" (*Threshold*, 72f.), though having a humorous touch about it, equally suggests the severity of fasting. The sonnet starts with a reference to taking the discipline:

> It is a day of fasting, and the whip
> Whacks through the air once more in every cell
> Ere, yawning, once again we gently slip
> Between our rugs to wait the morning bell ...

The sound symbolism of the phrase "the whip whacks through" audibly presents the sound of the whip cracking through the air. Taking the discipline is part and parcel of Carthusian life, its "naturalness" being implied by the conversational tone of the lines that follow. The mood then becomes peaceful again as the monks "gently slip" back to their beds.

These examples mirror various aspects of everyday life in the Carthusian monastery. The factual implications of the verse combined with the presence of honest feeling affords the reader glimpses of a life otherwise unknown to him. It is the daily routine which emerges from these poems, the daily penance the monk is confronted with. The poems add a very human touch to the figure of the Carthusian monk, who by most of us would indeed be classified among the "saints",[55] as Alun Idris himself observed.

3.1.1.2. SOLITUDE AND SILENCE

Solitude and silence form the very essence of life in a Carthusian monastery. They represent the basic means to create an inner void, which can then be filled with the divine presence. Being bathed in this completely silent and solitary atmosphere one has to bear in mind that silence is the common ground to all of Alun Idris' poems written in the charterhouse. It is essential to read them in the spirit in which they were written, in a spirit of silence. Many of them are meditations, and were born from felt and interiorized silence. Silence is ever present in them. In order to experience that silence in the poems the reader has to tune in on

---

[55] "After receiving Miss W.'s letter" (*Threshold*, 56).

the same "wavelength". Thus the very essence of life in a charterhouse, solitude and silence, often form the theme and inspiring source of Alun Idris' poetry.

Voluntary quasi perpetual silence is difficult to imagine in all its consequences for one who has never experienced it. In some of Alun Idris' poems, however, he manages to convey the nature of silence, its consoling as well as threatening aspect. In "3 a.m." (*Threshold*, 19f.) silence is presented as the monk's peaceful companion, his faithful friend:

> O Silence deep ... deep, deeper still ...
> O dew of Peace, thy peace distil;
> Come, tingle softly in mine ears,
> Thou Song of Time, voice of the years.
> Thou art the hermit's company,
> Of Solitude, the symphony -
> O! soundless Sound, how strange thou art,
> Thou searcher of the human heart!

The atmosphere created in the very first line is one of gentle peace, which is continued and developed to an idea of comfort and experienced peace as the stanza progresses.
"O Silence deep" - the three-fold repetition suggests its absoluteness, which is completed by the striking metaphor "dew of Peace": the idea of softness, gentleness, and naturalness is firmly implied. The natural pause after "Come", inviting silence to "tingle softly" in l.3, adds a human touch to the plea. Another metaphor is introduced in l.3 and continued throughout the stanza: "Song of Time", "voice of the years", "symphony" yet "soundless sound". It is paradoxical to ask silence to "tingle softly in mine ears"; however, the sound of silence is suggestive of that inward sound which can be heard in silence, and which can turn into a "symphony" when filled with divine presence. The s-alliteration abounding in the closing lines of the stanza add a strong sensual element, suggesting the presence of a still, small voice. Silence appears as the "searcher of the human heart", an effective means of finding access to one's soul.

The poem consists of five stanzas of equal length and rhyme scheme, eight lines of iambic tetrameter rhyming in couplets, developing the idea of solitude. The poet is willing to submit, to experience this solitude, but is also impatiently waiting for a sign:

> I listen to the emptiness
> That led those men to holiness;
> I wait ... I wait for some small word,
> Some message from the great unheard -
> And hear instead the noise within,
> The rustling of the restless din
> Of words ... more words ... more worrying,
> And unbecalmèd hurrying.

The gentleness dominating the first stanza is gone, and soberness prevails. Prepared to experience what others have experienced before, he is willing to wait. The three full stops which appear three times in this stanza accompanied by repetitions underline the mood of waiting, of the patience required. Instead, all he hears is the "rustling of the restless din": the alliteration on "r-" and "stl-" conveys a feeling of triviality, of failure.

The cardinal role of silence in a contemplative order is metaphorically expressed in the following lines:

> O Buzz of solitary thought,
> By thee my fathers here were taught:
> The grammar of the art of pain
> Doth sound, resound again, again -

"O Buzz of solitary thought" recalls the sound symbolism apparent in the first stanza, where the presence of fricatives provoked a buzzing sound. Another metaphor is introduced in l.3 which poignantly describes the function of silence: as "grammar of the art of pain" silence is basic to the skill; it is a tool which has to be studied hard until it can be used well. The question of what the "flesh" of the "language" in question may be, words and phrases, is not resolved. The image of the "art of pain" is highly suggestive as well, openly expressing the difficulties involved on the way to unification. The closing stanza again refers to the dichotomy involved but ends on a positive note:

> Where are ye now, my brethren, where -
> 'Neath nameless cross so stark, so bare?
> In death, e'en as in life forgot,
> Your silent lives in silence rot ...
> "Our little brother, wait awhile:
> These gaping skulls one day will smile,
> Will hold thee close in tight embrace
> In silence love's deep face-to-face. [corr.]

While the first four lines approach silence in a sober, direct, almost appalling way ("Your silent lives in silence rot"), the sense it makes to live in silence is all the more dominant in the closing lines. The "gaping skulls" represent a vivid image for all those who have gone before. It is certainly no euphemism, however. It reminds one of the fact that death is ever present to the contemplative monk; as it is the bliss of afterlife he is aiming at, death does not frighten him. One day he will be close to them, "In silence love's deep face-to-face ". This closing line has been restored to its original form, concentrating all the more on the central role of silence which is then combined with love, indicating that love and silence are the monk's principal tools. We are reminded of the metaphor already used and realize that what grammar is to words in a language, silence is to love in the "art of pain".

"Face-to-face" indicates that "contemplation is really gazing eye to eye with God. And God gazes at the soul" (letter, 8.7.1990). H.N. Fairchild stresses the significance of contemplation: "The only way of obtaining a foretaste of the perfect heavenly truth is not through the senses, not through books, but through contemplation." (Fairchild 1939, 109).

The poem has been set to music by Father Laurence Bévenot. Music and love have always been firmly connected, singing the poem places additional emphasis on the idea of love conveyed.

The following poem can be sung as well. It was composed to fit "Mozart's tune, 459"[56], a gentle song which, it is said, can be used to quieten children and lull them to sleep. "Nightfall, St. Valentine's Day" (*Threshold*, 21f.) is written in trochaic tetrameter as a basis, a metre which is normally only rarely to be found in Alun Idris' poetry. The first stanza beautifully expresses the nature of silence:

> Silence ... silence ... deep, deep silence
>   Seeps into my tingling ears;
> All Earth's noise, all Pleasure's violence
>   Shouts in vain across the years.
> Here mine eyes meet Thine, O Master,
>   Here none other enters in ...
> Broken lies the alabaster,
>   Broken every tie with sin.

The first line of this poem bears similarity to that of "3 a.m.". Repetition is again used to express the nature of silence, this time the word "silence" itself being repeated. The s-alliteration in the first two lines is gentle though ever present, suggesting a subtle buzzing sound. The assonance on the diphthong /aɪ/ and the long vowel /iː/ help to create this atmosphere of gentleness.

The second half of the stanza forms a firm unit: the embracing rhyme is completed by the use of anaphora (which is not employed in any of the other five stanzas). The idea of meeting God "face-to-face" in silence is explicitly expressed: "Here mine eyes meet Thine, O Master".

The "alabaster", that tiny antique oil can, conveys a biblical reference to Mary Magdalen, to be found in Matthew 26:6-13, John 12:1-8, and Luke 7:36-50, who falls on her knees, grasps Jesus' feet and washes them with precious oil, while Martha considers that to be a waste - "Ut quid perditio haec" (Matthew 26:7). Giving God the most precious thing you have as a gift certainly does not imply that it is a waste. The three biblical passages mentioned indicate the importance of love, which in a way sums up the essence of contemplative life. Living a life in silence in a contemplative order seems to be a waste of time. To think of such a life as being of no utility is tempting. The subtitle of the poem, "Remembering the Call on this night ten years ago" indicates the date of his call, the call to contemplative love, when the "romance with God" began.

The closing lines of the third stanza point out the importance of song in the contemplative monastery, when in the early morning "As the Breath to mortals given, / Changed to Song, regains the air". It refers to the consecration of the air by chanting the office of God for His honour.

At dawn the following morning, as is indicated in a note, Alun Idris added two more stanzas which are entirely different in tone. The power regained is to be felt, his soul has been nurtured with new energies, which finds expression in the structures he uses: short sentences prevail, the

---

[56] The given number is a reference to the Welsh Baptist Hymnal the tune can be found in. The melody is Mozart's Sonata KV 300i (331).

frequent exclamations and direct invocations replace the gentleness of silence. Now the tune does not, of course, really correspond to the tone conveyed in these lines any more:

> Night! O Night! Thy tight hold weakens -
>   Truth is leaping o'er the hills.
> Life, new life, Creation beckons,
>   Song, contagious, dances, trills.
> Dawn, arise! These stone walls shatter!
>   Shine in this sad hermit's heart.
> Heav'nly light, Hell's dank mists scatter.
>   Hail, fair Morn! Sweet Grace impart.

The lines overflow with joy and exultation, the short sentences and enumerations adding to that feeling. Using conventional imagery, the dark night of the soul gives way to that heavenly light he waits for, "sweet Grace" to impart. The first line of the closing stanza implies that he is still waiting, "Unseen Light, Thy prisoner seeks Thee", while in the last line he openly asks the Lord to "Point to me the Walls of Light" [corr.]. The image of the "Walls of Light" bears a reference to the last chapter of the Apocalypse, Apoc. 21:9-14, where the holy city of Jerusalem is described as shining with the glory of God, surrounded by a great high wall. Light, splendour and glory is what "Thy prisoner" is seeking.

Latin is still frequently used in the Carthusian monastery as the language of prayer, being very much alive in that sense. Nevertheless, it is remarkable that Alun Idris feels inspired to write poems in that language as well. Several poems written in Latin bear the mark of prayer and silence, the spirit they were composed in. "Quadragesima" (*Threshold*, 29f.) is one of these poems, consisting of 14 quatrains which rhyme in couplets, each line having eight syllables.[57] The poem illuminates different aspects of silence and solitude.

> Silentium! Silentium!
> Sodalis dormientium
> In clausula dulcedinis
> Stillantis solitudinis.

The genitive is used as an adjective, which is a Hebrew construction. The meaning of the closing lines is a combination of the nuance "in the capsule of sweetness of solitude distilled" with the literal sense "in sweet capsule of distilled solitude" (cf. letter, 19.10.1990). In the word "clausula" there is, of course, also a certain connotation of "prison", another aspect of life in a silent cell.

In the third quatrain we find a further aspect of silence:

> O Quies! fac quiescere
> In dulci tuo pectore
> Hoc pectus quod in strepitu
> Quietem quaerit sonitu.

---

[57] An unpublished French version of this poem exists as well, though with a different layout.

The paradox of seeking rest through agitation, i.e. anything which distracts the mind from tranquility, is implied here. The "art of pain" has special rules, the difficulty of coping with silence and using it fruitfully being firmly conveyed.
The fourth stanza introduces the idea of the void central to "successful" silence:

> O Absens! reple Vacuum!
> Fons silens horum fluctuum
> Qu*i* in aëre nunc tinniunt --
> Audisne tu qui t*e* audiunt?

"O Absens!" metaphorically addresses God, the absent one, which powerfully evokes the idea that God's presence cannot always be felt. This metaphor is of sobering effect on the reader, who may be surprised at the implications. The word "Vacuum" is capitalized which implies that the void is to be seen as a sign of God.[58]
The inner void enables us to experience God, we empty ourselves so as to meet God, to let Him enter into us; we need to be empty of all created things in order to meet Him. In Christianity the aim of the inner void is neither to meet oneself, nor to meet God through oneself but it is to empty oneself to meet God and be filled with His grace. In the Gospel of St. John we read: "He must increase, but I must decrease." (John 3:30)[59]
The sound of silence, the sound of the absent One is heard by the poet. The question which arises now is whether or not the absent One hears the ones who hear His sound, i.e. the sound of absence, the sound of silence tingling in the ears. The tone then changes, the question turns into a strong yearning, a plea:

> O Tacens! Tacens! Loquere!
> Inanitas! te capere
> Me do*ce* ac hanc praesentiam, [corr.]
> Palpa*re*, ut nos*cam* Essentiam.

He asks the silent one to speak, the void to teach him to capture itself, so that he may know its true essence. Despair creeps in, particularly in lines like "O vasta devastata Nox!" referring to the "vast, waste night". Is it all in vain?
Alun Idris' predilection for word play is apparent in this Latin poem as well when we read e.g. in stanza twelve: "Abscondor in Abscondito / Ignotus - n*isi* Incognito." - I'm hidden in the Hidden / Unknown - except to the unknown. And he continues:

---

[58] The idea of experiencing the inner void and emptiness links the Christian to Eastern religions, especially to Buddhism. According to Hubertus M. Blüm the main difference lies in the fact that Buddhism tries to find a "negative" emptiness and void, utter nought and nothingness, whereas the Christians aim to use the inner void as a vessel to be eventually filled will God's presence. According to Blüm, the Buddhists do not try to find God: their only aim is to have access to the inner core of themselves (cf. Blüm 1983a, 16). It might be argued that this is a matter of a point of view as trying to seek one's inner void, the inner self is also a way of trying to find the Divine in oneself. "One tends to go towards a presence, towards a fullness in Christianity, whereas in the Eastern type of mystical tradition one tends to go towards Nirvana, an utter emptiness." (letter, 28.2.1990).
[59] King James Version.

> Tacentem tacens sentio
> Hic solus cum Silentio
> Beatae Solitudinis -
> Solae Beatitudinis.

The word play in the closing lines is an echo of St. Bruno, "O beata solitudo, sola beatitudo", O blessed solitude, the only beatitude. This is the paradoxical nature of solitude, difficult to grasp for those not living in monastic surroundings, and equally hard to experience for those who have decided to enter a contemplative monastery. The poem closes, however, with a stanza full of hope:

> Nam sol*um* in solitudine,
> Umbrante multitudine
> Ala*rum* invisibilium,
> Non solus, nam cum Solo, sum.

The image of the multitude of invisible wings shading the solitary suggests the presence of all those who have gone that way before and who have already achieved their aim: union with God. He is therefore bound to say "Non solus, nam cum Solo, sum". The poem can also be sung to "Mysterium Ecclesiae".

In the charterhouse at Sélignac the cells are designated by letters, and each cell has an inscription over the door beginning with the letter of the cell. Brother David was living in cell "N", the door next to his therefore had "O", bearing the inscription: "O beata solitudo, sola beatitudo" (cf. letter, 8.7.1990). This quotation is also reflected in the first stanza of "Following day" (*Threshold*, 26f.), where we read:

> O Solitude! O Solitude!
> O Hell bathed in Beatitude!
> Encounter with Eternity,
> With Truth, hard Truth, Reality!

St. Bruno's quotation is slightly altered and completed by another central aspect of solitude: the image "Hell bathed in Beatitude" vividly expresses not only solitude's blessed aspect but also its frightful component. Solitude means "Encounter with Eternity", which can be full of bliss but may turn into "hard Truth" as well, though this image is less frightening than that of l.2. In the second stanza, however, the negative, frightful and harsh side of silence is taken up again, and is reinforced by sound symbolism - the lines abounding in plosives:

> A man is what he is with thee:
> The well-made mask that others see
> Here cracks; - the great Act takes to rout:
> Upon this rack the truth will out.

The two stressed syllables at the beginning of l.3 "Here cracks;" followed by a pause receive special emphasis: in solitude it is impossible to gloss over one's innermost kernel, any mask which might hide things from other people is bound to crack. The sound symbolism of "*cracks*", the accumulation of voiceless plosives completed by a hissing /s/, visualizes the encounter, the laying bare of the soul. The same sounds are to be found once more as the line proceeds, "*Ac*t ta*k*es", partly taken up in "thi*s rack*" of 1.3: this repetition reinforcing the harsh nature of the encounter.

However, the tone changes abruptly as the third stanza begins, turning from the brutality of the experience to the idea of suffering through loneliness; the contrast in sound to the previous stanza is striking:

> Alone! - t'is life endured and known;
> Alone! - t'is Stamina full-grown;
> Alone; - alone, alone, alone,
> 'Tis naked Man's lewd bareness shown.

The employment of anaphora, the excessive repetition of "alone" increases the effect of the message. The sound dominating in this stanza is the mournful diphthong /əʊ/, which suggests the idea of painful, interior suffering on a very subtle level. The capitalization of "Stamina full-grown" implies the powers of endurance gained through divine guidance on the one hand; on the other it is a stimulating metaphor taken from the field of botany: as the plural form of "stamen" it conjures up an idea of all life's powers full-grown through solitude, ready to spread and fall on fertile soil, ready for the encounter.

The mood, however, continues to change. In the fifth stanza an increasing balanced vividness is noticeable through the accumulation of /l/ and light /i/ sounds: "O Stillness! Make my spirit still; / O teeming Void, its void fulfil;" [corr.]. However, disillusionment is not long in coming by calling fruitful silence "strange friend of Loneliness". The awareness of the closeness of the terms is frightening. And yet in the final stanza the poem returns to a more positive mood. Relief is to be felt in the lines, their smoothness adding to this impression:

> O blessèd, blessèd Solitude!
> Thou sole, yea sole, Beatitude!
> Surrounded on all sides by thee,
> I'm stranded ... in Eternity.

The repetition in 1.2 "Thou sole, yea sole" implies that after all, despite the difficulties involved, solitude is and remains the only "Beatitude". "Nunc Sancte nobis Spiritus, solemn tone" offers the notation to which the poem can be sung, reflecting the spirit expressed therein.

The central role of silence and meditation for the contemplative monk is also apparent in "At night (mid-Lent)" (*Threshold*, 30), where we read in the first stanza:

> When I'm alone, away from all that bustles,
> Far, far away from all that howls and hustles,
> When round mine ears the sound of Silence rustles -
>   Then am I human.

The first two lines begin with a spondee respectively, and are thus united to the accumulation of stressed syllables of the closing line, which through its shortness attracts special attention:

"When I'm alone", "Far, far away", only when fully silent, "Then am I human". This short line bears four stresses in sequence, thus adding the emphasis of a weighty pronouncement. This emphasis on that line adds to the contrast, the paradoxical relationship established between the first three lines and the closing one, which is supported by the rhmye scheme. This structure is maintained throughout the entire poem. In the third quatrain he openly declares that his faith is his life:

> Yea, I believe. Nay, Faith, 'tis all my being.
> Earth rolls and rolls, towards Nirvana fleeing:
> Born of a Star, my native starlight seeing,
>   Homeward I travel.

To say "I believe" is not enough: faith has not just become the purpose of his life, it is his life, "'tis all my being". There is an opposition in movement to be noticed in this stanza: while the "earth rolls and rolls", flees "towards Nirvana", moving away from the very essence of life, he remembers his origin, he looks back, seeing his own "native starlight". "Let there be light" was the first command; each of us is a new spark of light when life is created. "Homeward I travel" implies his going back to that light of the very first hour, back to the origin, back to eternity. How this is achieved is described in the following lines:

> Deeper and deeper, into deep'ning Presence,
> Inward I swim, toward the inward Essence,
> Holding the hand of that familiar Absence,
>   Lost in Love's ocean.

The apparent contrast between "deep'ning Presence" and "familiar Absence" aims to express that God is not always felt to be present, His absence even being described as "familiar". The image of the second line is taken up again in "Lost in Love's ocean", the epigrammatic close summarizing the essence of the life of a contemplative monk: God is Love, eternal, boundless Love impossible to grasp by human nature, therefore enfolding the poet in its abundance. The tune which goes with the poem, "Ut queant laxis / Iste Confessor", is a very monastic, contemplative one, underlining the mystical nature of the poem.

The tone created in "At Meditation" (*Threshold*, 23) reflects the very essence of meditation, the experience of drawing everything inwards is well conveyed; i.e. nothing should distract you:

> Colour of darkness, land of recollection,
> Blindfold my senses, dampen each reaction,
> Fasten the world; in one, one sole direction
>   Draw all mine inwards.
>
> O tranquil Void! Come, make my vision single,
> Unruffled Calm, come, let me hear thee tingle,
> Virginal Stillness, let me with thee mingle,
>   Stepping in Silence.

The images Alun Idris uses to describe meditation are carefully chosen. The "colour of darkness" is highly suggestive of the invisible world which is there, although it cannot be perceived by the human eye. On a more literal level, employing the senses, it suggests the idea that, when closing one's eyes, one can still see some colours, a few impressions remaining of what was seen before. He firmly desires to "blindfold my senses", exclude them, forget their existence, to "fasten the world" and make himself secure. Here "fasten" is used in the sense of "lock out, exclude": firmly lock away. One is reminded of the meaning of the word "monastery", which comes from the Greek μόνος: all is unified in the one.

The rhyme scheme of the poem is aaab, cccd etc., and a trochaic pattern prevails. The first two lines of stanza one are split into two halves, each half starting with a stressed syllable. The third line is split into three parts, with an additional pause after "in one". The rhythm of the stanza is kept very slow. In the second stanza the order is reversed, with the first two lines consisting of three parts, and the third of only two. The repeated "come" suggests a plea. The imagery is again well-chosen and rich in associations. He steadily moves on:

> Inward I walk, toward mine inmost kernel;
> Deeper I dig, to summits, orbs supernal,
> Each thick'ning hour I palp into th'Eternal,
>   Walking on Absence.

It sounds like an adventurous journey, the stony way towards one's "inmost kernel", the only companion being silence while "Walking on Absence". "Absence", the absent one, refers to the physical presence of the void. The idea behind it is "vacate et videte quoniam ego sum Deus." (Psalm 46 (45):11), as we read in the psalms: the monks are emptying themselves for God, they are constantly striving inwards. When the center of the soul is harmonized, it will affect every other layer around it, so that eventually the whole being will be subsumed, and thus can disseminate itself afterwards. It is therefore essential to strip each layer away in order to reach the center and to harmonize it. The "summits" are in the depth of the soul. In the land of the invisible, in absence we find the essence, the absolute. "God is not visible, He seems to be absent, yet in this absence lies it all" (interview in Fraham, 1.7.1990).

"Each thick'ning hour" is a powerful image involving once more the senses, being completed by the rather unusual use of "palp" as a verb: trying to grasp "th'Eternal", he is "Walking on Absence". The closing stanza leads to the climax:

> Strange is the dark; and stranger is the darkness
> That darkened minds unveil in their aloneness:
> One with the One, all one with utter Oneness,
>   Solitude thunders.

"Solitude thunders" is a vivid image describing the experience of deep meditation, thereby offering the reader glimpses of what happens inside when "all [are] one with utter Oneness". The "darkened minds" convey a two-fold meaning: on the more literal level the term refers to the soul absorbed in meditation, when nothing is visible, but in a more figurative sense it alludes to the fact that we are darkened by the fall of man; that we tend to go astray. "There, at meditation, we unveil the darkness in us, the darkness of anything else but God. There you are eye to eye with God, nothing and no one else would be there" (interview in Fraham, 1.7.1990), therefore "Solitude thunders".

The closing line of each stanza acts as a reinforcing summary, an epigrammatic close which serves as a phrase to meditate upon.

"'Connais-tu l'épître de Saint Jacques?'" (*Theshold*, 65) was the question the novice master at La Trappe asked Alun Idris when he visited the monastery during the holidays in 1974 (cf. interview, 13.8.1990). The biblical passage in question talks about the importance of silence, the most famous verses being St. James 3:2-12. The sonnet is a general meditation on the importance of silence, both in a contemplative order as well as outside monastic walls, and was triggered off by memories of the past. In a silent order one is bound to realize the power of the tongue, as is indicated in the first quatrain:

> The Silence of the cell hath taught me, Lord,
> The power of this wee thing we call the Tongue.
> For those who enter here, the spoken word
> Is banished - for it doth to Thee belong.

By the rule of silence the monks consecrate their vocal chords to God, they only speak to God, use their voices for God. Silence brings into relief the power of the word ("the Force / In each inanimate, yet living, sound"), words become more important when there are fewer. And yet, he knows "what meant / The meeting of two souls entwined by Talk", as he made the discovery apparent in the closing couplet: "... And I perceived, as she talked on in song, / That Contact starts where stops the nervous Tongue" [corr.]. The capital letter in "Contact" is used to emphasize that the actual contact started in silence. The whole of the final line conveys a feeling of nervousness, due to the accumulation of voiceless plosives, thus forming a contrast to the previous line which refers to song, where talk has stopped, dominated by long vowels.

The following lines taken from "Are you there, Lord?" (*Threshold*, 67) reflect the experience so much longed for, the feeling of divine presence in solitude:

> 'Tis strange! E'en when we're utterly alone
> Th'unuttered word can speak so loudly that
> The workings of the heart be full o'erthrown
> As though we with a living being sat.

The two stressed syllables followed by a pause "'Tis strange!" form the forceful beginning of this sonnet which is bound to make the reader wonder and be filled with inquisitiveness as regards the origin of such amazement. The spondee in the second line ("so loudly") successfully emphasizes the seemingly paradoxical idea conveyed, "th'unuttered word" speaking loudly "when we're utterly alone", but this paradox implies the incomprehensible which is experienced when the divine presence is felt in solitude. "The workings of the heart", the striving for a sign, longing for a hint of love is "full o'erthrown": all the pains and doubts disappear as soon as He is felt. The word play on "utter", using it twice though with a different meaning, has a quizzing effect. The very title of the sonnet reflects an atmosphere of intimacy; a presence was felt, which made the poet pose the question.

"Michaelmas, 29/9/81" (*Threshold*, 88) demands special attention because of its structure. The rhyme scheme is aaab, cccd etc. with the first three lines having eleven syllables each, while the closing line has only five. The poem can be read with a trochaic pattern underneath, but also as iambic pentameters, each line starting, however, with an inversion. All the dimeters, i.e. the closing lines, have the grammatical form of a question, except for the last line, which is a statement. Thus we progress from uncertainty to certainty. The poem starts with a question:

> Am I alone in this unreal Silence
> 'Twixt these great walls, unstormed by this world's violence?
> When with one click I drive out noisy radiance,
>   Am I in darkness?

The opening line lacks one syllable, which is compensated by the pause after the second foot and the slow progression of the line. The rhythm requires two stresses on "unreal" followed by another stressed syllable, which indicates the strange nature of "Silence" on the one hand, and also points to the idea that this silence is in fact not real, as someone is present. In the third stanza we read:

> This tingling Void that patters on the ear-drum,
> Th'echoing Yawn of Solitude's huge Boredom,
> Is it but Sound, or can it be a syndrome
>   Of hidden Meaning?

The image of the "tingling Void" has appeared before, the metaphor of the second line, however, is original, the capital letters indicating that these aspects belong to God's creation just as everything else does. "Th'echoing Yawn of Solitude's huge Boredom" vividly conveys this aspect of solitude, which cannot be dispelled and is hardly made to appear less forbidding. The choice of the word "syndrome" is unfortunate. Its scientific connotations do not fit into the body of the poem; it only fulfils its duty as part of the rhyme scheme. This poem can be sung to "Christe Sanctorum decus Angelorum", a subdued and pleasing tune.

The examples given present silence in all its aspects, as a fountain of bliss as well as a source of almost unbearable pain. They clearly demonstrate the importance of silence to the Carthusian monk as the basic means to find the inner void. Alun Idris succeeds with significant poignance at conveying the nature of silence in the rhythm and sound symbolism of his verse.

3.1.1.3. RETREAT

To the contemplative monk retreat represents an occasion of inner, spiritual purification acting as a form of concentrated silence. Retreats differ in length: once a year the monks go into a retreat which lasts eight full days, but there are shorter forms as well, such as the one-day retreat, which is practised every month. During that period the monks often read the bible, sometimes meditating on only a few lines. Other monks do not read at all, they just meditate and wait to experience the Lord (cf. interview in Fraham, 1.7.1990).

In the volume *The Threshold of Paradise* we find several poems written in retreat, which reflect the spirit and the atmosphere they were written in. The mood varies considerably.

"Beginning of retreat" (*Threshold*, 32) was written in 1981 during a period of calm and tranquillity, as is reflected in the rhythm of the poem. Peace and calmness form the very essence of the first stanza:

> Time, time again
> Have I knelt here before,
> Yet in this quiet eventide
> I sense a Presence at my side
> And I adore.

The two stressed syllables separated by a pause at the very beginning prescribe the solemn tone of this verse. With minor alternations, the stanzaic structure of the first stanza is maintained throughout the entire poem: both the stanzaic opening and closure employ iambic dimeter, l.2 is written in trimeter, while ll.3 and 4 use tetrameter, with an iambic pattern prevailing. Embracing rhyme is employed in ll.2-5.

The meditative tone of the opening line is followed by a certain excitement caused by the "Presence at my side", indicated through the quicker rhythm in ll.2-4. The closing line, however, leads back to the original mood of solemnity. The idea of utter peacefulness and inner unrest mingled in this first stanza are taken up separately in the two quintains to follow:

> This is the night
> On which I turn aside
> From all that is not Thee alone
> And tread into the great Unknown
> That Thee doth hide.
>
> O! sacred peace
> That bathes that blessèd Face!
> Come, enter this my troubled breast;
> In this retreat teach me to rest
> On gentle Grace.

The poet is determined in his entire and exclusive concentration on the Lord in this retreat, as is firmly implied in the second stanza of this poem; he longs to separate himself "From all that is not Thee alone". The dominance of elongated vowels and diphthongs stress the decision to watch for God in silence and peace. However, the yearning to make it happen, the wish to accelerate the attainment of inner peace and equilibrium is felt as well. Thus a certain impatience creeps into the rhythm of the third stanza. The exclamation at the very beginning suggests the urge and yearning to be filled with God, whilst the opening spondee of l.3, "Come, enter", and the inversion in the middle of that line, "teach me" convey his own longing to be more active, to accelerate the procedure, encouraging grace to come. This determination is also apparent in the fourth stanza: "the hollow word / Draw me no more: my soul hath heard / The still, small voice." The spondaic "no more" underlines his determination to turn aside from all "terrestrial noise". The image of the "still, small voice" echoes a passage in the Old Testament, where the prophet Elijah tries to find God first in the tempest, then in an earthquake and finally in fire, but he cannot hear anything. In silence, however, God speaks to him: there is a light wind, a small voice of calm, some inner wind (cf. 1 Kings 19:11-13). The poet is fully aware that God can only be found in silence.

At the end of the eight-day-retreat the monk makes resolutions which he will read again the following year. These resolutions are also meditated upon during the monthly one-day-retreat and function as a kind of spiritual guide-line, enabling the monk to learn by his own personal experience (cf. interview in Fraham, 1.7.1990). Reading these lines brings back memories, which explains the sad mood of a poem simply titled by the time of its composition, "(3.30 a.m.)" (*Threshold*, 32f.). It was written in retreat a year later than the previous one, though using the same metrical pattern:

> When I look back
> On all that hath gone by:
> The days and hours that I have passed ...
> The memories that still cling fast -
>   I weep, I cry.
>
> Nay, nay, ne'er more
> May I again recall
> The opportunities of love,
> The grace once given from above
>   That I let fall.

The parallel structure and the pause used in the closing line of the first stanza, "I weep, I cry", the poignancy, yet irrevocability of this utterance rhyming on the plaintive diphthong /aɪ/ with l.2, reinforce the mood of sorrow and pain. The idea of not having used time and grace well is striking. Despair is firmly implied at the beginning of the second stanza, where the repetition suggests the sober realization of having missed a chance which will not be given again. "Given" (l.4) requires a pause when read aloud, which places emphasis on the succeeding phrase "from above", thereby pointing to the divine nature of grace "once given": the spondee employed suggests a tone of lament, as it is a past moment which is referred to, "once"; at the same time, however, it implies the unique nature of grace which is given once only and never repeated. There may be other chances at other times, but a chance missed is a grace lost for ever, which the poet is bound to realize: "once, only once, / Is every grace bestowed."

"Here begins retreat" (*Threshold*, 31f.) was written during the same retreat, apparently amidst a period of unease.[60] The rhythm is anything but smooth:

> Lord, once more I lie at thy feet,
> Here once again we pause to meet
> Deep in thy Heart, whose gentle beat
> Calls on, calls on.

The two pauses in the first line, one after the stressed "Lord" and the other after "more", the rapid movement in the termination "at thy feet", create a feeling of unrest. The second line can be read with two pauses as well, while there is only one in l.3. He pauses to meet the Lord, but is apparently still filled with unrest, as is implied by the unevenness of the rhythm.
The third stanza has fewer pauses but uses additional stresses:

> Yet this Lent is not as the rest;
> Nay, this retreat is one great quest
> For what vocation richly blest
> Calls on, calls on.

We move from five stressed syllables in l.1 to six in l.2. The accumulation of stresses points to the vital importance of this retreat, in which the poet aims to find out about his call, his future: "what vocation richly blessed / Calls on, calls on." The use of "richly blest" suggests that the range of possibilities lies within the domain of the religious life; they concern vocations blessed by God. The refrain employed throughout the entire poem, "Call(s) on, call(s) on." (which only in stanza five takes the form of a question) emphasizes the important problem to be resolved. Furthermore, the repetition enforces the idea that time cannot be halted in its flow.
Despite the inner strain caused by the difficulty of the decision, the poet's belief in providence is unshakeable, as is apparent in the penultimate stanza:

> Lord, is't all? Or can there be more?
> Thou, Thou alone dost hold the door
> Of Providence, whose teeming store
> Calls on, calls on.
>
> Mystery! How rightly thou'rt named!
> Veiled Destiny! In vain thou'rt tamed.
> Who knows? Who knows what Plan unframed
> Calls, calls, calls on.

God is the creator of providence and its "teeming store". There seem to be several possiblities at times ("can there be more?"), yet these are foreseen by providence as well. The poet is at a complete loss; he seems not to know at all where his future path will lead him, as is firmly implied in the closing stanza: "Veiled Destiny! In vain thou'rt tamed". Providence is only known to the Creator, the "Plan unframed" never seen by human beings. The refrain is slightly

---

[60] The poet was combining the two poems so as to furnish a sort of diary. As it happened, by the time he had finished the diary, he had to stop writing as it was "beginning to be very uncomfortable" (cf. letter, 8.7.1990).

altered: on the one hand the three-fold repetition emphasizes the lengthiness and weariness of the process, but on the other hand, a steady, inexorable progression of time and providence is implied as well.

"Lines jotted in retreat (and left in their crudest form)" (*Threshold*, 33f.) is another example for a poem written in retreat which is characterized by doubts and a strong feeling of uncertainty. Apparently retreats can become a touchstone of a monk's vocation. The poem is a catharsis rather than a balanced lyric, but none the less touchingly honest:

> "Too late! Too late!" I'm cracking, Lord.
> My heart swells up and heaves again.
> Am I where Thou wilt have me, Lord?
> Or am I labouring in vain?
>
> How can I know? What should I do?
> O silent One! Thou, Thou alone
> Must speak in this unending night.
> Ere't be too late, make, MAKE IT KNOWN!

The desperate need to know, the yearning to receive a sign, is apparent in these lines. In the first part of the poem, subtitled "the voice of the past", various voices expressing such yearning from his own biography appear, reminding him of missed chances in his youth ("too late, too late"). A notion of "hiraeth" is already present in these thoughts, a longing for things lost and gone beyond recall which can be found so often in his verse.[61]

The second part called "The voice of the present" projects the mood of failure and despair into the present. The pain experienced as a result of having missed a chance anew seems to be too much to bear now: "I'm cracking, Lord." The difficulty of the situation is firmly implied in the desperate plea addressed to the Lord: "Thou, Thou alone / Must speak in this unending night." The repetition as well as the metaphor of the "unending night" point at the hopelessness of the situation; only God can liberate the poet from the dreadful dead end. The urgency of the matter is powerfully suggested in the final, rather dramatic line, "Ere't be too late, make, MAKE IT KNOWN!"

In retreat, while meditating on various passages in the bible, the importance of the Word of God becomes all the more obvious to the monk. Lectio Divina is not only spiritual

---

[61] The following biographical details are etched in this poem: Alun Idris did not apply for the Universities of Oxford and Cambridge, as he intended to go on to the priesthood after having taken A-levels in 1971. His parents, however, wanted him to apply for Oxford, but when he asked for the application forms, his master told him that it was too late for that year. ("You are too late," the master said, / And drew upon his pipe ...".) Alun Idris eventually went to the University of Wales at Aberystwyth, having been granted a scholarship. A number of his friends, however, went to Oxford University, which explains the presence of the feeling of regret in the poem; the feeling of having missed a chance. "These are the things that come into your mind when you are on retreat, the chances of the past that you have missed" (letter, 8.7.1990). Another circumstance which encouraged the mood of having missed a chance was the life-story of a fellow-brother in Sélignac, who had studied at a French University. Under his influence, Alun Idris felt that he had not taken the academic life seriously enough, he could perhaps have done better. (It is interesting to note that this meditation on the "vast Unknown" of his future was written in 1981, i.e. at a time when the difficulties which finally arose as a result of his writing poetry had not yet appeared.)

nourishment but also represents a means of intellectual stimulation, as we read in the poem "In retreat: Lectio Divina" (*Threshold*, 35f.):

> Here in my hands I hold
> The Word that holdeth me;
> These leaves I turn my self unfold -
> Writ, I am read of thee. [corr.]

The word play used in this stanza beautifully suggests the power of Lectio Divina, mingling the literal and figurative meanings of a word. The poet holds the "Writ", the old English word for scripture, in his hand, but actually it is the other way round for it is the contents of the bible which have captured the poet's soul. It is he who is dependent on the "Word", gripped by and bound to the Word of God. A similar reversal occurs in ll.3f.: by reading in the bible, turning the leaves, his own "self" begins to "unfold". Also implied is the cooperation necessary to achieve union, man's willingness to "hold" the "Word". To turn "these leaves" is essential; one has to be open to divine grace. In the charterhouse, the power of God's Word is ever present: usually the monastic day starts with Lectio Divina, the monks imbibe the Word of God to be strengthened thereby for the rest of the day. In retreat, the monks savour a few verses of the bible, then ponder over them, and interiorize them. By reading the word of God, the monk is able to penetrate to his innermost kernel; he strips all the layers away, tearing him open for the Spirit to come.

> In the eternal peace
> Of unengendered Void
> Truth thought aloud and bade Silence cease,
> And with its echo toyed.

Lectio Divina is a powerful source for meditations: the "eternal peace /Of unengendered Void" is a striking image, pointing out that even before the creation, there was only God's thought, and nothing else, only the great silence of nothingness. However, He "bade Silence cease, / And with its echo toyed". He played with what He owned; He was the great omnipotent, forming things by His energy out of utter nothingness. The "echo" refers to all that happened afterwards and is happening still. The image of the "unengendered Void" goes back to beyond the beginning of the universe: "in the silence of Lectio Divina one is trying to get tuned to that eternal silence, the Word of God that was spoken in this great silence" (letter, 29.10.1989).

Such an attitude appears bizarre to the modern western mind. In general people are afraid of experiencing the void, using it as a means of calming and to find peace. However, experiencing the void, being entirely filled with peace and consequently God's presence, is what contemplative monasticism is all about, being always in touch with His great silence.

> Verb of unceasing Act,
> Logos of triune Thought,
> Thy quiet Fiat uttered Fact,
> Dreamt, and its dream-world wrought.

The image of the "Logos of triune Thought" in l.2 obviously refers to the Holy Trinity revealed in the bible. "Fiat" echoes what the Virgin Mary said to the angel, "let it be" (cf. Luke 1:38). However, it is also a reference to the original fiat, "Let there be light", "Fiat lux." (Genesis 1:3), which marked the beginning of creation. It is the first command, the first word utterd by God. God's word is incarnated in the bible, as is implied in l.1; it is there for us in print, a silent form of God's presence, "Thy quiet Fiat uttered Fact". The alliteration employed underlines the firm connection between God's command and the world He created thereby. Lectio Divina, "divine reading", is significant in that respect because it suggests that we are dealing with divine material. It thus contains the idea of epiclesis, which occurs when the priest spreads his hands over the offerings and asks the Spirit to descend upon them. The same happens during Lectio Divina when the Holy Spirit is asked to descend and elucidate the Word of Scripture and make the Word speak, thereby making Him speak to the monk personally. This question of receptivity before the Word of God is central to monastic spirituality, this special way of tuning in to scripture and ruminating upon it. The Carthusian tradition is a four-fold process: lectio (reading), meditatio (meditation), ruminatio (ruminating) and oratio (mental prayer, prayer of the mind and heart).[62]

In the sixth stanza God appears as a poet:

> "Be!" thought the Poet's Mind;
> "Am," was the Clay's reply ...
> "Thou, Adam, shalt become Mankind.
> Earth! with his will comply."

A poem is something which is created, is made, "poet" actually meaning "maker". God appears as the creator of the world, as "the Poet", the world being one of His many poems.

The imagery used implies that Alun Idris does not see any contradiction between priesthood or monasticism and poetry: "The poet sanctifies creation in the sense that he sings on its beauty, on behalf of the dumb creation" (letter, 29.10.1989). In Alun Idris' opinion the whole of creation is sanctified, there is nothing which is not sacred, as the whole of life is God's.

The poem terminates with a plea to receive a sign:

> Deep is the Silence, Lord,
> The Silence of the years,
> Lord! But a word, just one small word!
> Speak! for Thy servant hears.

L.3 in particular, with its pauses and additional stresses conveys a tone of impatience and longing. The closing line is directly inspired by Lectio Divina, when in 1 Samuel 3, verse 9+10 we read "Speak, O Eternal, Thy servant is listening". In the silence of Lectio Divina the poet is prepared to receive "a word, just one small word", he yearns to be given a sign. The poem was composed to be sung to "Bod Alwyn", a well-known tune in Wales.

---

[62] These four words are also written on the four windows in the scriptorium of La Trappe (cf. letter, 8.7.1990).

Retreats thus represent a source of philosphical and theological meditations. The following poem, simply called "In retreat" (*Threshold*, 34f.), merely tells of the curious relationship between the monk and the cell; living in a cell meaning to live at the edge of existence. This precarious personal situation involves extreme and contradictory feelings and attitudes. On the one hand there is an endless affection for the cell as it becomes the monk's home, representing a means of access to the Lord; on the other hand, however, it involves inmeasurable suffering as well. To deny the negative aspect involved would be self-betrayal.

> O! blessèd Cell, so quiet and so lonely,
>   Yet ever speaking to my crowded heart,
> Stark are thy walls, thy windows - yet, so homely!
>   Suffered, endured, yet loved, is this strange hearth.
>
> Known, so well-known, is every stone that holds thee
>   To these mine eyes, as unto theirs of old
> Who studied, prayed; slept, laboured here before me
>   In this same stifling heat and aching cold.

The monk is fully attuned to his cell; he has accustomed himself to it, and yet, or perhaps just because of its familiarity, there is an element of human suffering involved. In the cell there is nothing to please the body, the monk is "completely divorced from anything humanly satisfying" (letter, 29.10.1989), as is suggested in l.4 of the second stanza, "this same stifling heat and aching cold". The Carthusian is exclusively living on divine grace, the whole attention being centered on God and the cell. In a way it is a prison for the body so that the soul can be freed and fly to God; there being no distraction whatsoever. The contradictory adjectives employed (blessèd - lonely, stark - homely, endured - loved) suggest a kind of love-hate relationship towards the cell. However, it is the place to experience solitude:

> Known was the stillness of these sacred moments
>   That seem to freeze the very march of time
> To all who tasted Solitude's sweet torments,
>   Who bent their wills to this relentless chime.

The imagery used to convey the idea of a monk's solitude in his cell suggests both positive as well as negative connotations. While in l.1 an idea of peace and sacredness is conveyed, the tone changes in l.2, "freeze" implying a rather painful, forced standstill of time. The oxymoron of "Solitude's sweet torments" is highly expressive, pointing to its contradictory nature. Involving the senses by the choice of "tasted" adds another dimension to the experience; i.e. the interiorization of solitude. The imagery of the closing line hints again at the dominant role of the bell in the monastery, its "relentless chime", to which all have to obey. The tune that fits this poem is called "Rhys, 433" (the number refers to the Welsh Baptist Hymnal), which in its gentleness rather emphasizes the consoling and positive aspect of the cell. In "Beginning of retreat" (*Threshold*, 32) we read in the closing stanza:

> Yea, Lord, we're twain
> In this Carthusian cell.
> I "come apart to rest awhile"
> Alone upon this desert isle
> 'Twixt heav'n and hell.

This is what the Carthusian cell is, a "desert isle" positioned somewhere between heaven and hell. On the one hand it represents a source of bliss, offering comfort to the monk through the divine presence, the Lord always being there as the monk's faithful companion ("we're twain"), but on the other hand it is also a kind of hell.

The examples given in this chapter present the retreat as an occasion of spiritual purification, fostering spiritual growth. This form of concentrated solitude allows and encourages the monk to take decisions in the Lord's presence, to work out problems and achieve inner peace and equilibrium. The way to purification, however, is often linked to the experience of struggle, pain, even despair. In retreat Lectio Divina is of utmost importance, offering the monk both spiritual and intellectual nourishment. The poems clearly suggest "Divine Reading" as a fertile soil for meditations.

3.1.1.4. MAIN FEASTS

Religious feast days are one of the highlights in the life of a Carthusian monk, remembering these occasions and celebrating them being of great consoling and spiritually nurturing value. Feast days often stimulate meditations on the feast itself as well as subjects connotated to them; they act as a driving force for spiritual and emotional development. This idea is conveyed in the poetry of Alun Idris, given the fact that a great number of poems were sparked off on the occasion of church feasts. The poet had felt the urge to write a collection of semi-liturgical poems: "I was aware that there was a possibility of creating something for God rather than literature" (letter, 29.10.1989). This aspect of creating a work of beauty for God, of being creative for His honour is of utmost importance. Alun Idris has always felt the need for embellishing the liturgy, the work of God, and enhancing its beauty. The idea of conveying this beauty is supported by the fact that he often chooses to create a combination of song and writing, i.e. a poem which can be sung, prompted, of course, by the poet's own love of music, which seems to be a general characteristic of Welsh people.

"Candlemass" (*Threshold*, 16) is an early representative of this series. The feast prompted the author to write a poem where he uses the light of the sacrificial candle as a model for the Christian way of living, the candle's light being a part of the Light of lights, the Lord.

> O noble sacrifice indeed!
> O lesson for the world to heed!
> Thou teachest me, O martyr sweet,
> My life to lose in light and heat.

The metaphor is conventional; and yet the rhythm in the first three lines quoted suggests the poet's wonder at so "noble" a sacrifice, presenting the candle as a "martyr sweet". This oxymoron suggest the joy of sacrificing one's life for God. The alliteration and assonance in l.4 imply the poet's yearning to burn like the candle with love for God.

The regularity of the rhythm of the closing stanza, bearing a reference to Luke, chapter 2, firmly reminds one of a prayer:

> Lord, when this flame is wholly spent,
> And shadows bathe once more this tent,
> In peace may we, at Thy behest,
> Go forth, and, 'neath Thy radiance, rest.
>   Amen.

"O lux beata Trinitas", an old, well-known hymn sung on the first and second vespers of Trinity Sunday[63], offers the notation to which this poem can be chanted.

"Immaculée Conception" (*Threshold*, 7) has an interesting structure: the poet's own personal experience is mingled with religious ponderings and meditations. In the first two stanzas he seems to regret the fact that in his early youth he had not been aware of the blessing he was receiving, it had all been so easy then, so "simple". He realizes how close he had been to Grace in those days which are now gone, and laments his blindness:

> When I was young how simple things did seem:
> Earth then did bathe in Heaven's gentle gleam ...
> Lord, why, oh! why did I not then perceive
> How rich that Blessing I'll ne'er more receive?
>
> Had I but one small moment to re-live,
> How, oh! how would I not Thee glory give!
> Lord, my dear Lord, how blind I was to Grace
> In those dim distant days spent 'neath Thy Face!

The poem consists of ten quatrains written in iambic pentameter rhyming in couplets. The majority of the lines start with inversion or two stressed syllables. "When I was young", followed by a pause, indicates that life was different then, the extent to which it differed being suggested by the image presented in l.2. The rhythm of the third line corresponds to the poet's inner strain: the stresses on the two "why's" and on "not then" emphasize his despair, completed by the stresses that fall on "ne'er more" in l.4. The lament continues in the second stanza, starting with a nostalgic spondee: "Had I but one small moment to re-live". The spondaic third foot emphasizes that he would already be content with one short moment given again. The exclamatory "How, oh! how!" underlines how differently he would use that moment now, while the alliteration in the closing line suggests the feeling of how far away those happy days seem to him today.

---

[63] Cf. letter, 8.7.1990.

The feast of the "Immaculée Conception" records when Our Lady was conceived, not when she herself conceived: "One tiny *grain* of Love's st*ra*nge quick'ning leav'*n* ... / One *h*eav'*n*ly hour *h*ath made one heir of *H*eav'*n*." The repetition of sounds is striking in these lines, although the excessive use of syncope does not add to their beauty. The imagery used to describe the conception is forceful because of its visual impact.

Life which begins in only a moment of time goes on for all eternity, having a beginning but no end. The moment of life's beginning or conception, is therefore a very dynamic moment, releasing a new eternity. The rapid and dynamic rhythm of the fifth stanza takes up this idea, referring to a child growing up; each line of the quatrain starts with a spondee, which adds to its dynamics:

> L*i*fe! O! new l*i*fe, behold the r*ay*s of d*ay*!
> Spin, t*iny* world, on th*ine* uncharted w*ay*.
> Hour after hour drink T*i*me's unebbing gift ...
> Each r*i*sing d*ay* that lovely head shall lift.

The stanza makes elaborate use of assonance and consonance, as is indicated in italics, long diphthongs and vowels prevailing. The imagery in "Behold the rays of day" evokes the moment of first seeing the light of day, the moment of birth when we leave the dark night of the womb to step into the light of day. This light of day is free: "Bathe in the stream of freely given light", as we read in stanza six. In the succeeding stanza the poet addresses Mary herself, wondering about her own thoughts that might have come to her mind after having realized the Grace she had been given:

> What wilt though feel, small, uncreated Queen,
> Waking to find what unearned favours mean?
> - Yet is this not Life's crown each laurelled night,
> Nirvana's child, made for unmade delight?

What is the delight of heaven compared with the delight of the night? Ecstasy on earth cannot bear comparison with the joys of heaven, this idea is firmly implied in these lines. We are "made for unmade delight": the classical allusions evoked by the image of "laurelled night" suggest sensual pleasures which are firmly attached to classical mythology. Night is "Nirvana's child": "Nirvana" means "extinction", "gone with the wind", "nothingness", but is also the equivalent of bliss in Buddhism, therefore suggesting paradise. We come from nothingness, the night, from non-existence, i.e. Nirvana, but we also go to Nirvana in the sense of bliss. Moving from nothingness to bliss is man's destiny; for the Christian soul the Nirvana is "not non-existence, but fulness of life, it is sharing God's life" (letter, 10.6.1990).

The feast of the Immaculate Conception triggered off this meditation on life, on the poet's own origin, his existence, and how much he used or abused the graces which he has already been given. Hiraeth is apparent in this poem, the longing for a state of grace, a period in time which cannot be given again, a longing for something impossible to be grasped anymore:

> ... Were I a cell of embryonic Hope
> That with its new-found gift of life doth grope,
> With my first breath this would be my first word:
> "Fairer than all I thought is this fair world."

Determined to make better use of his opportunities if only there were a second chance, the poet knows that he is striving in vain: "Once, only once, is each blest hour bestowed - / Grace! Grace! In vain thine unused flood hath flowed." The mournful exclamation sums up the idea of endless sorrow for a chance missed.

The self-criticism in his retrospective is fostered by the difficult situation the poet was in at the time; it was not clear then whether he would continue to live in the order or not:

> Yet is it true that Youth is wholly o'er?
> Ye unborn years, what holds your pregnant store?
> Lord, is life lived, or is it just begun?
> O Mystery of Life! Where wilt thou run?

The imagery of the yet unborn child is once more employed in this closing stanza, having been used throughout the poem. "What holds your pregnant store?" is a striking metaphor for the future which cannot be known beforehand and also, on a very subtle level, pointing at the idea of providence; life has been pre-arranged ("pregnant store") for us by a guiding hand, although its ways and means are still hidden and unknown to us, it is there. You cannot behold the child before it is born; similarly, we cannot know our future from the present or the past, although divine providence has already arranged our days for us.

Septuagesima, the ninth Sunday before Easter, is of special importance in a monastery: on this day the community starts to read and chant the early books of the bible, a task which stretches over a two-year cycle; the chants about the creation of man, however, are sung every year. The Carthusians sing it in all its entirety, slowly and in Latin, without any ommissions.[64] This special day recalls the creation of man and the subsequent curse that was laid upon him, as we read in "Septuagesima" (*Threshold*, 18). The poem, which consists of four stanzas of eight lines rhyming in couplets, conveys a strong sense of sadness, which is reinforced by the effective employment of sound symbolism:

> When sorrow *paints* i*ts pa*le lament
> In colours of the firmament,
> When earth drinks deeply heaven's tears
> And Nature Life's great sighing hears,
> And when, alone with Loneliness,
> I think on what was happiness,
> Then, then alone is all in tune,
> Then doth my heart with Earth's commune.

The first four lines describe the early morning atmosphere on that day and metaphorically evoke a strong feeling of sorrow. The alliteration and the assonance on the mournful diphthong

---

[64] It is the only order that sings these passages in their entirety (cf. interview in Fraham, 1.7.1990).

/eɪ/ in l.1 and the dominance of long vowels underline the notion of lament conveyed. The entire stanza is pervaded with sorrow at the great tragedy described in Genesis, the fall of man, his curse. In ll.4-8 the poet remembers the happiness before the fall of man, the union of God, man and nature, which makes the present situation all the more painful.

"For Sorrow is the world's refrain: / The melody of stifled pain", as we read at the beginning of the second stanza, our world seems to be made for sorrow, "Recurring o'er the rhythmic years / On each new generation's ears". The lines suggest man's utter nothingness, having no right to any joy at all. Any joy a man receives being a gift; therefore it is important to free oneself from desire ("The hollowness of wanted bliss"). The stanza closes with the following lines: "And cries to highest heav'n above / The void of love devoid of love." The word play in the closing line emphasizes the severity of the hidden message. "In a charterhouse, you sacrifice everything, even yourself. Then, when joy comes, it really comes from above and causes deep fulfillment. [...] The important thing is to look for God, not for His consolation" (interview in Fraham, 1.7.1990).

Indeed, the "soothing joy of the evening" is to be felt in "Sunset on Septuagesima Sunday" (*Threshold*, 19), a poem written on the very same day. "In monasteries it was calm in the evening, the struggle was over as it were" (letter, 8.7.1990). A beautiful sunset can provide an unexpected joy. Indeed, the poem implies that joy only seems to come unexpectedly, "Giv'n always when I sought it least - / And never when I sat to feast": in other words bliss and joy cannot be forced to come, but they appear at unexpected moments. The absence of Joy, i.e. God ("We call thee Joy") is a most painful experience, for the poet has "known a little of the hell / Where thou art not, where sweetness sours, / And Pleasure lives on borrowed hours." The imagery used to describe the absence of Joy is striking. The closing stanza is a powerful testimony describing the poet's innermost experience:

> I sought thee ... and will seek again,
> E'en though I know I seek in vain
> Thy presence in th'e'er absent lust
> Of dust for its own native dust -
> Forgetting that thy blissful fire
> Burns only when allumed Desire
> Burns out, and, deadened, feeling nought,
> Feels that for which it ever sought.

The spondaic "will seek" in l.1 underlines his firm decision to continue his search, "E'en though I know I seek in vain". The initial spondee prepares the paradoxical idea to follow. He will continue to seek the Lord, although he is aware that only when all desire is gone, when the soul is completely empty, feeling nothing at all any more, as is powerfully conveyed in the penultimate line, only then the soul might feel "that for which it ever sought". The stony way to be filled with God, with bliss, with Joy finds expression here. The image of "allumed Desire" bears heavy French influence, the poet using a French word and anglicizing it.

In "First Friday in Lent" (*Threshold*, 25f.) the poet remembers the painful experience of our Lord when suffering from solitude in the desert : "Eternal solitary God, / This Solitude thy feet have trod". He also suffered the pain of fasting and hunger, a pain which has not changed during the years: "The taste of hunger changes not, / Nor hath the Fast his bite forgot". The monastic experience is the desert experience that the Lord underwent, an idea which is fundamental to this poem.

It is only in the fourth stanza, after having remembered all the pain He had to suffer, that the poet openly addresses the Lord, encouraging Him like a friend:

> O Son of God, now son of Man,
> O Light of Life, now lifeless, wan,
> Walk on, walk on, in search of shade
> From rays of light thy Light hath made.

Both divine and human natures are united in the hypostasis of Christ, in one person. As the "Son of God" he is now "son of Man"; as the "Light of Life" he is lifeless now, as being truly human, the man Jesus is bound to die ("wan"). The poet encourages Jesus to go on and pursue his painful march through the desert, "in search of shade", in search of shelter from the burning rays of the sun which, as it were, originate in his own divine nature. The poet continues his encouragement in the succeeding stanza, "With Lucifer await the night": Lucifer means "the bringer of light"; however, as the great angel who fell (cf. Isaiah 14:12) he is waiting for the night, which symbolizes the time of evil. The truth expressed in the closing line of this stanza, "The war within within is won", offers the link between Christ in the desert and its parallel, life in solitude. The final stanza is full of encouragement, almost of a spurring character:

> Yea, conquer, Christ, the Tempter's power,
> Serene, await his last dark Hour,
> And then, 'neath thine own weeping Light,
> Extinguish this Star's blackest might.

The shouts of encouragement become almost audible when reading these lines, the poet managing to vividly convey his own outburst of feeling, his compassion for the Lord. As a result, the sufferings of Christ lose their historical character and become relevant to present times, to this very moment, the intimacy of the lines helping to visualize the sufferings of Christ in a most powerful manner.

The allusion to classical mythology in l.2 aims to emphasize the bewitching force of the devil. "Thine own weeping Light" symbolizes the hour of Christ's death approaching, the eclipse when the Lord was crucified, while the "Star" in the final line refers to Lucifer who is deprived of power through the death of Christ.

On Maundy Thursday the eucharist was given to the church, and the priesthood instituted.[65] This occasion prompted a meditation on a theme fairly common in mysticism, the abuse of grace. We thus read in "Maundy Thursday" (*Threshold*, 43f.):

> When suffering is felt in Bliss
>   And ecstasy grows pale,
> Rejoicing sings a note amiss,
>   Th'eternal Sirens wail.

The common measure is employed in this poem consisting of ten stanzas. The tone is one of mourning and sorrow, which gradually increases in degree and finally culminates in reproachful accusations; "ecstasy grows pale" is a powerful image which suggests the diminishing of the first love for God. The image of l.3 completes this idea, emphasizing how the love starts to wane, just being "a note" amiss at the beginning. "Th'eternal Sirens wail" firmly conveys the idea of lament and pain involved when realizing how grace is abused, or not used well. The following lines of stanza six already convey the tone of accusation: "The very souls who hold Thy Word / Are damned by what they knew". "The very souls" refer to priests who hold the knowledge of the sacraments and who also hold the power to utter the word which makes the Lord present. Yet, they "are damned by what they knew": those who have studied theology and act with this knowledge in a guilty way being doubly guilty.

This question of responsibility is classic in monastic theology. More grace is offered; however, there are also more possibilities of abusing that grace, therefore making the monk's responsibility greater. The same applies to priests, of course. The lines in question refer to monks who are completely unrepentant. The problem the poet takes up is the danger of becoming used to things holy, of being hardened to sacred mysteries and then abusing them.

In the seventh stanza we are explicitly told that "This Particle can Bliss afford, / Or shut for aye its gate." The consecrated host can "Bliss afford" if it is well used; however, when you receive the Body of Christ in a state of severe sin, you even add something to this sin; i.e. blessings can turn to curses.

> "The hatred of the Food of Love
>   Hath grown too great, too great.
> The very gates of Heaven move:
>   Its blessings Hell now sate."

"The hatred of the Food of Love" is a reference to the abuse of the eucharist, and to the people who should show greater devotion to it. So great has been the abuse that "the very gates of Heaven move". To read that heaven's blessings "Hell now sate" strongly conveys the idea of dismay and horror, reinforced by the diction employed: to use the verb "sate" in this context clashes with the dreadfulness of the meaning conveyed, although it fits in style to the other

---

[65] Cf. letter, 19.11.1989.

carefully chosen words. "'Of souls unwashed a filthy horde / Among the just doth blend.'"[66] is a metaphor for those coming to communion unworthily.

As is indicated in a note in brackets, this poem can be chanted as well, it fits an adaptation of a Psalm melody picked up at La Trappe.

The Holy Week represents a very special period for the monks: the approach of Easter. This most important feast of the year is, of course, also reflected in Alun Idris' poetry. In his poems he tries to convey his own experience and feelings during that period, using them as a means for meditations and for pointing out general truths in connection with the feast day in question. Thus we read in "At dawn, Good Friday" (*Threshold*, 45):

> O dawn of dawns! O day of days!
> How strange, how eerie seem thy rays!
> The Light of lights thy light's own beams
> This day will darken as He screams.

The "Light of light", of course, symbolizes Jesus, the stanza metaphorically presenting the happenings on Good Friday. The first line of the poem is striking in as much as it conveys a tone of excitement, leaving a very positive impression, which certainly surpasses the mournful tone conveyed in the other lines. The poet thereby manages to convey the idea that God has saved mankind by sending His only son and by letting Him die for us, which turns this day into the "day of days", despite the horror and pain involved. The parallelism in the opening line, "O dawn of dawns! O day of days!" underlines the uniqueness of this day. In the third stanza this idea is explicitly presented:

> Walk on, O Christ, the end is nigh.
> Stretch out thine arms, look to the sky;
> Bathe in the Blood that sets us free,
> In death nail Death to this strange Tree.

The initial spondees in the first two lines, the inversion in the third foot of l.2, and the initial inversion in l.3 lend them a tone of urgency. The poet encourages Jesus to "walk on" and not to give up, for "the end is nigh". L.3 explicitly refers to Jesus as the saviour of the world, saving us through his death. "Bathe in the Blood" suggests a mingling of positive and negative associations, provoked by the contrasting connotations of the imagery used. The poem closes with the following strong appeal to carry on:

> O Christ, thy piercèd feet have trod
> The winepress of the wrath of God.
> March on, O King, tread earth and sea!
> Hold forth thy Sign of Victory.

The "winepress" suggests crushing and the flowing of red liquid, which becomes a metaphor for the blood of Christ. Christ is pressed like the grape, and the redemptive blood flows.

---

[66] The quote echoes the work of the Italian mystic Helena Leonardi (cf. letter, 19.11.1989).

"Torcular calcavi solus" (Isaiah 63:3) is the biblical reference to this metaphor.[67] The "winepress of the wrath of God" suggests God as being angry as a result of man's sin; the idea of justice having to be satisfied is firmly implied. There was a debt on man's part, there was a fault which had to be rectified. The question of the Atonement is touched upon, as the Son took the weight upon Himself. The tension present in this poem echoes the intense experience of solitude and fasting at that time, the monks live the Triduum, the three sacred days, to the full.

The following poem composed on the same day, "Good Friday" (*Threshold*, 46), takes very much the character of a prayer. It consists of five quatrains written in iambic tetrameter rhyming in couplets. Here again, the striking feature to be noticed is that the mourning over the approaching death of Jesus does not dominate the tone of the poem. It is a spurring on rather than a lamentation, encouraging Jesus rather than mourning for Him:

> O Tree of Life, my Saviour's Cross,
> Repair the Tree of Eden's loss;
> Stretch forth thine arms o'er all mankind,
> That wand'ring Adam shade may find.

The rhythm is calm and regular, only the medial break in l.1 and the initial spondee in l.3 offer a slight variation. The rhythm echoes a steady and continuous progress. The first two lines imply that there has always been a connection between the wood of the cross and the wood of the tree of knowledge, as well as with the wood of the tree of life, which is suggested by their combination and minglement. Alun Idris uses several images to evoke the idea of the cross: "Tree of Life", then later "Victorious Tree, triumphant Tree", "crux" and finally "O Gibbet". The subtitle of the poem "STAT CRUX DUM VOLVITUR ORBIS" represents the Carthusian motto,[68] which is referred to in the second stanza: "Unmoved thou standest o'er the world, / Unrocked, as this small globe is whirled." The cross stands firmly while the world goes round. In the closing quatrain we read:

> O Gibbet, thou shalt judge the world:
> The echo of thy final word
> Shall sound, resound from end to end
> Of Space that doth for e'er extend.

"Gibbet" is the "judge", the word also suggesting an association with condemnation. We detect a reversal of values: normally a person who has been judged is sent to the gibbet, the gibbet as such has no role as judge. However, in this case, the judged one is the final judge of the world in the end. The echo of His final word will never end, the echo being suggested in l.3 by the two-fold repetition. There will be no end to it.

---

[67] The verses of Isaiah 63:2+3 throw light on the passage (cf. letter, 29.10.1989).
[68] Cf. Heimbucher 1933, 385.

The following poem "Holy Saturday (at dawn)" (*Threshold*, 46f.), which uses the same stanza form as the previous poem, "Good Friday", is a poetic reflection on the specific nature of that day:

> Where wast Thou, Christ, on this dark day,
> So dark that none in church may pray,
> That o'er the earth no Sacrifice
> May be received in Paradise?

On Holy Saturday the Eucharist is not celebrated in the church: the tabernacle is empty ("The real Absence fills the Tent"), the altar is bare, with the sanctuary lamp extinguished. The poem is based on the question of where the Lord was on that day. The spondees at the beginning and at the end of the first line place additional emphasis on the question. A third spondee is employed at the beginning of the second line "So dark", which, as it is followed by a pause, reinforces the idea of our ignorance. The poem successfully conveys the pain of His absence, a strong feeling of abandonment:

> O Absence! O vast Emptiness!
> How hollow this day's Loneliness!
> No song, no office, not a face
> To bring one tiny ray of Grace ...

The third line echoes the fact that in a charterhouse Holy Saturday is spent in a very solitary way, there is no community exercise at all; the monks remain in their cells the whole day long, no office being celebrated in church. With the exception of the night office, though, but there is a void between the two night offices of Holy Saturday and the vigil of Easter Sunday (cf. letter, 22.7.1990). The whole day consists of mourning and waiting, which is conveyed in these lines. The exclamations, the mournful diphthong /əʊ/, the stress on "one tiny", all these devices add to this atmosphere.

In the sixth stanza we read "O Void! Where is my other Half?" The affection involved in this mystery, the pain felt at the absence of his "other Half", forms the very essence of this line; there is a strong yearning conveyed to see the beloved again. "On this dark day the Hidden One / Is hid e'en from the very Sun."[69] Jesus is hidden from all human beings, no human eye may see Him, "Thine least of all, poor carnal soul! / Await, await ... Let Fate unroll". Here the author addresses himself as "poor carnal soul" emphasizing human ignorance. The poem closes with a stanza which firmly suggests the utter nothingness and unworthiness of mankind, using harsh derogatory imagery:

> "All that we know is that full nought
> Is all the knowledge ever sought

---

[69] The Apostles' Creed talks of *descent ad inferos*, the official translation runs "he descended into hell", *ad inferos*, the so-called "harrowing of hell"; a better translation is "He descended to the dead" (which is used in the German version: "Hinabgestiegen in das Reich des Todes"), as *inferos* does not necessarily imply hell, the place of damnation and punishment, it rather suggests a place of waiting.

By little hominides like thee
Who know but half Eternity."

Several poems which are inspired by a church feast take the form of a dramatic dialogue. Such a technique adds a notion of dynamics to the subject treated, increasing its immediacy, and enabling the poet to present his thoughts in a more direct, appealing and electrifying way. By taking the point of view of the people involved, by letting them speak, Alun Idris increases the poems' authenticity and vividness.

In "The First Day of the Week" (*Threshold*, 49) the poet does not shrink from describing the apostles in despair and full of doubts after Jesus died:

> Despondency ... despondency ...
> O what dejected company.
> He's dead! He's dead! The Master's dead!
> For three whole years vain hopes we've fed.

The repetition in the first line suggests the weariness of the experience, while the repeated exclamation in 1.3 increases the tension; naming "the Master" after twice using the personal pronoun adds to the feeling of utmost despair. The heavy stresses on "three whole years" emphasize their despondency, all was in vain. "And yet we thought that it was he"; the pause in the middle of the line conveys an explanatory notion of excuse for their behaviour. The apostles had believed in Him, but now, of course, the situation is different: "It's over. He is dead and gone. / We've lost. We've failed. The Jews have won." The shortness, the abruptness of these sentences combined with the use of parallel structure intensifies their feeling of surrender. The reader comes to realize that the disciples were real human beings, critical and completely incredulous:

> A world-wide church built by twelve men!
> We must have been stark raving when
> We put our trust in this strange man
> From NAZARETH! - that backward clan! -

The alliteration and the long diphthongs in the opening image convey a notion of grandeur, which is utterly destroyed by the biting sharpness of 1.2. Presenting the apostles in their doubts and uncertainties diminishes our distance towards them, they cease to be abstract figures by being presented the reality of their weakness. "Forget that Bread ... Forget the Cup ..." powerfully implies their feeling of deception. However, the situation changes abruptly at the beginning of the penultimate stanza:

> What hit me? Ouch! What's shining there?
> Ow! Stop it! Stop that dazzling glare!
> "It's Him!" - "It's not?" - "Yes, look! It's Him!"
> "You're joking." - "No, it's not a whim ..."

The colloquial tone in this short conversation adds to the immediacy of the message, which is a characteristic of the entire poem. It strongly conveys the Apostles' own astonishment and wonder at the Resurrection of Christ.

The following poem, "Easter Monday, after mass" (*Threshold*, 49f.) deals with the episode of Maria Magdalena, Maria (James' mother) and Salome going to the grave in order to anoint the body of Christ. The refrain at the end of each stanza, the repetition of the Angel's question "'Quem quaeritis'", makes the reader re-experience the dialogue between the three women and the angel. The poem reminds one of a short mystery play in verse form.

> Good Sir, if thou know'st ought of this,
> Or canst explain what is amiss,
> Pray, tell us where our Treasure is.
>   - "Quem quaeritis?"

The women seek the Lord, the hope that perhaps this "Good Sir" knows something about His whereabouts is apparent; however, as the angel keeps asking them doggedly whom they are looking for, they lose their patience:

> But Sir, thou surely must have heard
> Of this great Name at least a word:
> We seek the Lord, the LORD, THE LORD!
>   - "Quem quaeritis?"

Their dismay at such ignorance finds expression in the exclamatory "But Sir", which receives additional emphasis by the pause that follows. The three-fold repetition in 1.3 is accompanied by a rise in the tone of their voices, as is indicated in the notation. Yet the angel continues to ask his question with unimpressed stubbornness. And it is only in the closing stanza that his motivation for such seemingly inexplicable behaviour is revealed, with much dramatic force:

> "Seek if ye wish, But why seek here?
> Why seek a living in a bier?
> SURREXIT." - "What?" - "Nay, thou didst hear."
>   "You mean- ?" - "Yes. Yes."

The inversion at the beginning, "Seek if ye wish" helps to convey the angel's apparent indifference, but it serves as a means to emphasize the futility of their search. The tone changes, and the rhythm of "But why seek here?" suggests kindness and understanding. "Surrexit" is a direct reference to the Introit of the Day Mass of Easter Sunday, "Surrexi, et adhuc sum tecum", the first verse of Easter mass, the first word sung (cf. letter, 22.7.1990).[70] "Temps Pascal" (*World*, 5) is a similar poem in French which uses the same dramatic structure. It was written years later at La Trappe.

---

[70] In the Introit the first person is used, while the angel in the poem uses the third person: He has risen! The biblical reference is Luke 24:6 or Matthew 28:6.

The closing stanzas of "Sunset of same day" (*Threshold*, 50f.) effectively visualize the change in the two disciples from Emmaus after having realized that Jesus has arisen. The immediacy of their experience is captured in lines such as: "He takes; he pauses to adore ... / Nay, wait! We've seen this done before ..." The slow, calm description of what happens sharply contrasts with the rhythm of the line that follows; the heavy stresses on "Nay, wait" mark the start of a change. Their enthusiasm is captured in the closing quatrains:

- Of course! We knew it all along!
Those tones to Him alone belong;
That lovely tingling in our hearts
Nought but the Master's grace imparts.

We must go back. We must go back.
The road is long, but these hearts crack
With Joy that will to folly drive -
We've seen Him! Jesus is alive!

The assonance in 1.2 suggests both solemnity and the sorrow of not having seen clearly earlier. The spondee at the beginning of "That lovely tingling" emphasizes the peculiarity of the tingling which is completed by the spondee in "Nought but"; it was the Lord Himself they had met. Their conviction to go back is firmly implied by the repetition of "We must go back", where the second "must" is firmly stressed. The enjambement of the second line, "these hearts crack / With Joy" has a special effect of emphasizing the wonderful nature of the "Joy" experienced. The capitalization points to the divine presence in that joy. The disciples' enthusiasm thus expressed is predestined to be re-experienced by the reader. "In solitude these biblical events become much more alive because one is living, re-living them, the liturgy is far more than just a commemoration: it is bringing the past into the present" (letter, 19.11.1989).

The critical, yet very personal examination of the nature of Corpus Christi led to the writing of a poem simply named after the feast, "Corpus Christi" (*Threshold*, 79), where we read in the first stanza:

Is this the Bread that those fair Hands divided
    On that last night before they piercèd were?
Is this the Cup that Love itself provided
    For mortal thirst before it thirsted here?
        Is this the Body? Is this the Blood?
        Is this the Presence of the living God?

The mental struggle to find an explanation for the inexplicable, the search for intellectual analysis and comprehension, is apparent in these lines. The use of parallel structures underlines the poet's repeated and intense search. The questions of the first four lines, which are united by alternate rhyme, are taken up again in the closing couplet, where the essence of the question is summarized in the final line: "Is this the Presence of the living God?" The difficulty of comprehending the mystery is apparent in the second stanza:

Hid is the essence of this hidden Manna,
    Hid from mine eyes - I see but bread and wine;

> Yet on mine ears steal sounds of distant Cana -
>   Power at work, Authority divine.
>   Hearing alone can here be believed:
>   Sight, smell, touch, taste are utterly deceived.

The same structure, as used before, is also employed here, the couplet representing the summary of what has been said in the preceding lines. The repetition of "hid", "hidden" emphasizes that the poet has not yet found access to the truth. All that he sees is "bread and wine", but not the Body and Blood of Christ. "Yet on mine ears steal sounds of distant Cana" - the opening accumulation of stresses mark the beginning of a change. The conciseness of 1.4, concentrating on the very essence of the message, emphasizes the idea of wonder conveyed at the happenings of "distant Cana". The closing couplet firmly implies that he puts all his trust in the divine word, which contains the truth and which is the truth. "Hearing alone can here be believed": in his cell he can only rely on the words spoken by God, all the other senses are "utterly deceived". The poem closes with a declaration of his faith on the one hand and dismay on the other, dismay at the unworthiness and sinfulness of man:

> Lord, I believe! I trust, I bend, I follow ...
>   Tears blur my eyes, so strange a Bread I break:
> That sinful Man the Son of God should hallow,
>   And with a word the unmade Word should make! -
>   Nay, 'tis too much! My heart will not withstand.
>   I hold who holds Creation in his hand.

The parallelism in l.1 powerfully suggests the poet's unbound belief in God. The strong affective bond towards the Lord is implied in l.2, the spondaic opening underlining how much he is moved by the presence of God. The alliteration and assonance in "*so strange a Bread I break*" emphasizes the precious nature of the Body he holds in his hands. So strong is his awareness of the sinfullness of man that he is seized with horror at the very idea of man hallowing the "Son of God". In the closing couplet, however, the poet once more returns to celebrate the divine presence. The solemnity expressed in the line "I hold who holds Creation in his hand" mirrors his wonder at the grandeur of this moment, experiencing the presence of God.

For a complete understanding of "Lest we forget" (*Threshold*, 65) it is important to look at the exact date when the poem was written, which is indicated in the subtitle in brackets: "written on the fourth of May". The fourth of May is the day when the Carthusians celebrate their martyrs. The Carthusians were among the first martyrs of the reformation in England. On that day, for example, Maurice Chauncy's account is chanted. The first two quatrains of this sonnet bring us back to the days of the early martyrs:

> Had I *b*een *b*orn *b*eneath another star
> A few *m*ore *m*oons ago - yet still *h*ad *h*eard
> The Calling of *m*y *M*aster from afar,
> And let my feet to walls like these be stirred,
> I'd not - as I am now - be nibbling *b*read,
> Or *b*rooding o'er who might have been a wife,

>   But offering a slip-knot my starved head,
>   And waiting for the kind castrator's knife.

The alliteration in the first three lines (indicated in italics) is striking. By imagining himself to be one of them, having been born just "A few more moons ago", he powerfully visualizes the dramatic situation of those martyrs who were soon to be killed. The imagery used in ll.7f. is particularly effective: the alliteration in "*k*ind *c*astrator's *k*nife" underlines the sharpness of the knife. The oxymoron suggests that their death, despite the torture and pain preceding it, redeems them from their physical pain ("my starved head") and brings them close to God, providing the union which they have always striven for.

Although the poem has the outer form of a Shakespearian sonnet, the break (underlined by indentation) already occurs after the second quatrain, similar to the Italian form. The scene changes as the third quatrain starts, the descriptive passage of the happenings of the past turning into a more meditative section, containing a number of allusions:

>   O England! on this day thy pastures green
>   First drank the blood of those, like me, who loved
>   The Sacrifice that all thy kings had seen,
>   Ere for one's night of bliss 'twas e'er removed.
>   ... And yet, need I have been so stubborn too?
>   The priests he made can do just as we do.

The "pastures green" are taken from the hymn "Jerusalem" by William Blake. The person addressed in "Ere for one's night of bliss" is, of course, King Henry VIII, which lends an ironical touch to the closing couplet: were the priests he "made" really priests that God was ordaining? The intention of consecrating a Catholic priest was certainly not there.

The poems discussed in this chapter help to reach a deeper understanding of a mystery or truth celebrated on feast days, the truth expressed in the bible. They are critical as well as highly personal meditations, which offer insight into the poet's own experience of specific biblical verities. At times the poetry offers an outlet for his own inner struggle to find access to the truth as well as for the joy he feels when grasping it. The musings invite the reader to reach a deeper, fuller understanding of the background of a religious feast. Some poems employ dramatic dialogue, which helps to increase their immediacy, the power radiating from the verse being heightened by the vividness of the scenes presented.

3.1.1.5. THE DOUBT, FEAR AND DESPAIR OF CARTHUSIAN LIFE: POETRY AS AN OUTLET

The borderline between overwhelming joy and utmost despair can be very thin, in particular in the solitude of a Carthusian cell. Whenever despair creeps in, which is a very relevant part of Carthusian life, the pain suffered is immense. The monk can only share his pain with the Lord who is his faithful listener and companion. However, in the work of Alun Idris the poems also function as an outlet for inner tensions, the silent verbalization being a means to overcome the pain, helping to console the desperate soul. Thus we read in "Trinity Sunday" (*Threshold*, 78f.):

> Born of the earth, and earthly-born,
> Made to be loved, unloved, forlorn,
> This Heart cries out, in pieces torn,
>   Within, within.

The first line emphasizes his "earthly" nature, which contrasts with the divinity referred to in the title of the poem, thereby underlining the poet's own unworthiness. The enumeration in l.2, "loved, unloved, forlorn" is very dramatic: the main emphasis lies on "unloved" where both syllables are stressed. The positive outlook, "made to be loved", is opposed to two negative perspectives, which are dominating at present. "This Heart cries out", and it virtually does, with all four syllables being stressed.

> No, no; no more is comfort found
> In the great Void that doth rebound
> With echoes of the empty sound
>   Within, within.
>
> All, all without is passing ..., passed;
> Youth's deepest bliss one hour doth last ...
> O! heart of Man! no rest thou hast
>   Within, within.

The repeated negation conveys an idea of finality, underlined by the spondaic "no more". The "great Void" (which receives additional emphasis as the two syllables, which are firmly stressed, follow a pyrrhic) does not offer comfort any longer, it rebounds "with echoes of the empty sound". The sound is empty, there is nothing left anymore, God is absent. The repetition in l.1 of the stanza below continues the lament, turning to the outward world. The idea of transitoriness of all human outward things is climaxed by the short appendix "passed". Attaching the past participle in this way powerfully suggests that there is nothing left anymore. Our time is short, which is metaphorically implied in l.2, much too short as the tender image of "Youth's deepest bliss" implies. The mournful exclamation and the consonance in "rest" and "hast" complete the feeling of utmost frustration. This line is an echo of a line in St. Augustine's confessions, "Our heart was made for thee, Lord. It cannot find rest until it rest in Thee" (cf. letter, 16.9.1990).

> I turn aside and, weeping, cry
> For some companion to draw nigh.
> O! Essence! Heed th'unuttered Sigh
>   Within, within.
>
> Deep calls on deep, deep in this breast.
> Made for its maker, 'twill not rest
> Till it have seized Thee, Triune Guest,
>   Within, within.

The desperate longing "For some companion" is firmly implied in the penultimate stanza, as the poet feels he is utterly alone and deserted, suggested by "some". He longs desperately for a sign. The feeling of abandonment, defeat, and resignation, dominating the preceding stanzas, gives way to an emotional sigh, lending the lines a very human touch. "Deep calls on deep" is a reference to Psalm 42, verse 7 (cf. letter, 16.9.1990). The poet realizes that it is still not too late, he remembers that "this breast" is "made for its maker": he was made for God, and he is bound to fulfil his destiny. Now, at last, the will regains power, as is obvious in 1.3 which abounds in stresses (spondees alternate with iambic feet). The "Triune Guest" is a metaphor for the Trinity, which implies that, as a "guest", the Lord's company cannot be taken for granted. The closing refrain attached at the end of each stanza emphasizes that the struggle is fought entirely within, in the depth of the soul, alone.

In particular towards the end of Alun Idris' time as a Carthusian monk, several poems were written on his unknown future; the fears, the anxiety of what lies ahead finds an outlet here. The following poem called "After Reverend Father's refusal" (*Threshold*, 90) serves as an example:

> And I had thought that it would be for e'er
> When once, still green with Youth's first beaming smile
> I looked not back at what again ne'er, ne'er [corr.]
> I'd see, - those angel forms I'd loved awhile, [corr.]
> And which, today, have flown to the unknown, - [corr.]
> But at the Cross - that standing on the world -
> And took it for my bride, my only Friend,
> The one that would stand firm as all else whirled,
> For I had vowed to bear it to the end.
> But now that world is crumbling round my ears,
> And what I thought changed not now slowly blears.
> In one short morn the length of seven long years
> Hath flowed away 'neath torrents of hot tears.
> O thick Unknown! I walk alone, alone
> From what I knew so well that 'twas not known.

This poem, which seems to be a sonnet at first glance, has one line too many to be a proper sonnet. It is 1.5 which stands out, but it incidentally rhymes with the closing couplet. Furthermore, the third quatrain does not have an alternate rhyme but uses "eeee" as its rhyme scheme. "And I had thought that it would be for e'er": the rhythm of the opening line sets the tone of the poem. The first four syllables are stressed, the nucleus lying on "thought", which is then followed by a pause. The second, slightly shorter pause is inserted before "for e'er". These pauses add a notion of solemnity to the message conveyed. The first quatrain represents a metaphorical flashback of the days when he decided to become a Carthusian monk, when "still green with Youth's first beaming smile". He decided to turn away from everything profane, as is indicated by "those angel forms I'd loved awhile", a metaphor which not only suggests the beauty of these "forms" but also their descendence from God, as everything comes from the Lord. "And which, today, have flown to the unknown": the line, which is the surplus one to the sonnet, seems to imply that they have completely disappeared. However, on a more subtle level, when bearing in mind that the "unknown" simply refers to the future outside the Carthusian monastery, which can be concluded from the title and the date of composition, we realize that this line suggests rather the contrary, emphasized by the insertion of "today": "those angel forms" will be a part of the future again, the "unknown". In the second quatrain the poet beautifully describes what and whom he embraced, the Cross: "And took it for my bride, my only Friend", in all its firmness, even when the rest of the world is whirling around him, echoing, of course, the Carthusian motto. The firmness of his decision, implied in these lines, to look at the Cross forever, contrasts sharply with the third quatrain: "But now that world is crumbling round my ears", the two initial words indicating the change. The quatrain is firmly united by the rhyme scheme "eeee", which puts additional emphasis on the weightiness of the present situation. "And what I thought changed not now slowly blears." The rhythm is quick until the heavy "changed not", when the slowness of the destruction, which is therefore doubly painful, is underlined by the employment of long vowels and diphthongs. "Now slowly blears" is a fine choice of phrase which effectively visualizes a gradual disintegration. The contrast in l.12 ("short morn" - "length of seven long years") increases the notion of pain and shock at what is happening. The image "torrents of hot tears" adds to that idea, having been skilfully foreshadowed by the word "blears" in l.11. The closing couplet is a meditation on the impossibility of knowing the future beforehand: "O thick Unknown! I walk alone, alone / From what I knew so well that 'twas not known." The repetition of "alone" indicates the painful sufferings he has to bear. The word play in the last line ("knew so well" - "'twas not known") emphasizes the paradoxical nature of the meaning conveyed. The poem, despite its "irregularities", or perhaps in fact because of them, succeeds in conveying the poet's difficult and painful situation; the feeling of being at a complete loss, facing his past in ruins, is firmly implied.

In "The sixth of August" (*Threshold*, 83)[71] Alun Idris makes excessive use of repetition using a number of different techniques. The repetition in the closing line of stanza one, "Thou brought'st me here, apart ... apart ..." is taken up in the second stanza and used as an anaphora, which leads to a kind of culminative climax:

> ... Apart from all that is not Thee,
> Apart from what one day must flee;
> Apart from men, apart from life,
> Apart from Love, Youth, Friendship, Wife ...
>
> "Thabor! alone I stand on thee:
> God, God alone looks down on me.
> Naked I lie, I wait, I cry;
> Bare with bare truth, for Truth I sigh.

---

[71] The background to the poem is a holiday in Greece enjoyed with his parents in 1972. There Alun Idris had seen several monasteries perched on top of a perpendicular rocky mountain. He assisted at the liturgy one morning - it was the morning of the 6th of August - and climbed the mountain afterwards. On top of that mountain he was sitting and meditating, thinking about the Feast of the Transfiguration he had heard of in the liturgy that morning (cf. letter, 16.9.1990).

The note at the end helps the reader to realize that the poem is a meditation on the Feast of the Transfiguration. The Transfiguration is mentioned in various passages of the gospels: in Mark 9:2 the word "apart" is important, that word which in Alun Idris' poem is taken up and used for the parallel structure. In Mark 1:35 the Lord goes to a lonely place ("He got up and went away out to a lonely spot. He was praying there.") which finds an echo in the second stanza quoted.[72] All these passages are key passages for monasticism, especially eremitic monasticism (cf. letter, 16.9.1990).

The idea of sharing in the divine nature, being caught up in divinity to such an extent that we are deified, is important in Eastern theology. God transforms the very deepest level of our being, takes us up into Him. It is exactly this which is suggested by the Transfiguration. This is essential to the contemplative life, attaining the uttermost of human capacity. For that to happen, however, a great mortification of the senses is necessary, the dark night of the soul: "Naked I lie, I wait, I cry; / Bare with bare truth, for Truth I sigh." The asyndeton increases the urgency of the message, underlined by the word play in the line to follow. The senses must die, it is only the spirit which is left free. And then God can start working:

> Stripped of my self, I have no more;
> Stranded, I stand on this world's shore.
> Upward alone may I now look -
> Nay! Heav'n itself heav'n from me took. [corr.]
>
> Nought, - nought! nought! nought have I left now.
> Wisdom! walk on: to Thee I bow.
> Walk o'er me, Lord; pass by, pass by ...
> My will is Thine. I ask not "why?"

The inversion at the beginning of the first three lines quoted suggest the inner strain, the despair present, while l.4 rhythmically represents an emotional outbreak, his despair being fully conveyed. The four-fold repetition in l.1 of the second stanza emphasizes the utter non-existence of the senses; nothing at all is left anymore, with the exception of pain. The urge to make something happen is implied in l.2: the inversion, followed by a spondee, reinforces the utmost necessity the poet feels to change something about his deplorable state. The urge is continued in l.3, again emphasized by the use of repetition. It is only in the fourth line, however, that the poet seems to have overcome the period of inner strain and despair. The sudden regularity of the rhythm evokes the idea of the equilibrium regained. This glimmer of hope which now, after all the struggle, seems to have reappeared once more, is taken up in the final stanza:

> ... Or can it be -? Is't here that starts
> The meeting of two broken hearts:
> Thine own - because I knew not Thee,
> And mine - on Thabor's Calvary?

---

[72] Another passage is Mark 1:12, where we read: "Then the Spirit drove him immediately into the desert."

"The meeting of two broken hearts" suggests that there is an indwelling of God which is so intense that we almost share God's nature, we belong completely to God, consecrated utterly (cf. 2 Peter 1:4). "Thabor's Calvary" is used both in the literal sense, referring to the place where Jesus was crucified and, in the figurative sense, the poet alludes to the death of his own senses, a prerequisite for being able to experience the transfiguration.

The examples given demonstrate that poetry also functions as a means to release inner strain, thereby becoming an outlet for doubts, fears and despair. These factors are inherent parts of Carthusian life, which the monk has to face constantly. Expressing thus the "overflow of powerful feelings" certainly has a consoling and healing effect on the poet himself, serving as a means to work out difficult situations.

3.1.1.6. RECENT, UNEXPECTED EVENTS AS A FREQUENT SOURCE OF INSPIRATION

The silent, solitary life in a Carthusian monastery does not offer much variety. As a logical consequence, any kind of unexpected event tends to be a powerful stimulus and prompts the poetic vein to start to flow. We thus find a great number of poems which originate in recent, unexpected events: they reflect the unsated human need for surprises and variety, even in the Carthusian monastery.

During a "Retraite mensuelle" (*Threshold*, 42) the poet happened to come across an envelope of a letter he himself had written to the monastery in 1975 (cf. interview in Fraham, 1.7.1990). The sudden joy he felt in that very moment is expressed in this sonnet:

> I came across an envelope one day
> Among the sheets with which Carthusians speak,
> And suddenly Monotony gave way
> To bubbling Joy, as like a flash did streak
> Across the screen of Memory a horde
> Of utterly forgotten minutes spent
> In Youth's fair prime, when word was put to word
> To form the letter that in this was sent.
> ..."Le Maître des Novices" read the first line ...
> And "France" had been left out, - yet nonetheless,
> The writing I beheld was really mine,
> And Providence its journey deigned to bless ...
> And I recalled how thick the question mark
> That hung o'er what I sent into the dark.

The regularity of the rhythm of the first two lines suggest the "Monotony" which usually prevails, although the melodious tone of "I came across" already hints at some kind of special incident which is about to follow. The voice is raised in 1.3, the rhythm, slow at the beginning in order to emphasize the surprise which follows, accelerates as the line progesses, ending with a spondee in the last foot. The medial pause in 1.4 places additional emphasis on "bubbling

Joy", the voice has reached its top pitch. The capitalization reinforces the idea of joy conveyed, and also implies the divine origin of joy, which usually comes unexpectedly, and is therefore all the more powerful. The inversion after the pause ("as like a flash") creates a quicker rhythm, and leaves a heavy stress on "flash": this image beautifully conveys the idea of a sudden, unexpected joy. The accumulation of harsh /k/ plosives in "streak / Across the screen" suggests the quickness of the process, how everything all of a sudden changed. The sound symbolism of the line which follows, which is dominated by t's - "a horde / Of utterly forgotten minutes spent" - suggests the quantity of numberless short actions, "minutes" which he had already forgotten. L.7, however, which is characterized by the repeated use of long vowels, conveys a solemn tone, which aims to point out the beauty of youth, which has, unfortunately, already passed. The third quatrain deals exclusively with the envelope he found, the rhythm being quicker again, more lively in a way; the memory of sending the letter has apparently lightened his heart. The tone changes once more in the closing couplet, becoming meditative again. L.13 contains two pauses: the spondaic "how thick" is both preceded and followed by a short pause, which emphasizes the grade of uncertainty he felt. This uncertainty is underlined by the closing image, "into the dark".

At times it is a seemingly trivial event which stirs the author to write a poem, as with "After an accident at excitation" (*Threshold*, 18), when Alun Idris as "frère excitateur" woke up the community too early (he was responsible for the night excitation at the time).

> I wind thee once again, sweet little clock,
> And, winding, turn another full-writ page:
> This grinding key one yawning day doth lock
> To sleep 'neath the sarcophagus of Age.
> Good night, good friend. I take a moment's rest,
> Relying on thy faithful watch the while
> Tick on, tick on, tick on, tick on ... on ... - lest
> I rave, unfrocked on Hypnos' desert isle
> ... And fail to pull in time each little bell
> That pulls a brother-lark from his soft planks.
> Alarm me out of Heaven into Hell,
> To shiver, yawn, and fragrantly give thanks
> For what this world that those small fingers move
> Forgets, while lying deep in unfelt Love.

The poem is self-explanatory and fairly straight-forward. Some of the diction and imagery employed is, however, unusual: the "sarcophagus of Age" (l.4) is striking as it conveys the idea of the coffin which waits for us while sleeping. This image is picked up in l.8 when "Hypnos" is mentioned, the Greek God of sleep, who was the son of the night and also the brother of death. L.8 contains powerful imagery to describe the poet asleep, dreaming, "unfrocked on Hypnos' desert isle": "unfrocked" is a striking neologism in the context, pointing to the fact that when the monk is asleep he wears a special night cowl instead of his normal one. L.7 tries to evoke the ticking of the alarm clock, which gradually fades as the monk falls asleep. The term "brother-lark" is a word creation as well, firmly pointing out that Carthusians rise very early. The last four lines present a vivid picture of what it is like to interrupt night's rest, every night. "Alarm me out of Heaven into Hell" implies that the monk feels heaven when he is still asleep, while waking up is like returning to hell, sleep being an escape from the frustration and penance of monastic life. Despite the shivering and the yawning though, he "fragrantly" gives thanks. The use of this adverb surprises at first sight, forming a sharp contrast to the preceding half-line: on the one hand getting up every night takes a lot of will power and hardly becomes less painful to the body in the course of the years. On the other hand, however, giving thanks to the Lord does not lose its savour or its beauty. Monks "give thanks" for the whole of mankind, in the name of creation, as people forget the grace they are given. According to the poet himself, the monks are the "lighthouse in the dark keeping vigil for the world" (interview in Fraham, 1.7.1990). The closing line implies that God's Love is present in human love: when deprived of it one feels it all the more. The lamentable incident occurred again, as the title "After another accident at excitation" (*Threshold*, 40) indicates.

Another poem inspired by a recent event is the sonnet "Le Manuscrit du Purgatoire" (*Threshold*, 52): the manuscript mentioned in the title had only just become known to him, the excitement about it triggering off this poem:

> The manuscript that lies before my eyes,
> Unknown to this wide world, - unknown to me
> Till yesterday - hath travelled through the skies,
> And comes directly, gracious Lord, from Thee.
> I hold the greatest gift that I e'er held
> (- Save those, e'en greater, common to each soul -):
> A joy unknown within my heart hath welled,
> My little body bursts my massive cowl -
> THIS MUST BE KNOWN! - It is an atom bomb
> That Providence hath planted in this cell.
> The choice is mine ...: It can once more become
> Forgotten - as desires the ruse of Hell,
> Or, passing through the filter of my brain,
> It can, in English, walk the world again.

A feeling of amazement and wonder characterizes this poem. The first quatrain presents the situation, telling us of a certain manuscript which is now lying in front of him: "Unknown to this wide world, - unknown to me / Till yesterday -". The spondees on "unknown", the dominance of long diphthongs and vowels, and the w-alliteration suggest a tone of mystery prevailing, which is abruptly broken by "Till yesterday". The second quatrain describes the poet's own reaction, his wonder finds expression in long vowels and diphthongs, the rhythm moves gently, utter amazement is conveyed which, later, turns into thrilled excitement in 1.8, as is indicated by the imagery used. A joy "unknown" - the word appears for the third time now - a joy which he can hardly bear, "My little body bursts my massive cowl". The alliteration is employed as a means to emphasize the discrepancy between the frailty and smallness of his body and what he considers to be his natural boundaries, i.e. his cowl, and not his skin as one might have expected. The third quatrain depicts his growing excitement with the exclamatory

"THIS MUST BE KNOWN!" The capitalization underlines his thrill. In addition the utterance receives special emphasis as every syllable is stressed. The poet realizes that "it is an atom bomb / That Providence hath planted in this cell". Rather than the excitement about the discovery he made, his awareness that he must do something about it is conveyed, for the future of the manuscript now lies in his hands: "It can once more become / Forgotten -" The pause after "forgotten" adds a dramatic note - "as desires the ruse of Hell": the dominant voiced /z/ fricative suggests the seductive manner of the evil serpent. The closing couplet presents the idea in the poet's mind that a translation of the manuscript might save it from oblivion: "it can, in English, walk the world again."[73] The lines convey a certain light-footedness and ease which point to the realistic possibility of having it translated.

What kind of an "atom bomb" the manuscript indeed is we read in "Ces pages jaunissantes ..." (*Threshold*, 63f.), an elaborate French poem written in alexandrines. It informs us about the contents of *Le Manuscrit du Purgatoire*, as well as the poet's own reaction to it, by addressing the lady involved. The manuscript documents an extraordinary, unique form of communication between two souls towards the end of the last century. A nun who had died suddenly, unprepared for death, was experiencing a terrible purgatory of twenty years. With divine permission she was allowed to communicate with another nun still alive, who had tried to help her while yet on earth:

> O! Soeur oubliée de ce monde,
> Enterrée sous la boue d'une haine profonde
> Par ces grands raisonneurs qui entendent refaire
> Les décrets éternels régissant d'autres aires,
> Avec tout ce qui plane en ce Vide si plein
> De surprises, fournies par ce Dieu en déclin,
> Que ton âme, ma Soeur, a trouvé vigoureux
> Dans un ciel "réformé" un peu plus rigoureux
> Qu'une soeur - même bonne - ne l'eût jamais pensé -
> Surtout si celle-ci avait trop offensé
> Cette Fable innocente, incapable de nuire
> À une âme qui sait en ce monde la fuir.

The "haine profonde" is a reference to the anti-clerical movement at the end of the 19th century and the beginning of the present one, whilst the image of "ces grands raisonneurs" points to the dominating role of reason. "Ce Vide si plein, / De surprises" is the first reference to the strange, surprising events which were to take place. "Ce Dieu en déclin" reinforces the idea of that profound hatred caused by all too dominant reason; apparently it is used ironically as well, as in fact the poet aims to indicate God's undoubted grandeur, in particular when bearing the very existence of the *Purgatory Manuscript* in mind. "Qu'une soeur - même bonne" contains a word play, as "une bonne soeur" is a common way of describing a nun, a good sister.

---

[73] As it happened, it did: the translation was published as *The Purgatory Manuscript* by Edwin Mellen Press in August 1990.

> Oui, ma Soeur, j'ai eu peur en relisant ta lettre -
> Lettre? Non! - très précieuse - oui, unique - fenêtre [corr.]
> Sur ce monde inconnu que connaît maintenant
> Et ton âme et la mienne, car ce Continent
> Qu'on reproche de rester voilé à nos yeux
> Se devoile en ses traits les plus nus et hideux
> À travers ces messages, ces cris si étranges
> Reçus jour après jour et transmis par cet ange
> Inconnu comme toi, comme toi effacé,
> Dont la plume sans voix fait hurler le passé [...]

The "fenêtre" opening onto an unknown world, a whole "Continent" indeed, as the poet calls it: the word play on "voilé" and "se devoile" emphasizes how the unveiling takes place. "Ces messages, ces cris si étranges" refers to the strange kind of communication which took place between the two nuns. In the introduction to the manuscript we read: "[...] Soeur M. d. l. C., décédée à C. le 11 mai 1917, perçut tout à coup, près d'elle, en novembre 1873, des gémissements prolongés [...] A cette sommation, aucune réponse ne fut faite, mais les plaintes continuèrent ... en se rapprochant d'elle de plus en plus." (*The Purgatory Manuscript*, 79). What started as strange cries developed into a verbal communication which was to last for several years: between 1874 and 1890 Sister M. of the C.[74] recorded these mysterious relations (cf. *The Purgatory Manuscript*, iv.). "Inconnu comme toi, comme toi effacé, / Dont la plume sans voix fait hurler le passé" - the internal rhyme employed sounds pleasant to the ear. Yet, what the voiceless pen wrote down was all but pleasant:

> Vingt années de souffrance! - et cela bien moins
> Que le taux général qu'en ce pays lointain
> Les nouveaux-arrivés trouvent sur leur bilan
> Le matin où se trouve au delà de l'Écran
> - Sans le vouloir, d'ailleurs - tout leur être - et cette âme
> Qui a trop souvent bu à ce ruisseau infâme
> Que les savants dénomment - sans toujours le fuir -
> (Sachant où son absence pourrait les conduire)
> "COMPROMIS".

The shortness of the last line, only consisting of one single word, and not having a line which rhymes with it, emphasizes the importance of this word: "Compromis" is that which guided this sister, the entire stanza centralising this word. The terminology taken from book-keeping as an analogy to "cash up" one's life is striking but has a long tradition.[75] The succeeding stanza deals more explicitly with the nature of compromise:

> O! gros Monstre cornu, plein d'astuce!
> - Qui se plante en nos coeurs comme l'oeuf d'une puce
> Et qui pousse et qui pousse en beau gras parasite,
> Puis arrange à ses goûts et le lieu et le site
> De son action -

---

[74] We are not given any more details as regards the identity of the nun.
[75] It was already used in the middle-English morality play *Everyman*.

The poet has a decidedly strong sense of sin; the simile used ("comme l'oeuf d'une puce") effectively and vividly presents the idea of this sly and cunning monster gradually growing. The poet then includes two lines of direct speech, where the personalized compromise has a chance to defend itself. The statement, however, is immediately followed by a contradicting response:

> "Allons donc! A-t-on vraiment à être si dur?
> Une entorse ici ... là ... ne te rend pas impur" -
> Et c'est fait! On a cessé de viser le but,
> Et perdu pour toujours cet "amour du début"
> Qui eût su nous conduire à ce Seul Nécessaire

The seductive element is strongly present in the first two lines. "Et c'est fait!" abruptly interrupts, however, thereby emphasizing how quickly it happens, how easily it is possible to lose that "amour du début" (cf. Apocalypse 2:4), that first love for God which has been mentioned in other poems before. "Ce Seul Nécessaire" is a veiled scriptural reference to Luke 10:42, where Jesus tells Martha that she is "fretting and fussing about so many things; but one thing is necessary. The part that Mary has chosen is best; and it shall not be taken away from her." To never lose that first love is essential for finding the way to God. There are more references to be found in the poem: "O ma Soeur! O ma Soeur! Que c'est triste! / Oui, SUNT LACRYMAE RERUM! Quelle affreuse piste!" The capitalized Latin quote is taken from the fourth book of Virgil's *Aeneid*, which tells the tragic story of Dido. The poet continues to describe her tears which are now "Transformées en cette encre qui nous dépeint [corr.] tout / Ce que tu as trouvé derrière le Voile, / Et pourquoi tu as pleuré la nuit sans étoiles / De l'Aurore." The veil of the beyond has been lifted, the documentation allows us to take a glimpse at her experience in the beyond. The nun had died in an accident as a result of her compassion for other people. It seemed as though she was all too ready to enter heaven but no, "Mais non! / Tu attendais toujours / Quand ta voix sans larynx cria grâce un beau jour". The idea implied is that a large proportion of the human race is doomed to damnation or purgatory, no matter how virtuous their conduct may appear in the eyes of mankind. The poet closes by drawing personal consequences:

> Chère soeur, soeur aînée! Tu m'apprends où je vais:
> Car l'état de mon âme, Dieu seul le connaît -
> Mais je sais tout au moins que si tu nous dis vrai,
> Le Plaisir que j'ai eu, je l'ai eu à mes frais.

Alun Idris translated the original French manuscript into English. The translation, which is called *The Purgatory Manuscript*, was published in August 1990. In his poetry we find several references to this manuscript, also in later periods as for example in "Photocopying" (*World*, 46), a poem written at Roscrea, where a certain frustration at not being able to publish it then is apparent.

> I just wanted to preserve it from being lost because, in a way, it is a precious document. The diary which this nun kept from 1874 until 1890 gives insight: she

was allowed to ask any question she wanted about afterlife. The whole process of purification comes through. (interview, 13.8.1990)

The Purgatory Manuscript was not read in the monastery; it was withheld from general circulation, as, particularly in a contemplative order, such a story can "make the monks' imagination reflect" (interview, 13.8.1990).

The "protagonist" of the first two quatrains of "Ruminating over Father Laurence's letter" (*Threshold*, 64) is not the contents of the letter, as might be assumed, but a useful instrument which had been used only shortly before:

> My brother held one morning in his hand
> A little tin but half an inch in height.
> He placed within its gizzard one small band
> And left it in a corner out of sight ...
> And chattered on as though nought were amiss,
> As brother talks with brother when alone
> 'Twixt four thick walls, in silence such as this,
> An hour or two, like any, quickly flown.

The trivial subject of these lines, "a little tin but half an inch in height" (the assonance "tin"-"inch" emphasizing the small size of the tool) is a BBC tape recorder which Huw Jones used in order to record the conversation with his brother, Frère David. The interview, which was approved with exceptional permission, was broadcast on Radio Cymru on 22nd November, 1981 and was to be repeated on the request of the Welsh listeners.

The word "band" shows French influence: the French word for "tape" is "bande". The rhythm is regular and moves steadily onwards; the only variation occurs in l.7, when in "'Twixt four thick walls" the last three syllables are stressed, a pattern which is repeated in the second half of the line. It is a simple description of this ordinary tool, yet some of the diction employed to describe it is original: "gizzard" is a vivid image, letting the tool appear in a more human light, but also pointing to the process of "digesting" the material it is fed by. He finishes the sonnet with the following lines:

> The words we spoke tipped slowly to the past
> Like those of any day, that no more thought
> Recalls - for seldom doth our mind e'er cast
> A second glance o'er what returns to nought;
> - And yet, it seems that what we said that day,
> Through that small listening tin, was said for aye.

The enjambement in the second line puts special emphasis on the word attached to l.2 but placed at the beginning of l.3, "Recalls". And yet, it seems as though the words were frozen, preserved for the future.

"While dusting I came across a yellowing sheet of paper in a rarely read volume. It bore a versified prayer to the Sacred Heart on it. The author had left no signature, only the date: 'Feast of the Sacred Heart, 1882.'" This detailed note attached to "Meditation on the little sheet" (*Threshold*, 80) fully explains the context which inspired the poem's composition. Alun Idris takes it as a starting point for a meditation on time:

> Sleep on, my brother, take thy rest, 'tis o'er.
> Far, far away repose from what awhile
> Thou too didst know while yet on this same shore
> Of Time, that laps each hour this desert isle
> Called Solitude ...
>   A hundred years have passed
> And still it stands - alone in Chronos' sea.
> I have, like thee, on her mine anchor cast
> A day or two, unmapped of History.
>   Canst thou recall how once thou too didst stroll
> O'er these baked sands that seemed so numberless,
> How day on endless day did seem to crawl
> From East to West, to endless Emptiness,
> How far away did the Horizon seem
> On which tonight this isle seems but a dream?

L.5, which is optically split into two halves, indicates the length of those hundred years of solitude which lie between the date the yellowing sheet bears and the present. The solitude has not changed with the years, "still it stands", with the alliteration reinforcing the unchanging continuity. "Chronos' sea" is the symbol for time, while the "desert isle", "this same shore" represents solitude. The imagery used in the poem sticks to this symbolism. "I have, like thee, on her mine anchor cast / A day or two, unmapped of History": the special nature of this desert isle is indicated by its personification. The term "unmapped" fits well to the imagery of navigation: nobody knows that he is living there in solitude, forgotten by the whole wide world. The anonymity goes so far as to not even put names on the crosses in the cemetery. "These baked sands that seemed so numberless" points to the austerity of the daily life as a Carthusian, which is reinforced by ll.11 and 12. From l.9 onwards the poet keeps asking his fellow monk whether he still remembers the life on this desert isle, thereby stressing the difficulties involved. Asking these questions seems to be consoling for the poet, as they suggest that the other monk's life was no less austere than his own. In particular the closing line is of soothing effect, as it implies that one day for him, too, this isle will appear like a dream. For the time being, however, it is only his brother to whom "this isle seems but a dream", as is indicated in l.1: "Sleep on, my brother, take thy rest, 'tis o'er."

Letters from the outside world, rare as they are, provide, of course, fertile soil for poems. The subtitle of "After receiving a letter from home" (*Threshold*, 12) indicates that in the letter he was informed about the Pope's preparation for a journey to Wales and his taking Welsh lessons.[76] The idea that the Holy Father was visiting his home country was apparently very moving to the poet:

---

[76] The name "Andrew O'Neil" mentioned in the sub-title of the poem is quite well-known in Wales: the O'Neil-family used to sing together. One of them, Andrew, was studying for the priesthood in Rome at the time and the Holy Father went to him for Welsh lessons. He eventually decided to go full time into music rather than enter the priesthood (cf. letter, 10.6.1990).

> Can it be that distant shadows
>   Lengthening 'neath this fair moon
> Reach out o'er those far off meadows
>   That once knew a fuller noon?
> Is this night like any other
>   In that land so near, so far?
> Wales! O! Wales, my gentle Mother,
>   What did thy first beaming mar?

The poem contains a reference to Dominic Savio, the schoolboys' saint, who had a vision of the Holy Father standing in a great field enveloped in mist holding the lamp of faith. It seems as though this was an indication of what was going to happen to Wales and England: the Catholic Christians bringing back faith to the protestant country.[77] Those "distant shadows" mentioned in l.2 refer to that vision, while the fourth line indicates that there was a time in the past when the situation of the Catholics in Wales was much better than it is nowadays. The outburst in l.7 "Wales! O! Wales, my gentle Mother" well reflects the poet's love for his home country, a love which is still much alive and has not at all diminished in the course of his solitary years. This idea is underlined by the tune Alun Idris chose for the poem to be sung to: Blaernwern. This famous Welsh folk-tune completes the notion of hiraeth implied in the verse.

The creative mind picks up suggestions of many different kinds; apparently unexpected incidents and events act as an additional stimulus, which the poetic vein can only conserve in the form of a poem. Trivial as an event may seem at times to people in the outside world, it is of a different, more immediate significance to one who is living in a contemplative monastery, where any kind of deviation of the daily routine is much more intensely experienced. This idea is frequently reflected in the poetry of Alun Idris.

3.1.2. POETRY AS A FORM OF MEDITATION

The Carthusian monk spends his life in contemplative prayer and meditation. Many a poem of Alun Idris' reflects this idea, and very often the poems not only mirror a meditation but actually turn into a form of meditation themselves. As a result, they not only offer insight into the interior proceedings and developments of the poet but also prompt the reader to join in and continue the meditation individually.

Alun Idris' poems echo the most important, the most essential bases of meditation in a Carthusian monastery. Some ideas constantly recur. They keep providing a fertile soil for further meditations. Such recurring ideas are presented in this chapter.

---

[77] Alun Idris had heard of the visions of Dominic Savio at a time when he was looking for confirmation as to whether the Catholic church was the 'true' one (cf. letter, 10.6.1990).

3.1.2.1. GRACE AND PROVIDENCE

The idea of grace is implied in many a line of his poetry; Alun Idris tends to drop a word, make an allusion to grace time and again, which underlines its importance in his philosophy of life. Some poems are entirely dedicated to the question of grace, representing a meditation on its nature. In "Sacred Heart" (*Threshold*, 80) we read:

> What is this Light that men call Grace,
> By which we see Thee face to face?
> This Peace ... this Warmth ... this inward Might,
> This Distillation of delight ...
> - What is the source of this pure Stream?
> Of what is made this quiet Gleam?

The opening line summarizes the essence, the basic nature of the question of what "Grace" really is. An answer cannot be found, yet the stanza supplies descriptions of grace as it is experienced by the poet. The enumerations in ll.3 and 4 suggest a certain notion of rapture on the poet's side at the very thought of grace. The image of "This Distillation of delight" attracts attention, underlined by the alliteration used. Mingling a chemical term with so emotional a word as "delight" is unconventional and surprising, yet "distillation" provides all the connotations the poet intended to convey: cleansing and separating, in order to receive a certain liquid in its purest form. On a second level, of course, the term also evokes the idea of the production of whisky; the intoxicating effects of the liquid thus produced reinforce the idea of delight conveyed. The image of the virtual flow of grace, its liquidity, is continued in the closing lines which lead us back to the very beginning of the stanza: "What is the source of this pure Stream? / Of what is made this quiet Gleam?" The second stanza develops the idea further:

> O mystery! O mystery!
> Angels alone its essence see.
> Bathed by its tide, each wave they feel,
> Dazed by its wine, they revel, reel.
> Seraph and Saint in this are one -
> Grace here below is Glory won.

The stanza differs rhythmically from the previous one: while the first line is to be read in regular iambic pentameter, all the other lines start with inversion, which tends to provoke a pause in the middle of each line. There is a rhythmical connection to ll.1 and 5 of the first stanza, the question exposed there and the respective answer given here are rhythmically alike. This "answer", however, is all the poet can strive for at the moment. He is bound to realize that human beings are not in a position to see "its essence", that "Angels alone", who are closer to the Creator than we are, are capable of doing so, and that they seem to fully enjoy it: "B*a*thed by its t*i*de, each w*a*ve they feel, / D*a*zed by its w*i*ne, they revel, reel." The internal rhyme of this couplet adds to the mood of perfect harmony implied. "Seraph and Saint in this are one - /

Grace here below is Glory won." The amount of grace we are able to hold and operate with is the degree of glory that will be ours. The communion of saints is glorified, including the Seraph, the angel with the six wings in the Old Testament. The abuse of grace has eternal consequences, missed graces have an effect on one's capacity for eternal things.[78] "Grace" is a Greek word meaning "free gift", it is the free gift of God, God's favour. "Grace is a quality of the soul, not a substance" (letter, 28.2.1990).

The rhythm of the closing stanza differs from the other two, which successfully underlines the plea contained therein, the plea to receive grace:

> Whate'er thou be, my need is great:
> Grace, fall on me! My thirsting sate.
> Lo! Lord, my mouth I open wide,
> Nay, more, I press it to thy Side.
> More! Give me more! Cease not, sweet Flood.
> Full Hippocrene, fill me with God. [corr.]

The excitement and thrill, the need to receive grace, is powerfully conveyed by the rhythm of this stanza. The smoothness and regularity of the first line suggests the idea of taking breath, of building up one's strength to make the outburst that follows all the more powerful and expressive. The spondees at the beginning of all succeeding lines convey an almost demanding mood, the need to be filled with grace is desperate. "Lord, my mouth I open wide, / Nay, more, I press it to thy Side." is a direct reference to the Sacred Heart. From the open wound in Jesus' side, i.e. from His Sacred Heart, the waters of life flowed, which is the source of the church's sacrament.

The metaphors used in the closing lines are highly suggestive. They imply on a very subtle level Alun Idris' attitude towards the relationship between poetry and faith: "Full Hippocrene, fill me with God". "Hippocrene" means "underground stream": it is a hidden stream suggesting, thereby, that in a sense grace is similarly hidden.[79] The metaphor not only refers to this one particular aspect of grace, it also perfectly combines the two vocations. By addressing Hippocrene, the source of inspiration of poets in Ancient Greek culture, to fill him with God's grace, His love, the poet indicates the closeness, if not the identity of the sources for both divine and poetical inspiration, suggesting that poetic inspiration is a divine grace. The following quotes from letters of the poet to the present writer underline his attitude: "God is the source of all beauty, all creation, including poetic creation, inspiration. [...] God comes to us in different forms; beauty and the ability to create and interpret beauty certainly is God coming through that form, using that form to give himself" (letter, 19.11.1989). "In as much as the art of creating beauty is unchanged and unchanging in the experience of Mankind, there is

---

[78] The idea also finds powerful expression in a sonnet called "'Having your voice, I needed your touch'" (*Beyond*, 151), where we read the following line: "how heav'n ungrasped is deeper hell".
[79] It was a fountain which sprang from the northern slopes of Mount Helicon in Boeotia (Greece), and was sacred to the Muses and Apollo (who was thought to be the source of poetic inspiration). It received its name from the wingèd horse, Pegasus, which had caused it to gush forth by striking the rock with its hoof.

no contradiction in the linking of the Source of Grace with the Source of Inspiration" (letter, 11.11.1990).

In scripture we find a reference to poetic inspiration as well when we read about the divine blowing in 2 Timothy 3:16: "All scripture is inspired by God and profitable for teaching, for reproof, for amendment and for moral discipline." The spirit inspires in many different ways: good actions, active charity and also manifestations of beauty. What is essential, however, is: "We have to be receptive, aware that He might want to use us to produce something" (letter, 19.11.1989). Such an attitude reflects the romantic identification of the transcendental faculty with poetic genius.

Grace must be used well, the grace of a moment is only given in that moment, and cannot be repeated. There may be other graces at other times, but a missed chance is a chance lost forever. This idea, which has been indicated in other poems before, is firmly conveyed in the first stanza of "Thinking aloud" (*Threshold*, 41f.):

> There'll never be another chance.
> O Lord, you gave me one, but one.
> I took it, Lord; I used it, Lord;
> Abused, misused it; now it's gone -

Resignation is the prevailing mood: the asyndeton and the word play in ll.3 and 4 emphasize the idea of failure. The poem was triggered off by seeing a picture on a calendar, as is indicated in the subtitle. The picture caused the stirring of memories of the past, which in turn led the poet to a meditation on grace bestowed on us. The poem consists of ten quatrains, most of them are run-on-stanzas, like the following ones:

> Goodbye, poor, uncorrected Past!
> Goodbye, unfelt, unvalued Youth!
> Could I but have you back one day
> Within my hands, now that the Truth
>
> Has taught me what is meant by Grace -
> That is, the meaning of a Gift -
> What is the value of a choice,
> The art of knowing how to sift
>
> Importance from its brother, Air,
> Worthwhileness from its sister, Noise,
> And how, how precious is one hour
> That in the Here and Now does poise
>
> My wobbling soul 'twixt what may be
> And what, if 'tis, must be ruled out
> For ever, ever, evermore
> By Fate that from all time does shout:

The run-on-stanzas intensify the feeling of lament conveyed, which leads up to a climax, when at last the voice stops to listen. The poet laments on his past which, apparently, he did not use well. The adjectives "poor" and "uncorrected" imply its faulty, imperfect nature; "unfelt, unvalued Youth" intensifies the feeling of moaning. He did not even feel or estimate his youth, but now it is too late. Now he knows, as the "Truth / Has taught me what is meant by Grace". The final position of "Truth" in the stanza adds emphasis to it, being thereby linked to the last word of the following line, "Grace", which in turn gains importance through the pause after it; thus the firm linkage between "Truth" and "Grace" is implied. The poet continues by describing the nature of Grace and its inherent characteristics. The image of the precious hour which "in the Here and Now does poise / My wobbling soul" suggests the frailty of his inner equilibrium. The weary lamentation culminates in a line anticipating a certain message which fate "from all time does shout":

> "Take care, take care, child of an hour:
> Reflect before you burn its oil.
> I give it once, once only. Hear?
> One tick Eternity can spoil."

The repetition in l.3, followed by the short exclamatory rhetorical question, emphasizes the uniqueness, the irretrievability of each grace given: one "tick", one grace "abused, misused" "Eternity can spoil". How important it is to use grace well is firmly implied.

"(5 p.m. as I write)" (*Threshold*, 48)[80] contains a meditation on grace combined with a reflection on the idea of providence. The title refers to the time of the poet's own baptism, as we are told in a footnote, the poem being triggered off by the commemoration of this event. It is full of allusions to the poet's own past which make it appear rather obscure.

> Grace! How thy ways are nebulous!
> The clock strikes out the hour, the day
> On which the most ridiculous
> Came true, and brought that drummer gay
> Upon his knees before a Saint
> Who, though the drummer little knew,
> Had traced for him in letters faint
> A word that soon his heart would woo.

The exclamatory statement in the first line is illustrated by presenting an anecdote of the poet's own personal life. The pause in l.4 after the first foot places emphasis on the preceding phrase: "the most ridiculous / Came true" - Grace works in surprising ways indeed. The "drummer gay" is a reference to the author himself (cf. letter, 19.11.1989), who used to play the drums in his youth. The "Saint" provided a mysterious "word that soon his heart would woo" - the sound symbolism employed in this line (the alliteration and assonance, the use of long vowels) firmly implies tenderness towards the word in question, in particular the choice of "woo" suggests the presence of love and attraction. In the second stanza Alun Idris explicitly introduces the idea of the "Book of Life":

---

[80] The poem is a continuation of "Evening of same day" (*Threshold*, 47).

> O Book of Life! Two columns bright
> Are marked on these thy gilded leaves:
> The one, writ in eternal Night,
> Marked with the Plan that Wisdom weaves,
> The other void, to be yet filled -
> Though filled a little every hour -
> With one short question: "Was't fulfilled?"
> - And one last space: "Which of the Four?"

The first six lines describe the "Book of Life", a term which is mentioned in other poems as well.[81] The spondee on "Two columns" emphasizes the dual nature of this image. One column has already been filled, having been written wisely beforehand, "writ in eternal Night", "with the Plan that Wisdom weaves". The idea conveyed is that providence has foreseen the whole of our life, - our life has been written into the Book of Life previously.[82] Yet, we do not have any knowledge of its contents, which leads us to the second column, - the "void to be yet filled". As time and our lives progress, the empty pages of the Book of Life are steadily filled ("Though filled a little every hour") till the last page is completed. The "short question" mentioned in the closing couplet refers to the question of whether or not the purpose of one's life has been fulfilled, while the ultimate question is a reference to St. David (cf. letter, 19.11.1989). The "Four" mentioned therein are explained in the third stanza:

> Heav'n waits, and so doth Purgatory;
> One last faint hope in Limbo lies;
> Hell sings Despair's invitatory,
> And hides its music from our eyes ...
> O Lord, I dangled o'er the last:
> Precocious sinner, had I left
> My body in my putrid past
> My damnèd soul by Hell were cleft.

"Limbo" (l.2) refers to that interim state of hope for those who died without having been baptized, in particular infants; the third line contains a refence to Dante's "Abandon hope, all thee who enter here", written on the gate of hell.[83] Bearing in mind that the invitatory is the first psalm sung at matins, the psalm which invites people to come to worship (psalm 95), the combination with hell and despair surprises. The closing lines shock because of their ruthless and open self-accusation, using vivid imagery.

> Of course one does think about these things in retreat. The whole point of the annual retreat is that one thinks about the last things, death, what one is doing in life, how one is using it. It is certainly not morbid! If one isn't thinking about these things in retreat, when will one think about them? It is too easy to go through life without reflecting sometimes about the whole optic of one's existence, what one is aiming for, who one is trying to please. (letter, 22.7.1990)

---

[81] The "Book of Life" is a reflection of Apocalypse 20, 11-end of chapter. Verse 15 is quite explicit about the Book of Life, as is verse 12: "Another book was opened", i.e. the book of life. The dead were judged according to the things written in the books in relation to their works (cf. letter, 22.7.1990).
[82] Julian of Norwich's teachings are reflected in this attitude; she believed that for all eternity providence has been forseeing things, arranging things (cf. interview in Fraham, 1.7.1990).
[83] "Lasciate ogni speranza, voi ch'entrate." Dante, *Inferno*, Canto iii (Dante 1957, 30).

The "Saint" is mentioned again in stanza three, this time, however, a direct reference is made by a note in brackets to the identity of the person: Billy Graham is the "Saint" in question, the famous protestant preacher, well-known in all English speaking countries, who makes use of satellites and television to reach as many people as possible.[84] "From thence Thou bad'st me slowly climb, / From that abyss of graceless strife": the metaphor used to describe his former life firmly implies that providence had arranged for him to choose a different way of life, the former restlessness lacking grace has been gradually diminishing since he had known this mysterious word. The solution is given in the very last stanza: "Xxxxxxxxxx was the graven word". A note explains that "The Xxxxxxxxxx in the text stands for the name of the monastic Order who wish to remain without mention here." It is, of course, the Carthusian Order which is referred to.

Many of Alun Idris' poems reflect his strong belief in providence as part of his philosophy of the world. We detect an unreserved confidence in fate's guiding hands. "New Year's Day (and following), '81/'82" (*Threshold*, 10f.) progresses from meditations on the factual past to the "possibilities" of the future. Each of the twelve stanzas consists of three rhyming lines written in iambic tetrameter (starting with an inversion or a spondee), followed by an incremental refrain in iambic dimeter.

The stanzas dealing with the past are full of lament:

> Ah! Could I but begin again
> Each ill-writ phrase that doth thus stain
> These leaves of history that wane
>   'Mid what hath been!

The stains of failures are indelible in his Book of Life. The awareness of the invariability of the past is a constant source of lamentation, the hiraeth to start anew is ever present.[85] The Book of Life is implicitly mentioned in the following stanza:

> Yea, as I turn the hours, the days,
> As on each distant page I gaze,
> This welling sigh my thought betrays:
>   "It could have been!"

The rhythm appears irregular; however, as is indicated by the stress marks in the very first stanza, the poem is meant to fit to a tune the poet himself has composed (cf. letter, 10.6.1990), which explains the rhythmical "irregularity". The refrain implies the idea that we have to choose, and yet it is all foreseen. Alun Idris' attitude of mind is clearly expressed in the following quote:

---

[84] In March 1993 he visited Germany. His preaching was also watched in other European countries via satellite transmission.
[85] Lament on the unchangeableness of the past can be found in other poems as well, as e.g. in: "Immaculée Conception" (*Threshold*, 7), where we read: "Had I but one small moment to re-live, / How, oh! how would I not Thee glory give!"

> The Lord has a will, but there is a question mark to that will in the sense of whether we conform to that will or not. And even if on one occasion we miss the right turning there will be a new grace: He always meets us where we are, and if we go astray, He meets us there as well. (letter, 29.10.1989)

This idea finds expression in the following stanza, where the free will of man is explicitly mentioned:

> Chain linked to chain of un-lived facts,
> Destined, predestined free-will acts
> That were not made, that Fate subtracts
>   From what hath been ...

The incremental refrain underlines the progress, a new idea is added to the thought expressed in the repetition. We move from the factual past "'Mid what hath been!" to the hypothetical past "'It could have been!'", from starting to question the hypothesis: "Could it have been?" back to reality again: "Cause of each cause, Thou'rt the Lord: / Thy 'Yea' hath been." [corr.] He closes with a vision of the future:

> Ancient of Days, didst Thou e'er see -
> Nay more, e'en ere Thou wast, decree
> That one, sole, POSSIBILITY
>   That could e'er be?

The poet refers to "le futurible", things that could have happened: history is made up of a chain of events, one fact leads to another ("chain linked to chain"). The question arises of the existence of other possibilities, other combinations, different chains in history apart from the one which actually becomes reality. The poem is a meditation on the possibilities of time. Alun Idris shows a predilection for such hypothetical meditations on what could have been, - there are a number of poems which echo this special liking.

The importance of making decisions and being aware of their consequences is implied in "24th of March" (*Threshold*, 36), a poem consisting of ten quatrains written in iambic tetrameters. The poem reflects Alun Idris' last day in noviciate, the 24th of March 1982:

> I walk alone into the dark
> That shrouds the hiddenness to come.
> Noviciate! Familiar sound!
> Ne'er more may I thee call my home.

What lies ahead the poet does not know: the imagery used in the first two lines emphasizes the idea of the great unknown which is to come, as his time in the "Noviciate! Familiar sound!" is over now. The quick rhythm in this line and the dominance of the light vowel /ɪ/ suggests the happiness, the carefreeness of that period which now is gone; the fourth line is dominated by long mournful vowels and diphthongs, just as the first two lines are.

> Twelve hours to freedom - or to death
> On Solitude's slow-writhing rack ...
> A choice, a word - nay, but a nod
> Draws onward, or for e'er pulls back.

The lines show the poet's awareness of the importance of his decision, of making such a step, rather than reflect a deep crisis. They mirror his realization of the importance of taking the step: his decision may lead "to freedom - or to death", which in a rather dramatic manner emphasizes the importance of the option he takes. The idea is reinforced by the imagery used in 1.2: "Solitude's slow-writhing rack" powerfully visualizes the dreadful and terrifying aspect of solitude which becomes unbearable if the decision he is to make happens to be the wrong one. The asyndeton in 1.3 suggests the simple nature of the ceremony, reflecting the very nature of Carthusian silence: a nod is sufficient to indicate the decision. "And in this choice all choices rest. / Each 'possible' hangs on one whim." The idea of the "chain linked to chain" finds an echo here. In the seventh stanza we read:

> Good Lord, what else is there in life
> Besides the "possibility" of grace,
> The chance to gain new merit, ere
> Be fixed for aye our heav'nly place?

The "'possibility' of grace" is a veiled reference to *Le Manuscrit du Purgatoire*, the diary which formed the basis of a retreat the poet had made (cf. interview, 13.8.1990).[86] The message of this book finds expression in the stanza quoted: while we are on earth, there is still the possibility of receiving grace, of acquiring merit through using grace well, merit both for ourselves and for others. However, once we have left this world, the possibility of winning this merit is gone, as then "our heav'nly place" is "fixed for aye".

The "'possibility' of grace" not only suggests the possibility of grace being offered but also refers to our own infidelity, which prevents grace from exercising its full effect.

The concept of providence and grace is difficult to grasp, which is reflected in the meditations just presented. Alun Idris' own belief in the existence of providence, his full awareness of grace being given to man by God shines though his verse most powerfully.

3.1.2.2. TIME, DEATH AND AFTERLIFE

Time is much more consciously experienced in a contemplative monastery than it is in the outside world. On the one hand time ceases to exist insofar as Carthusian life has not changed in the course of the centuries.[87] In a sense the Carthusian monk takes the place of his predecessors, he continues the tradition, being integrated into and absorbed by the community of all Carthusians praying for the world:

> For in this place, e'en for the book of Time,
>   The story's told:

---

[86] See above, pp.88ff.
[87] "Cartusia nunquam reformata quia nunquam deformata." Their Order was never reformed because never deformed. Cf. Thompson 1930, 108.

> To those of old.
> This eventide I do as they have done
> In ages past
> Who now their rest have won.[88]

On the other hand, however, the importance of using time well makes every single moment a precious, unique one. The monks are constantly reminded of the flow of time, the bell will not let them forget it, as we read in "New Year's Eve" (*Threshold*, 9f.):

> What sound, what distant melody
>   Steals thus upon my hearing?
> - The hourly chime, the voice of Time
>   Its ancient message bearing:
>
> Now, now, this very Now -
>   The sole through all eternity -
> Once, once will it come to me;
>   This Now must I live, not the morrow.

The "hourly chime" of the bell acts as the "voice of Time", it bears an "ancient message" which has not changed throughout the years. The second quatrain is the refrain which recurs after each of the four stanzas. The "Now" refers to the now of the present moment, which includes all other moments, even eternity. When one has departed, all the other nows merge into that "Now", time ceases to exist, they are all incorporated in the one, the last, the final moment, with the moment of death really being the moment of life. The present now is a preparation for that final moment which, when added together, will make up the great "Now" at the end.

> As hour by hour the past is spun,
> Our future Time is weaving:
> Each pain, each fight, each sweet delight,
> Once gone, flees all retrieving.

The metaphor used in the first two lines visualizes the correlation between the quality of our eternity and our use of time - the quality of the fabric depends on the quality of the thread spun. As the title indicates, the poem was written on new year's eve, a day which naturally encourages meditations about one's nows, the use of time. The metaphor of the weaving of time is continued in stanza three: "From day to day, in endless coils, / This globe is ever turning:" The world's past is spun and rolled up in "endless coils". The final stanza employs forceful imagery to describe the float of time:

> Yea, with the year my life slips by -
>   Each flow'r must slowly wither:
> From opening womb to gaping tomb -
>   Oh! Time, lead on! Lead thither!

While the conventional metaphor of the withering flower in l.2 has a notion of melancholy about it, powerfully suggesting the sorrow linked to the passage of time, the loss of youth, the

---

[88] "The eve of my 27th birthday anniversary" (*Threshold*, 4).

imagery used in l.3 is striking because of its directness, forcefully and relentlessly indicating the flow of time. The internal rhyme adds to the feeling of rush conveyed. The poem was composed to be sung to an old well-known folk tune, "Greensleeves", which perfectly reflects the message of the poem.

Representative of others, this poem mirrors the tendency in Alun Idris' poetry to combine time and meditations on time with reflections on death and afterlife. Afer all, the afterlife is but a continuation of our life here on earth on the axis of time, with death as the zero in the coordinate system.

The dual nature of time powerfully experienced in the monastery, its flow on the one hand and its standstill on the other, is conveyed in the closing stanzas of "Day before visit" (*Threshold*, 81):

> For here the Time hath passed not on.
> The silence of these silent walls
> Doth testify that nought doth change
> In each Today that softly falls.
>
> We meet again ... We part again ...
> This joy that we ENCOUNTER call
> Embraces Past and Present tears
> One hour ... ere Future onward haul.

As the title indicates, the poem was written on the day before his family came to visit him. In a way, for him time has not passed on, as the "silence of these silent walls" is still the same, not having changed at all. In a Carthusian monastery the days are all alike, his "Today" is like his yesterdays, which are the same as those of his predecessors. Despite this monotony time passes on relentlessly, as is implied in stanza two; the parallel structure employed in l.1 indicates the rush. The "ENCOUNTER", a special moment to the Carthusian monk (underlined by the spelling in capital letters) as he is not allowed to receive visits from his family very often, only lasts an hour though. The flow of time cannot be stopped, we cannot prevent time from irrevocably pressing onward. The imagery used in the closing line forcefully indicates the rush of time.

In the Carthusian monastery the bell acts as the constant reminder of the relentless flow of time. In "The eighth of September" (*Threshold*, 86) the poet remembers when in September 1976 he returned to La Grande Trappe for a prolonged stay (before entering the Carthusians in December):

> Now as I write I think again
> How at this hour on this great day
> I took one step o'er one small stone
> And left the world behind for aye.
>
> Eleven o'clock was striking then
> As it rings now within mine ears -
> The only sound that I have heard
> Through these five solitary years.

> Ring on! - I listen to your song.
> Ring on! - Your voice alone may speak.
> Ring on! Ring on, as ye have done
> Each quart ... each hour ... each day ... each week ...

The tone of the first stanza is smooth, and yet full of silent enthusiasm. The inverted first foot in l.1, the stresses in l.2 ("how", "this hour", "this great day") emphasize the importance and wonderful nature of this step, when he "left the world behind for aye". Just as then the bell is ringing now, as we read in the second quatrain, the chime of the bell is "the only sound" he has heard in all these years. How ever present, at times even intruding the bell is, is firmly conveyed in the third stanza; the anaphora emphasizes the inexorability of the bell, - it keeps ringing all the time. The enumeration in the fourth line gives an impression of the fading sound of the chime until it disappears completely.

The closing stanza implies that the bell can be tiresome at times:

> O Lord, my Lord, did Jewry too
> Have engines that their makers rule
> Long, long ago when Thou wast here
> In Solitude's unchanging school?

The two-fold apostrophe in l.1 suggests an uncertainty whether to address the Lord or not, asking Him this question. The poet wonders whether Jesus had known the sound of the bell and its dictational nature too, thereby implying how tiresome he himself experiences it to be at times.

Poems dealing with time are often mingled with meditations on death and afterlife. The Carthusian monk is confronted with death every day when he goes from his cell to church, thereby passing the graves in the cemetery. Numerous wooden crosses without any names on them stand there in mute testimony. The following poems reflect the inescapable presence of death and afterlife.

For the full understanding of "Back to the convent (in thought)" (*Threshold*, 55f.) it is necessary to know that the incident which provoked this sonnet was sitting in a Dominican convent[89] on the public side while waiting to go back to the charterhouse, - his passport had to be renewed, therefore he had spent some time outside the monastery (cf. letter, 19.11.1989). The element of time, its passing nature, is the theme of this sonnet.

> It struck eleven as I said my prayers
> In that small convent, on the Public's side
> Of that huge grille that sealed my world from theirs - [corr.]
> And both from the great sealed-off world outside.
> The office that I prayed was for the dead

---

[89] The convent in question contains the pulpit used by St. Vincent Ferrer, who had preached near Bourg-en-Bresse. He was a powerful preacher, discoursing in Latin: hardly anyone could understand a word, yet the congregation was moved by his manner of delivery. ("St. Vincent Ferrier" (*Threshold*, 55) is dedicated to him.) The difference between life as a preacher and the life of these sisters devoted to prayer is obvious. The contrast of the diverse means for furthering the gospel is very apparent.

> Who, 'neath another grille, another world, [corr.]
> Recall these Psalms that they, like us, once said
> In unchanged manner, word for unchanged word.

The "grille" appears twice in the first two quatrains, the first time referring to the visible grille, which separates the public side from that of the nuns, the second time talking about the grille which separates the living from the dead. The mentioning of the exact hour ("It struck eleven as I said my prayers") functions as an additional reminder of time passing. The flow of time is contrasted with the timelessness of prayer: "In unchanged manner, word for unchanged word."

As the title indicates, "Histoire Vraie" (*Threshold*, 13f.) is a poem dealing with a supposedly true story. Consisting of 15 quatrains, the poem takes the form of a dialogue between a believing soul and a famous statesman of the past, Napoleon Bonaparte. In the first two stanzas the believer seems to remind Napoleon of his faith by asking him whether he was aware of "Le Bien" and "Le Destin" which guide him. But Napoleon has lost his faith in God entirely and only believes in his own personality and strength:

> "Je n'y crois plus. Mon Dieu est mort.
> Le Néant - voilà l'au-delà!
> C'est moi le maître de mon sort.
> Ma gloire est ici, ici-bas."

> J'espère, ami, que c'est le cas:
> Pour toi j'espère que ma foi
> Se trompe - oui, que l'au-delà
> Est vide - au moins, AU MOINS POUR TOI.

The believer's answer is surprising: he declares that he would prefer Napoleon's attitude to be true and his own faith to deceive him, rather than the other way round, for Napoleon's sake only. The believer hopes that there will be a void, an emptiness to save him from the pains of hell. In the seventh stanza the poet introduces two more characters who talk to each other: two officers[90] in the Russian campaign had doubts about the afterlife. They decided to make a pact and agreed that if one of them should die and the other survived, the one who died should come back in some form and report to his comrade, for they had heard this might be done:

> Si l'un de nous part sous ce feu
> Et laisse l'autre avec sa peau,
> - Et s'il y trouve quelque dieu -
> Qu'il vienne en dire à l'autre un mot.

Eventually one of them died, and somehow a voice was heard, as we read in the final stanza:

> Et laissa l'autre, un peu moins gai,
> Et moins encore après le bruit
> Qui cria de l'Eternité:
> "L'enfer existe ... Et moi, j'y suis!"

---

[90] From metrical necessity Alun Idris called them "sergeants", needing a word with two syllables.

"Apparently, there is no communication between souls in hell and those on earth. It has to happen through the mediation of the Lord" (letter, 10.6.1990). A monk's task is to pray and do penance for souls in order to avoid their going to hell. "Hell is a great reality for people who live in a monastery because you are living face to face with the eternal questions of why we are here, what we are doing, what our people are doing" (letter, 10.6.1990). This reality of the hell, the dread of damnation, is a prominent feature of this poem.

"Lettre de l'enfer" (*Threshold*, 58) is another French poem dealing with the afterlife. The sonnet is based on an unpublished manuscript, containing the story of a young girl who had died unprepared in a car accident and who later communicated with a Carmelite.[91] The poem ends with a quotation from the letter "'Écris ... pour que nul autre n'entre ici!'"

Considering the relatively small number of French poems in comparison with his English ones, it is striking that the French poems very often deal with afterlife and purgatory. One feels that these poems are written to convey a warning to the living. Naturally a contemplative monk thinks and ponders about the last things a great deal:[92] "The contemplative monk is trying to sacrifize himself for the souls, both living and dead, who need his prayer: this is his purpose" (letter, 19.11.1989).

Many a poem contains hints referring to our transitoriness and the afterlife, either in form of a reference to departed brethren who have already fulfilled their course or by referring to the poet's own death. Alun Idris lets his dead brethren speak in lines like "'Walk on, our brother, tread where we have trodden'"[93], or addresses them, as in the final lines of an early poem called "The eve of my 27th birthday anniversary" (*Threshold*, 4), which has already been quoted earlier in this chapter: "This eventide I do as they have done / In ages past / Who now their rest have won." His brethren are just one step ahead, tomorrow others will do as he has done "this day", and he will be among those who will have attained their rest then. The poem radiates peace as well as inner equilibrium; the novice is firm in his resolve to stay in the charterhouse until the end of his days.

Amongst those poems which bear reference to his own death we find "Ash Wednesday" (*Threshold*, 25), one of his earliest musings, which is a touching form of prayer in essence. The tone of the opening stanza in particular suggests this idea, underlined by the diction employed:

> Father Almighty, King of all creation,
>   Whose gentle nod bade constellations be,
> Thou knowest how one cell became a nation,
>   And how the Void was given eyes to see.
>
>   Each living thing was fashioned by that Hand -
>   And at the last before its Lord must stand.

---

[91] The story is similar to the one in the *Purgatory Manuscript*.
[92] "One has the office of the dead once a week", as the poet pointed out in a letter of 19.11.1989.
[93] "In retreat" (*Threshold*, 34f.).

The attached couplet is used as a refrain: the rhythm of these lines, with the additional stresses at the beginning, conveys both an idea of finality as well as reminding one of a choral response which the community gives to the priest. The poem concentrates on the poet's own unworthiness, his insignificance and minuteness in comparison with God who created him:

> There was a time - yea, ages without measure -
> When none on earth of me had ever thought:
> All that I have is mine by Thy good pleasure;
> How can I boast, or think that I am ought?

The refrain which follows acts as an emphasizing force, it stresses the validity of what was said before. In the succeeding stanza the poet introduces the idea of death:

> Age after age, each twinkling star still flashes - [corr.]
> Yet every flame must flicker and must die:
> Dust unto dust, yea, ashes unto ashes,
> From earth once drawn, in earth again I'll lie.

The first two lines suggest in conventional metaphors the contrast between the eternity of things divine and the finite nature of man, underlined by alliteration, while in the closing lines he displays in concrete form man's mortality by visualizing his own death. The parallel structure employed in l.3, separated only by a colloquial, reinforcing "yea", emphasizes our finite nature, - there is no escape from death: "From earth once drawn, in earth again I'll lie." However, the outlook in the closing stanza is a decidedly positive one:

> Lord, wilt Thou end in dust Life's tragic story?
> Canst Thou forget this dust's great sigh for Thee?
> Nay! - Death is but the portal unto Glory -
> Freed from my chains, Thy Smile at last I'll see.
>
> Praise for all life, free gift of that vast Hand!
> Lord, at its end before Thy Throne I'll stand!

All the lines start with a spondee or inversion, which adds a notion of urgency. The rhythm of the third line, the spondee followed by a pyrrhic, places heavy stress on the word "portal", which lets death appear in a different, positive light. The ultimate refrain, which has been slightly changed, reflects the positive outlook suggested before, the glory of salvation. As we read in a note attached to the poem, Father Laurence Bévenot set these verses to music. They were written after the death of Fr. Laurence's brother, Maurice Bévenot, S.J., to whose memory "Ash Wednesday" is dedicated. Most of Alun Idris' early poems can be chanted, which turns them into hymns, with the prayer element coming out strongly. Some of his hymns have been published in various religious periodicals and are sung in Wales (cf. letter, 29.10.1989). Many of the poems utilise Gregorian tunes which Carthusian monks often chant.[94]

---

[94] "In solitude one doesn't hear much else, one lives in music" (letter, 29.10.1989).

The following poem, "3.30. a.m." (*Threshold*, 32f.), can be sung as well, fitting to the notation of a Welsh Catholic hymn. The closing stanza contains a vivid reference to his own death:

>Passage of Time!
>This slowly-marching bell
>Calls me to sleep and rest awhile ...
>Ring on, great Bell! - till Time thee style
>My passing knell.

The bell can be heard the whole time in a monastery, it tends to organize one's life. "It's the Lord's will for us" (letter, 29.10.1989). In its role as an organizer it also rings in the day of his death.

The title "On hearing of Roger Howells' tragic illness" (*Threshold*, 15f.) explains the origin of that poem. A note at the end informs us that "c'est un jeune prêtre de la haute église."[95] The Anglicans are allowed to marry; but the question arises whether they are therefore true priests or not. The meditation is prompted by the hour of death, which seems to be near:

>Art thou a priest, O man of God,
>That liest on this bed of pain
>Awaiting th'eerie Reaper's nod
>And medicating Fate in vain?
>
>Thou leavest here no progeny,
>For thou didst choose, as those above,
>The blissful double agony
>Of love denied for scalding Love.

The proximity of death is firmly implied by the imagery used in the first stanza. "Th'eerie Reaper's nod" picks up the idea of death as the Reaper cutting off our lives with his scythe: a nod is enough to execute death. The second quatrain concentrates on the question expressed in the opening line of the poem, "Art thou a priest?". Apparently, Roger Howells chose not to marry, although to practice celibacy is not obligatory for Anglican clergymen. The final line explains the reason why: it was "The blissful double agony / Of love denied for scalding Love" which made him decide not to marry. He preferred the Love of God to human love ("love denied"), with the image of "scalding Love" powerfully pointing to the tremendous power which emanates from the Love of God. The closing stanza expresses a longing which can often be found in Alun Idris' verse: the poet's wish to receive some kind of proof is firmly expressed, - he longs to have a sign from God, seems to be desperately seeking for it:

>But when thou'rt there, O man of God,
>When eaten flesh tastes no more pain,
>If thou canst gain thy Maker's nod,
>Come, bring me word: didst bow in vain?

---

[95] Roger Howells, an Anglican priest of only 30 years, suffered from leukaemia (cf. interview in Fraham, 1.7.1990).

The opening spondee reinforces the urgency of the message. The imagery used to suggest death in 1.2 is vivid and striking, almost of morbid explicitness. The two initial spondees in 1.3 firmly imply his need to know, yet at the same time suggest that receiving a sign would only be possible in accordance with the Lord's will. The rhythmical irregularity continues in the final line, underlining the poet's excitement and anticipation.

The timelessness of the Carthusian life, whose course has been the same for centuries, parallels a high awareness of the importance of using time well, which makes every single moment precious. In solitude time is felt more consciously, life is lived to the full. As the door to afterlife, death loses its frightening aspect. The preparation for death and afterlife is of the highest importance to the Carthusian monk, which becomes evident in Alun Idris' poetry.[96] The misery of purgatory and the dread of hell are experienced as important realities, just as heavenly bliss is.

3.1.2.3. MEMORIES

Memories are of great significance to someone living enclosed in a contemplative monastery. Given the fact that there are not all that many outward stimuli, memories frequently act as an interior stimulant from within. In the poetry of Alun Idris we find a considerable number of poems centered on re-living memories of the past, happy as well as sad ones.

How important memories are can be seen in the following lines taken from "Evening of same day (10/4/82)" (*Threshold*, 47):

> Ah! memories! How sweet they are -
> And yet how painful to the heart
> That sees each one as from afar
> And reaches out lest it depart,
> In vain, for part it must ... it has ...
> It will ... yet will again return
> As sweet as at the first it was,
> To rouse Pain's embers that still burn.

The dual nature of memories becomes evident in these lines. The mournful exclamation at the very beginning sets the tone of the poem as a whole. The poet touchingly describes how the heart "reaches out lest it depart", the diction he uses is carefully chosen, gently suggesting the sweetness of a memory. The pause after "In vain" adds much to the power of the line. Grasping a memory to hold it forever is impossible, memories come and go, as is implied by the parallel structure used. The poem is a meditation on the occasion of the anniversary of his reception into the Catholic church.[97]

---

[96] The first Friday of every month is usually dedicated to a greater degree of recollection, when the monks can reflect on and prepare for their own death (cf. letter, 8.7.1990).
[97] "The writer was received into the Catholic Church on Holy Saturday, 10/4/71, and baptized SUB CONDITIONE between 5 and 6 p.m. in St. David's Chapel, Ampleforth." (*Threshold*, 48).

> It hurts, good Lord, and yet I feel
> Some little spark, deep, deep within,
> Some faint, faint echo that doth steal
> Across the grinding Past's loud din
> On these calm eremitic ears
> Now stabilized with frozen Time
> That, station'ry, surveys the years
> And freezes them anew in rhyme.

The anaphora and the repetition used in ll.2f. emphasize the non-tangible nature of the origin of memories, yet somehow they "steal / Across the grinding Past's loud din". The image used to describe the past contrasts sharply with that depicting the present. For him, time has ceased to exist ("frozen Time"). The "faint echo" will always be there though, remaining the same ("station'ry"), as the original sound of his "Past's loud din" does not change anymore. The closing line subtly conveys that by writing these verses memory "freezes" his "calm eremitic ears" anew, - they are preserved forever. The last stanza brings back explicit memories of that important day in the distant past, describing other people's reactions to the step he took:

> O inward sigh! Thou art repressed,
> And yet thou'rt heard on Heaven's height ...
> "Who would have thought, who could have guessed - ?
> A monk, him, HIM!, E'er hid from sight. ..."
> Ah! such a childhood, protestant,
> Impassioned, rowdy, impish, rude,
> Epitomy of Discontent - [sic!]
> Content this night with crusts for food...

The rhythmical pattern of l.3, the medial pause separating two identical halves of a spondaic followed by an iambic foot, emphasizes the feeling of wonder and astonishment conveyed. The spondaic repetition in "him, HIM" (1.4), reinforced by the notation in capital letters, completes the idea of wonder evoked. The mournful "Ah!" reappears once more, which points to the happiness of the memory of his childhood. The crossed alliteration in 1.6 (imp-, r-, imp-, r-) reinforces the vividness of his boisterous youth, while picking up "-content" from the penultimate line to start the last one sharpens the contrast between the past and the present.

As indicated in the title, "Memories" (*Threshold*, 73) explicitly deals with the nature of those recurring thoughts. It consists of seven stanzas written in iambic tetrameter, each stanza being made up of two alternate rhyme quatrains, and is a meditation on the poet's own experience of memories:

> When memories return once more
> From whence they came, deep in the breast [corr.]
> That stores its bulging treasure store
> Of yesterdays today that rest,
> Then doth my spirit heave a sigh
> And sighing, touches whence 'twas heaved -
> The depth of the unfathomed Cry
> That none e'er heard or e'er perceived.

The imagery used to describe the moment of memorizing an event of the past is carefully chosen and evokes a flood of associations, which in turn suggest the very process of memorizing as such. The "bulging treasure store / Of yesterdays" implies the abundancy of precious memories which are stored in his breast. The inversion of the third foot in l.2, "deep in the breast", suggests their hidden nature, an idea which is picked up in the two closing lines of the stanza. The accumulation of stresses at the beginning of l.5 - "Then doth my spirit" - emphasizes the preciousness of the experience. The end of the second stanza vividly completes the experience of memories:

> And marching past before mine eyes
> In pageant after pageant bright
> Of reincarnate living lies [corr.]
> That, mocking, dance before my sight.

The imagery used is striking: "pageant after pageant bright" suggests the grandeur of memories, their sumptuousness. However, our illusion is destroyed by the image that follows: "Of reincarnate living lies". The poet is bound to realize that memories belong to the past, and they will stay there.

> ... And when these spectred parts of Yore
> Rouse in that unparedèd breast
> That bursts 'neath its too bulging store
> Those yesterdays today that rest
> Far, far more present than the Past
> Was ever when it came this way,
> Then yields that breast one mighty blast
> Of Longing, for sweet Yesterday.

The honesty of the feeling conveyed is striking. The image of the "spectred parts of Yore" powerfully evokes the sudden appearance of a memory of the past; the noun "spectre" used as a verb emphasizes this impression. In l.3 the poet picks up imagery used in the first stanza, slightly altering it: the breast, which formerly "its bulging treasure" stored, now "bursts 'neath its too bulging store". The heavy weight of memories is too much for him to bear. Now his spirit does not "heave a sigh" any longer, but "yields that breast one mighty blast / Of Longing, for sweet Yesterday." The imagery used strikingly conveys his inner tension, which is finally released in one great "blast": hiraeth has entered his soul. This strong feeling of longing dominates all four stanzas which follow, the fourth starting with a mournful sigh "O Yesterday! how fair thou wast!". He laments on his own incapability to fully appreciate those happy moments of his past. If only he had known before: "Then, how, Oh! how would I have sucked / Each tiny dew-drop that distilled, / Would I have fondled each flower plucked / In that fair Paradise." The closing stanza culminates in directly invoking "Yesterday" to come back:

> O Yesterday! come back again!
> Lend me but one, one tiny hour,
> Send upward thy descending rain,
> Replant awhile each withered flower ... [corr.]

> \- Nay, 'tis absurd! This miracle
> Omnipotence itself works not.
> Time! - None e'er crossed this obstacle.
> None; ever. None!
>   Nay, one -
>   Thou, Thought.

The rhythm of the first two lines conveys the urgency of the message, the spondee at the beginning of l.1 and on "come back", the inversion of the first foot of l.2 and the spondee on "one tiny" increase the strain. The paradoxes in ll.3 and 4 reinforce the urgency, yet equally hint at the absurdity of the wish expressed. Now disillusionment takes the place of longing. The short sentences and exclamations, the uneven rhythm, the diction which is harsh, not at all pleasing to the ear ("omnipotence", "obstacle"), all these devices help to create the feeling of utter disillusionment, which is reinforced by the repetition at the end, "None; ever. None!" Yet, there is one: the shortness of the phrase "Thou, Thought.", with the pause in the middle, suggests the solemn tone in which it is uttered, the inner wrestling so dominant before vanishes.

"Memories that linger" (*Threshold*, 40f.) is an example of the lasting effect of memories, of how they can give the impetus to further meditation. The note at the end "I.S.C.F. Camp, Harrow, 1970" provides the context to this memory. I.S.C.F is the abbreviation for the the "Inter-School Christian Fellowship", a Christian organization promoting cooperation between schools:[98]

> "What are you?" said the little head
> That touched the head on which it leaned,
> When I held Childhood on my back,
> Myself from childhood barely weaned.

The word play in this stanza suggests the closeness the poet felt towards this child. What she wanted to know was "'Are you a boy? Are you a man? / Which is it? Tell me, tell me, please!'", as we are told in the second quatrain. She kept asking, the shortness of the question emphasizing her curiosity. How much he enjoyed playing with the children there is implied in the third stanza:

> We walked a little further on,
> And I remember how I thought
> How sweet it was to be embraced
> By Innocence unsoiled, untaught."

The incident of the stubborn questioning of this child was not forgotten. It is a memory which is still vividly present to the poet's mind. Remembering the incident makes him reflect on the girl's present life, what might have happened to her, picking up the question used before:

> O Childhood! Art thou rightly named -
> With thoughts so deep in heads so small?

---

[98] Camps are organized by this organization during the holidays, particularly in the London area.

> And thou, sweet load, where art thou now?
> Should I thee "Girl" or "Woman" call?

In "Whitsun" (*Threshold*, 75f.) the memory of the first time that he ever saw a Catholic mass[99] enters into a meditation on the feast of Whitsun.

> O living sacramental Life,
> The same, whate'er the noise, the strife
> Of Earth, of Time, of Human Kind -
> A timeless Peace in thee I find.
>
> The sight of those great outstretched hands ...
> The crimson form that yonder stands ...
> This sacred Stillness of my Lord ...
> The silence of the silent Word ...

The "timeless Peace" the poet experiences is conveyed in the rhythm of the first stanza; the mood of inner equilibrium triggers off the memory of a peaceful experience described in the second quatrain, - the first time he ever saw a Catholic mass. The enumerations successfully convey the idea of catching glimpses through the windows. Furthermore, they suggest the vivid memory of the scene, and also his being moved by just observing the ceremony. The priest was dressed in red ("crimson form"). The notion of wonder and meditation is interrupted, however, by the succeeding stanza, which brings us back to the present in a rather abrupt manner:

> - The bell rings out. We bend the knee.
> It rings again. We wait for Thee.
> Thine epiclesis, Holy Ghost,
> Draws Thee, yea Thee, into this Host.

The presence of the almighty bell is firmly conveyed in these lines: the short sentences imply an urging, almost an insistance, a stubbornness, a rigorous subjection to the outward rules. There is no time left now to indulge in reminiscences.

The following day, however, another memory triggered off a poem simply called "Lines jotted on Whit Monday" (*Threshold*, 76), where the poet recalls the memory of a friend during his student days, an elderly lady, which bore fruit in the poem:

> "Remember me ...," the lady said
> With tears beneath her failing eyes,
> On that last night before I left,
> That night of hid, repressèd sighs.
>
> "Remember me," she said again,
> Her wrinkled face now touching mine,
> "When you're alone in that dark cell ..."
> And harder pressed in tight entwine.

---

[99] The first time Alun Idris ever witnessed a Catholic mass occurred at a place near Oxford, where he saw through the back windows of a modern church what was going on inside. The poet was 13 or 14 at the time (cf. letter, 16.9.1990).

The stanzas recall the evening of their last encounter before the poet quit the world. The memory of that event is still vividly present. The parallel structure used in the first line of each stanza (it is also repeated in stanzas three and four) conveys the idea of memory rising and fading again, yet returning steadily. Thus we read in the fourth stanza:

"Remember ..." - How could I forget?
Where art thou now, my agèd friend?
At ninety-two where dost thou lie?
Thy wilting hours where dost thou spend?

Or dost thou listen as I write?
Art thou gone on where all must go?
Canst hear my young heart beating still,
The memories that haunt me so?

The lines convey the strong affective bond which still exists between the poet and this lady. The inquisitive nature of the questions, one asked after the other, suggests his curiosity to know what has happened to his dear friend. They show that the memory of the lady is still vividly present to the poet, as is explicitly mentioned in the closing line, "memories that haunt me so".

The examples given demonstrate the importance and significance of memories in a contemplative monastery. Memories are experienced differently in solitude than elsewhere, - they represent a precious quota of stimulating thoughts which can hardly be amplified or increased anymore, given the monotonous nature of the daily life of a Carthusian monk. The joy and sorrow involved in recalling the memories of the past find an outlet in Alun Idris' poetry.

3.1.2.4. THE POWER OF THE WORD

The Carthusian monk leads a life in solitude and silence. He consecrates his voice to the Lord only, to His praise. Apart from the recreation on Sundays and the weekly walk, the monks do not converse with each other, - they use their voices for prayer and chant alone. Such exclusive usage turns the voice into a precious instrument and makes the power of the word, especially in its written form, highly expressive to the monk. The word is a means to praise the Lord. To Alun Idris the writing of poetry represents a beautiful, effective way of celebrating his love towards God, of giving Him honour. It does not surprise, therefore, to find that the power of the written word represents the origin of many a meditative poem. In "After receiving Huw's present" (*Threshold*, 17), Alun Idris refers to the pen as:

A little gadget that can move the world,
An instrument of Man that men doth turn,
The voiceless herald of the silent word
That thou, whoe'er thou be, e'en now dost learn:
Its tiny body heaves my Now to thine
And freezes for e'ermore one drop of Time [...]

The sonnet meditates on the tremendous effects of the written word created by this "little gadget". Ll.5 and 6 are particularly striking in their imagery: the role of the pen as an intermediary vehicle to heave "my Now to thine" beautifully expresses how a person's presence is captured in a letter, a poem, anything written. Writing involves freezing a moment for posterity.

The sonnet "Lines written on Feast of the Compassion of the Blessed Virgin" (*Threshold*, 42) deals exclusively with the idea of writing poetry in the order. Apparently, certain difficulties caused by his poetic vein had already arisen. The honesty is striking:

> I write in vain. I write in vain, in vain.
> 'Twere better not to take my eyes from Thee,
> Good Lord, and do as doth the Rule ordain
> That bids full peace vain correspondence flee. [corr.]
> None e'er shall see this sentence that I write,
> This page, like me, will end its life in dust:
> Through life, through death, removed from human sight,
> The hermit and his scribblings vanish must.
>   And yet, is't vain the message that a friend
> Writes to his friend, e'en should the latter know
> Each syllable from aye, ere he aught send -
> As Thou, Lord, this small WORD kept hid till now?
>   For Thee alone I write, my Lord ... My Lord,
> For Thee alone shall burn each unread word.

The three-fold repetition of "in vain" at the very beginning of the sonnet emphasizes the poet's despair experienced at that moment. By referring to the Rule that "bids full peace", prohibiting "vain correspondence", Alun Idris implies the troubles which had arisen as a result of his poetic creativity. The possibility of his verse ever being read by others was practically non-existent, as is suggested by forceful imagery: "This page, like me, will end its life in dust ... The hermit and his scribblings vanish must." The third quatrain, however, is different in tone, - the feeling of disappointment and frustration is replaced by a tenderness and silent enthusiasm for God: it powerfully implies that every word was written for God only, his faithful companion, as "a friend / Writes to his friend". Given that the Lord has seen every word from eternity ("know / Each syllable from aye"), the question arises, however, whether it is not absurd to write down what He knows already. Everything comes from the Lord, including poetry, as is implied in the line "ere he [a friend] aught send - / As Thou, Lord, his small WORD kept hid till now". God is the inspiring source of all the words which had been kept hidden for all eternity. Absurd as it may seem to write down what He knows already, it is not: the writing of poetry is a means of giving honour to the Lord. "If I was asked to burn them, they would burn for the Lord alone, and the smoke would rise up for Him alone. He alone would see what was in them" (letter, 8.7.1990). This statement in a way implicitly summarizes the whole nature of the Carthusian life, - everything that is offered is burnt for the Lord. The holocaust is for Him alone.

The following two poems also deal with the power of the written word. In "After receiving Easter letters" (*Threshold*, 51) the poet meditates on the nature of a missive:

> An envelope is but a tree grown old,
> And chopped and treated till at last 'tis made
> A little square, whose emptiness can hold
> The fulness of the human heart out-weighed
> On sheet on sheet of script inanimate
> That nothing knows about the force it holds
> Upon the brain that soon shall permeate
> The travelling Truth this packet now unfolds.
>   How many hearts have leaped to see this square
> Bear their own name, for that they knew within
> The Presence of the other to be there,
> Enclosed, incarnate, 'twixt two walls so thin ...!
>   Ignited missile, loaded with my soul,
> Explode far, far away, beyond control!

The poet starts with a certain innocence and carefreeness, underlined by the regular rhythm, to describe the nature of an envelope, "whose emptiness can hold / The fulness of the human heart": the contrast "emptiness" - "fulness" emphasizes how much can be contained in an envelope so small. The imagery used to describe the reading of a letter by the addressee skilfully suggests the process of reading, - "the brain that soon shall permeate / The travelling Truth this packet now unfolds." The spondee at the beginning of the third quatrain, which is given additional emphasis by the indentation, points to the vast number of "hearts" which "have leaped to see this square / Bear their own name": the inversion of the first foot followed by a spondee in l.10 serves as an additional means of emphasis. How much it means to receive a letter, in particular in a contemplative monastery, is implied when we read about "The Presence of the other to be there, / Enclosed, incarnate, 'twixt two walls so thin ...!" Letters contain more than just a written message: the personality of the sender is contained therein as well, - the addressee is able to feel his presence when reading the lines. The synecdoches used to depict the addressee, i.e. the "brain" and the "heart", reinforce this idea.

The subtitle of the poem, "and sending a missive that could have important consequences", explains the origin of the meditation. The consequences were important indeed, as the "missive" in question was a letter which eventually led to his not being allowed to continue in the Order. The Grande Chartreuse had been informed of an interest in publishing some of the novice monk's verse (cf. letter, 28.2.1990). Thus the use of the metaphor "ignited missile" is justified, - indeed, it did explode later on.

The inner and outer tension increased, - the writing of poetry started to become problematical, as is apparent in "After receiving news" (*Threshold*, 51). The poet knows of the possibility of having some of his Welsh verse published, which causes a terrible conflict:

> The Hidden is my portion and my cup;
> Thy force doth turn to sin all other sound.
> - I WILL NOT SIN: it would defeat the end
> Of this strange life, and turn to ridicule
> The Prayer sent to the One that I offend
> E'er adding to this noisy monticule.
> ... Yet, if I stop, th'unsaid rests e'er unsaid,
> And what ne'er was ne'er shall be, can be, read.

The poet certainly did not want to break the Rule. The heavily stressed, capitalized assertion "I WILL NOT SIN" firmly implies his decision not to write anymore. The poet proceeds by trying to explain why a continuation of writing verse in the monastery would be absolutely impossible, even sinful: every poem added "to this noisy monticule" would "offend" the Lord. The metaphor used to describe the number of poems he had already written is strikingly derogatory. The word "monticule", rarely used in English, is actually a French word, which the poet employs to rhyme with "ridicule". However, despite the awareness of the possible sinfulness involved, the poet does not really seem to be fully convinced that giving up writing poetry would be the right decision, as is implied in the closing couplet. There is a certain melancholy conveyed in the idea of not being able to, not being allowed to write anymore.

3.1.2.5. A MISCELLANY OF MEDITATIONS

The present chapter aims to demonstrate that the origin of meditative poems is varied and manifold. There is a whole variety of different aspects which can be used as the basis for a meditation, as becomes apparent in Alun Idris' work. By pointing to the wide range of potential sources, the following selection of meditative poems mirrors the life in a Carthusian monastery as well.

As they bear witness to God's power and goodness, the beauties of nature offer such ground for meditation; however, such moods never approach a pantheistic confusion of God and nature. We find several poems which meditate on stars sparkling at night.

"Petit été de S. Martin" (*Threshold*, 1f.) is a mingling of meditations: it is a reflection on Venus on the one hand and on the other on the phenomenon of stars originating in and radiating from the past. Some of them have stopped burning by the time the light reaches the earth:

> Let me gaze into th'Empyreon [corr.]
> T'ward the Night,
> T'ward this Light,
> Child of vast Hyperion.

The poem consists of eleven quatrains in embraced rhyme. The number of stressed syllables per line of each stanza (4-2-2-3) is constant throughout the entire poem. A trochaic pattern forms the base, although the ryhthm is fairly irregular at times. The poem is an early one which fits to the notation of the tune "Thanet". L.4 of the first stanza contains an allusion to one of Keats' fragmentary poems. "Hyperion" is a term suggesting various associations. The actual meaning of the term is "highest heaven" (cf. letter, 6.5.1990). In Greek mythology Hyperion was the father of Helios, the sun God, but the name was also used as an epithet for Helios himself, the incarnation of light and beauty (cf. Homer 1990, 548). Mankind has always admired the stars, which fascinate through the idea of otherness and power they suggest. Admiration for the powers of nature can also be found in the psalms. As Christians we abscribe all majesty to God, to the creator.

The poem is bathed in ancient Greek culture. "Alpha", "Omega", and "Hesperus" also appear. The fact that the morning star is called "Matutina" ("Alpha, thou art Matutina") adds a Christian element to it. The notion of combining classical mythology with Christian poetry has a long tradition. Early Christian poets frequently combined classical allusions with Christian notions.[100]

In "A clear night" (*Threshold*, 59) Alun Idris meditates on the "Morning Star"; he closes the poem with the following two stanzas:

> Soft boreal Light, thy life is short:
> Thine own eclipse thou dost escort.
> Efface thyself before thy lord,
> Recede ... recede ... without a word.
>
> And when this day is fully spent,
> And man hath used what God hath lent,
> Shine forth again, 'neath altered name -
> Sweet Vespera, e'er, e'er the same.

The poem is a meditation on the nature of the morning star, whose life is short. In the morning it has to recede, which is well conveyed by the repetition in l.4 of the first stanza quoted. The idea of the light fading away slowly is subtly implied. However, "when this day is fully spent" the star will return once more, though with a different name, yet still the same. The rhythmical regularity of the first two lines of the succeeding stanza suggests the unstoppable flow of time, which marches on relentlessly, while the spondaic openings of the two closing lines convey a notion of the wonder experienced at the beauty radiating from this star.

Anything that strikes the human mind can become the ground for a meditation, and, as a result, a poem might develop. The title "Dreams" (*Threshold*, 60) clearly hints at the origin of the meditation:

> When *I* am wrenched from Hypnos' gentle arms -
> In *time to* wrench *my* brethren in their *turn* -
> And leave behind a world of *Ea*stern charms
> And in a seco*nd* all *I* learnt unlearn.
> O Wo*n*derla*nd*! Had *I* but at m*y* s*i*de
> When lost in thee, one t*i*ny wr*i*ting pad,
> The *ga*tes of this str*a*nge heav'n *I*'d open w*i*de
> And *freeze for* e'er the *fri*zzling joys *I* had.
>   It is bizarre! How rarely doth my soul
> Walk proudly through thine absent alley-ways
> Clad, as it should be, in the sacred cowl
> That should preserve it in this naughty maze!
> Dark Land! Did men know what monks did in thee,
> They'd flee till death the Saints' bad company.

---

[100] Prudentius is an outstanding example of a Latin Christian poet who combined the two elements in his poetry. He was writing in the period of transition from pagan to Christian culture, when Christianity was becoming the accepted and official religion of the Roman Empire. *Cathemerinon Liber*, *Peristephanon* and *Apotheosis* are his most famous works, including hymns, religious and didactic poetry (cf. Hauck 1971, 185ff.).

Although it is a Shakespearian sonnet, the mental structure reminds one of the Italian form, despite the fact that the closing couplet surprises. The smoothness in sound of the first two quatrains is striking, as is indicated in italics - they indeed seem to be bathed in the gentleness of Hypnos' arms. The dominance of long vowels and diphthongs, in particular /aɪ/, creates a peaceful and solemn atmosphere. The frequent appearance of the voiced /nd/ provides an effect of humming and singing. The occasionally sinister touch of such a combination (cf. Boulton 1972, 58) finds a vague echo as the poem progresses. The phonetic pattern of /f-r/ in combination with the voiced /z/ and the expressive /dʒɔɪz/ in 1.8 is striking and suggests the sweetness of the experience. It is only 1.2 with its alliterating explosive t's and the repeated "wrench" of l.1 which forms a contrast in sound with the other lines of the first two quatrains, emphasizing the cruelty of being woken up; additionally, the rhythm of this line is much quicker than that of the others. The three stresses in a row in "all I learnt unlearn" (l.4) attract attention, emphasizing how very different a dreaming from the alert mind is. The spondee in l.5 ("Had I") reinforces the notion of longing to be able to write down what he sees and feels when dreaming, despite the impossibility of ever being granted that wish.

The exclamatory "It is bizarre!" at the beginning of the third quatrain indicates the change in tone which is about to follow, although the gentle fricative /z/ establishes a connection to the preceding line. The meditative tone dominating so far is superseded by a tone suggesting surprise at the fact that when dreaming his soul does not walk "Clad, as it should be, in the sacred cowl", with the dominance of the uncompromising /k/ suggesting a notion of order, and as a result disobedience. The closing couplet surprises, reinforced by the contrast in tone. While l.13 suggests some of the smoothness of the first two quatrains ("Dark Land!"), the closing line is but a sober insight, although a humorous notion is contained therein as well.

The following French poem, "Was it Théophile Gautier?" (*Threshold*, 17) is an interesting meditation on a poem which apparently had left traces on the poet:

> Est-ce toi le poète qui sema ces vers
> Qu'un beau jour, dans un livre que j'avais ouvert
> Par hasard, je rencontrai, et, les ayant lus,
> Méditai longuement, dans un rêve éperdu?

The poem referred to is called "A Zurbaran", written by the French poet and critic Théophile Gautier (cf. letter, 8.7.1990). As a teenager, Alun Idris happened to come across this poem, which apparently had a great and lasting effect on him. The poem is about a painting of Carthusians sitting at table, with their hoods up, presumably looking rather emaciated. Gautier closes his poem with the following lines:[101]

> O moines! maintenant, en tapis frais et verts,
> Sur les fosses par vous à vous-mêmes creusées,
> L'herbe s'étend: Eh bien! que dites-vous aux vers?

---

[101] Gautier 1970, 311.

Quels rêves faites-vous? quelles sont vos pensées?
Ne regrettez-vous pas d'avoir usé vos jours
Entre ces murs étroits, sous ces voûtes glacées?
Ce que vous avez fait, le feriez-vous toujours? ...

Théophile Gautier suggests how senseless it all is that those depicted in the painting are now being eaten up by worms and all their painful sacrifice was in vain. This idea finds an echo in Alun Idris' poem:

Est-ce toi qui prononças ce verdict hautain
Sur ces rangs capuchonnés qui marchaient en vain
Vers le Néant qu'ils priaient - que tu connais mieux,
Éclairé que tu es par l'éclat lumineux
De la Raison.

The shortness of the closing line consisting of four syllables rivets attention. Furthermore, while all the other lines rhyme in couplets, this one does not have a complementary rhyming line; it stands on its own, which conveys on a very subtle level that reason as such does not comprise truth in its entirety, - something is missing.
"I was very moved by that, I thought, if there are monks who live such an austere life, I'd like to join them. I was eighteen when I read that" (letter, 8.7.1990). Alun Idris continues the poem by pointing to the paradox of philosophy, making fun of those rationalized philosophers:

O Philosophie Souveraine!
Connaissance assurée, connaissance certaine
Du plus grand Inconnu, - connaissance, assurance
Dont la base solide est la ferme Ignorance. -

Here the poet points out the paradox of philosophy trying to find answers to questions which cannot ever be answered. The paradox and the oxymoron employed emphasize the impossibility of finding the answer. The idea of the absolute inscrutability of God is implied: God is imbued with a sense of mystery. As the poem progresses we find a reference to the original stimulus of Gautier's poem in inverted commas:

Ta pitié pour ces gens que tu voyais assis
À leur "table frugale", tous à la merci
D'une immense illusion, qui, hélas! aboutit
Au lugubre repas que ton barde décrit,
Me transperça le coeur [...]

The "table frugale" echoes the original image of "à table au frugal réfectoire" (Gautier 1970, 311). Gautier's compassion "Me transperça le coeur": the line skilfully implies that it is actually the other way round, namely that the poet feels compassion for Gautier, who apparently was not able to pass the frontiers of reason.
The structure of the poem is arresting: the closing stanza returns to the very first lines of the poem by using the same words and phrases which were employed earlier on:

... Oui, ta vie est vécue ... Et la mienne commence -
À la merci, hélas! d'une illusion immense
Ensemencée un jour par hasard par des vers
Que je lus dans un livre que j'avais ouvert.

The contrast in the first line firmly conveys the idea of their utterly different attitudes towards God, apart from the literal meaning conveyed. The verb in "le poète que sema ces vers" of the very first line of the poem is picked up again in the last line but one in "Ensemencée" as a past participle. It seems as though this very poem by Théophile Gautier, which presents the Carthusians as pathetic souls, striving and suffering in vain, had a lasting effect on the poet. It caused an attraction and an interest on the part of Alun Idris in the Carthusian way of life, paradoxically the very opposite of what Gautier had intended.

"After receiving Blake's poem"[102] (*Theshold*, 57) is a meditation on the poet's identity. The sonnet itself is exceptional, as herein Alun Idris experiments in five different languages, trying to find out who he is, where his roots are and where he really belongs, where his future lies, what his identity is. The poem starts *in medias res*:

I often wonder what I am -
An Englishman baked in an Oxbridge school,
Ai Cymro pybyr, mab i bybyr fam
A brawd i frawd a gân i Saeslyd ffŵl,
- Ou même si je ne suis devenu
Tout autre chose par ce long exil
Si différent de tout ce qu'a connu
Un Gallois, pourtant bien anglophile;
An "neutrum" quid sim - sicut omnes qui
Sub hoc cucullo antiquo cantant quæ
Antiqui semper solitarii
Cantarunt ubi et ego hodie ...
Ἢ εἰμι ὥσπερ σύ, ὦ Κύριε –
τις Μελχισέδεκ, ζῶν μὲν, ἄπων δὲ; [corr.]

The use of all these different languages reflects the poet's search, intensifying the difficulties of finding the answer. He seems to be torn apart: the first quatrain concentrates on the contrast between his two native languages, English and Welsh. The two Welsh lines are translated and explained in a note below: "Or a staunch Welshman, son to a staunch mother / And brother to a brother who sings to an Englishy fool (the latter being a reference to the record for which, among other things, he [his brother] is known by all Welsh-speaking people.)" His Welsh background, his firm roots in Welsh culture seem to clash with his English education. The French quatrain proposes the possibility that he has changed completely, having perhaps become "Tout autre chose par ce long exil". The Latin quatrain seems to dissolve his personality insofar as he is completely absorbed by the community of the Carthusians, both past and present, - he has become a part of the Carthusian quest. The closing couplet in Greek, which means "Or am I just as Thou, O Lord: / Some Melchisedek, alive indeed, but absent?"

---

[102] The poem in question was Blake's "The Little Black Boy", which his next door neighbour in the monastery had given to Alun Idris (cf.letter, 6.5.1990).

contains a fascinating suggestion. Melchisedek was the priest-king who seemed to appear from nowhere, without father, mother or geneology; he blessed Abraham, received his offering, and then disappeared into the oblivion whence he had come (cf. letter, 6.5.1990).[103] In a way the poet has detached himself from his past, the family ties do not really exist any longer. Life in the Carthusian monastery is like disappearing into oblivion, "alive indeed, but absent": more alive in a way than others, yet absent, non-existing for the outside world.

Music is of great importance in a monastery; for a Welsh monk it seems to be even more important, as the Welsh in general are said to be very fond of music. This is certainly the case with Alun Idris, who is particularly attracted by music and song. The tunes attached to his poems, the fact that many a poem can be chanted, underlines his love for song. Alun Idris dedicated a sonnet to the beauty of music, simply calling it "Music" (*Threshold*, 53): "A word that means the Muses' own blest art": the long vowels of the opening line of this sonnet convey an element of the bewitching nature of song. After pointing out that music was an art man learnt even before he knew how to speak, he closes with the following emotional outburst:

> O! Beauty's language, I was rocked of thee;
> A little older I half-felt thy trance
> And glimpsed what cloisterers shall never see
> The hour thou'rt linked to Love's high rhythmic dance.
> ... This night I heard thine echo once again
> Rise up and fall and fade on Time's refrain. [corr.]

The first line quoted implies that music has been important from his earliest childhood onwards, he grew up in the presence of music: "I was rocked of thee". The expression "I half-felt thy trance" in l.10 and the use of the word "glimpsed" in l.11 suggest that in his youth he was able to feel the firm union of love and dance, a most natural experience in the life of adolescents. The poet seems to be glad to have known that feeling, as such experience cannot ever be repeated: "what cloisterers shall never see".

The closing line, "Rise up and fall and fade on Time's refrain." suggests the idea of hearing an echo. In a monastery the echo can be heard for a few seconds, reverberating until it fades. In church there are two choirs chanting alternately: one choir's chant rises and fades, then the choir on the other side begins to sing. "You can almost hear time passing. The timeless chant goes on for two or three hours." This chant provides time to reflect, while praise is ascending, "fading into heaven", "the prayers of the past are fading, you are taking their place, you are the choir doing what they have done on that spot" (interview, 13.8.1990).

Miraculous, inexplicable events may provide fertile soil for meditations as well. Such is the case in a French poem called "Laveline devant bruyère" (*Threshold*, 2f.),[104] which is a meditation on a catastrophe in 1978: a church was gutted, everything was completely and

---

[103] Cf. Genesis 14:18ff. and Heb. 7:1ff., also Psalm 109, which is a "significant psalm for someone doing priestly studies. I used to like this psalm a lot" (letter, 6.5.1990).
[104] Other examples can be found in "Castelnau de Guers" (*Threshold*, 5) or "Christus Rex" (*Threshold*, 5f.), the latter dealing with a prophesy made by Helena Leonardi, an Italian mystic.

utterly destroyed by the fire, the only remnant being the wooden tabernacle and the Blessed Sacrament contained therein, as we are told in a note. The poem consists of six stanzas following the metrical pattern axaxbbbx cxcxdddx etc., where the "x" represents the constantly recurring refrain: "À Laveline". Laveline was the first place where the (then) Prior of Sélignac used to say mass regularly after having been ordained. The memory of those days is placed at the beginning of the meditation:

> As-tu chanté, jeune prêtre,
> À Laveline,
> Seul, ici, devant ton Maître,
> À Laveline,
> Ces douceurs eucharistiques,
> Ces récits évangéliques [corr.]
> Qui se montrent authentiques
> À Laveline?
>
> Cette négligence heureuse
> À Laveline,
> Cette invention désastreuse
> À Laveline,
> Prévue par la Providence,
> Guidée par sa Main d'avance,
> Prêche au monde sa Présence
> À Laveline.

While the first stanza seems to indulge in happy memories, the second turns to the catastrophe which had happened there.

The constant repetition of "À Laveline" emphasizes the special nature of that place, it rivets the attention of the reader by reminding him/her stubbornly of the miraculous happening which occurred there. The paradox "négligence heureuse" in l.1 of the second stanza, which suggests human error as the cause for the catastrophe, is taken up in l.7 and used to point to the positive effect of the fire: the world was reminded of the Lord's presence. Had this disaster not happened, the holiness of the blessed sacrament could not have been shown in such a clear way. Certainly there is no scientific explanation whatsoever for why the wooden tabernacle did not burn, while the rest of the church was reduced to rubble. "Providence had admitted something to happen and had used it for its greater glory" (letter, 6.5.1990).[105]

The third stanza vividly presents the church on fire:

> Vieilles vitres, carbonisées
> À Laveline,
> Chaire sculptée, pulverisée
> À Laveline,
> Cloches fondues, tombées, cassées,
> Poutres, orgues, croix entassées, - [corr.]
> Tout crie: "Assez! Assez! Assez!"
> À Laveline.

---

[105] The phrase "négligence heureuse" is an echo of St. Augustine's "O felix culpa" - o happy fault - "quae talem nobis meruit Redemptorem - which has merited for us such a great Redeemer. The Exultet at Easter reveals that even disasters can be foreseen and in a sense arranged or included in God's plan (cf. letter, 6.5.1990).

The asyndeton employed in this stanza suggests the idea of a documentary report, with all the terrible details given. The scene is vividly presented. Thus the emotional outbreak in 1.7 seems to be a natural consequence.

The closing stanza reinforces the inexplicability of how it was possible that not everything was devoured by the flames:

> Petit tabernacle boisé
> À Laveline,
> Petits, petits cercles croisés [corr.]
> À Laveline,
> Resté jaune comme l'arbre,
> Restés blanchis comme marbre,
> Restez là. Que se délabre
> Tout Laveline.

The image of the "petits cercles croisés" refers, of course, to the hosts which remained inviolate as well, - "les hosties ne portaient même pas de trace de brûlure", as we are told in the note.

The small selection of poems presented in this chapter suggest the great variety of subjects for meditative poems. The musings deal with matters both sacred and profane.[106] They reflect the poet's thoughts and ponderings, which are often apt to arouse further meditation on the part of the reader. The poems eliminate the sense of other-worldliness frequently attached to a contemplative monk and let him appear in a very human light, thereby suggesting that human nature is still preserved even in so strict a monastery as a Carthusian one.

3.1.3. POETRY AS A FORM OF PRAYER - THE IMPORTANCE OF MUSIC

The border line between meditative poems and poems as prayers is not always easy to draw. Thus a considerable number of poems already mentioned belong in this chapter as well. Frequently a meditation has a prayerful notion about it or turns into a prayer. The following section concentrates on those poems which share characteristic features of what is commonly called a prayer. A distinction will be made between "community prayers" and "personal prayers": while the simplicity and straightforwardness, the diction and rhythm of the former resemble prayers in church, the latter are prayers on a highly personal and intimate level, poems of much greater literary value.

---

[106] The volume also contains a series on the senses: "Father Prior is becoming more and more deaf" (*Threshold*, 67), "'You have problems of Turvey dimensions.'" (*Threshold*, 67), which is a meditation on the blindness of a friend, or "'Votre nasalissime client ...'" (*Threshold*, 68), a sonnet which, as is indicated in the title, deals with the sense of smell.

3.1.3.1. COMMUNITY PRAYERS

The volume *The Threshold of Paradise* contains a number of comparatively short poems, which can be used as prayers for the day. On pp.22-24 there is a whole series of poems for mardi gras, i.e. French for Shrove Tuesday. These poems with their simple rhythms are suitable for community prayers. Most of them can be chanted as well, as "Grâces" (*Threshold*, 23):

> We thank Thee, Sun of Righteousness,
> For moments of sweet Happiness
> At morn, at noon, at eventide,
> To mark Time's hourly ebbing tide.

The poem was written to fit the notation of "O lux beata Trinitas", a famous ancient hymn sung at first and second vespers of Trinity Sunday (cf. letter, 8.7.1990).
There is a second "Grâces" to be found on the same page, which has a similarly regular rhythm:

> We thank Thee for this gift of love
> Descending from those stars above
> That now recede to where they were
> Ere Love from Love for love did stir.

The first movement was a stirring of love, the whole of creation focuses on love. The word play in the closing line reinforces this idea. "It's from this invisible maker that all good comes, out of love" (letter, 8.7.1990). This poem can be sung to "Iam lucis orto sidere", as is indicated in brackets.

At noon the monks pause to say grace before eating. Louis Veuillot observed: "Les chartreux ne mangent jamais de viande, et l'on n'en mange pas chez eux. Mais frère Jean n'a pas son pareil pour accomoder les choux. Et je trouve pour ma part que rien n'ouvre l'appétit comme un Benedicite" (Veuillot 1877, 91). In "Benedicite (noon)" (*Threshold*, 24) Alun Idris writes:

> Descend upon us, blessèd Grace;
> Bless with the blessing of thy Face
> This restful boon that bids us pause
> One hour, 'neath Time's unhurried Cause.

This poem can be sung as well: Alun Idris himself composed a tune for it; both the poem and the tune were used in the charterhouse (cf. letter, 8.7.1990).

"Grâces" (*Threshold*, 24) follows to thank God at noon for the food he gives us. The food is borrowed, just as is the present hour:

> We thank Thee, hidden Source of Good,
> For this new gift of borrowed food,
> Not ours to take, not ours to give -
> No more than this new hour to live.

In a charterhouse the feeling of food as a borrowed good is strongly present: food is passed through the hatch. It is given to the monks, which emphasizes the idea of the gift they receive. The poem was composed to fit the notation of "Rector potens", a tune which is used regularly in monasteries at midday.
This series of short prayers reflects the monastic spirit of the necessity to give thanks to the Lord from morning to evening: everything is the subject of thanksgiving, even hunger, as we read in "Mercredi des Cendres" (*Threshold*, 24):

... And thank Thee for this hunger, Lord,
This void that savours thy sweet Word:
We feed on fasting for one day,
Lest we forget our tasteless clay.

The rhythm of this poem is different from the prayers mentioned before. The paradox of "We feed on fasting" is underlined by the use of alliteration. The diction of this short poem is carefully chosen, a tone of solemnity prevails. The contrast between "sweet Word" and "tasteless clay" suggests human weakness and triviality in comparison with God.
The void, this emptiness opens us to grace and to the coming of the Lord, - it "savours thy sweet Word". This poem again fits the notation of "O lux beata".

Many of Alun Idris' poems can be chanted. They either fit the notation of well-known hymns or old monastic tunes, or they have tunes which were composed especially for them. All the prayers mentioned can be sung. The Carthusians hardly converse with each other. They use their voice to praise God only. Chanting this praise is an even more affective and powerful form of praying, which explains the presence of tunes and melodies in this chapter.

3.1.3.2. PERSONAL PRAYERS

Praying means talking to the Lord. In this sense we find many poems of Alun Idris' which correspond to this definition of prayer. The conversation with Christ in silence is central to many a poem. Frequently, it is even more than just a conversation: the poet is encouraging Christ as a fellow man, as a friend, in particular in poems written during Lent, when we are most of all reminded of Jesus' being a true human being as well. Such a vivid "dialogue" can, for example, be found in "Palm Sunday" (*Threshold*, 43), where we read:

March on, march on, O Victor, march
T'ward this strange throne prepared for Thee;
For one short hour bend 'neath this arch
That subjugates Eternity.

And then lift high that Head again
To see the light that doth await
Beyond the dark that felt Thy pain:
Ride through Heav'n's newly opened gate.

The three-fold repetition and the apostrophe used in 1.1 evoke a strong notion of encouragement for Jesus to continue and not to give up, - an idea which has been seen before. The "strange throne" is a metaphor for the cross, which suggests His exalted position, both in the literal and in the figurative sense. The spondaic opening in the closing line reinforces the idea of encouragement and excitement conveyed, the poet being fully aware of the importance of the completion of Christ's suffering for the atonement. The lines show Alun Idris being impelled to write by deep spiritual passion. Especially the poems composed during Holy Week abound in such personal incitements. "Palm Sunday" fits the notation of "Exultet coelum laudibus, Ascension Day", an old monastic tune which lends the poem an even more stirring character.[107]

Similarly, in "At dawn, Good Friday" (*Threshold*, 45) the poet encourages Jesus to "Walk on, O Christ, the end is nigh. / Stretch out thine arms, look to the sky", and later continues: "March on, O King, tread earth and sea! / Hold forth thy Sign of Victory!"[108] The poem can be chanted as well: here it is "Vexilla Regis" which lends the poem an additional affective component.

All these examples strongly express the close relation the poet feels he has with Jesus, whom he considers as his companion. By talking to Him in such a personal, direct way we feel the poet's closeness to Christ, his love for God, his compassion for the tragic events. The life of Jesus, in particular Christ's Passion, is re-experienced, - it is a great reality to the poet.

The Threshold of Paradise contains a number of poems which are addressed to the Virgin Mary. In later periods their number is greater. "25th of March" (*Threshold*, 37) meditates on how this little maid, who is now queen of heaven, experienced the message of the angel. The poem also ponders on the question of whether she is able to hear all the pleas and prayers of these hordes of people who are praying to her. It is a very human approach which the poet attempts, following Julian of Norwich's idea of Mary and how she saw her. The poem represents both a meditation and a kind of prayer, in the sense of his addressing her personally:

> Is this the sound that thou didst hear
> Long, long ago when thou wast here,
> When that strange messenger drew near,
>   And said, "Hail, little maid."?

Mary is never addressed by "Thou" written in capital letters. The use of capitalization is restricted to the Lord only. The rhyme scheme of the poem is aaab / cccb / dddb etc., with the first three lines being iambic tetrameters, and the closing line written in iambic trimeter, which

---

[107] "Palm Sunday is a moment of glory in the midst of passion, and I felt that it was fitting that the ultimate march to the heavenly Jerusalem be reflected in the choice of Ascension music to accompany His entry into the earthly. [...] On both Palm Sunday and Good Friday, the Church honours a triumphant King by using bright red vestments and altar frontals." (letter, 18.11.1993).

[108] Cf. pp.74f. for a more detailed discussion of the poem.

represents a kind of incremental refrain. This closing line always refers to the angel's salutation to Mary:

> ... The hush of this becalmèd night,
> The darkness of Prayer's fastened sight,
> The warmth of this angelic light
>   That whispered, "Hail, sweet maid!" ...

The rhythm is very smooth, thereby suggesting the calmness of the night, which was suddenly interrupted by the angel's question. In the fourth stanza we read:

> And tell me, gentle maiden dear,
> This Song of Silence that I hear,
> Hath it much changed since in thine ear
>   'Twas broke by: "Hail, sweet maid!"?

The rhythm in l.3, starting with an inversion followed by a spondee, reflects a certain impatience to know about it. In the closing stanza Mary is asked in the refrain whether she can hear all the prayers wafting up to her: "Dost hear th'unheard 'Hail!' prayed?", a line which is not as smooth as the closing lines of the other quatrains. This poem fits an adaptation of a psalm tune learnt at La Trappe, as we are told in a note. Here again music supports and strengthens the affective component of the poem.

Sometimes saints are invoked in the poetry as well: as a representative of these poems the following one addressed to St. David, the patron saint of Wales, to whom Alun Idris has always felt a great devotion, may be cited. The poem was written on the saint's feast day, simply being called "St. David's Day" (*Threshold*, 27):

> In ages past upon these timeless mountains
>   Myriads of saints once toiled in silent prayer.
> With joy their soul drank from Salvation's fountains -
>   Joy in the Cross the flesh was giv'n to share.
>   Scarred were the hands that tilled these hills and dales,
>   O David, raise those hands once more o'er Wales.

This poem is one of his earliest musings, it was written to fit to the notation of a tune the poet's mother had composed.[109] The first stanza recalls the missionary activity of St. David in Wales: the image of "Myriads of saints" underlines how strong the Catholic faith was in those days. "With joy their soul drank from Salvation's fountains" (l.3) firmly implies the power and strength flowing from faith. The fountain of salvation spends the vital water for the soul, which keeps it alive. The memory of those days is depicted in the stanzas which follow:

> At night their chant, like incense, rose to heaven;
>   As Earth rolled on, these stars their vigil kept.
> At morn their praise was heard, - at noon, at even -

---

[109] Olwen Jones had composed the tune for the Cardiff Eisteddfod in 1978; fond as he was of the tune, her son decided to write a poem to be sung to the tune. The first poem was a Welsh one on this metre; the hymn to St. David followed, first in Welsh, later transposed into English (cf. letter, 8.7.1990).

>When twilight failed their souls 'mid Angels slept.
>Sweet to thine ears these singing hills and dales;
>O David, hear the beating heart of Wales.

The idealized picture of those days in the distant past reflect what the poet longs to happen again in Wales. The images which he uses to describe those days are full of affection and tenderness, which also reveals Alun Idris' own love for his home country. His bonds with Wales are very stong. Therefore he wishes St. David to come again, to think of the country once more. The explicit wish to make the saint return is to be found in the ultimate line of each stanza, where Alun Idris uses a parallel structure to reinforce his yearning: "O David, tread once more the roads of Wales", "O David, cast one last sweet glance at Wales." The final stanza contains a reference to the age of the saint: "Those hundred years grew dim in that strange passage / From pain to unknown realms of bliss for aye." St. David is supposed to have reached an age of almost one hundred years, dying around 601 (cf. Farmer 1978, 103).

The poems mentioned can be considered to be prayers in the sense that here Alun Idris addresses Christ, the Virgin or a saint in order to talk to them, share their experience, encourage them, beseech them. It is striking that the majority of these poems can be chanted as well, which underlines the role of music as a vehicle to convey an additional affective component. Singing a prayer is more affective and emotional than merely reciting it.

3.1.4. THE AFFECTIVE COMPONENT:
POETRY AS A MEANS OF DECLARATION AND CELEBRATION

"And above all you must be loving, for love is the link of the perfect life", as we read in the letter of St. Paul to the Collosians (Col 3:14). Love is what we have to strive for, particularly in the solitude of a contemplative monastery. According to H.M. Blüm love is of three-fold importance to the contemplative monk. First, love is the motivating force in contemplation, which allows the soul to think of God and things divine continuously and with ease. Second, love is the primary means to reach a state of contemplation. Love should not only guide reason to God but also inflame it, in order to reach that loving insight which forms the very essence of contemplation. Third, love is the perfection and the crowning of contemplation, as increasing one's capacity of love is both the aim and the fruit of contemplation (cf. Blüm 1983a, 18).

This tremendous, burning love for God, this joy to be near the Beloved can be felt in many a poem of Alun Idris. It appears as though poetry was an excellent means of capturing this wonderful feeling and making it glow all the more: "Love [...] of the Beloved accounts for many of the most intense moments in most lives; moments generating the emotion that, recollected in tranquillity, may crystallize into poems" (Stallworthy 1973, 19). Such intense moments are conveyed in the poems included in this chapter which celebrate the enthusiasm for God, the love for God, and also the love he feels towards La Trappe.

3.1.4.1. ENTHUSIASM FOR GOD

The joy of receiving the Holy Spirit, the poet's excitement at being filled with it, is apparent in "Whitsun" (*Threshold*, 75f.), where we read in the seventh stanza:

"Nay, Spirit, come! I'll come. We'll meet.
Marana thà! My God I greet. [corr.]
I kiss Thee, Lord, upon the lips,
Thy love outpoured by being sips.

One is immediately impressed by the sustained tone of joy, breathless, beyond breath, that provides the dominant feeling of this verse. It is a song of praise, an evocation of the special pentecostal ecstasy. "Marana thà" is a scriptural reference (1 Cor 16:22) and means "Come Lord" (cf. letter, 19.11.1989). The excitement is conveyed by the short exclamatory sentences he uses. It does not surprise to see that this poem is meant to be chanted as well: it fits to the notation of "Veni Creator Spiritus", a well-known monastic tune. Doubtless, the verbal emotional outburst is reinforced by the music.

A much more silent declaration of love can be found in "Renouvellement des Voeux" (*Threshold*, 39). First of all discussing negative motivations for renewing his vows, he moves on to a striking declaration of his love for Jesus:

'Tis not the fear of Hell that moves my soul
To seek the Face that sought me ere I breathed,
Nay, nor the sight of those great clouds that roll
Across the vault of Heav'n, with glory wreathed,
That bid leave now behind whatever moves
Outside the orbit of one tiny cell,
And clip the wings of unfledged angel loves,
And throw away the key of this strange hell ...
But someone that I met long, long ago
When yet unwarned of what this stranger did
To those who, unawares, did near him go,
Unarmed against his slow, sly cunning bid:
"Wilt give me this ... and this ... yes, p'haps and this? [corr]
This too? ... p'haps this as well ... in turn for bliss?"

The sobering nature of the first two quatrains prepare us for the message of the closing lines: what or who can it be that makes him lead such a life? The metaphors used to describe the Carthusian way strikingly convey the pains, the suffering involved: to "clip the wings of unfledged angel loves" is a very strong metaphor, which arouses a feeling of dismay as well as lack of understanding. What can be so strong a force to allow this to happen? "And throw away the key of this strange hell ...": who can it be for whom one's whole life is left behind to dwell in "the orbit of one tiny cell"? The third quatrain tells us why, though referring to the cause just with "someone that I met long, long ago". The stranger is, of course, Jesus Christ: the poet merely makes allusions ("When yet unwarned of what this stranger did"), thereby declaring his love; by not naming Jesus he powerfully implies that one has to be careful, - one can be caught just as he was caught, "unawares", - it is almost like a warning: beware! He takes more and more of you! This is what the closing lines seek to imply, although the repetition used is not very pleasing to the ear, which makes the message less convincing.

The short Latin poem without a title (*Threshold*, 39) aims to reinforce the message of the previous one: we cannot flee from the Lord's presence.

> Jam jacta est alea! Heu! nunc
> Migratus sum in locum hunc
> In quo introducti pereunt
> In Oculo quem fugiunt.

At times, the poet uses most striking imagery to declare his love to God, as in the following stanza of "11 a.m., 25th of March" (*Threshold*, 37f.). With tremendous enthusiasm and overflowing feeling the poet is bound to cry out:

> The die is cast! O Rubicon,
> Thou'rt crossed. Henceforth I must go on.
> What might have been ne'er more may be.
> O Cross! Now am I nailed to thee.

The finality and irrevocability of his decision is underlined by using Caesar's words when crossing the Rubicon, "alea iacta est". The poem was written immediately after having renewed his vows for another two years in a small ceremony which had taken place in chapter (cf. letter, 29.10.1989). On that day, the 25th March 1982, Brother David passed on to the group of solemnly professed monks. The stanza quoted powerfully conveys that now the course is set and that his decision is irreversible: "O Cross! Now am I nailed to thee." Apart from the enthusiasm apparent in this line, the imagery used also suggests the pain and suffering involved in leading such a life in a Carthusian monastery. The importance of this moment is stressed in the second stanza:

> In two years' time 'twill be too late
> To re-arrange my earthly fate.
> Now, now, e'en now the choice is made.
> Short vow! On thee one life is weighed.

The monks make solemn profession after seven years, which will bind them forever to the Carthusian Order; however, the poet feels that it is "Now, now, e'en now", i.e. after having lived in the charterhouse for five years, that the decision has already been made. The repetition reinforces the importance of the decision, "On thee one life is weighed." His enthusiasm is firmly implied in the closing stanzas:

> O grace! O grace! How could I doubt?
> O Satan! Now thou'rt put to rout
> By these three words that crossed the lips
> Of one that from thy claws now slips.

O David! Bruno! On I come.
This Charterhouse shall be my home
Till ye shall deem it well to hail
And draw from these small hands each nail ...

- And open wide some unknown Door
That none shall close, e'er, evermore,
And say, "Behold what's laid for thee,
With us, till fades eternity!"

The short sentences and exclamations used express the poet's excitement. All seems to be so clear now, the former doubts are hard to understand anymore. Addressing Satan and telling him that "Now thou'rt put to rout" is another means to emphasize the finality of his decision. Normally Satan is only mentioned in his poetry, but never directly addressed, which underlines the importance of the step in question. In the second stanza quoted, which is the penultimate stanza of the poem, Alun Idris returns to revelling in his enthusiasm for the decision he has made. The image of the very first stanza is taken up again. Now that he is "nailed to Thee", the charterhouse shall be his home until at last "each nail" will be drawn from his hands; at last he will be released. The spondee on "some un-known" in 1.1 of the final stanza suggests the special nature of that door, reinforced by the three stresses on "none shall close" (1.2).

Enthusiasm for the cross is also conveyed in "The fourteenth of September (Holy Cross Day)" (*Threshold*, 87) where the poet celebrates the cross and its releasing and redeeming nature. It is a successful attempt in elevated religious lyric:

Hail, Glory! Hail, glorious Tree!
O Cross, thou hast set us free!

Shine o'er the vast Creation,
Illumine Earth's starless night;
Assemble every nation
Beneath thy radiant light.

The first couplet is the refrain, which is repeated after each stanza. The rhythm of 1.1 expresses the poet's enthusiasm and happiness (//x//x/)[110], which the second line continues in the metrical pattern of x//x/x/. The poem is an adaptation of verses originally written in French, which is reflected in the metrical pattern used in the English one: "Victoire! Tu règneras! / O Croix! Tu nous sauveras."[111] The first stanza reflects the poet's overwhelming enthusiasm for the cross, thereby implying the firm relation he feels he has with it. In the third stanza Alun Idris addresses the cross with loving tenderness:

O! sweet, sweet little acorn
Predestined for such a tree!
The death-bed of Life's first-born,
The seed of Eternity.

---

[110] "/" symbolizes a stressed syllable, while "x" represents an unstressed syllable.
[111] In French one has to count all the syllables when singing, which means that the final "-e" has to be counted as well (cf. letter, 16.9.1990).

The metrical pattern is again shaped by the original French poem, which makes it appear uneven in rhythm. The imagery of this stanza is skilfully employed: the acorn as the seed of the oak becomes the symbolical seed of Eternity. The "death-bed of Life's first-born" attracts attention because of the contrasting images employed: the term "first-born", which has a deeply human notion about it, opposes the "seed of Eternity", a contrast which functions as a means to suggest the hypostatic union. The lines convey the poet's reverence as well as his love for the cross.

Alun Idris has also composed a tune for this poem, the music underlining his wish to celebrate and honour the cross.

As could be observed in the examples included in this chapter, outbursts of unbounded affection manifested in a longer piece of verse are not all that frequent in his poetry; they are interspersed in the verse, concentrated in a line or one particular stanza. We find such a particularly forceful manifestation in the closing stanza of "Corpus Christi" (*Threshold*, 79):[112]

> Lord, I believe! I trust, I bend, I follow ...
> Tears blur my eyes, so strange a Bread I break:
> That sinful Man the Son of God should hallow,
> And with a word the unmade Word should make! -
> Nay, 'tis too much! My heart will not withstand.
> I hold who holds Creation in his hand.

3.1.4.2. THE LOVE FOR LA TRAPPE

During the long vacation of 1974 Alun Idris visited La Grande Trappe for the first time. He returned to this Trappist monastery for a prolonged stay before finally entering the charterhouse at Sélignac. However, La Trappe had been the poet's first love, - a feeling he never lost. The sonnet "After night office" (*Threshold*, 59) tells us of his sorrow at not having gone there:

> The voice of Prayer is ever heard on high:
> I sleep, but others keep the lamp alive.
> My resting lungs now heave a little sigh
> As slowly it strikes on from four to five
> - As they recall how each unthinking beat
> Calls forth the brethren to those stalls that knew
> That gyrovague who in his youthful heat
> From cloister unto cloister madly flew -
> And fell in love too often with that Love
> That did without a word reverberate
> In those arched tunnels through which e'en now move
> Those hooded mysteries that contemplate.
>   La Trappe! I fell too early in thy jaws.
> The hiraeth for my home mine inwards gnaws.

---

[112] For a detailed discussion of the poem see pp.79f.

The first lines of the sonnet echo the idea of the lamp of prayer being handed on from one order to the other during the whole of the night.[113] Those "brethren" mentioned are the Trappists, as they commence their office when the Carthusians have concluded theirs. "Gyrovague" refers to R.S.B. 1:10, where St. Benedict talks about the different types of monks. The gyrovague is described as follows: "[...] girovagum, qui tota vita sua per diversas provincias ternis aut quaternis diebus per diversorum cellas hospitantur." (Seidle 1978, 62) - "From cloister unto cloister madly flew": he is not a true monk, - he is someone who has no roots (cf. letter, 29.10.1989). And yet, the reason was Love: the poet is someone who "fell in love too often with that Love", - the affection he felt for God and the different forms of being His servant were the reason for his decision to join the Carthusians, yet the feeling of that first love which he had felt for La Trappe is still burning. He still longs that he might have gone there, which becomes most apparent in the closing couplet. The exclamation and the imagery used show the strong affection he feels for La Trappe. In the closing line the poet explicitly uses the word "hiraeth", this typical Welsh form of longing and yearning: the longing for his "home", i.e. La Trappe, is gnawing painfully at his heart.

The hiraeth he feels for La Trappe is also apparent in "'OCCUPATION: Religieux trappiste'" (*Threshold*, 54f.), a sonnet written "after coming across the first 'permis de séjour' and recalling what 'frère Secrétaire' wrote on the form", as we are told in a note in brackets. The residence permit arouses floods of memories of La Trappe, which are characterized by a strong notion of longing:

> Je pense encore à ce cher monastère
> Que berça ma jeunesse en son doux chant ...
> La Trappe! - Ah! Qu'est-il? Quel est ce mystère
> Qui tire, attire, et puis déchire tant
> Le coeur de tout jeune homme qui entend
> Ton grand Silence, dont l'aiguë Sirène
> Perce à jamais le Plaisir que défend
> Ce vaste mur qui rompt la cantilène
> De tout ce qui peut tirer sur les cordes
> Des coeurs inconnus entrés par ici, [corr.]
> Qui portent seuls le monde qui déborde
> Cet être jamais fait pour être ainsi.
> ... Pourtant! ... Ce mot "RELIGIEUX TRAPPISTE"
> Me parle!! ... Aurais-je fait mauvaise piste???

The imagery used to describe the poet's memory of La Trappe is bathed in affection: from the very first line onwards the reader is bound to feel how much the poet is in love with La Trappe. "Ce cher monastère / Qui berça ma jeunesse en son doux chant ..." powerfully evokes that La Trappe had been his home, almost a mother to him, as is suggested by the imagery used. The third line starts with a mournful sigh: "La Trappe! Ah! Qu'est-il?" The longing to be there is firmly conveyed. The poet then tries to explain what it is that attracts him so powerfully, "ce mystère / Qui tire, attire, et puis déchire tant / Le coeur de tout jeune homme

---

[113] Cf. "Just another day" (*Threshold*, 61f.); see discussion of the poem on pp.34-38, in particular p.35.

qui entend / Ton grand Silence". The cumulative enumeration suggests a certain inevitability of not being able to escape the attraction La Trappe exerts on one whose heart can understand "Ton grand Silence". The use of the intimate form "ton" adds to the feeling of closeness conveyed. Furthermore, the second meaning of "ton", i.e. "sound", is noticeable as an overtone, suggesting thereby the paradox of the sound of silence. Further "paradoxes" are implied as the poem progresses: "Plaisir" defends "ce vaste mur", which is, however, destroyed and penetrated from within, "la cantilène / De tout ce qui peut tirer sur les cordes /Des coeurs inconnus entrés par ici". It is a call to the heart one feels, and it is only if the heart responds to the call that a soul enters the monastery. Trappists are unknown to the world, and remain unknown throughout the rest of their lives. They normally do not speak, their heart is hidden ("coeurs inconnus"). It is a strange, indeed almost inhuman life, as the Trappists bear alone the weight of the world, as is suggested in l.11. Inhuman as it seems, since man is a social being, they nevertheless joyfully embrace such a life. The closing couplet firmly implies how much La Trappe still means to him. "Ce mot "RELIGIEUX TRAPPISTE" / Me parle !!" is followed by two exclamation marks to emphasize the strong bond of attraction he feels. The final question is not only an indicator to show how much he loves La Trappe but most of all a sign of inner struggle: was the decision to become a Carthusian the right one, with his heart still burning for La Trappe?[114]

The love he feels for La Trappe culminates in "The twenty-fifth of March, 1984" (*Threshold*, 90), the sonnet written on the day when Alun Idris' vows expired. It is the last poem contained in the volume *The Threshold of Paradise*: on that day he changed canonically from being a Carthusian to becoming a Trappist postulant. The poet was thus officially still a Carthusian, but the poem was actually the first one to be written at La Trappe, where he arrived the same evening (cf. letter, 30.12.1990):

> This is the day that changes all my days,
> And makes me what so long had seemed untrue.
> La Trappe! Who, who could e'er have known the ways
> That were to bring me back to thee, and you
> My quiet, quiet brethren, who still smile
> As you did smile before, from 'neath your hood,
> At one that knew your goodness for a while
> And cast it off, to seek an alien good.
> I have come home, and in your arms I feel
> Th'embrace that said, "Goodbye; but thou'lt return."
> O massive walls! O Altar! Here I kneel,
> As long, long, long ago, where't 'gan to burn.
> And thee, my father! In thy arms I cried,
> For thou wast right. And yet I tried.
>   I tried!

---

[114] In an interview (Fraham, 1.7.1990) Alun Idris mentioned that "In fact I went straight home to La Trappe". The poet's use of the word "home" is in itself striking and underlines once more the love he feels for La Trappe.

This sonnet reflects a historical moment in the life of the poet. It tries to explain how it had all come about. The honesty behind it is striking. The love he feels for La Trappe radiates from every single line. In this poem Alun Idris found an outlet for an interior "volcano". It reflects the outburst of his innermost feelings. The essence of the very first line is ever present in the succeeding ones, - the conviction that everything will change from this day onwards: "This is the day" - the initial spondee and the pause after "day" set the tone and emphasize the special importance of this day. The stresses on "so long" in 1.2 indicate that a lengthy process had preceded the happenings of that day, it had been a dire, fierce struggle, as the hiraeth to go back to La Trappe had already been felt for a long time.[115] The exclamatory "La Trappe!" reminds one of an enraptured sigh uttered in a moment of great emotional passion. This idea is reinforced by the spondee and the inversion which follows, i.e. three stressed syllables in a row, which add to the impression of the utter improbability of such an event. The rhythm of the fourth line puts heavy emphasis on the word "back"; the idea of coming home to the place where he belongs is firmly implied. The pause after "thee" in 1.4 isolates the last spondaic foot; "and you" is given a highly solemn tone, in particular as it rhymes with the repeated "who, who" of the previous line. The components thus unified by interior rhyme suggest that the monks ("you") possibly foresaw his return. Ll.5 and 6 describe the Trappist brethren: the slow rhythm, the repetition and the pauses underline the quiet but balanced life in the Trappist monastery. Their life has not changed at all: they "still smile", with the spondee reinforcing the notion of stability. The inversion at the beginning of 1.6 indicates the flashback in time which follows. The pause in the middle of line 8 places heavy emphasis on the preceding word: "And cast it off", which points to the gravity of the mistake. The accumulation of accents makes the phrase "I have come home" in 1.9 the one which receives most emphasis. Indeed, it is the basic message of the entire poem. The series of exclamations which follow suggests the poet's excitement at having returned. It seems as though he does not know where to begin; all he is able to stammer is merely an enumeration of what he sees, what he is impressed by. The three-fold repetition in "As long, long, long ago, where't 'gan to burn" reinforces his excitement. He seems to be at a loss for words in the face of the significance of the moment. La Trappe was the poet's first love, "where't 'gan to burn", - it was here that he felt the pull, the love of God for the very first time. The closing couplet is full of regret for what had happened, why he had not stayed there in the first place. The final repetition "I tried!" attached to the poem in an additional line emphasizes the poet's sorrow, while at the same time it suggests his urge to find an acceptable explanation for his behaviour.

Although this poem is based on real events which occurred in monastic surroundings, it describes a universal experience, and on reading the lines a chord of one's own past will be struck in the reader. The poem tells of a man's experience who is bound to realize that a certain idea, a certain plan has not worked out, but that others foresaw this development in advance. The universality of this experience, combined with an honesty apparent in every single line,

---

[115] This hiraeth is apparent in the poems mentioned earlier in this chapter.

makes this sonnet particularly attractive and powerful. The rhythm helps to convey the message in an even more stirring manner. All these devices add to the poem's effectiveness, yet it is most of all the presence of love which makes it so powerful.

The examples included in this chapter demonstrate how poems become a means of celebration: the love Alun Idris feels for La Trappe is firmly conveyed, - affection is ever present. The reader is bound to be touched by the power which radiates from these lines, reflecting thus the poet's innermost being.

3.1.5. (IN-)COMPATIBILITY OF
THE CARTHUSIAN AND THE POETIC VOCATION

The poems in *The Theshold of Paradise*, written at the charterhouse of Sélignac, stem from the intensity of Alun Idris' religious experience and are written in the spirit of deep faith in God. They almost exclusively deal with religious matters. In view of the creative output and the quality of many of his poems we must rank him among the vocational poets: a Carthusian monk who, apart from his monastic vocation, also has a truly poetic vocation. It must be emphasized, however, that originally the poet had no intention of publishing his verse, the poems being written for God only, to praise the Lord and worship Him. The poetry echoes all the facets of the Carthusian way of life. Thus the musings represent a documentation of the novice monk's own spiritual path on his way to perfection, - a stony and laborious march.

The poems on solitude and silence convey the very essence of contemplation and help to understand the ultimate goal of silence and meditation: the emptying of earthly vapidness, finding the inner void, which creates room for the spirit to enter.[116]

In some poems he is able to catch glimpses of a soul in utter silence, in retreat. Retreats often turn into touchstones for finding out about one's vocation, or taking important decisions. The essential characteristic about retreats is that they represent a search for a solution in union with God, i.e. in the presence of God. The monk does not decide on his own, for he always tries to listen to God's voice.

Many a religious feast is the inspiring source for the composition of a poem. Celebrating a religious feast in a contemplative monastery is of great consoling spiritual effect; it is always a happy moment for the monks. The poet frequently meditates on the very essence of a certain religious feast, which enables the reader to understand more about the occasion by feeling its importance, as conveyed in the poem. Frequently, the poet presents the historical background to a feast, or uses dramatical dialogue to describe the happening, which intensifies the experience of reading and which also helps to actualize the events portrayed in the Bible.

---

[116] The difference to other Eastern religions, in particular Buddhism, where much emphasis is placed on meditation and finding the void as well, is clearly demonstrated.

By presenting the apostles in a most human manner, they cease to be distant, vague figures but turn into real human beings, who suffered from doubts and endured difficult periods as well.

The Carthusian monk spends his life in contemplative prayer and meditation. Numerous examples have demonstrated that Alun Idris' poetry is a means to catch moments of intense meditation, at times even becoming a form of meditation itself. The honesty present in the verse encourages the reader to grasp the spirit conveyed therein and continue the meditation him/herself. Rather than teach or instruct, these meditations invite to share. However, the way to perfection is a process involving many periods of struggle and wrestling for God's love. Such painful interior clashes are part of the Carthusian life as well, whose terror is not glossed over in the poetry.

> Born of the earth, and earthly-born,
> Made to be loved, unloved, forlorn,
> This Heart cries out, in pieces torn,
> Within, within.[117]

At times the pain is so great that it is difficult to detect the original love which caused it all: the poet fiercely fights for access to that love, be it perhaps in the form of some little sign. However, such signs are rarely offered to the searching soul in despair, the soul having to cross the desert by its own powers.

The themes which occur frequently in his meditative poetry reflect the fields and ground of meditation which continuously form the fertile soil for prayer in a Carthusian monastery. Thus the poems on grace and providence reflect the poet's unbounded belief in divine providence, God's guiding hand, which is always there. Grace is of particular importance. The poems mirror a strong awareness of how essential it is to use grace well, to be aware of the grace given. Repeatedly the poet points out that other chances might be given at other times, but a missed chance, a misused one, is a chance lost for ever.

The meditations on time, death and afterlife mirror that time is much more consciously experienced in a contemplative order than elsewhere: the monk is highly aware of how important it is to use our share in time well, which makes every single moment precious. Simultaneously, however, there is a certain timelessness to be observed in the contemplative monastery. There, life has not altered over the course of the years; it is still the same as in the early days of the Order. This duality of time, its non-existence and yet its tremendous importance is mirrored in many a poem of Alun Idris', offering insight into its two-fold nature. Death, as the doorway to heaven, loses its frightening aspect. It is the afterlife which the contemplative monk is striving for, which turns death into a happy occasion, into his second birthday even, the birth in God. The bliss of heaven is a great reality in the contemplative monastery, and so is the terror of purgatory and the dread of damnation. The poems reflect the

---

[117] "Trinity Sunday" (*Threshold*, 78f.).

monk's belief that these terms are not of an abstract nature but are real. Alun Idris shows a strong awareness of the effectfulness of sin, which can ruin the whole of one's afterlife.

Most of this poetry can also be considered as a form of prayer. A distinction has been made between so-called community prayers and personal prayers. The short and rather simple community prayers can be used in church, reminding one very much of prayers recited during mass. Their simplicity and straightforwardness makes them all the more suitable for hymns, which they often are; the poet frequently composed a tune for the prayer, or used an already existing melody to be sung with the poem. As the language of love, music reinforces the affective level of the hymn, and allows the praying soul to burn with fervour all the more. The so-called personal prayers are on a much higher literary level. They are addressed to God, to Mary or a saint and represent the fruits of intense religious experience. The writing of poetry at Sélignac provided an outlet for Alun Idris' religious conviction and enthusiasm on the one hand, and a vent for accumulated feelings, thoughts etc. on the other, as a result of the impossibility to communicate them verbally. We find many poems directly addressed to Jesus Christ, the only companion in the cell; they become a very lively form of prayer.[118]

Love is of outstanding importance to the contemplative monk. Without the presence of love life in the monastery would not be possible, as love is the driving force for the monk's whole being there. The joy experienced at the presence of God, the tremendous love the poet feels to the Lord finds expression in the poetry.[119]

From the literary point of view Alun Idris' Carthusian poetry is characterized by a strong sense of perfection: the poet is always trying to find the precise expression and takes particular care in the metrical regularity of his poems. The style he uses can be called an archaic one, old forms like "thou", "art", "canst" etc. appear with such regularity that they can be called a distinctive feature of his verse.[120] These forms aim to underline the solemnity conveyed, the grandeur of the Lord. It should not be forgotten that the Bible, which uses, of course, a similarly elevated style, is read with such frequency in the charterhouse that the language used therein to describe those holy incidents was certainly influential on the poet. In order to keep the rhythm regular, all forms of phonetical licence are employed, such as apheresis (e.g. in 'tis), apocope (th'eternal) or syncope (maj'sty, pow'r, o'er), which also become an outstanding feature of his verse.

Alun Idris uses changes in rhythm to underline a change in mood, and often succeeds in conveying the tone he aims to imply. Rhyme and rhythm are very important. When they are jettisoned he feels there is a danger of not being able to maintain the link between the harmony of creation and the order and beauty of poetry (cf. interview, 13.8.1990). Another characteristic feature of his verse is the careful choice of diction, using rare words frequently. The imagery employed often succeeds in reflecting and intensifying the idea expressed.

---

[118] "All Saints' Day" (2), "The eve of my 27th birthday anniversary" (4), "Christmas Night" (8) or "Ash Wednesday" (25) are a few examples of such deeply prayerful poems.
[119] See chapter 3.1.4.
[120] Archaic forms appear in his English poetry only, not in the Welsh nor in the French.

In his early period, different stanza forms are employed: the stanza form of the iambic quatrain written in tetrameter ("Christus Rex", *Threshold* 5f.) or pentameter ("All Saints' Day", *Threshold*, 1), united by cross rhyme, is often used. The poet also frequently combines two quatrains to form one stanza ("Septuagesima", *Threshold*, 18). The iambic rhythm almost always prevails, only rarely is a different rhythm used. Another stanza form to be found in his poetry is the quatrain consisting of three rhyming lines in pentamer, and a closing dimeter line which does not rhyme ("At night (mid-lent)", *Threshold*, 30). The common measure occurs with frequency as well ("Lines jotted in retreat", *Threshold*, 33f.). Many poems employ a refrain, which is used as a means of emphasis, in particular the incremental refrain to create a special effect ("Ash Wednesday" *Threshold*, 25). The French poems are usually written in alexandrines.

During the last two years at the charterhouse the poet started to write sonnets as well, which was to become his favourite stanza form. While at the beginning we only find sonnets occasionally interspersed in his poetry, they grow steadily in number with time. It is the Shakespearian sonnet which he uses, although at times a break occurs after the second quatrain, which unites the closing six lines, and is thus reminiscent of the Italian form.

It has been demonstrated that the writing of poems as such does not represent an obstacle to the quest for spiritual perfection. The poet uses his poetic vein to create beauty for God. However, the situation becomes problematical as regards the publication of poetry written in a Carthusian monastery. One has to bear in mind the Carthusian motto, outlining the objective of their vocation: "Non sanctos patefacere sed multos sanctos facere." - "To make many saints but not to publicise them" (Lockhart 1985, 35). The Carthusians do not invite attention, although their way of life might arouse curiosity. Naturally, the superiors discerned some danger in Alun Idris' poetic output and did not regard his creativity benevolently, in particular the idea of publishing the verse was not met with approval. Such oppression of the creative urge involves, of course, immense suffering, most of all to the poet who does not see any contradiction between the two vocations ("Cease not, sweet Flood. / Full Hippocrene, fill me with God").[121] The poet writes for God alone: "For Thee alone I write, my Lord ... My Lord, / For Thee alone shall burn each unread word."[122]

Alun Idris becomes aware of the problem his poetry has caused for his superiors, who consider the two vocations as irreconcilable. He therefore decides to stop writing completely, so as not to endanger his religious vocation: "I WILL NOT SIN", as we explicitly read in "After receiving news" (*Threshold*, 51), emphasizing his decision not to write poetry again.[123] Nevertheless, his Carthusian vocation could not be saved.

---

[121] "Sacred Heart" (*Threshold*, 80).
[122] "Lines written on Feast of the Compassion of the Blessed Virgin" (*Threshold*, 42).
[123] "Regret" (*Beyond*, 114) describes the difficulties he faced during that period.

3.2. THE TRAPPIST PERIOD

2 General view of La Grande Trappe

3.2.1. POETRY AS A MIRROR OF TRAPPIST LIFE

3.2.1.1. THE "DAILY ROUTINE"

Most of the poems dealt with in this chapter were written at the Trappist monastery of Roscrea, describing the daily routine there. They offer glimpses of the silent life of a Trappist monk, inspired by events which characterize the day-to-day life in the monastery. As a result of the limited number of poems written at La Grande Trappe, we do not find many which give an idea on the daily life led there. The first two examples given, however, were written at La Trappe, the former being one of the first poems Alun Idris composed there; it is called "After trying on the new habit" (*World*, 1f.):

    Seven years have flowed since I knelt on this grass
    And, lying on my elbow, read a book
    Beside thee, little lake, as thou didst pass
    As now, 'neath Rancé's bridge. Again I look
    At what I looked on then, and little knew
    While looking, what strange look Time's visage held
    Well veiled. O! little stream, the only voice
    And ear in this great tomb, how oft beheld

> Mute saints their hooded heads in this thy noise.
> This morn I wore a second what for days
> And hours and years and ages whole have worn
> Th'unmarried fathers that have walked these ways
> And of whose sexless progeny is born
> Another and another dumb from birth
> Who multiplied in turn, and filled the earth.

The poem was triggered off by his trying on the new habit for the very first time, yet it also offers a few impressions of life at La Trappe. The rhythm of the very first line attracts attention: starting with an inverted first foot, three stressed syllables follow, "Seven years have flowed", which adds a tone of solemnity to the time span indicated, as well as underlining the length of these seven years. A short pause separates this first part of l.1 from the second, which consists of two anapaestic feet. This pattern conveys a feeling of rapid movement, which thereby contrasts sharply with the solemn, calm progression of the first half of l.1. This contrast in rhythm helps to underline that, although many years have passed, the poet yet vividly remembers his first encounter with the monastery. The clear memory of those days is also indicated by the inversion of the fourth foot in l.3 and the spondaic first foot in l.4, "As thou didst pass / As now", which makes his memory sound all the more vivid. Ll.6 and 7 attract attention because of the accumulation of stresses: both the third and the fourth foot of l.6 are spondaic, just like the first two of l.7, what "strange look Time's visage held / Well veiled". The idea of the absolute unpredictability of the happenings of his past is firmly implied, - one could not have foreseen what time and providence had pre-arranged for him. The poem which appears to be a sonnet at first sight is not, as there is one line too many: "At what I looked on then, and little knew" (l.5) is injected into the poem as an extra line, a line apart. It could have been intended to underline how absolutely impossible it was to foresee events; however, equally possible is a faux pas in the course of composition, as normally the poet takes much care in the form he uses. The imagery used to describe the little stream near the monastery at the end of the second quatrain strongly implies that the Trappists are a silent order: "O! little stream, the only voice / And ear in this great tomb, how oft beheld / Mute saints their hooded heads in this thy noise." The stream is both "voice" and "ear": the only voice to be heard, the only ear which listens to the silent words of the "Mute saints". The image of "this great tomb" is very forceful, and powerfully suggests how forgotten their silent lives are by the rest of mankind. In the third quatrain the poet remembers all those monks who went that way before, wearing this same habit through long ages, while he is only at the very beginning, he has only just started, - "I wore a second". "Dumb from birth" refers to the extremely silent life they lead. Trappists hardly ever talk. The "sexless progeny" of "th'unmarried fathers" has "multiplied in turn, and filled the earth": the Trappists have their own means to multiply on earth, which is suggested by using the imagery of progeny in a slightly altered and adapted form.

The second example, which was also written at La Trappe, reflects the often extreme climatic conditions in the monastery. The sonnet called "The upturned fingers" (*World*, 6) illustrates the daily penance in winter caused by the lack of heating:

> The cold is cold. It was so yesterday
> And yesteryear in this cold house of Cold.
> Yet - strange! - unchilled we plod our cloistered way
> Barefoot in sandals, nor doth one here hold
> A handkerchief against a streaming nose ...
> 'Tis strange! 'Tis oddly strange. Whereas before,
> 'Mid corridors of heaters, these wee toes
> Would through a fondled body keenly gnaw
> With one degree of Comfortlessness heard,
> Here once, but once, have I e'er seen it mimed,
> The sign that signs this Arctic in a word -
> And 'twas by me - and 'twas indeed well-timed,
> For 'twas too cool one Rancéist too warm
> Who with closed doors found th'ice above the norm.

The cold has not changed over the years, - it is still as penetrating and harsh as it was in ages past. The sonnet visualizes the extreme customs of the monks, walking "barefoot in sandals" or living in a room with "th'ice above the norm". The body has to become used to the cold, and it certainly does to some extent. In the second quatrain the poet remembers how in his own past he froze fairly easily, - a room could not be warm enough for his "fondled body"; now, however, the situation has changed; he does not experience the cold in the way he used to. Only on one occasion, as we are told towards the end of the sonnet, did he use what is mentioned in the title of the poem, "the upturned fingers", which refers to the sign for cold. A note in brackets explains that one member of the noviciate had a passion for open doors and windows, even in winter, which is extreme behaviour even for a Trappist monk.

The splendour of a high mass celebrated at Roscrea led to the composition of the following meditation simply called "Pontifical High Mass" (*World*, 47). The poet meditates on the question of for whom it is that man creates beauty. Several different suggestions occur to his mind:

> The beauty that man makes, is it for man [corr.]
> Or for the hidden cherubs that, men say,
> Are flitting 'twixt our quires, and whose wings fan
> The gentle clouds of opium that convey
> Our prayers euphoric to th'Ancient of Days;

"There is a mystical action involved when one is in choir", the poet explains in a letter to the present writer, and he continues:

> One is actually representing the church as the higher choirs of angels who spend their time adoring the divine majesty, and not having any ministery, except this ministery of grace [...] During these moments of liturgical praise one is doing someting angelic, one has a role in this mystical body which is unseen, very deep and very powerful. The angels are there with us. (letter, 26.8.1991)

The presence of these "hidden cherubs" is firmly implied in this first quatrain. The "clouds of opium" are, of course, the clouds of incense, referred to in psalm 140:2, which talks about prayer rising up as incense (cf. letter, 26.8.1991).

The poet continues to mention other possible causes for creating beauty: "for the growing souls" (l.6), i.e. for the children and young adolescents, the schoolboys in particular, as there is a school adjacent to the monastery at Roscrea; or "for the vulgum pecus who,/ Though dust, are dust divine" (ll.9f.), which refers to the ordinary people, who are very precious; on a Sunday many would come to church. The closing couplet presents the ultimate possibility, "Or is it also sometimes for Thee, King / Of hosts who smile to think we think we sing?". It appears that at times we forget for whom we actually celebrate mass, why we prepare it in such an elaborate, painstaking way as is required for the celebration of a pontifical high mass, with the abbot presiding, wearing his mitre and carrying his crozier. In Roscrea, in particular, much emphasis is laid on an appropriate celebration of the mass, the monks taking great care in making mass an aesthetical experience.

The split nature of human beings is central to a sonnet entitled "Meeting St. Aelred" (*World*, 47),[124] which talks about the two halves of the human psyche, "Animus and Anima". Finding one's other half, the union of the two components, allows new forces to stir: "And in this two-fold hollowness to let / Well up a double fulness made of Worth". The search to find this other half is not only an interior quest, seeking one's inner equilibrium, but can also be seen symbolically: the search is normally performed in human society, - it refers to finding one's partner in life; however, it is possible to find one's other half in God as well.

> And yet, good teacher, thou'ldst here seem to say
> That in our hidden, hooded, hardened rows,
> 'Twixt like and like, I say, a little ray
> Of sacred Amicitia oft flows.
> And yet 'tis strange, 'tis oddly strange, 'tis hard
> To know how the sealed heart can share its nard.

The apostrophe in l.9 is addressed to St. Aelred, who was aware of the importance of friendship: he sensed that it was possible to be very close to each other even in silence. The alliteration in "*h*idden, *h*ooded, *h*ardened rows", however, suggests a mood of scepticism: the monks' hearts are hidden, not at all revealed to their brethren. "Hooded" implies that their hearts could perhaps be uncovered, though "hardened" suggests that that would be fairly difficult. "Hardened" implies that the monks are like statues in their silence, not exchanging words at all. The "nard" of the closing couplet is a reference to Mark 14:3, and also to John 12:3, where we read about Mary bringing a very costly perfume to Jesus, an oil of pure nard. In both biblical passages, there is explicit reference to the odour of the precious oil. Mary shared the most valuable thing she had with Jesus, and similarly the monks share the most

---

[124] St.Aelred, the famous Cistercian twelfth century abbot of Rievaulx, is one of the most esteemed Cistercian spiritual writers.

precious thing they have, the heart, with each other, despite the fact that their heart is sealed by the rule of silence. The notion of the odour, however, points to the possibility of sharing, even without the use of words.

The study of St. Aelred had a profound effect on the poet. It made him realize how distinguished the family was he had joined, the great succession in which he was following (cf. letter, 26.8.1991). "Getting to know Aelred better" (*World*, 48f.) describes this experience, pointing out that in the person of Aelred so many things were combined which spoke to his heart: "For where else on this Trappist globe, where, where / Could these three paths that in thee did unite / Be held so clearly 'neath my frightened sight?" The "three paths" in question are those of the erudite, the spiritual and that of the loving father of his monastic family (cf. letter, 26.8.1991). Aelred was a classicist and a very erudite monk. "This emphasis on love, spiritual fatherhood, fellowship, and relationship between the souls was something which spoke to me very strongly" (letter, 26.8.1991). The "frightened sight" implies how much he was aware of what the future might hold.

How much Alun Idris had been formed by the silent years both in the charterhouse and at La Trappe is apparent from a meditation called "Vigils" (*World*, 55), which powerfully describes the peace felt in those tranquil moments, celebrating the company of the Lord. Vigil is the term for the night office in the Cistercian order. After the night office there is a period of meditation, followed by a quiet rumination on scripture until dawn. "That time is very special, it is a wonderful time to just keep vigil with the Lord, the Lord's presence, to be aware that one is representing the sleeping church. It is a sweet time" (letter, 27.9.1991).

> There are some moments 'mid the times we live
> That in their richness bear a double load
> Of living; and there are some hours that give
> To other hours a pause on their wild road.
> Nay more, at whiles, as earth dreams on and on
> Towards its rude awakening, an eye
> That, open still, keeps watch till dark is done
> With all its deep-drowsed myst'ries, 'wakes the sky [corr.]
> And, gazing yet, beholds what brings for some
> An ecstasy ne'er known before, a pain
> That others never tasted, and sees come
> The hour that bids its sweetness melt again
> Into the parting night from which it came
> When it burned not, when naught burned, save this flame.

The sonnet is characterized by a very calm and peaceful rhythm, the poet's happiness at experiencing such "sweetness" being felt in these lines. It is a silent celebration of his being in good company, keeping vigil with "this flame".

The first quatrain meditates on the "richness" of some quiet moments; the enjambement of l.2 surprises and bids the reader pause after "Of living", which places additional emphasis on these words: life is experienced and felt more intensely then. L.4 has a medial pause, which reinforces the "pause" mentioned there. The rhythm accelerates from the second quatrain onwards, - we find more short sentences and phrases. It is a sweet delight which is conveyed, an inward joy, a happiness which is felt when the poet describes these precious moments of keeping vigil: "an eye / That, open still, keeps watch till dark is done / With all its deep-drowsed myst'ries, 'wakes the sky". (ll.6-8) Apposition helps to convey a certain excitement, while the long vowels at the beginning of 1.8 suggest the vastness of mysteries, of the great unknown, which dominate the night. The day to come is full of mystery as well, - an "ecstasy" for some, while painful to others. At last the eye "sees come / The hour that bids its sweetness melt again" (ll.11f.): the hour of transition from darkness to light, pre-dawn to morning, approaches, in which the sweetness of that moment of gradual awakening, the sweetness of keeping vigil, will evaporate with the parting night from which it came. This sweetness belongs to the night, once the night is gone, it will disappear as well. In that night only the sanctuary flame is burning quietly: keeping vigil is similar to burning like a flame, offering oneself in sacrifice and vigil. There is also an implication that we came from eternal night: in that night there was nothing but the one living fire of God; everything else was ignited by this fire.

The importance and the beauty of contemplative prayer is central to "An hour in the Presence (beside the contemplative nuns)" (*World*, 58). A group of contemplative nuns had been present at a conference on contemplative life. They used to spend long periods meditating, one hour in the morning, one hour in the evening (cf. letter, 27.9.1991). Their presence in the monastery apparently reminded the poet of the importance of contemplation, its centrality in life, everything else was completely secondary:

> The quality of moments is not sure
> As is their quantity, e'en though this last
> Be sure to One alone in His one, pure
> Eternal instant, whence He views us cast
> Our splashes on the shore of Chronos' sea.
> But when I see and feel what in one hour
> Can lie, hath lain, and o'er each folded knee
> 'Neath wimpled tent-wear buried, Will's own pow'r
> Doth doubly daily bid to lie, I fear
> Lest I forget th'encounter this night known.
> For I perceived, respiring thus so near [corr.]
> The essence of our meaning, that outblown
> Were many, many urgencies that called
> T'wards walling out e'en that for which we're walled.

The idea of providence is firmly present in the first quatrain, as in "His one, pure / Eternal instant" God has known our lives before, everything is foreseen by Him. The metaphor used to describe His watching us suggests the smallness and insignificance of man in comparison with God: all we do is "cast / Our splashes on the shore of Chronos' sea", a line where the fricative consonants almost make audible the attempts to move on in the water. With 1.6, however, the poet turns his attention to these contemplative nuns whose own will it is to "*doubly daily bid to lie*", to contemplate the Lord twice a day. They are always faithful to these precious hours of prayer. A certain insisting tone is noticeable in this accumulation of plosives and the /l/, -

- there is no exception to the rule. The pauses in 1.7 suggest the long tradition which they have followed. "Can lie, hath lain, and o'er each folded knee / 'Neath wimpled tent-wear buried" - the imagery used describes the nuns in prayer, who devote themselves entirely to God, who are seemingly "buried" in the eyes of other people. Their presence reminded the poet of the "essence of our meaning", which is to contemplate the Lord. The closing couplet stresses the problem which is touched upon in other poems as well, - that even in a monastery other activities can become more urgent, more important that the one activity "for which we're walled": contemplation. This is the irony contained in the closing line: it seems as though contemplation, for which they are walled, was the one thing which is walled out.

"After night office and meditation" (*World*, 58) describes the role of the monastery for the contemplative monk:

> Each day there are so many things that come
> To wake our fastened eyelids. As men sleep,
> We taste already th'earnest of our Home
> In this its antechamber. Our eyes peep [corr.]
> Behind the stars that watch with us, ere too
> They fall asleep in watching, for e'en they
> Burn less long than the Am that pierces through [corr.]
> These aeviternities sparked in a day.
> There are but seven in the sacramental scheme,
> And yet, as now I ope my pores to Heav'n
> And, empty for a day, receive the gleam
> That here escapes the channels of the sev'n,
> I am aware as I stand on the shore
> Of hours, that beams have songs through which some snore.

The capitalized "Home" in 1.3 refers to our final home,[125] i.e. heaven; its "antechamber" is the monastery, although the quatrain also suggests that sleep functions as its "antechamber" as well. There is one further ambiguity in 1.6 where it is not fully obvious what exactly "they" refers to: it seems as though the poet was referring to "our eyes", which at last fall asleep in watching, although, as the lines continue, it becomes clear that it is the stars which "Burn less long than the Am". The "Am" is, of course, a reference to the great "I am" pronounced by God (Exodus 3:14). The "aeviternities" echo a theological term: man's soul is aeviternal, it has a beginning but no end.

"Our eyes peep / Behind the stars that watch us", a line which implies that there is something mysterious about the stars: regarding a star in contemplation, when keeping the vigil, implies looking at time; one is observing the past, beyond time, and therefore looking towards God, the author of the stars, who existed long before any star was sparkling, long before any human soul was "sparked". The expression "These aeviternities sparked in a day" emphasizes the relativity of the stars in comparison with their creator. We have been "sparked" in a day. We had a starting point in time, and we shall go on, like the stars, though even longer than they do, for our souls will not be annihilated.

---

[125] "Th'earnest of our Home" is an indirect reference to 2 Cor 1:22 and 5:5 (cf. letter, 27.9.1991).

The third quatrain meditates on how God's grace comes to us in different forms, one of these forms being the silence of the night, the blessing of the vigil period. The poet has always felt that this early period between rising and dawn, the vigil period, is very sacred and holy, both in the monastery and outside in nature. It is special to Cistercian life. At this point of the day, it seems as though the soul was particularly receptive, "empty for the day, receive the gleam": the soul is open to receive grace at that point, because the body is still, the heart is beating slowly after night rest, the body is fasting; the monk is empty to receive the gift of the day. God's grace comes in different forms, "the gleam / That here escapes the channels of the sev'n" (ll.11f.): He imparts truth to us through scripture. Spiritual reading in silence becomes a sacramental channel, a real channel of grace. "The shore / Of hours" refers to the border line between sleeping and waking hours: a threshold, a new land, a new day is approaching; it is the frontier of non-being (sleep) and new being, the life of a new day. The closing line implies that those sacred moments can remain unobserved, unreceived, untasted, unfelt, even unsensed by some who snore through them, because they are not awake: some are thus not open to grace at that particular point, unaware of its existence. It can happen to contemplative monks as well.

The verse referred to in the title of the sonnet called "Holy Rule, chapter 7, verse 56" (*World*, 59) is of special importance to the contemplative monk: the ninth degree of humility tells the monk how to control his tongue and keep silence, not saying anything unless asked.[126]

> There is a word that changes all my words
> To list'ners, for I 'gin to hear the truth
> In these consignèd messengers that cords
> Have plucked along the ages since the youth
> Of this monastic genus, in the heart
> Of every hooded voyager within.
> For in the hours 'neath which I saw depart
> The doubled fulness of two dwellings, thin,
> Nay, microscopic was the leak through which
> The wastage drained me. For 'twas my own soul
> That hovered o'er the moving of a switch
> That could record, nay, densify the whole
> Or lose for e'er the harmony engraved
> On this band by unbinding soon depraved.

"Every hooded voyager within" in l.6 is a metaphor for the journey inwards, the discovery of one's own interior sea. It is the object of monastic life, although, of course, the whole of mankind is engaged on this journey, to meet God in the depths of one's innermost being. The "doubled fulness of two dwellings" (l.8), which is explained in a note attached to the poem [corr.] as referring to Sélignac and La Trappe, echoes the density of prayer and thought which had been stored up and accumulated in those almost ten years in France. Here in Ireland the poet apparently seemed to be at a loss in the process of speaking. Speaking was slightly less rigorously handled at Roscrea, "thin, / Nay, microscopic was the leak through which / The

---

[126] "Nonus humilitatis gradus est, si linguam ad loquendum prohibeat monachus et, taciturnitatem habens, usque ad interrogationem non loquatur." (Seidle 1978, 88).

wastage drained me". However small it was, it existed and had an impact on him. The metaphor introduced in 1.10 presents the idea that it is only one little decision which had opened the leak, which had allowed the process to start, a "switch". "The harmony engraved / On this band" was still there. Turning the switch on, which means talking, could "record, nay, densify the whole / Or lose for e'er the harmony engraved". Playing the band too often affects its quality. The band was unbound, the danger to be "soon depraved" was strongly felt. It was a crucial switching on each time the poet talked. The possibility of communication seemed to destroy what was on the band before. It is the sacred silence which makes the monk seek inwards, find God and speak to Him alone; doubtless, a great deal is lost by talking. In the contemplative life one is habitually orientated towards God and interior prayer; however, being involved with the human side of things more than before means that one's attention is drawn in a different direction. "The moving of the switch" also suggests Alun Idris' departure from La Trappe, as this was the point when his life started to change radically.

The timelessness of prayer, which has continued in the Trappist monastery for so many years, is central to "'Clocking up the hours'" (*World*, 59), which suggests how much prayer is going on day and night.

> 'Tis well, 'tis well to be thus ever bound
> To turn upon the axle of a gong.
> For in the gentle echoes of one sound
> Are called, recalled th'antiquities of Song
> That have in eightfold intervals all time
> Since our far Syrian birth, their pauses giv'n
> To Hurry's respiration. Now, as climb
> High, high the depths of chasmic Age, half-riv'n
> Are these great clouds of incense that them bear   [corr.]
> On chanted memories of ones that were
> Awhile before us on this road, to where
> They are, where trancèd melodies now stir
> No more the hearts that dreamt them, for withal
> Are strains unthought that nought save th'eons call.

The bell reappears in its role of "managing director", whose echoes urge the monks to gather for prayer. The bell is situated in the center, the monks rotate around it, as is implied in the first two lines. The chime of the bell also echoes its long tradition, a tradition which originates in Syria and Egypt ("Syrian birth"). The "depths of chasmic Age" in 1.8 suggests the prayer of all the monks throughout the ages: this pattern has gone on for so many years, the psalms which used to be prayed by the monks in the Syrian desert still being chanted today. Therefore, they are somehow still coming from the past. It is a timeless prayer, as it has been the prayer of so many generations. The "clouds of incense that them bear" (1.9) is ambiguous, as the pronoun "them" refers to "th'antiquities of song" but also to the "depths of chasmic age". Both imply, however, the connection with the past, which is now rising up towards heaven. It seems as though their past prayer was still ascending, therefore going back to them, "to where / They are, where trancèd melodies now stir": the "chanted memories of ones that were / Awhile before us on this road" can entrance us, as old Gregorian melodies do, but they do not stir them anymore: "now stir / No more the hearts that dreamt them, for withal / Are strains unthought that nought save th'eons call." These chants have no longer power to stir them anymore, although the monks were entranced by them when still on earth. The song of time, the song of eternity, of the unseen world beyond is what is calling forth the melodies, giving them the power they exert on us today.

"'Non Christianus, sed Ciceronianus.'" (*World*, 60) was written after talking to a Carmelite, as we are told in a note in brackets: she used to be a teacher before she decided to enter the community - "erstwhile teacher (now from sight / Of children and their clamour barred)", in order to experience the void which is necessary to provide the soil for the Lord to till.

> And thou art right, my sister, thou art right.
> The value of the utterness of void
> Doth from thee, erstwhile teacher (now from sight [corr.]
> Of children and their clamour barred), the cloyed [corr.]
> Attirance of starved, stifled letters push
> Behind horizons massive: these that break
> At thy long hours of knocking. Now the rush
> Of knowings from thy brain no strain shall take.
> But having all its forces aimed at one,
> One only point within, nay, far beyond
> Its innermost, it hath without undone
> Left all that could be filtered past this bond [corr.]
> That seems, alas, through thee to come again
> Its hold o'er Mind's withholdings to regain.

How much he agrees with what the nun told him is explicitly expressed in the very first line. The repetition, the apostrophe, and the fact that it is an endstopped line reinforce the firm impact her message had on him. She experienced the "value of the utterness of void" (l.2), which she preferred to anything else. Having talked to her made the poet realize how the emptiness of pure contemplation penetrates behind "massive" horizons, as, for instance, the temptation of doing academic work, which was certainly there, the "A*tt*irance of *s*tarved, *s*ti*fl*ed le*tt*ers": the plosives and fricatives suggest a notion of agitation and disquiet, contrary to the peacefulness of contemplation. This attraction for intellectual work suddenly cloyed as a result of hearing her words. "These [horizons massive] that break / At thy long hours of knocking" describes the Carmelite nun's experience: she had been working as a teacher for a good while. In that period she had "knocked" at the monastery door, - she desired to enter. In her decision to return to the void of prayer, the emptiness of anything else but prayer, her distant horizons of academic work had been shattered. "Now the rush / Of knowings from thy b*rain* no st*rain* shall take" (ll.7f.). Being involved with academic work, in her case with teaching, means that there is hardly time available for God, but now she is liberated from the "strain". The interior rhyme in that line emphasizes that she is completely at the Lord's disposal. The third quatrain presents the beauty of her availability now, as all her brain's forces are "aimed at one", fully and exclusively concentrating on the Lord. "It hath without undone / Left all that could be filtered" (ll.11f.): by leaving undone all that work outside her mind, not projecting herself outwards at all, everything is now enclosed within her. The mind is kept free for God. "This bond", however, reappears again. It is now perceived by the poet himself, as is implied in the final line. He feels the bond which binds the monk to God, to be for Him alone.

As the title indicates, "A lecture on the history of the mansion" (*World*, 28f.) stirred the writing of this sonnet. The building in question is the mansion of Roscrea, which belongs to the community. The poem starts with almost excessive use of sound symbolism and alliteration:

> So many eyes have looked upon these hills
> And grown and dwindled 'neath this selfsame star
> That, smiling with same visage, here distils   [corr.]
> Still on our risings settings from afar,
> Where others were, where others ere they were
> Breathed too this gentle air that bids us die,
> And in th'unhurried war-march, some sounds stir
> E'en now the ears that hear these reaped fields lie.
> O children of a summer's day, did ye
> At times the winter's hungry gnaw too feel,
> And when still green did ye too stop to see
> The meadows ye had covered? Did ye steal
> A sheaf of Pleasure ere ye walked, walked on   [corr.]
> Along these walks to where the years have gone?

In l.1 and l.4 the voiced /z/ fricative dominates, while in l.2 and 3 the voiceless version /s/ is of predominant power (with the exception of "vi*s*age" and "distil*s*"). The "selfsame star", which is the sun, of course, is "smiling": this is a Welsh influence as in Welsh the sun smiles rather than shines. The poem continues with more alliteration and assonance: "*W*here others *w*ere, *w*here others ere they *w*ere / Brea*th*ed too *th*is gentle air *th*at bi*d*s us *d*ie" (ll.5f.): the almost exact repetition of the first half of the line in the second half places strong emphasis on "ere", though it is not too stimulating in its effect. The internal rhyme "were - air" is a pleasant surprise, however, followed by a phrase full of contrast which comes as a shock; the sober way of presenting that truth quite unexpectedly surprises the reader: "this gentle air that bids us die". Indeed, it seems as though the idea of approaching death was ever present to a Cistercian monk. For him death has lost its frightening power as it is the door to afterlife, which he is ultimately aiming at. In a Cistercian abbey the monks walk one behind the other, the elders go first, the younger ones behind. In the same way, the older ones go to the tomb before their younger brethren, but eventually they are all approaching the ultimate goal. The following two lines are highly metaphorical: "And in th'unhurried war-march, *s*ome *s*ounds *s*tir / *E*'en now the *e*ars that h*ea*r th*e*se r*ea*ped fields lie" (ll.7f.). The monks' lives that have walked their way before us have been reaped, like the fields which they themselves have harvested before. The fields contain the harvest of their souls. The "ears" refer to those who listen to the silence of graves, meditating on the last things.

The third quatrain uses striking imagery: the metaphor of the "children of a summer's day" refers to a period of great growth and flowering in the Cistercian Order, - the great old days when the monks were fervent in their belief and the monastery was abounding with young people. They were full of the spirit of their youth, enthusiastic about their lives led for God only. It was summer compared with the present situation. As the author was writing these lines, winter has come.

The "children of a summer's day" is also a metaphor for those who are gifted with a special grace of God. Being used to warmth, i.e. filled with divine emotion, the divine presence, "Winter's hungry gnaw" refers to those painful periods when doubts come up and gnaw, "gnaw" being a most striking expression to describe what happens to your belief and conviction then. It must be added, however, that doubts as such are not necessarily negative, as Alun Idris himself pointed out in the interview with his brother:

> Doubt is very healthy. But there is a doubt within faith. There is a doubt to strengthen faith. Fides quaerens intellectum, the faith looking for justification for what it believes. I think that basic doubt is necessary in the spiritual life. (Jones, Elwyn, producer 1981)

"Winter's hungry gnaw" can also be taken on a literal level: the winter in that part of Ireland where Roscrea Abbey is situated is usually rather cold; the interior of the building is freezing, outside biting winds blow. These Celtic winters must have scarred our ancestors as well; indeed, the Cistercians are famous for their harsh regime. "Did ye too ..." suggests the idea of the timelessness of monastic life: becoming a monk means to enter a tradition, a family, with all your ancestors being linked to you. "[...] stop to see / The meadows ye had covered?" contains the suggestion of looking back over the time one has spent already. These lines convey the linkage between past generations and future ones: "it is really a belonging to the ground in a very deep, certain way in a Cistercian monastery, belonging to the place itself, belonging to time because time is beaten out by the rhythm of the bell, the same bell which has rung out, called the succeeding generations to prayer, the same prayer basically which they have chanted" (letter, 10.12.1989). The monks of past ages walked along these paths on which their feet are treading now. They are wearing their habit: "You cannot but feel very close to them. When you pass their graves you see their pilgrimage is over, they are still resting. There can be a very strong link with them."

A monk is regularly called back to prayer. Nothing should take precedence over prayer, for the monk represents the whole of creation before God, at all hours (cf. letter, 10.12.1989). This pattern of life, which was followed by numberless ancestors, applies to the modern monk as well. The possibility of losing one's first zeal, which had menaced earlier generations too, is still actual today, - a problem which the forbears mastered. To think of "children of a summer's day" is a way to memorize the glorious past, emphasizing that they tried not to lose that first zeal, that first love. However, to the poet it seems as though this danger of losing the original zeal had already, to some extent at least, effected the contemplative life in Roscrea. It seemed to him that parts of the tradition had gone. He felt that something very precious had been lost (cf. letter, 10.12.1989).[127]

The closing lines suggest a certain innocent pleasure which can be enjoyed by anyone gazing at the beauties which are common property: the air, flowers, fields, simple joys granted by God and shared by all of God's creatures. Roscrea is a very pleasant place, a fine monastery with beautiful gardens. "I felt the timelessness of pleasure, experience which comes to all children of time" (letter, 10.12.1989). "And when still green" is ambiguous in meaning: on the one hand it refers to youth and one's youthful enthusiasm, on the other it implies a state of experiencing God's grace, being filled with true life, therefore the adjective "green" is used. The question arises, however, whether one ever ceases to be green if one has grown in grace.[128] "There is a certain freshness in monastic life; it's all very old but it's always very new: one is always getting up again after falling, one is always meeting God again in every new office which starts, as though it were the first one ever" (letter, 10.12.1989).

Sunday is the day when the monks do not have to do much manual work, - it is reserved for the Lord only. The special nature of that day is meditated upon in a sonnet simply called "Sunday" (*World*, 35f.) where we read:

> There are some hours that travel doubly blest
> Across our spiral path; there is a morn
> That wakes not as its brethren, whose behest
> Pulls oft against the grain, for sometimes dawn
> Bespeaks the pain soothed by the eve awhile.
> There is an hour for each thing 'neath the sun,
> But only one, and this too we beguile
> In doing then what then could rest undone.
> We merit ill in working at repose
> And guiltiness ill-rests our heaviest load.
> Yet this aged brazen song today still knows
> The sweetness of a linger ere this road
> That onward walks without us, call us on,
> And bids us naught but look one hour, just one.

The diction employed to describe the nature of Sunday in the first five lines mirrors the solemnity and venerability of this day, as, for instance, "blest", "morn", "behest", "oft", "bespeaks", "soothed" or "eve". The pause in l.2 adds additional emphasis to the message conveyed in the first one and a half lines, indicating the blessing this day conveys. "Our spiral path" suggests the cyclic progress of time, one week following the other, forever returning to the first day of the week, though having slightly progressed on the axis of time. Ll.4 and 5 make the reader feel that the night is very short in a Cistercian monastery, which makes it at

---

[127] This clearly refers to the process of aggiornamento after Vatican II, which was a painful experience in many communities.
[128] The concept of *viriditas* ("greenness") was peculiar to Hildegard of Bingen. The Celts were close to nature, which explains the affinity between the Welsh, Irish and Gaelic spirituality and that of Hildegard. The idea of "greenness" is also reflected in "Corpus Christi" (*World*, 40) where we read: "There is an ageing in our growing old / That need not be, and many have grown young." What is important is never to lose one's enthusiasm, never to get used to divine grace, as this might cause stagnation of one's spiritual development.

times difficult and painful to rise ("whose behest / Pulls oft against the grain"). L.6 is a quotation from the Book of Ecclesiastes 3:1 ("Everything has its appointed hour, there is a time for all things under heaven") (cf. letter, 25.8.1991); the central point about it is that, since "each thing 'neath the sun" has its hour, "But only one" (the successive pause emphasizes the uniqueness of that hour), we should use time well; however, we tend to fritter away the moment that is given for sacred purposes ("this too we beguile") by using it for other tasks ("In doing then what then could rest undone."). The third quatrain reminds one of a plea not to misuse Sunday, not to transform our repose into work, not to fail to obey the Lord's command to rest on Sunday: "We merit ill in working at repose / And guil*t*iness ill-*rests* our heavies*t* loa*d*." The accumulation of plosives and the hissing /s/ fricative underlines the attempt to demonstrate that in addition to our work there is the weight of guilt we have to bear. There will not be peace at heart, which results in a very bad use of Sunday, not being lived in accordance with the Lord's will. At the beginning of l.11 the poet resumes his praise of the beauty and the blessing of Sunday, when he refers to "this aged brazen song", a metaphor for the chime of the bell, which still "knows / The sweetness of a linger" and "bids us naught but look one hour, just one". The bell reminds us of the hour, it is calling people to mass, to celebrate the moment of sacred time. The "sweetness of a linger" suggests the beauty of the hour, the hour at the beginning of Sunday - the subtitle mentions the time of the day: "as bell rings for first Mass, 6.30 a.m."

Trappists are not allowed to talk without permission. At La Trappe unauthorized conversation is a very serious offence, though in other houses this kind of misdemeanour is not always so rigorously handled today. Such an unauthorized exchange of views is central to a poem called "A conversation" (*World*, 40), whose importance is suggested from the first line onwards: "A life, two lives and more hang on a word / And in robbed murm'rings something mighty stirs." Apparently it was a significant conversation: Alun Idris shared his fears and sorrows as regards the future of the community with another member of the order in a quiet conversation, "in robbed murm'rings". "Something mighty stirs" refers to the possible outcome, suggesting the possibility of working with the Charismatic Renewal. The sonnet reflects the period of strain the poet was enduring at the time of writing; he closes with the following lines:

> For soul meets soul but when a meeting-place
> Is found in the unlearning of our all;
> And in the rippled water, little trace
> Was left by one wave passing, yet too small
> To stir above the stirrings of a tide ...
> And yet, who knows what charged thoughts, discharged, hide?

The "unlearning of our all" suggests utter disillusionment, - the protective mask having been cast off, all the illusions gone, when one is completely oneself in the sense of laying bare one's true face and soul: in this honesty there is a "meeting-place" of souls. No one knew about the conversation, - "little trace / Was left by one wave passing". Monastic life continued as usual. The wave it stirred was "too small" for the tide of time. It did not bring about any effect noticeable at that moment. And yet, who knows what might result of their sharing thoughts in the future, "what charged thoughts, discharged, hide". The thoughts might be transformed into actions one day, - this possibility is certainly implied.

Manual work forms an important part in the life of a Trappist monk, - monasteries usually form a fairly autonomous entity. He is bound to work in different areas. "Going to the bog (to dig turf, and coming back with four stitches)" (*World*, 40) reflects one of these necessary activities in the monastery. Of course, "going to the bog" has a double sense in English-speaking countries, but the note in brackets does not leave any doubt about what exactly is intended; apparently the poet had an accident that day, which involved being taken to the surgery. Thus, the memory of that day stands out from the course of other days.

> Amidst grey working days as they float by,
> There fall at times some beams that still shine on
> In Mem'ry's crowded cells. And as we lie
> In eves to come on re-dreamt hours long gone,
> Some will not go unseen, but standing there
> As milestones on this little path we trod,
> They will recall where passed this thoroughfare
> And laugh where we once laughed at thrills so odd.
> For there are that would buy lost hours of joy
> And map fair days to hold them, and go far
> And further still to find how all did cloy
> At th'hour they passed them by, where they still are
> Awaiting our return. For only he
> Who little wants n'er wanted more to be.

The first line is built on an anapaestic rhythm, which conveys a feeling of steady movement, the very float of time. The spondees in l.2 ("some beams", "shine on") suggest the outstanding nature of some events which are remembered forever, "In Mem'ry's crowded cells". Indeed, "Some will not go unseen": the trochaic inversion in the first two feet underlines the message conveyed. The inversion at the beginning of l.7 continues the description of those days. While the first two quatrains concentrate on presenting the nature of these outstanding events in our lives, the third one introduces the idea of planning such events in advance, - "buy lost hours of joy", "map fair days to hold them", - indicating the wish to influence and plan happy moments. This is not possible, of course, thus the poet presents us with his own formula to avoid such disappointment in the closing couplet. "For only he / Who little wants n'er wanted more to be." Desiring little means that one is satisfied with what there is, with the moment of joy he has. The important message implied is to banish desire. This will ultimately lead to an inner harmony and balance. It reflects the Buddhist principle of abandoning desire so as to attain tranquillity.[129]

The examples given offer glimpses into the life in a Trappist monastery, providing insight into spheres which are normally not known to outsiders. They range from the banal

---

[129] This poem, amongst others, was set to music by David Solomons, a London musician, who has specialized on setting to music twentieth century poems.

daily round of the monk's existence to important spiritual attitudes and convictions. The honesty behind these musings not only lends them a deeply human touch, presenting the Trappist monk as a truly human being, with thoughts and feelings common to us all, but also makes the poems more powerful and striking to the reader.

3.2.1.2. FEARS AND CONCERN ABOUT THE FUTURE

The first three examples given in this chapter were composed whilst a member of the Cistercian Order of Strict Observance at La Trappe. They reflect the poet's uncertainty concerning his future path: the possibility of becoming a hermit seemed to realistically exist and the temptation to live as a recluse was strongly felt. The poems function as a means to sort out his own mind, also to find personal consolation, as writing about the problem was a way to release the inner strain caused by this uncertainty whether to continue as a Trappist monk or to become a recluse.

In "Writing an unsent letter" (*World*, 13) the poet seems to have made a decision, which now causes considerable strain. He feels the call to become a recluse, yet at the same time he is aware that this call might not be in accordance with the plans of his superiors, - an idea which is particularly implied in the first quatrain:

> They asked me, Lord, to ask Thee for a sign.
> The sign I feared and longed for has been giv'n.
> They asked me, Lord, and asking, thought that Thine
> Would follow theirs. O Waste! Alas! I've striv'n   [corr.]
> Six months in vain, to follow Thee by flight
> From where Thou'ldst lead ... And yet was it in vain,
> The coming to the Voicelessness where Light
> Doth shine more inwardly? 'Mid Noise profane
> Would we have seen the writing on the wall,
> And 'mid mine ancient shackles, Habit-worn
> And screwed by Institution, would the Call
> That on th'unfettered gusts of Grace is borne
> Have found a way into the land of Law
> To whisper, "Let's embrace. - But lock the door."?

The end-stopped lines at the beginning of this sonnet convey an idea of finality, describing the facts as they occurred. The repetition of "They asked me, Lord" underlines that at that point there was a certain opposition, separating the rest of the community from "me", which is reinforced as the quatrain continues: they had thought that the sign the Lord would give him would be identical with what they considered to be the right decision, which, however, was not in concordance with his own wish. The emotional outbreak in 1.4 underlines the inner strain from which the poet suffered. He longs to become a recluse, but his yearning and struggling seem to have been in vain, as is indicated in the second quatrain: "And yet was it in vain, / The coming to the Voicelessness where Light / Doth shine more inwardly?" These lines describe life as a recluse, a life in perpetual solitude and silence, which exerts tremendous attraction on the poet. "The coming to the Voicelessness" implies that his personal decision has already been made. He is fully aware of his longing to become a recluse, whether it will be possible to do so or not. It seems as though his striving was not in vain, for he realizes that otherwise, had he not striven for the possibility to become a hermit, he would never have felt the call of reclusion which he experiences now, - "the Call / That on th'un*fettered gusts* of *Grace* is borne": the imagery used describes how strongly grace can be felt, the explosive and hissing consonants even suggesting that it can be a fairly rough experience, - there is no way of not noticing the power, the impetus of grace. "Institution" and "the land of Law" represent life in the Trappist monastery. They seem to be opposing factors to his call; yet the call has found its way into this "land of Law / To whisper, 'Let's embrace. - But lock the door.'?" This closing line offers opposed interpretations: the call is felt, has reached the poet, but, as it cannot be implemented at the moment, it is better to keep silent, - "But lock the door." On the other hand, it also suggests the call's imperative invitation to live as a recluse in perpetual solitude.

The theme is continued in "Seeking an envelope" (*World*, 14f.): the poet wonders about what will happen, whether his plea to become a hermit will be heard or not. The message has not been sent yet, as is implied in 1.2:

> What *is* to b*e* *e*nclosed and s*e*aled *i*n th*ee*,
> That mayest or may'st no*t t*omorrow par*t*
> Beyond the s*ea*s, to bear one quiet pl*ea*
> For *L*one*l*iness, to *fill* my *l*one*l*y heart,
> Will it be h*ear*d, will it without a w*or*d
> Do what the pow'r of ink inanimate
> *H*as in the *h*istory of *h*earts been *h*eard
> *T*o do *t*o *M*an, *M*an's thoughts, *M*an's though*t*less Fa*t*e?

A feeling of wonder about the future is conveyed in these lines. The poet seems to be fairly optimistic as regards the outcome of his letter, though, of course, the ultimate decision is unknown to him. The two quatrains quoted are characterized by a balance in sound, as is indicated in italics: the assonance in l.1 (long /iː/ as well as short /ɪ/ abound) suggests a feeling of wonder in his meditation on the future, which is interrupted by the harsh "not" of l.2, followed by a series of plosives pointing to the activity involved. The wonder is continued in l.3, underlined by long vowels and the assonance in "seas" - "plea". The alliteration in l.4 suggests the flowing of the "plea / For Loneliness" to fill his heart, - he aims to inhale solitude. The repetition in l.5 emphasizes his yearning to let the plea be heard, to let his silent words speak. The poet's belief in the power of the written word becomes apparent. The influence it exerts cannot be stopped, - there is something inexorable about it, which is suggested by the alliteration on /h/. L.8 is fairly balanced in sound, implying a feeling of continuity. The image of "Man's thoughtless Fate" echoes the poet's belief in providence, how all has been foreseen by God. The poem closes with "Fly, Lick that seals me. Part, sweet dove!" The imagery used strongly conveys on the one hand that the poet is prepared to wait for the result before taking any further step, - "Lick that seals me". On the other hand it also suggests the utter solitude and silence of the life of a hermit he is heading for. Using the dove, the conventional symbol of peace, as a metaphor for the letter containing his plea suggests his intention not to cause any trouble or annoyance, and underlines that he himself cannot see anything harmful contained in the letter.

"Questions" (*World*, 26) is a key poem, written after seeing the Bishop and Bardsey Island, as is indicated in a note in brackets. It was the last poem to be written at La Trappe, due to the novice master's decisive remark that writing poetry was "tout à fait anti-cistercien" (*World*, 42). The poem is followed by a long pause: Alun Idris stopped completely and only started again in Roscrea, where he was encouraged to resume (cf. Mörwald 1990, 79f.).

"Questions"[130] is dominated by the feeling of uncertainty of how to continue, whether as a Trappist monk or as a recluse. Both paths seem to be possible:

> Is there one way or are there sometimes two
> To climb a hill? When we start out to walk
> The path that leads us o'er Life's roamings, to
> Our starting-point, do pathways sometimes fork
> Already in our Maker's mighty brain?
> Are there two beings that respond to one,
> One sole, one only name: the one whose reign
> O'er Time and Being had his chance, whose sun
> Rose up and fell o'er his sweet chosen game,
> And th'other who ne'er had a voice to speak,
> Who ne'er could answer to his rightful name,
> For that he was not called. And yet, unique
> He also could have been, - and yet could he?
> Are there two patterns to Eternity?

As is characteristic of many of his poems, Alun Idris poses a question at the very beginning of this poem. However, this particular sonnet consists of questions only, thereby fully corresponding to its title, with no answer being given. The final line summarizes the question central to the entire sonnet: "Are there two patterns to Eternity?" The three quatrains are not clearly to be distinguished, - it is only the rhyme which reminds us of their existence: they flow into one another. Yet, together they point towards the one great question uttered at the end, which remains unresolved: does providence at times offer two ways, either of which could be taken? ("Do pathways sometimes fork / Already in our Maker's mighty brain?") The poet ponders on the possible existence of the two "beings" as a result of the different ways he might opt for: "one whose reign / O'er Time and Being had his chance", referring to the way which materializes, that "sweet chosen game". The other, though equally potentially existing, "ne'er had a voice to speak", although "he also could have been - and yet could he?" Two different ways of life, therefore two different beings lie before him, hypothetically speaking. The poet does not yet know which of the two will be the one to materialize. The poem well reflects Alun Idris' feeling of uncertainty as regards his future life.

---

[130] To restore the chronological order, the first poem written after "Questions" was "'Home, sweet home,' she said" (*World*, 43) (cf. letter, 7.4.1991).

The following sonnet called "Ireland" (*World*, 35), written already at Roscrea, is another meditation on the unknown future, a pondering on different ways and possibilities, apart from describing the beauty of the countryside there. The poem starts with "Fwyn dír na nÓg, sweet land yet bathed in grace", which means "gentle land of perpetual youth" (cf. letter, 25.8.1991), and aims to suggest that Ireland has kept the faith till now, the means of grace are still there, despite negative influences which, of course, threaten the island, just as many other countries are afflicted. The poet is concerned about Ireland's future and ponders about the possibilites of how he might be of help to the country, as we read in the closing lines of the sonnet:

> And could I, Erin fechan, save thy soul,
> What would I not thee give? Shall I thee leave
> A cell? A song? - a morsel of the whole
> That in its thinking moves, or wouldst thou grieve
> Should something roar in Juda o'er thee too
> And these thine unfed ears with Beauty woo?

"Erin fechan" means "little Ireland", which adds an affective note, he is personally concerned about the country's future fate. The synectoches in l.11 point to the various possibilities which are at his disposal: the "cell" indicates the possibility of becoming a hermit and praying for the country in solitude; the "song", of course, refers to his own poetic vein, suggesting thereby the possibility of igniting new religious fervour through his poetry, using poetry as a means to express his love for God, which might exercise a certain influence on the Irish people. Another possibility is indicated by the "morsel", which is specified in the closing couplet: the Line of Juda is explicitly mentioned, - the poet wonders how the country would react to the Charismatic Renewal. "And these thine unfed ears with Beauty woo" suggests the beauty which comes from the worship and celebration of those young people involved in the renewal, to which Irish ears are as yet unaccustomed. The awareness, even the pull to work actively in the Charismatic Renewal, is implied in these lines.

The enthusiasm for the Charismatic Renewal is also present in "Eve of Pentecost" (*World*, 36), a feast which is certainly apt for pondering on such a movement, a "noise":

> There could yet be a noise upon this land.
> It waiteth but the willingness to say,
> "I will," and in small shifting much can stand
> Beyond our last soft step that ends this way.
> The dying of the heaved, stretched, slow-racked death [corr.]
> Could gaze on the beginning - that 'gins not
> For that one seed ne'er came. Nay, something saith
> Deep, deep within that blasted years will rot -
> And this when there are oceans that o'erflow
> From one small spring, one hid, that some have trapped.
> And by the secret of its sacred use, let go
> In their full flood the forces they have tapped,
> O! but a word could yet hold back the tide:
> There are two seas that dammed 'hind one thought hide.

The sonnet is bathed in the poet's autobiography, - the meaning he intended to convey can hardly be grasped if the reader is not informed about his situation when writing the poem. What is clear from the poem, however, is that the "noise" originates in some kind of revolutionary movement, which is about to spread in the country. The movement Alun Idris referred to when writing this poem was the Line of Juda: he was aware of the possibility of bringing the spirit of this movement from France to Britain and Ireland, "There could yet be a noise upon this land". The message is given additional emphasis by the fact that the sentence stops with the first line. The spondaic "I will" at the beginning of l.3 underlines how much it is up to him to decide about the movement's future development. "And in small shifting much can stand / Beyond our last soft step that ends this way:" the "small shifting" suggests his personal decision to leave the monastery. The accumulation of monosyllabic words in l.4 reduces the speed of the rhythm, thereby conveying a notion of solemnity, which underlines the tragic end the poet foresees as regards the future of the Cistercian community in Ireland. L.5, however, is even more explicit: "The dying of the heav*ed*, *stretched*, *s*low-*racked d*eath", - the enumeration of attributes, separated by a pause each time, intensifies the idea of the slow, lingering death, while the accumulation of sharp, hissing consonants add to the feeling of horror conveyed. Those "blasted years will rot": life was, it seemed, in the Charismatic Renewal, - an idea which is elaborately presented in the third quatrain. "The secret of its sacred use" points to the beginning of the renewal, switching on the power of the spirit, as it were. The movement has maintained its fervour. The participants have not lost the glow of the first love for God: "let go / In their *f*ull *f*lood the *f*orces they have trapped". The alliteration firmly implies the motion of that torrent, the tremendous power of the renewal. The closing couplet summarizes the situation, and also contains an allusion to the very first line, telling us how the "noise" could be brought into the country. The decision has to be made, - one word, "I will" would be enough to allow the energy, the powerful stream, the "two seas" to flow. Whether this will happen, however, cannot be known yet.

The examples given illustrate the poet's concern for the future. They act as an outlet for the inner strain accumulated by the "forking path" in front of him. In that sense the poems certainly helped to alleviate the strain.

3.2.1.3. INNER TENSION AND DESPAIR

The present chapter will demonstrate that poetry not only offers release in periods of uncertainty as regards the future, but that it also represents a means to express utmost inner tension, even despair. In the Carthusian period, this function of poetry as a vent for despair was already noticeable. During his years as a Trappist, however, it is omnipresent, as the tensions attain new dimensions.

The despair which stirred the composing of "Upset" (*World*, 45) is underlined by the structure of this poem: it consists of one sentence only, with the first eight and a half lines describing situations "when" in distress, the remaining lines concentrating on what happens "then". The entire poem reflects its title:

> When, in distress, we wonder what can come
> And fear the morrow for that we see not
> Its unshaped form nor hear the voice still dumb
> Of unspoke Fate, when still the Gordian knot [corr.]
> Of tangled, ravelled Happenings unbound
> Remains, and, lying, drains the inner sight
> Of curious energy, and when the sound
> Of the unanswered question fills the night,
> When, when, I say, we look and nothing see
> Except the look of looking, then, O Void,
> Dost thou at times look back, or doth a plea
> Of unvoiced asking reach thy depths unbuoyed, [corr.]
> And do these sometimes answer en sourdine,
> "Each morrow's child one yesterday had been."?

The origin of the despair is not mentioned but it apparently caused considerable inner struggle.[131] The repetition of the structure starting with "when", enumerating all these incidents which describe a state of inner tension, increases the feeling of despair conveyed. The images he uses add to that feeling: the "Gordian knot" is yet "tangled" and not cut, - there is a problem which still must be solved, - its "lying, drains the inner sight / Of curious energy". The imagery used here powerfully conveys the idea of how his enthusiasm gradually diminishes until nothing remains anymore. He seems to be at a complete loss, not knowing what to do, and yet he desperately longs for the answer ("the sound / Of the unanswered question fills the night"). L.10 summarizes his state of depression. He cannot see anything anymore, "Except the look of looking". There is nothing which may guide him to find a solution. He is lost, completely on his own. He has reached a state of "Void". In the closing lines the idea of providence emerges, when the poet asks the void whether his pleas of despair find their way to the depths of the universe ("doth a plea / Of unvoiced asking reach thy depths unbuoyed"), adding the potential answer: "'Each morrow's child one yesterday had been'", - which, of course, suggests the existence of providence, and that everything was planned beforehand.

The rapid rhythm of the poem is only interrupted as "when" appears once more. It is as though the poet was taking breath anew to continue his lament. The repetition of l.9 "When, when, I say, we look and nothing see", followed by the short sentence "I say", underlines his excitement. The turning point is reached at the end of l.10: "then, O Void" - the "then" is given a firm stress, indicating a certain change, although the rhythm does not decrease in speed. In the eyes of providence our lives have always been. They are pre-arranged, events have their

---

[131] The poet had found himself obliged to talk against his will in places which used to be reserved for strict silence. Someone had said to him: "You are not a Carthusian now." He was taken aback by this utterance, as thereby he would have to repudiate his past in a way (cf. letter, 25.8.1991).

cause, and all our worries will be one day answered. This is the auto-suggestive message of the poem.

The two pulls Alun Idris felt strongly in his heart caused considerable pain: on the one hand there was the will to be completely separated from this world, but on the other, the longing to be involved in the renewal was equally strong. The conflict is central to "Setting up a modern oratory" (*World*, 53), which is an "extended" sonnet: it has four, instead of three quatrains.

> There are two wills and more within my breast,
> That heave and pull against each other's force.
> To want to do the perfect, nay, the best
> While knowing that its doing is far worse
> Than all one e'er has done - the pain! the pain
> Of this slight Yea that would be Nay ... The thought
> That the Anathema declared profane
> Had but this morn a benediction sought,
> Aches 'gainst an ache, for two share ill one home.
> To walk beyond this sign, my soul doth fear
> The thought ... and yet they said, "Nay, we shall come",
> And these two steps would bring two worlds so near ...
>
> When angels say that they will pray with us,
> And when their Lord we have bid pitch His tent
> Before us in the midst, with one lamp thus
> Recalling His thick Presence, why the scent
> Of this wide world, the incense fumes of Hell
> Dread more without than here where locked fiends dwell?

The first quatrain presents the conflict: the rhythm is quick, with irregular pauses. The spondee in 1.4 ("far worse") followed by the stressed long vowels in "all", "e'er", and finally "done" suggests the terrible situation the poet faces at the moment, until at last the struggling finds release in the reiterated outburst in 1.5, "the pain! the pain". The four successive stressed syllables in 1.8 ("Had but this morn") increases the tension, - the strong feeling of lament expressed. The rhythm finally slows down in the second half of 1.9, when he seems to face the problem again in a calmer way, "for two share ill one home". The long vowels and diphthongs make the line sound very calm. He realizes that a decision has to be made. The "Anathema" of 1.7 refers to the hankering after what he had been told at la Trappe, i.e. the radical difference between the religious and the secular, for which they had two signs (cf. letter, 27.9.1991). "This sign" in 1.10 refers to the sign of enclosure: there was an urge to walk beyond this sign outside the enclosure to the guesthouse, yet he had been taught at La Trappe that going to the guesthouse was equivalent to going outside the enclosure, which should be avoided at all costs. The strong influence of his French formation is strongly implied. The "extra" quatrain attached to the poem seems to resolve his struggle in a sense. The "angels" are those aspirants, fervent in their love for God before the tabernacle, the "tent". The closing couplet is full of self-criticism, implying how arrogant it is to think that contemplative monks are "better" than these aspirants: they were keeping themselves for a greater holiness, keeping themselves away from what is a part of our world, which is deeply sanctified, more perhaps than they are, these "locked fiends". Such severe self-criticism underlines the period of strain the poet was undergoing at the time.

At Roscrea, the poet was disturbed by the seemingly gloomy prospects as regards the future of the community: he felt he was still young, young at heart. The awareness of not being able to share his enthusiasm with the elderly community led to a period of depression. His anxieties find expression in a poem called "Apathy" (*World*, 33f.), whose title already suggests the basic nature of the problem. The poem celebrates the qualities and powers of youth: "When we are young, untarnished of aged sloth, / There is a dew in new-filled skies still held". The freshness and wonder implied in the highly melodious second line contrasts sharply with the imagery used in the first line, "untarnished of aged sloth", which is immensely accusative in tone. It is not a wise equilibrium which is obtained as the years pass by, but "aged sloth". The contrast between youth and age is constantly implied as the poem proceeds: "And 'tis known / That there is yet Tomorrow o'er the hill / And that Today's fresh flame while yet unblown / By belching crassitude, can warm us still" (ll.5-8). The attacks are continued, a feeling of abhorrence being added by the imagery used on the one hand ("belching crassitude") and by the positive presentation of the ideals of youth ("Today's fresh flame") on the other. "And when the young a younger self still finds / That its soft growing follows" (ll.9f.) aims to express that as a young person one sometimes thinks of the ideals one had considered to be important earlier in one's life, - "its soft growing follows". The ideals accompany the young person. They are not forgotten. On the contrary, "nothing grows / In this terrain of Ageing". The generalization of such an obviously intolerant as well as intolerable statement evokes an idea of the circumstances in which the poem was written. Doubtless the sonnet was a means to mitigate the inner strain which had become unbearable. The discrepancy of what the poet considered to be the ideal life as a Trappist, i.e. the way he had been formed at La Trappe, and how this Trappist ideal was realized in Ireland he found impossible to reconcile.[132]

The tension which now has virtually turned into despair is central to "Corpus Christi" (*World*, 40). Utter disillusionment is apparent. The dreams of the past are broken:

> And I had thought to be a priest for aye,
> But 'twill not be; nay, nay, it doth not come.
> There are too many turnings on this way,
> And though I see a light, it is not home.
> There is an aging in our growing old
> That need not be, and many have grown young.
> I would not ope this chapter were it told
> And 'tis Youth's wanderings that give morn its song.
> For though I be a while in being aught,
> I would be my becoming to the full;

---

[132] The situation was difficult: on the one hand he would have preferred the order to be more austere, which made it difficult for him to stay, while on the other hand the members of the community were very kind and full of love. In the end, the growing tension led to his leaving the order, a fact which the poet regretted later on: "I regret not having been more prudent." (letter, 25.8.1991).

And though in oft becoming we be naught,
A dream more than delusion doth growth pull.
And yet, to hold awhile this little Hand ...
- 'Twas dreamt for long, but dreams ne'er understand.

The tone of frustration and bitterness concerning the present situation is obvious from the very first line onwards. The pause after "And I had thought" is the first indication that a certain hope had been in vain, that it had not worked out. L.2 explicitly mentions the impossiblity of hope being realized, intensified by the pauses interspersed in this line. The repeated "nay, nay", which rhymes with "aye" of l.1 eliminates any remaining rays of hope. The medial pause in 1.4 emphasizes the phrase which follows, "it is not home". The eye rhyme, rare in Alun Idris' poetry, does not disturb the flow of the poem; it acts as an additional means to convey the idea of deception, - what seems to be alright at first sight is not. The second quatrain mentions that problem which was touched upon before, - he feels that his youthful energies cannot develop and be used properly in the order. L.8 is an appendix to 1.6; its location underlines the excitement of the poet, who seems to wish to express all his thoughts simultaneously. The third stanza refers both to the poet's past and his future. He certainly does not make compromises in his vocation; he intends to live his calling "to the full"; and yet, he realizes, when pondering about his past, that "in oft becoming we be naught": starting too often afresh can mean that one ends up by achieving nothing at all. Even so, he still wants to pursue his dream. In the dark night of the soul he was experiencing there was nothing to "pull". The closing couplet refers to the title "Corpus Christi": holding the blessed sacrament is like holding the hand of God; although it is only a tiny host, it is the link with the creator; we are in direct touch with God. The final line expresses how long he had dreamt of becoming a priest, but dreams do not "understand" how they are to be worked out. And yet, he certainly does not renounce his dream, however unwise and unrealistic it may seem.

"After compline" (*World*, 41) continues to present the inner strain prevailing at the time, although this sonnet already echoes the feeling that his time as a Cistercian was coming to an end.

There is a mighty throng upon my back
And in this whitened robe a hidden cloud
Doth hover and oft sing, "Thou'lt here not lack
The ordinariness that saints doth shroud."
And in this dying song at eventide
I hear the voices that have hailed my Queen
From Hist'ry's heart well up, borne on this tide
Of Beauty oft made deep where depths have been.
Yet Cîteaux in its newness also grew
And there is whiteness in the Bride's robes still
That woos me home to newness truly new,
Where many many beauties wait to thrill
The weariness of newness growing old,
That was young once: but found its youth too bold.

The "mighty throng upon my back" in l.1 is a metaphor for his being a Cistercian: after compline, the time the poem refers to, as the title indicates, the monks take off their habits, thus the habit which he is, metaphorically speaking, still wearing, simply suggests the order he belongs to. The "hidden cloud" of witnesses in l.2 is a scripture reference to Romans 12:1 (cf. letter, 25.8.1991). The quotation in ll.3 and 4 is bound to provoke associations for a Cistercian: the word "ordinariness" does, in a way, sum up Cistercian spirituality, - the ordinariness of ordinary things.[133] Cistercian life is characterized by the routine of day-to-day activities. This ordinariness "saints doth shroud": the habit shrouds the monk, who is buried in this Cistercian silence, - he is unknown to the world, dead to the world in a sense. The image of death is taken up in the second quatrain, "And in this dying song at eventide" which refers to the last song to be chanted in the day, the *Solemn Salve*, the Cistercian *Salve Regina*. At the Trappist monastery of Roscrea it was chanted as the Cistercians have chanted it over the centuries (cf. letter, 25.8.1991). The beauty of the *Salve* is firmly implied when we read "this tide / Of Beauty oft made deep where depths have been": it is a chant which is of tremendous affective power, deeply spiritual, characterized by that Cistercian simplicity and dignity which is a mark of the order. "Yet Cîteaux in its newness also grew": with the beginning of the third quatrain the poet returns to his painful present situation, - the feeling that here the newness has been lost, that it is to be found elsewhere, "That woos me home to newness truly new". Once more the feeling of frustration becomes apparent, - "The weariness of newness growing old, / That was young once: but found its youth too bold". There is a note of capitulation apparent in these lines, apart from the despair implied. To face his enthusiasm "growing old" seems more than he can bear.

It was noticed in the monastery that Alun Idris found it very hard to settle at Roscrea. "After the disclosure" (*World*, 61) refers to a talk the poet had with the abbot (cf. letter, 27.9.1991), who was fully aware of the poet's suffering. The poem is an outcry of the drama which was taking place silently:

> There echo oft hewn chasms 'neath a sigh,
> And what the mouth sounds not the breast ill seals.
> The language of the heart that dares not cry, [corr.]
> Th'unheld of what we are its flow reveals.
> O Happiness that held me for a while,
> Wilt thou too now betake thee to the past?
> Will these that here in gentleness still smile
> Upon this oft blocked road now smile their last?
> Must I haul in this anchor once again
> And drift so far away from what I am?
> The heart of man was made for unfelt pain
> And he lives well that well hath walled this dam
> That holds the ocean of our sufferings,
> And keeps his sorrow for e'en sadder things.

---

[133] "The novice master at Sélignac told us that only one extraordinary thing was allowed: to do the ordinary things extraordinarily well." (letter, 25.8.1991).

The frequency of end-stopped lines in this sonnet is remarkable, as usually run-on lines dominate in his poetry. The first quatrain presents the poet's deplorable state, "There echo oft hewn chasms 'neath a sigh" - the sigh is the only sound to be heard, emanating from the "hewn chasms" he is facing at the moment. He does not verbally articulate the pain ("what the mouth sounds not"), but "the breast ill seals": there is a sigh which escapes from his heart.

The second quatrain reflects on his immediate past, the time he has spent in Roscrea: he was happy there "for a while", but it seems as though the happiness had evaporated. "These that here in gentleness still smile" refers to the goodness of the monks at Roscrea. The poet continues by glancing at his future in the third quatrain. He fears that he is bound to alter the destination of his voyage once more: "Must I haul in this anchor once again / And drift so far away from what I am?" All he ever strove for was living in silent union with God, but the inner struggles caused by the severe conflict of what he expects a Trappist monastery to be like and what he found there, makes it impossible for him to live and experience that union. He concludes that "The heart of man was made for unfelt pain" (l.11): the line suggests that the pain has grown to such an extent that he has become accustomed to feeling it so intensely so that he does not feel it anymore. The "ocean of our sufferings" indicates the vast quantity of anguish the human soul has to assimilate. The metaphor of the dam holding back the ocean of sufferings conveys well how some seek not to be drowned in pain, encapsulating themselves behind thick walls, to keep their "sorrow for e'en sadder things".

The poems mentioned in this chapter no doubt function as the mouthpiece of the poet's heart. They gain their strength from the intense pain which inspired their composition and which is skilfully reflected in them. The honesty behind them is strongly felt, which reinforces the power these poems exert on the reader.

3.2.1.4. RECENT EVENTS AS A STIMULATING SOURCE OF POEMS

Like the Carthusians, the Trappists lead a life which does not offer much variety. It appears logical that any special, unexpected event, however insignificant, can have a lasting effect on the monk, is more intensely experienced than might be the case in the secular world. Therefore it is not surprising that the creative mind reacts to such stimulations with effusions of the poetic vein. Special occasions are always more intensely experienced, all the more in a contemplative monastery. Many examples in Alun Idris' work reflect this facet, a small selection will be given in this chapter.

It is striking that at the beginning of his stay at Roscrea many poems reflect recent events. On the one hand this is caused by the complete change in the exterior situation, leaving France after almost ten years, and going to Ireland, back to an English speaking country. Such a change was bound to affect the poetic vein. On the other hand, the flow was encouraged by the fact that Alun Idris had ceased writing poems completely at La Trappe. Doubtless, he had been suffering under the suppression of the poetic impulse; at Roscrea, where he was asked to resume, it seems therefore natural that such a great number of poems were written.

The first poem Alun Idris was to write after the long break caused by the novice master's remark in La Trappe was "'Home, sweet home,' she said" (*World*, 43), a poem which was written while the poet was staying in the guest house at Roscrea, just before he joined the community. He had made a pilgrimage to the shrine at Ballinspittle with a lady who was staying there as well, as is indicated in a note, - a meeting which apparently left a profound impression on the poet, - naturally, as it seems, after having lived in solitude for almost ten years. His surprise and wonder is explicitly conveyed:

> Did e'er two worlds so far apart collide
> Or minds unlike vibrate such harmony?
> Th'enjambement that hopped the Great Divide,
> Was it e'en felt or heard? Monotony -
> That hours and days and months and round years whole
> Had raved of the Impossible, that Breath
> (That voiced a thought that one small second stole
> From Nothingness) bid rise from tombèd death -
> Could it have seen what this day saw, and lived? [...]

It seems unbelievable that the monotony of the past years (cf. 1.5), in particular those in the charterhouse, would have been able to foresee this day. Such a day would have seemed completely impossible. The very fact of talking to a lady again would have appeared absolutely ridiculous, as a Carthusian does not normally speak to women once having entered the Order, except for his mother and sisters or very close relatives (cf. letter, 25.8.1991). "The great Divide" in 1.3 refers to the division between the secular and the religious world.[134] The capitalized "Breath" in l. 6 turns that day into a kind of resurrection from "tombèd death". It was something entirely different from what he had experienced in all those past years and had a profound effect on him.[135]

The catalytic moment of being taken into his cell is reflected in a sonnet whose title simply indicates the occasion on which it was written, "Before being taken into cell" (*World*, 43).[136]

> A few small steps between a universe
> Of unexpected memories new-stored
> And unborn Fact no fiction can rehearse
> In one thick-wombed new world. In white, restored
> Will be the Quiet these few seconds lost
> Upon another planet. Three short dawns
> Do separate the ray that thawed the frost
> Of Solitude from this eve of all morns.
> Good Master, didst Thou weep or didst Thou smile,
> Nay, didst Thou, 'neath Thy gentle Mother's gaze

---

[134] The Cistercian sign-language has two signs for it. At La Trappe the emphasis laid on the difference is considerable (cf. letter, 25.8.1991).
[135] Alun Idris was still a Trappist monk at the time, moving directly from one house to the other, i.e. from La Trappe to Roscrea.
[136] The poem was written in the guesthouse of Roscrea (cf. letter, 25.8.1991).

Allow the great Forbidden one short while,
That the unsacred, it too, might amaze
The eyes that now re-close to all but Thine,
- Yet was't not Thine, what Thou too didst entwine?

The "universe / Of unexpected memories" (ll.1f.), just as the "ray that thawed the frost / Of solitude" (ll.7f.) and "these few seconds lost / Upon another planet" (ll.5f.), apparently refer to the poem just mentioned, an encounter which had a marked impact on the poet. But now "one thick-wombed new world" (l.4) lies in front of him: the imagery used conveys vividly an idea of the enormous dimensions of that new world which was awaiting him in Roscrea; the image also suggests the idea of home, - it was as though the poet was returning to the great "womb" of contemplative monasteries. "In white" points to the white habit he was going to wear as a novice. The question implied in the third stanza, as well as the closing couplet, is whether or not this encounter and the pilgrimage to Ballinspittle had not been foreseen as well by the Lord: "Good Master, didst Thou weep or didst Thou smile." Did He "allow the great Forbidden", talking to a woman? It is clear from the closing couplet that he is firmly willed to re-close his eyes "to all but Thine"; yet, as is indicated in the final line, such an encounter as he had had just a few days ago was part of the divine plan as well. The fundamental theological question behind is whether it is possible to divide the sacred from the non-sacred, a question which was already touched upon in the previous poem.

The title of the sonnet "After being put in cell" (*World*, 44) explains the origin of its composition: it expresses the joy and happiness experienced at this moment:

O little hole, hid, hidden from the world,
How peaceful are thy tiny new-found wings!
In one short minute all the earth was hurled
Outside thy soundless orbit. Each stone sings
Of loneliness with Him who is alone,
Of Happiness with Who alone gives mirth,
Of separation from what now undone
Can ne'er more be, for Time hath but one birth.
O Ocean of unknowns that comest yet [...]

There is a strong affective bond between the poet and the cell noticeable in these lines, he is filled with peace again. The alliteration in l.1 ("*h*ole, *h*id, *h*idden") emphasizes its separation from the world, which contrasts with the smooth sound of l.2, where long vowels and diphthongs prevail: such melodiousness implies the vast dimension of the possibilities now available, how far it will be possible to fly with those "new-found wings". Ll.5-7 enumerate the characteristics of the cell, which are awaiting him: loneliness, happiness and separation from the outside world. In addition, there is the presence of the one "Who alone gives mirth": the Lord is always at his side. The poet has made his choice, "for Time hath but one birth". He does not know what lies ahead, "O Ocean of unknowns that comest yet", but his decision has been made.

The following sonnet was written as a result of contact with Sr. Agnes, a novice mistress, as is indicated in a note to "After listening" (*World*, 44):

> And hast thou, Mother, sown a seed that I
> Did hardly see, and could have thrown away?
> Th'austerities that please the gawking eye,
> Shall they to most displeasing ones give way?
> And yet, the *c*old is *c*old as 'twas of yore.
> The *t*oi*l* is *t*oi*l*, and '*t*wi*ll* be *t*oi*l*ed again
> *T*omorrow and *t*omorrow as before
> When *h*our to *h*our each *h*our did yield its pain.
> But thou, dear sister, looking deep within,
> As thou'rt wont unto sweeter angel breasts,
> Didst with thine own soul's ears pick out the din
> That in th'unopened heart unuttered rests?
> "Fair is thy call. It foster," was the word
> That passed through thee, passed through me, and was heard.

The quotation in l.13 is apparently taken from the conversation they had: "Fair is thy call. It foster" were the words which fell on fertile soil, - they represent the "seed" she has sown in l.1. The "austerities" mentioned in l.3, which are more explicitly described in the second quatrain, are the daily penances, perhaps not spectacular, yet all the more effective. The pain of suffering the cold, for example, has not changed: it is still the same penance which was experienced by all the Fathers who have lived here before. The repetition and alliteration throughout the entire quatrain (as is indicated in italics) underlines the unchanging nature of the penance. The "din / That in th'unopened heart unuttered rests" suggests the immense power and enthusiasm the poet feels for God, the Love that is within his "unopened heart", making much interior noise, which cannot be heard by the human ear, only by the "soul's ears", by her heart. The inversion of the first foot in "Fair is thy call. It foster", the alliteration and the brevity, yet firmness of the statement, adds special emphasis and force to it. The closing line attracts additional attention as the rhythm is different: the two pauses reduce the speed and give the line a solemn tone. "That passed through thee" is written in regular iambics; a stressed syllable follows, which turns "passed through me" into a cretic, followed by a second one in the phrase "and was heard". A tone of grave solemnity is thereby conveyed.

The subtitle of the following musing indicates the occasion when it was written: Sr. Anthony had sent a tart to the noviciate on the first of March, knowing that Alun Idris' religious name was David. "After an act of kindness" (*World*, 44f.) meditates on the kindness of this sister, on how such ideas of charity in general occur, are sometimes forgotten again, with nobody knowing that the idea was originally there, "'Twere easily forgot, / The madness of th'uncalled-for calling sound;" [corr.] however, this sister heard the "sound", "sister of a child / Too long without a home that spoke of home", - the "child" refers to the poet himself, who had been too long without a home. In the closing lines we read:

> The mother in thee hid 'neath wimpled mild
> And quiet smiling, let not this wind roam
> Into th'oblivion whence it came. It came
> And in its going left not life the same. [corr.]

"The mother in thee hid 'neath wimpled mild" adds to the feeling of home which the poet experiences by explicitly referring to the mother in her, in this nun, hidden under her veil, "'neath wimpled mild". She seems to be goodness personified, and did not dismiss the idea she conceived. The "wind" is the metaphor for the surprise she had thought of, which came from the "oblivion", all of a sudden. Doubtless, this sign of sympathy had a great impact on the poet, as the closing line firmly implies, for it "left not life the same". The obsolete form of negation employed underlines this idea.

"After receiving a letter (from la Trappe)" (*World*, 45) describes the memory of his departure from La Trappe, provoked by a letter he had received. "As through the port-hole of that vessel comes / The sight of parting years that slipped away" (ll.7f.): the metaphor of the vessel which moved on, continuing his voyage of life expresses how he gradually lost sight of the seas of his past. The closing couplet reflects an insight he has gained: "We live, have lived, shall live where we live not, / And when 'tis lived our living is forgot." What these lines try to convey is the idea that we are always living either in the past or in the future, pondering about the past, dreaming or worrying about the future, but do not live this very now. The implication is to take more care over the present, to live it to the full: energy is wasted on something which is not the present, which is not life. The message has auto-suggestive character, for at the time the poet was certainly in danger of "wasting" much energy in ponderings and reflections on his own past.

Events which interrupt the flow of every day life can have lasting effect on the monk. In the case of a Sister's report on Ethiopia the effect produced on Alun Idris was greater than could ever have been foreseen: "A surprise" (*World*, 47) describes his utterly changed emotional state after having listened to the talk. The sonnet is characterized by a vivid, rapidly moving rhythm, which reflects the "re-mobilization" of his mind, - a chain of thoughts was triggered off.

> An afterthought that opened up a world
> So huge that all the mass of problems borne
> 'Twixt these sealed, insulated walls, was hurled
> Beyond the stars, as though this night were born
> Another planet hov'ring o'er the earth
> Of paltry thinking orbiting its thought -
> This earth, I say, that spun on its own worth
> And ne'er a core save its great axis sought ...
> Kind sister, nay, blest angel, thy two wings -
> I mean the sacred fingers that have sped
> These doubly damnèd souls to better things -
> Have touched this hour an unclassed demon fed
> For ten rotating years on thick'ning void,
> And burst the Paradise at which Hell toyed.

The consequences of this talk were surprising indeed. He was not only reminded of the problems that exist in a third world country, but above all also became aware that in his monastic past, "'Twixt these sealed, insulated walls", his thoughts, problems and sorrows had been too self-centered; the space imagery he uses to demonstrate this egocentricity is straight forward, which also points to the completely different world he was immersed in, as well as its degree of narrowness: "orbiting its thought", "spun on its own worth", "ne'er a core save its great axis sought". The third quatrain shifts the emphasis to the sister, who set the ball rolling, a lady whom he addresses with much affection. "These doubly damnèd souls" refers to those impoverished people in Ethiopia, who not only suffer from the lack of physical but also spiritual nourishment, which makes them therefore "doubly damnèd". She made the poet, this "unclassed demon", aware of how much he had been "rotating" around an empty centre, "ten rotating years on thick'ning void", on himself, only trying to satisfy his own spiritual needs. The poem does not spare the poet from sober, devastating criticism; it is full of self-accusation. The closing line even suggests that it was a fool's paradise he had been dreaming of, the "Paradise at which Hell toyed".

Shakespeare had always been one of Alun Idris' favourites. At Roscrea this interest was noticed and one day he was given two books on Shakespeare to read, which were very stimulating (cf. letter, 27.9.1991). They provoked a sonnet called "Two volumes on Shakespeare" (*World*, 58):

> And are there hours that roam yet o'er the earth
> That can beside the hurried way sit down
> And look at their own journey? Is there mirth [corr.]
> To be yet found in toil not made to crown
> The year with fulness solely in the void
> Of air's recycled needs? Do some e'en now, [corr.]
> Now, now as I write, live and avoid
> The Damoclean bell 'neath which years bow? [corr.]
> Are there beyond these walls some worlds that move
> As once, once long ago, I thought they could,
> Without such thought to endlessly improve
> The speed of their own moving? Is there good
> To be yet found above the level soil
> And will an hour yield Meaning to hours' toil?

Reading the two volumes provoked this meditation about the meaning of life and how to use it well. It seems at times that we are too much in a hurry, - people have hardly time left to sit down and "look at their own journey". We rush through our lives without reflecting on our aims. The image of "air's recycled needs" (1.6) refers to the machinery in which every one of us is constantly ensnared; it is possible, as probably each of us knows from personal experience, to spend more time on managing the practicalities of living without reflecting on the meaning of life. That this should also be the case in monastic surroundings, however, surprises. The other danger which lurks in a monastery is the tremendous influence and power of the bell, the "Damoclean bell", as Alun Idris refers to it in 1.8, which suggests a certain fear of its power. The bell regulates the monk's life. He can find himself always rushing to complete a task before the next chime is heard, as the monk has to stop everything immediately as soon as he hears the bell, as we read in the Rule of St. Benedict, chapter 43, paragraph 1. Indeed, it is the bell "'neath which years bow". The third quatrain contains more allusions to the way he was formed: "endlessly improve / The speed of their own moving" in ll.11f. suggests that he was taught to make good use of time. It is essential to use working time for God, doing one's tasks with all seriousness. This ethos is to be found in every house of the order (cf. letter, 27.9.1991). The closing lines suggest an echo of his yearning to spend more time on meditations and intellectual work than manual tasks. "And will an hour yield Meaning to hours' toil" questions the possibility of whether an equilibrium can be achieved when meditating on the meaning of life during one hour as a compensation for all the hours of toil: can such a short hour raise the "level soil" to a higher pitch?

The happenings at Chernobyl in May 1986 are still vividly present in our memories. The catastrophe stirred the writing of a sonnet called "May (and Chernobyl)" (*World*, 37), which is infused with memories of the poet's own childhood:

> Do children play the little games we played
> In our own time, itself a time foreknown
> By fathered times before? Have years betrayed
> The secret of the folly that no frown
> Hath yet with Worry wrinkled? Doth the day
> Now rise and fall still o'er some little lamb,
> Some nodding boy, some small girl's curds and whey?
> And doth a child still linger where I am?
> O mystery of sev'n ages, when are hours
> Called years, and are our years the years that were?
> The joys that, tumbling, lay once 'tween these flow'rs, [corr.]
> Will they again a child's own child still stir?
> And will the morrow we leave here for e'er
> See where we played, and know what was known there?

The poem consists exclusively of questions, a fact which underlines the idea of the instability of our future. No answer can be given yet as to what extent exactly we shall be affected by this nuclear catastrophe. The future will not be the same, though. The life of future, innocent generations will be affected: recollecting all those nursery rhymes which are interspersed into this poem helps to underline the question in how far their lives will be different from those of past children; however, it also emphasizes the innocence of the victims. The "little lamb" is apparently a reference to the nursery rhyme "Mary had a little lamb, its fleece is white as snow, and everywhere that Mary went, the lamb was sure to go". The "nodding boy" is a reference to "Noddy and big Ears", a figure in a children's book by Enid Blyton. "Curds and whey" is a line taken from a nursery rhyme which begins "Little Miss Muffet, sat on a tuffet, eating her curds and whey". The innocence conveyed by the employment of these nursery rhymes reinforces the threat expressed in the poem. To even question whether these flowers will "again a child's own child still stir" suggests the scale of the danger we are facing.

Experiences common to the whole of mankind, trivial as they may seem, equally form the origin of many poetic musings. Reading such a poem, which is not meant to stir deep philosophical thought, means being reminded of feelings common to all of us, and is bound to leave us with a smile, perhaps because of the truth involved, perhaps with a feeling of consensus, or perhaps because of the imagery employed for so trivial a subject, as, for example, "Losing a file" (*World*, 27), where we read at the beginning:

> There are some toys with which we play awhile
> And which, ne'er giv'n a breath, reanimate [corr.]
> The joy we lost in letting naught else smile [corr.]
> About us when we met our orphaned fate,
> In coming back twice smiling from the land
> Where this now seems to wander unobserved. [corr.]

Even though they are inanimate objects, they animate the joy we lost. When one has lost something, nothing matters except finding it, - a trivial but common experience. The image "orphaned fate" conveys our pain, when a part of us is gone. The object is all the more precious because of the wanting it ("twice smiling"). Later on he continues: "Marie Céleste of ages, thou wast here / And known and unknown unto all that sailed / On this side of the stars". Marie Céleste is one of the famous sea mysteries of Britain, a ship which disappeared to the unknown. Using this ship as a metaphor for things lost is striking and highly suggestive of their personal value. The image is picked up and continued by addressing the whole of mankind as ships that "sailed" in this our world, "on this side of the stars", implying on a subtle level that one day we all shall be lost in the great ocean of time.

"And is there goodness yet on earth? A thought / That voyaged thinly through the air can move / The universe within." These are the opening lines of "O Bonitas" *(World*, 52), a poem written immediately after receiving a letter, as a note in brackets indicates. The letter had an enormous influence to the poet, - it moved "the universe within". Later he continues: "And in our dark rouse long-becalmèd storms", which implies how memories can rend the veil of unruffled peace, inner tranquility, by making us think of the past, perhaps even upset us. The writing or receiving of letters inspired the composition of a considerable number of poems, which underlines the importance of the written word to the poet.[137]

The examples given in this chapter reflect the potential of the poetic flow, accumulated during the period of having stopped writing completely. The urge to be creative and unleash the spirit finds expression in the great variety of subjects. The seemingly trivial content of some of the poems mentioned reflect the poet's urge to write, - the joy he feels when letting the poetic vein free. These poems do not intend to stir deep philosophical thought, nor do they pretend to be filled with such: they are musings, which try to please the ear, offering the reader a facet of beauty.

---

[137] Other examples are, for instance: "After receiving a letter from a Carthusian nun" (*World*, 4f.), "'Gone away'" (*World*, 7), "Waiting for a letter" (*World*, 48), "Seeking an envelope" (*World*, 14f. - see above, pp.158f.) etc.

3.2.2. POETRY AS A FORM OF MEDITATION

3.2.2.1. GRACE

As in the Carthusian period, meditations on grace were composed in Alun Idris' period as a Trappist monk as well, although less frequently. Normally, ideas on the nature of grace are interspersed in the poetry; at times, however, they form the very subject of an entire poem. We even find examples where the poet addresses grace as a personification, as is demonstrated in this chapter.

The notes attached to "After discovering what chance was missed" (*World*, 8f.) explain the background to the poem. The missed chance was the possibility of becoming a hermit, a desire which had always been very tempting to Alun Idris. The poem consists of two sonnets, the first one glancing at the past, the second looking forward to the future.

> So thou, milord, wast, as I thought, my lord
> In Christ, who in thy clasping hands passed on
> An ounce of warmth. Ah! Ah! Had but that word
> That from within did well ... but nay, 'tis gone.
> The grace was there. I knew it, felt it well,
> But would not, could not, break the rule and speak ...
> And thou, fair Grace, of which those verses tell,
> Art thou another Time will ever seek?
> Ah! Time, thou comest once to passing man,
> Each hour each grace imparting, only once.
> What could then be, like lightning through me ran,
> But left no trace. For what in that small ounce
> Could have been giv'n, came not. For I would not.
> Would not? Nay, would. Would! WOULD!! But got it not.

The abundance of short sentences and exclamations conveys the poet's excitement, his agitation at having missed a chance like that. A note attached to the poem explains that "my lord / In Christ" refers to the bishop, who had tried to engage him in conversation, whose "clasping hands passed on / An ounce of warmth". The imagery used conveys the warmth and understanding that was present, however short the encounter might have been. The exclamations in l.3 are followed by four stressed syllables, "Had but that word / That from within did well ...", where the nucleus is placed on the last syllable of the line, "word", which emphasizes how much he regrets not having uttered a word to him about his longing to become a hermit. L.6 explains why he found himself obliged not to utter a word: "But would not, could not, break the rule and speak". The rule of silence, to which he firmly clings, prevented him from mentioning the "word" to the bishop. The medial break in l.5 emphasizes the message of the first half, which is a whole sentence, "The grace was there. I knew it, felt it well": the shortness of this sentence, its directness and touch of objective observation, lends additional power to it, leaving no doubt about the presence of grace. The second half of the line is once more split in two halves, which repeat the message of the first part of l.5 on a more personal level: now it is the poet himself who feels the presence of grace. The closing lines of the second quatrain ask a rhetorical question to grace about the possibility of returning once more to him. The answer is given in the third quatrain, starting with another mournful exclamatory "Ah! Time, thou comest once to passing man / Each hour each grace imparting, only once". Every grace is only given once, there might be other graces at other times, but one lost grace is a grace lost forever. As a simile for his awareness of the grace present he writes "like lightning through me ran, / But left no trace". He felt the presence of grace, was filled with its powers, but now it is gone, nothing is left anymore. The image used at the beginning of the poem is picked up again to point out that the meeting could have ended differently, "For what in that small ounce / Could have been giv'n, came not." Although it was perhaps just a "small ounce" of warmth, it would have been enough to change his life. The repetitions of the closing line reinforce how much he regrets not having used the chance, not having profited from grace. The rhythm is all but regular, which emphasizes his state of agitation. The question in the regular iambic first foot is followed by a pause, the succeeding answer is a spondaic foot, followed by another pause. The two exclamatory "Would! WOULD!!" receive heavy stresses as well, underlined by the capitalization. The adjacent pause is the longest of these three pauses in l.14: this stamps the closing phrase ("But got it not.") as a kind of superfluous appendix, not belonging to the rest of the line, which makes it sound all the more mournful and lamentating.

The second stanza presents a vision of the future. The poet seems to have overcome the pain and sorrow at the missed grace; he has regained his former inner peace, as the rhythm of the sonnet suggests, although the reader feels that he tries to calm himself, that he has not yet fully recovered from the shock, in particular towards the end:

> And yet, when I behold this little isle
> That looks each morn at me as if to say,
> "Thou there, dost think that thou'lt escape awhile
> The Grace that hunts thee, and once crossed thy way?"
> I ruminate what pleasant horrors yet
> Time holds unwound. For as I see his sun,
> The first of this dark summer, slowly set
> To rest its head, ere 'gain its course it run,
> Can I say, "There's no more", when there is one? -
> Tomorrow and tomorrow will revolve
> And now and now and now each now begun
> Till now no more, must into Then dissolve
> To make room for another. And Thou'rt there.
> And shouldst Thou be ... - But where? Lord, where?? Say where!!

The spondaic first foot "And yet" implies that the lamentation is over, suggesting a certain recovery from the shock, regaining his inner balance. The ease conveyed in the allegorical quote of the "little isle", which addresses the poet with that rather colloquial sounding salutation "Thou there", indicates the poet's recovery. "The Grace that hunts thee" (1.4) implies that, although he escaped grace on this one occasion, it does not necessarily mean that there will not be another chance: the image of the hunting grace rather suggests that one day grace will catch him. In the second quatrain the poet ponders about his future, the surprises which might be contained therein: "I ruminate what pleasant horrors yet / Time holds unwound." The oxymoron of those "pleasant horrors" points to the possibility of becoming a hermit one day: pleasant and joyful as it is to live in a hermitage, one cannot deny its horrors. How much peace seems to have filled his heart again is implied towards the end of the second quatrain when the poet starts to meditate on the beauty of the sunset on that evening, "the first of this dark summer". Watching the sun set has always been associated with peace and tranquillity, thus when taking this line on a literal level, as it is presumably meant to be, it underlines the notion of equilibrium regained; that it should be "the first" in this "dark summer", however, contributes a melancholic undertone. The personification of the sun ("to rest its head, ere 'gain its course it run") suggests the poet's compassion, a feeling of tenderness towards the sun, which additionally stresses the inner peace he feels once more. In the third quatrain the isle's utterance is picked up again. We see its fruits: the poet meditates on the question of whether or not there is a second chance, a second grace given to one who has not used the first well. "Can I say, 'There's no more', when there is one?" The possibility of receiving another grace seems to be there. The flow of time, its cyclic recurrence, is expressed in the closing lines of the third quatrain, where one "now" is constantly superseded by another "now", as it "must into Then dissolve / To make room for another": his past consists of all these one-time nows, which will have dissolved into thens one day, to let other nows have their share. The couplet reminds one in its structure of that of the first sonnet: there is a short sentence in l.13, which through its shortness and directness attracts attention - "And Thou'rt there." The poet is convinced that the Lord will be his companion. The final line is uneven in rhythm, which suggests that the former unrest and agitation is still prevalent and not yet overcome: "And shouldst Thou be ... - But where? Lord, where?? Say where!!" The pauses between the questions and the exclamation at the very end add to the urge conveyed: he longs to know where his future lies.

Grace in personified form appears in "After scratching the watch" (*World*, 9), a sonnet which tells of the presence of grace as it is felt and experienced by the poet:

> Yet Grace, thou blowest still, and wilt not let
> My heart go free from what a while ago
> Thou wouldst, it seemed, it free. Alone, we met.
> And here, alone again, I somehow know
> That Thou sit'st by me by this sleeping lake
> And callest in the ear of my calmed soul.

Grace is presented as a wind whose breeze is still felt by the poet, his heart has not yet ceased being captured by its presence. In solitude and silence he encountered grace; it appears as though solitude was a prerequisite for grace to come: "Alone, we met." And now, "alone again", he is aware of the presence of grace: he feels how grace is speaking to his heart, "And callest in the ear of my calmed soul". It is a sweet experience, his soul is calm and peaceful, the grace he feels even adds to that inner equilibrium. The "sleeping lake" can be taken both literally and symbolically: on a literal level it refers to the pond near La Trappe, which the poet might have envisaged when writing the sonnet. On a symbolical level, however, the "sleeping lake" also refers to his "calmed soul" which rests peacefully at the moment, - former periods of agitation have passed.

Silence is that fertile soil where God's grace can best be perceived. "In the cloister garth" (*World*, 11f.), a poem written after hearing the clockwork in the belfry being re-wound, as we are told in a note, deals with Alun Idris' consent to do God's will, - his firm disposition to be open to grace. The poem can be divided into four sections, each consisting of four stanzas. As a stanza form he uses three rhymed iambic tetrameter lines followed by an amphibrach, an extended iamb, which has been a common device of iambic verse throughout the ages (cf. Hamer 1966, 13). The first section deals with the unknown origin of grace, - its mysterious ways of operating, which cannot be known beforehand:

> Whence comest thou, sweet Grace divine,
> And thou, hid muse, from line to line
> That dost th'unthought with Thought entwine
>   In silence?
>
> And thou, great Bell, that now again
> For one more week by grating chain
> Art turned to turn returning Pain,
>   What strikest?
>
> And thou that art as yet not struck,
> Art long? Art short? And this god, Luck, -
> Thou, Chance - art real? Wilt Youth's vim suck,
>   Tomorrow?
>
> Who knows? Who knows their hidden face?
> Who knows the course of running Grace? [corr.]
> O Future! On thy past no trace
>   Thou'dst leave us.

The first stanza suggests an additional aspect concerning grace: following poetic inspiration complies with the will of God, - the hidden muse entwines "th'unthought with Thought". Human and divine thought are united in poems. The Muse, acting in silence, is presented as the inspiring spirit behind each poetic line. Thus the parallel to divine grace is clear. The amphibrach "In silence?" reinforces the idea that divine grace is best received in solitude and silence. The second stanza turns to the bell and its role as the "organizing principle" in the monastery. The repetition in l.3 emphasizes the monotony of life in the Trappist monastery, - it is a constant recurrence of "returning Pain"; however, this forms a contrast with the attached amphibrach, which suggests a notion of surprise and expectation of what the future will be like. The third stanza deals with the poet's future life: the short sentences and questions underline the impossibility to know beforehand. Finally, the fourth stanza, i.e. the last of this section, summarizes on a more general level what was implied previously. The image used of the future not having left any trace "on thy past" well conveys this idea.

The second section (stanzas 5-8), however, suggests that there is a way to have some pre-knowledge of grace. It starts by picking up the image used in stanza 4:

And yet! And yet, I hear thee call:
There is a trace, be't e'er so small:
Today Tomorrow can forestall
    By feeling.

For Grace, thou'rt felt, thy pull is felt,
As felt as e'er by aught that knelt
Within these Beams that did all melt
    Before them.

Feeling is the graven word: grace cannot be known or grasped mentally in advance, but it can be felt. This is the "trace" which grace leaves in passing. The imagery used in this stanza suggests that especially in contemplative prayer ("aught that knelt") grace can be strongly felt, "these Beams that did all melt", its power being tremendous.

In the seventh stanza the poet skilfully rewrites the message conveyed in the first one, leading from the general idea to his own personal, his individual situation:

Where wilt thou pull, sweet Pull divine,
And thou, hid Breath, from line to line
That dost my thought with thine entwine
    And passest?

By referring to the muse as "hid Breath", Alun Idris obviously has in mind the original concept of poetic inspiration, with the poetic ideas being breathed into the human brain.[138] The lines also convey the idea that we have to be receptive to divine grace and should be aware of the fact that the spirit exercises influence in many different ways, including poetic inspiration. Even in scripture we find references to the "divine blowing", when we read in 2 Timothy 3:16: "All scripture is inspired by God." To Alun Idris the connection between the beauty in poetry and God is obvious: "All art in a way is an expression of God. All beauty is an expression of God's beauty" (letter, 28.2.1990). Poetry therefore has an important function in its role of consecrating creation. Unfortunately, the attitude of the Cistercians towards his poetic aspirations was similar to that of the Carthusians; they, too, had reservations about such activities in a contemplative order, especially as regards publishing his poetry.

The question of becoming a hermit, a recluse was still unresolved. The possibility was there, and although he yearned to become a recluse, he was willing to surrender to the divine will, in whatever direction it might lead him.

    The darkness of thy veilèd face
    Bids me thee grope, and interlace
    My hands in thine, that one word trace:
        SURRENDER.

Giving in to the will of God is essential for the monk. Alun Idris had already spoken about it in the interview with his brother at Sélignac: "I heard within a voice saying, alright, who is having

---

[138] There is also a parallel to the well-known hymn "Breathe on me, Breath of God, And make me wholly thine ...".

his way, you or me? And here you have it Lord, I gave in, and grace did the rest" (Jones, Elwyn, producer 1981). When writing this poem, Alun Idris was still very enthusiastic about the idea of living in perpetual solitude. He had a strong yearning for reclusion, as he was not fully adapting to La Trappe. The third section exclusively deals with the phenomenon of reclusion, firmly implying how ardently he longs to become a hermit:

> I hear a word, a little word
> Too big by many to be heard,
> That something in my heart hath stirred
> For ever.

The paradox in 1.2 suggests the grandeur of this word and its tremendous consequences, too great to be grasped by the majority of mankind; however, he has heard the word and responded to it. The twelfth stanza leads to the climax, when at last the word is pronounced: "R-E-C-L-U-S-I-O-N!" The spelling reinforces the tremendous power the word exerts on the poet.

In the fourth section, the poet has calmed down again, - he tries to reflect objectively on the present situation:

> Along, along, I walk and talk
> With Thee, my Friend, their friend, whose walk
> I'd follow: for the way doth fork
> Before me.
>
> Could I but know which one to choose,
> - For to go wrong were both to lose -
> Thou knowest well I'd ne'er refuse
> To follow.

The appositions in 1.2 of stanza 13 ("my Friend, their friend") suggest how close the poet already feels to the hermits "whose walk / I'd follow". He knows that a decision has to be made, "for the way doth fork", but emphasizes once more in the fourteenth stanza that he would never do anything which did not conform to the Lord's will. And yet, how much he longs to know, to receive a sign pointing to the right decision, is revealed in the final stanza:

> But give me in my loneliness
> A little for my emptiness,
> A little ray of darkliness,
> From Thy light.

The poet employs a variation of triple rhyme, where the stressed syllable does not rhyme, however, with the other lines. This does not sound too pleasing to the ear; nevertheless, it does convey an idea of the poet's total loss, of how much he longs to receive a sign, be it just "a little ray of darkliness". The paradox is used to underline that he does not look for a miraculous, complete enlightenment; in his modesty all that he wishes is a tiny ray, which might show him the way. The final line differs from all the other closing lines in that here we find three stressed syllables, "From Thy light", which underline the divine nature of the light.

The importance of grace to the poet is fundamental. Meditations on grace are usually mingled with other subjects, in particular with his longing to become a hermit. The poet is aware, however, that the dream of becoming a hermit can only materialize if it is in accordance with divine grace.

3.2.2.2. TIME, DEATH AND AFTERLIFE

As in the Carthusian period, we find many poems dealing with the phenomenon of time, death and afterlife during Alun Idris' Trappist noviciate. Time is of special importance in a contemplative monastery, - it is experienced differently, more consciously than in the outside world.

The following poem, "Cierge" (*World*, 17ff.), is an elaborate meditation on the nature of time and its flow. Written to be recited in Community on a special occasion, the celebration of the fiftieth anniversary of the profession of one of the Fathers, as we are told in a note in brackets, a reflection on the passage of time was very apt. It is a long meditative poem in French consisting of 13 stanzas of varying length. There is a certain conversational tone about it, with many exclamations and apostrophes. It is addressed not only to the father who celebrated the anniversary of his profession but can be applied to man in general, "ô Homme". The title indicates how life burns itself up like a candle, although the image of the candle, "cierge", as such is not mentioned again throughout the entire poem.

> "Une vie, une vie ..." - Doucement ces deux mots
> Qui résument sans bruit tout le bruit de ton lot
> Ici-bas, viennent franchir tes lèvres, ô Homme,
> Sans te toucher, te bouger. C'est bien. La somme
> De minutes sans borne, sans nombre, sans poids
> Qui t'assaillent, ne peuvent qu'augmenter ta foi
> En ce copain d'enfance que tu as connu,
> Rencontré, embrassé, caressé, oui, tout nu
> Que tu étais le jour où tes deux yeux s'ouvrirent [corr.]
> Pour rencontrer les siens - ces bleus, bleus yeux qui virent
> Ton sourire. Car tu étais beau, et content
> De ton cadeau - ce cadeau, je dis, qu'on attend
> Sans le savoir, neuf mois - [...]

The mysterious "copain d'enfance" (l.7) with these "bleus, bleus yeux qui virent / Ton sourire" (ll.10f.) is not explicitly named yet: a strange companion with enormous influence, seemingly present from the very first moment onwards. L.2 contains a vague reference to the power of words silently abounding in meaning, "Qui résument sans bruit tout le bruit". The "cadeau" apparently refers to the gift of life, an image which is taken up again in the second stanza:

> "Ton amie, mon amie, fut ton grand ennemi;
> Son cadeau - ce cadeau qu'il te fit de ses mains
> Fut nul autre que lui, oui, lui-même - et demain
> Il le fera encore - ou du moins, tu le penses [...]

It is clear by now that the "cadeau" refers to time, which is later explicitly addressed as the stanza progresses ("Ah! le Temps"). In the third stanza the poet meditates on the flow of time, where he uses sound symbolism to underline the passing of time: "Je t'entends palpiter, petit temps palpitant / Eternel en ta fuite - éternel, et pourtant": here the ticking of the clock almost becomes audible, just as further down, in stanza 11, when we read "Je t'écoute ... t'écoute ... percuter ...".

The poem continues its meditation on the nature of time, consisting of a seemingly endless number of moments:

    ... Un moment, un moment ... - La fleur
Est si belle, si belle, si frêle - un moment;
Et des moments, par moments, si beaux - le tourment
Du passage d'un moment au passé, naguère
Omniprésent, non, absent ... Ah! Joie passagère!
En t'attendant, on t'aime, car tu es promesse;
En t'étreignant, on t'aime, car tu es caresse,
Mains on craint - on te craint, car parfois tu t'épuises;
On te craint, car on craint que tu ne te réduises
A un moment.

The beauty of moments is clearly conveyed in the first lines, although it is coupled with transitoriness. The flower is a conventional metaphor to describe the beauty of a moment, which is bound to fade. The rapid passing of time can be painful, which is strongly expressed in the exclamation "Ah! Joie passagère!". There is a certain joy in awaiting a special moment, - one is thrilled while waiting, and yet there is always the fear present that the joy passes too quickly, "on craint car que tu ne te réduises / A un moment", so that ironically, a moment of joy is but a moment, having vanished all too quickly.

    ... Un moment, un moment. Moments!
Ah! quand même! vous avez un moment de temps,
Un tout, tout petit moment de vrai - le bilan
Contre vous est dressé; quand je vois l'océan
De gros moments perdus, à jamais oubliés,
Je m'écrie: "Ah! à quoi bon? A quoi, Destinée,
Veux-tu mener?"

We allow many moments to pass, many chances remain unused. There is a whole ocean of such moments which could have been employed differently. And yet, it seems to be providential that these moments remain unused, although human nature cannot grasp the plan behind: "A quoi, Destinée, / Veux-tu mener?"

    Time is short. Monks know that it is essential to use time on earth well, reflecting also on time already passed. This idea is conveyed in "Stations" (*World*, 50), where we read:

How many things have separated these
From month to month across the growing years! [corr.]
'Tis good to pause awhile on bended knees
Where one has paused before, where one still hears
The echoes of faint yesterdays, now gone
But somehow there unceasing in still prayer.

In silent prayer these "echoes of faint yesterdays" are contained, and they will never cease to be present. The poet recommends to "pause awhile on bended knees / Where one has paused before": reflecting on one's past is important, to halt awhile and meditate is healthy for the interior equilibrium; unfortunately "some forgot this halt before". Many people rush through their lives without much reflection on what went before. Reflecting on one's past, however, helps to prepare the way for the future, which renders occasional pauses indispensable.

The following poem is a meditation on the poet's own remaining time here on earth, the time which lies between the present moment and the beyond. The title expains the origin of the poem, "After seeing a picture of a recluse, and recalling the photographs of Dom Damien." (*World*, 14). It is a sonnet, although the quatrains are printed as individual stanzas. The union between the stanzas is achieved by the repeated apostrophe at the beginning of each quatrain.

> My father, why didst die so young? And yet
> Why not? Alive or dead thou'rt as entombed
> As e'er entombed man was. 'Twere hard to get
> More close in life to what in death we're doomed.
>
> My father, why didst die so young? And yet
> Art dead? Which is't that loudest speaks? Thy voice
> That ne'er was heard, save by such as were let
> Into its faintness - or thy tomb's faint noise?

L.1 which is repeated in each of the two stanzas refers to the early death of Dom Damien, the last recluse at Camaldoli,[139] who had died suddenly just a few years previously. The first quatrain suggests in a rather direct, almost morbid sounding manner that there is no real difference between a man entombed in a hermitage and the corpse entombed in the grave, "why didst die so young? And yet / Why not?" The corresponding question in stanza two represents the positive counterpart, "And yet / Art dead?", which suggests that now he is probably more alive than before. The third quatrain turns to the poet's own death, concentrating on the period of time which is still left him, while in the closing couplet he tries to find a common bond between Dom Damien and the poet himself:

> My father, must I die so young? There's yet
> A time before the lapse of time that holds [corr.]
> Me from this Siren ... Père! what was't that set
> The great machine Coincidence unfolds?
>
> Who led us both to that obscurity
> Whose dimness let thee hand thy torch to me?

The "great machine Coincidence" allowed things to develop as they did. At the time the possibility to become a recluse seemed realistic to the poet. The "obscurity" refers to life in the hermitage, which seems to be dim and obscure; the "torch", the illumination of that place by living there as a hermit is handed on to the poet. It seems to be his task now to rekindle the light in the hermitage at Camaldoli again.

---

[139] Cf. *World*, 14.

The following poem is connected with the idea of reclusion as well, as it was written after reading about Saint Colette, a recluse (cf. *World*, 20). However, it is primarily centered on the approaching death of a brother at La Trappe, at whose bedside Alun Idris was keeping watch: "At midnight in the infirmary: keeping watch at the bedside of a dying Brother" (*World*, 20)

> The Silence of the night is doubly Great:
> The world sleeps on 'neath blankets of deep sin,
> The cloister snores; the brethren, dreaming, wait
> The call to Prayer. No sound doth stir thy din,
> O buzz of Peace - save this, the rhythmic breath
> Of dying lungs - and this, the rhythmic beat
> Of living Time. I am alone with Death;
> Thou too, cher frère; alone, th'Alone to meet.
> How many ticks, how many breaths rest thee?
> Thou knowest only that one tick, one gasp
> Shall be thine own ... Dimmed eyes, what shall ye see
> When in one twinkling, vistas new ye grasp?
> For death we're born. Good Lord, why more hold back?
> Grant, tombèd sisters, grant this blissful rack.

The most striking feature of this sonnet is its abundance of opposites: "the world" - "the cloister", "sin" - "Prayer", "No sound" - "save this", "dying lungs" - "living Time". We also find an oxymoron in "blissful rack" and such paradoxes as "dimmed eyes, what shall ye see" or "for death we're born". The word play in l.8 "alone, th'Alone to meet" also suggests a paradoxical idea which originates in the different use of the word "alone". All these devices imply the special nature of death, whose mystery is impossible to grasp, although in medical terms it is easy to define. The first quatrain describes the silence of that night which was "doubly Great": the capitalization implies the divine presence that night. The dying brother was to pass soon from this life to the afterlife. Seemingly a night as usual and ordinary as others, it is not: the second quatrain describes the situation, the "rhythmic breath", "the rhythmic beat" of his brother is still observable, but death is already waiting in the wings. "I am alone with Death; / Thou, too, cher frère; alone, th'Alone to meet." These lines describe the two different perspectives of death, one as it is seen by other people watching a person die, the other as it is experienced by the dying person himself. In the third quatrain Alun Idris exclusively deals with his brother, how much time may be left for him, pondering about what his dimmed eyes shall see soon. The closing couplet does not surprise when bearing in mind that it is the afterlife the monks are striving for: what is the point of holding back the "vistas new" he will see soon? The final line addresses the recluses, whom he beseeches to "grant this blissful rack". This closing oxymoron summarizes the contradictory nature of death.

The eventual death of Frère Marie, to whom the previous poem is dedicated, inspired a sequence of three sonnets called "On my knees beside Frère Marie" (*World*, 21f.). The sequence starts with a striking metaphor:

'Twas but one breath like any other, frère,
That, coming not, made thy soul's nostrils breath
The limpid ether of th'angelic air.
Or dost thou, silent brother, e'en now seethe
Awhile in unindulgenced flames that some,
Of having seen them, have decried, and that [corr.]
So loudly that their cry to us has come
In manuscripts o'er which for months we sat?
Yea, I say "we", for though all, all alone,
I knew another to be by my side,
Who did in ink one time what I have done
Another, somewhat further on its tide.
She waiteth for thee, Marie, on the shore,
Where many, many travellers went before.

The inversion at the very beginning of l.1 followed by a spondee, the pause after "breath", and the even stronger one after "coming not" in l.2, help to place even more emphasis on the metaphor, which is in itself stiking, - the breath "That, coming not, made thy soul's nostrils breathe". It visualizes the moment when life leaves the body, and passes on its living force, as it were, to the soul. The use of "nostrils" emphasizes this very first moment of afterlife, of breathing in the "limpid ether of th'angelic air". That moment is of paramount importance and also of great interest to the others, as the monks strive for that day when, at last, they attain the afterlife. The possibility of entering purgatory first is, however, considered as well, which is accompanied by a change of tone in l.4: "seethe / Awhile in unindulgenced flames", where the imagery used describes purgatory in a highly visual, though traditional way. The "manuscripts" mentioned here refer to a document Alun Idris had only shortly before translated from French into English, the *Purgatory Manuscript*. The woman mentioned ("She waiteth for thee") refers to one of the nuns who features in the manuscript.[140]

The first quatrain of the second sonnet echoes the Cistercian way of burying monks:

And this small cross beside thine own to come
In turn to rest on restless limbs here healed,
It will be like thine own, that marks the dumb
Cistercian's everlasting dumbness sealed;
It bears thy name [...]

As is indicated in a note, Frère Marie's brother had been buried there only a few months before. The two of them had been living at La Trappe for many years, and many a word appears twice in the lines quoted, reminding us of the two brothers ("rest" - "restless", "dumb" - "dumbness", "beside thine own" - "like thine own").

The third sonnet of the sequence was written after "A night has passed, thy first in untimed Time; / Art thou by now more used to the Beyond?" The poet addresses his brother like a friend who is right beside him, as though he was still able to answer his questions. There is no barrier between the two caused by the death of the brother, - their relationship has not

---

[140] For further details cf. pp.88ff.

changed. It still shows the same familiarity which was already noticeable in the previous stanzas. Death has nothing repulsive about it, for it is the door to eternity.

On the glass door that opens to the cemetery from the cloister, through which the dead are carried, there are two crosses marked on the stain glass, which describe death as the doorway to eternal life (cf. letter, 10.2.1991):

```
                C                         R
                I              ExspEctantes
     RequieScentes                        S
                T                         U
                E                         R
                R                         R
                C                         E
                I                         C
                E                         T
                N                         I
                S                         O
                E                         N
                S                         E
                                          M
```

Death being the doorway to afterlife, the cemetery loses its frightening aspect for the monk. Therefore it is not surprising to see that poems were also written in the cemetery itself, which represents just another aspect of life, - a particularly important one. To write poems in the cemetery seems macabre only to those of us who are still more concerned about their mundane lives on earth. "Au cimetière" (*World*, 12f.) supplies meditations and impressions received while sitting in the cemetery and pondering about the monks whose bodies are lying there.

> Le sommeil! Le repos! Vous dormez, mes chers Pères.
> Votre soir est venu. Dormez bien, mes frères.
> Oui, ce soir que le jour tous les jours veut revoir,
> Veut revoir revenir, devenir un espoir
> De répit momentané, de trêve à sa lutte
> Contre l'Heure et l'Ennui qui ennuie, qui rebute
> A chaque heure ennuyeuse qui arrive et repart
> Pour revenir encor, repartir nulle part [corr.]
> Sinon à son départ, d'où ne partira pas
> Cet Ennui renaissant qui toujours renaîtra. [...]

The use of repetition is not only observable in Alun Idris' English verse but also in his French poetry. The case is the same with enjambement. This poem is written in alexandrines, although some lines vary as regards the number of syllables. It consists of three parts differing in length; the first part is the longest one with 26 lines rhyming in couplets, except for the last two lines:

> Par ces croix où se croisent vos soirs et les nôtres,
> Par ces croix où est inscrit le plus grand des vôtres
> A jamais. Car ce jour du Retour ne venaint
> Qu'une fois.

The short closing line forms the first part of the inital line of the second stanza: "A jamais! A jamais! Oui, jamais", which rhymes with the penultimate line of stanza one. The anaphora emphasizes the importance of the double function of the crosses, as a reminder of all the souls which have gone this way before and also of the greatest of all days for the departed. The two dates on the crosses, the date of birth and the date of death, are two birthdays in a way, the birthday to this life and the birthday to the great life afterwards.

> The moment of death is the one at which the whole life had been aiming: in a monastery it is all towards God, all aiming towards eternity. One lives already in eternity, that's the point, when eternity dawns. (letter, 30.12.1990)

The second stanza consists of 8 lines: ll.2-7 rhyme in couplets, l.1 rhymes with the penultimate line of the first stanza, l.8 lacks three syllables which are supplied in the inital line of the third stanza. While in the first stanza he addresses all the brethren lying in the cemetery, the poet talks about them and all the other departed in the second stanza, starting with an emphatic repetition:

> A jamais! A jamais! Oui, jamais
> Pourra homme ni bête, ni bombe ni feu
> Reconquérir les jours qu'ont conquis en ce lieu
> Pour toujours et toujours ces seuls vrais conquérants
> Qui reposent. Car ici, saint, roi, mécréant
> Se retrouvent, et trouvent la grande Trouvaille
> Qu'a trouvé chaque tombé de chaque bataille
> En ouvrant les yeux bleus de son âme.

"Les yeux bleus de son âme" is a beautiful image, with the colour blue suggesting purity and crystal clearness, but also including the idea of spirituality, traditionally implied by this colour. The third stanza consists of 15 lines, with the first (which completes l.8 of the second stanza) and the last two lines not rhyming. The final two lines are actually only one phrase, which is given additional emphasis by using two lines and the special mode of orthography. The poet returns to his individual situation, involving the monks of the past, though by addressing them personally once more. Towards the end a certain yearning for solitude is apparent:

> En ce soir de mes soirs où je vole vers vous,
> - Va couler, découler, dis-je, jusqu'à la terre,
> Pour laisser une copie tracée dans la pierre
> De ce tout petit mot qui m'a parlé si fort
> Que je prévois déjà ce que sera mon sort ...
> De
>   RECLUS.

"De reclus" has a double meaning: it can refer to "the word of recluse", but also suggests "the lot of recluse". The poet himself explains: "This was the period when I was still not able to free myself of the Carthusian past and the yearning for solitude. Because I had intended to become a Camaldolese [...]" (letter, 30.12.1990).[141] Doubtless, these lines echo his hiraeth to become a hermit.

Voluntary death as a special mode of death is treated in a poem simply called "The suicide" (*World*, 28). It takes the form of a monologue and is addressed to two young people, personally known to the poet, who had committed suicide (cf. *World*, 28):

> An instant brought you home to your request,
> My parted brethren ne'er to be recalled
> This time from saddened Sorrow. Will's behest
> Commanded, and obeyed 'twas by appalled
> And knowing members whose own muzzled thought [corr.]
> Thought better. Ah! too late, the musings sweet
> Of sages cold that know not what was fought
> Between the first and last swell of birth's heat. [corr.]
> Upon the edge of Time, what did ye feel?
> What did ye know when its last notch had clicked?
> And would ye then have half-rewound its wheel - [corr.]
> Just one half-turn? A quarter? Were ye pricked
> Upon this little frontier of hid pow'rs
> By something, some small thing that wielded hours?

The spondee at the beginning of l.3, "This time", emphasizes the finality of the decision, the instant, completed by the pleonasm "saddened Sorrow". The capitalization reinforces the idea of sorrow conveyed. The natural pause before "Will's behest" and after "Commanded" places enormous emphasis on this phrase, making it sound like a verdict pronounced, not giving the "appalled / And knowing members", i.e. all the instincts of self-preservation which rebelled against it, the slightest chance of appeal. The pause after the exclamatory "Ah!" and the second one after the spondee "too late" (l.6) places additional stress on the sobering insight that it is too late for any laments.

The sound symbolism of "*musings* sweet / *Of sages cold*" in ll.6f. (long vowels, musical labials, voiced /ngz/ opposed to sharp plosives and the sinister /dʒ/) suggests the idea that it is easy for people to argue philosophically like a sage, even to condemn others for committing suicide. For a long time suicides were not given church burial. However, who can really plumb their agony? "Birth's heat" is a metaphor for the life energy within us, the energy to continue the process of birth from conception onwards. Everything in the individual is orientated towards self-preservation. L.9 forms a whole sentence, which is rare in Alun Idris' poetry: "Upon the edge of Time what did ye feel?" The question is prompted by a notion of curiosity, followed by four further questions on the same subject. "Some small thing that wielded hours" refers to the short break of conscience, the moment which might hold a person back. The poet meditates on the interior mental and emotional proceedures of a person who commits suicide. He does not

---

[141] Brother David was allowed to spend a few days in solitude by the Abbot of La Trappe: the poems "Lines written on Dom Damien's stone" (*World*, 22f.) and "Others written the following morning against a stone of his doorway" (*World*, 23) echo this occasion. After staying with the Camaldolese at Camaldoli, both at the Cenobis and at the Sacro Eremo, he visited Frascati and the more solitary Monte Rua before returning to his Abbey. The Coronese branch own the Frascati and Monte Rua hermitages. The Prior of Monte Rua would have been willing to let him try, but the General, at Frascati, hesitated greatly (cf. letter, 13.1.94). For further details as regards the poet's hiraeth for reclusion, cf. chapter 3.2.3.2., pp.210-217.

condemn the suicides for taking their lives, as he is aware of the impossibility of knowing the agony from which they had suffered. But he wonders whether they might have wanted to change their minds in the end, when it was not possible to do so anymore.

The death of a brother at La Trappe, who had been Alun Idris' neighbour in "quire, scriptorium and dormitory", inspired the following French sonnet, "Si tôt, mon frère?" (*World*, 31), written at a time when the poet was already a Trappist at Roscrea:

> Mon frère, as-tu vu maintenant ce lieu
> Si longtemps rêvé? Sais-tu maintenant
> Ce que tu voulais savoir? Tes deux yeux [corr.]
> En s'ouvrant sur ce lointain continent,
> Qu'ont-ils pu voir? Ce moment fut-il court -
> Ce moment qui séparait tous les tiens
> Des nôtres qui demeurent? Oui, tu cours,
> Etienne, mais un autre attrape bien.
> Tu es très occupé ce soir, à laisser faire
> Ce Temps, qui ne fut donné ici-bas
> Qu'en petits bouts trop courts pour pouvoir plaire
> A cette Hâte, amie de l'Au-delà
> Qui voit venir encore un grand coureur
> Sautant l'Eternité en sa fureur.

By talking and pondering about Frère Etienne's death, we are given a lively description of his character and personality. By nature he seems to have been in a constant hurry ("Oui, tu cours") - he was responsible for the the infirmary in the monastery, and worked part-time in the kitchen as well (cf. letter, 17.8.1991). The repetition of "maintenant" in the first two lines emphasizes how long he had already dreamt of attaining the afterlife. The first two quatrains are filled with questions about how he feels, what it was like to pass from this side to the other. As a summarizing statement, he adds "Oui, tu cours, / Etienne, mais un autre attrape bien". He was in a hurry all the time, but there is one thing in life which makes you stop immediately. The third quatrain deals more elaborately with this typical characteristic of his: "Tu es très occupé ce soir, à laisser faire / Ce Temps" - these extreme opposites help to underline how difficult it was for him not to do something productive, not to work, he always felt the need to do something. Thus, at last, he is now busy with "laisser faire". It seems as though he came to eternity in a hurry, therefore all the more quickly.

"Old age" (*World*, 38) is a lament on the passing of youth, on the inexorable progress of time, and also developing the unfairness of being remembered the way one was towards the end of one's life, instead of in the fullness of one's youth. The death of Fr. Canice at Roscrea stimulated the sonnet:

> The years have moods o'er these our greying hairs -
> As o'er these others that, still fair an hour,
> Re-see the light of day. Our body bares
> The load of Time as doth the new-oped flow'r
> That wafts the acme of its youth away
> Before our eyes - these eyes that have known friends
> Too fair to be fair long. It is a day,
> One more, just one, that sighs, "Here growing ends?"

> And be there some that were not meant to die
> But to be plucked still living? Lord, the years
> That cover their forerunners with a lie,
> Forgetting what they were, will they have tears -
> Not for the stooped and shrivelled that walks on,
> But for the shriv'lling of some day long gone?

The simile of the flower in blossom in l.4, which is to wither soon, is conventional; the diction used, however, is well-chosen: "as doth the new-oped flow'r / That wafts the acme of its youth away" - the process is a gradual one, almost unnoticeable, which is suggested by the verb "waft". The "acme" refers precisely to the point when we have reached the summit of our day, our full bloom, i.e. when the decline starts. The simile is then used metaphorically when the poet asks the question "And be there some that were not meant to die / But to be plucked still living?". This metaphor conveys the idea that some people do not "die" as a result of the process of slow decay but they lose their lives while still in blossom, "still living". The undertone present suggests the growing absence of life and energies as the years float by. L.11 introduces the idea of the unfairness that our old age covers up youth, people are remembered as they were when they died: will those years of our youth have their tears of regret and mourning for "the shriv'lling of some day long gone?", i.e. the day when the decay started, turning us into the "stooped and shrivelled that walks on".

Fr. Canice's death also stirred another meditation, "The burying of a saint" (*World*, 39) which is centered on the idea of death as such and what happens afterwards. "The wheel of Fortune turns but once for u*s* / And we thi*s* *c*ircuit run in our *s*ole ra*c*e." The hissing /s/ fricatives convey the idea of the inexorable progress of time; there is a certain balance achieved by the long vowel /i:/ at the beginning of both l.1 and l.2, which additionally underlines the firm connection between the wheel of Fortune and our lives. For his departed brother, an "unmapped journey" has begun, from which there is no return:

> Ah! dense Unknown, 'tis this to know thee well
> For that thy weight too great for little things
> Crushed all that e'er approached thee, heard thy knell
> Or stepped into the shuffling of these wings
> That blow out this our candle with a flick,
> For though we burn, we lose not this strange wick.

The "weight" of this great unknown, of the beyond we enter after our death, "crushed all that e'er approached thee", and cannot in any way be compared to anything experienced before. Alun Idris uses the candle as a symbol for our life: although it is easy to blow out our mundane lives "with a flick", there is no way to extinguish a soul, "we lose not this strange wick". It is the same person who carries on in death, we do not lose the link, "this strange wick".

Death in its intermediary function as the opening door to afterlife is often reflected in the Trappist period of Alun Idris' verse. The attitude of a Carthusian monk towards death does not really differ from that of the Trappist monk, as both basically seek the afterlife, the ultimate, eternal union with God. The meditations on time are less frequently to be found in the Trappist period than in the Carthusian one.

3.2.2.3. THE POWER OF THE WORD

Words have a different impact on monks in a silent order than they have on people living outside monastic walls. As the monks rarely talk, it is the written word in particular which receives special importance. To Alun Idris, the written word, be it in the form of a letter or a poem, exerts tremendous power: to him it is the vent for one's innermost being, speaking much more directly and honestly to others than in an actual conversation. The examples below clearly demonstrate this view.

"En écrivant les dernières lettres (avant d'entrer en retraite)" (*World*, 2f.) is an early example mirroring the importance of the written word for the poet: the sonnet addresses the writing tool, a pen.

> Une heure ou deux me restent dans ce bruit
> Sonore que tu es, doux instrument. [corr.]
> Je manie tes prouesses aujourd'hui,
> Te laissant découvrir mon dénuement
> A ceux qui par tes traits verront ma face
> Intérieure - celle qui échappe
> A tout regard. Car nul ne voit la Grâce
> Et nul ne saura ce que cette chape
> Qui cachera désormais tout mon être
> Va cacher. Car le coeur ici se cache.
> Un dernier regard, car la fenêtre
> Ouverte que tu es, se clôt. Et sache,
> Ami, qui relies tout ami, que toi,
> Toi seul, as transsubstantié mon moi. [corr.]

It is a love poem really, addressed to the pen: the affection expressed towards this little tool is striking, in particular towards the end of the poem. The note in brackets explains the forthcoming separation of "ce bruit / Sonore que tu es", which prompts the poet to write down a few lines in honour of that "doux instrument". The pen represents the means to express his innermost thoughts in the form of poems, his interior, "mon dénuement" (1.4) even finds expression and allows others to glance at it, as is conveyed in ll.4-5. The imagery used in 1.5, "A ceux qui par tes traits verront ma face / Intérieure" beautifully suggests the process of communication, and intensifies the personification of the pen already implied. "Celle qui échappe / A tout regard" underlines the special nature and function of the written word, which reveals man's interior face, which cannot be seen from the outside. The repeated use of the literary form "nul" underlines the firm separation between the hidden life of the Trappist monk and the rest of the world, his entire being is hidden, including the heart: "Car le coeur ici se cache." The shortness of this phrase intensifies the meaning conveyed. The pen used to have an intermediary function, which is suggested by the metaphor "la fenêtre / Ouverte que tu es, se clôt". However, this window now closes; and yet, it appears as though at last the poet wishes to confide a secret to the pen: "Toi seul, as transsubstantié mon moi." The bold metaphorical language employed here is highly suggestive, firmly implying the importance of the written word. The theological term "transsubstantiation" refers to the doctrine that the bread and wine in the eucharist are changed into the body and blood of Christ. In the metaphorical sense it implies that to the poet the pen is a means to find and express his true self; the poem is the true embodiment of his real inner being, just as the bread *is* the body of Christ after the consecration. Only the written word, the poem, is his true inner self. Only in this particular form his true face is visible. What is furthermore implied by the very use of this theological term as a metaphor is that the poet does not see any contradiction between the poetic vein and leading the life of a Trappist monk in silence.

"Answering the request" (*World*, 15f.) deals exclusively with the idea of writing and the Muse's central role. It is a French poem, despite its English title, and presents the poet's ideas about poetic inspiration. The poem itself has an interesting structure: consisting of nine stanzas of different length, it is an enumeration of ideas that come to the poet's mind while pondering about the subject. The lines rhyme in couplets except for the last line of each stanza, which is single. There is only one variation to that pattern, the fifth stanza does not have an extra line at the end, for it is placed at the beginning of the sixth stanza. Repetition of sentence structures, repetition of words, and parts of words is a characteristic of this poem. The beginning is startling:

"Pondez-nous!" disaient-ils, mais la muse est à sec.
"Pondez-nous!" disaient-ils; mais ce petit blanc-bec
De poète peu doué en langue barbare
Ne peut pondre, répondre, comprendre ... - Bizarre
Est ce drôle d'engin qu'on appelle la Rime
Qui exprime ou opprime le courant infime
D'une pensée ...

The image of the poet as "petit blanc-bec", unable to hatch for others on command, hints at the natural, spontaneous development of a poem in the poet's mind, which turns what starts out as a thought into a poetic line. The use of the word "Rime" is not to be taken literally, but rather as *pars pro toto*, although Alun Idris does, in fact, consider rhyme as fundamental to poetry. Rhyme, or rather poetry, is able to "exprime ou opprime", - a line of poetry is a source of bliss if used well and with skill, a burden if the thought does not find its proper expression. "Le courant infime / D'une pensée" is an effective image to describe the nature of the thought: the tiny current of a thought is there. It is important to use it well by clothing it into a good poem. The succeeding four stanzas all start with the same two lines: "La Pensée! La Pensée! Oui, drôle / Est ce drôle d'engin qui répond sans contrôle ..." The repetition of "La Pensée" has an alienating effect, for it is far from smooth in sound; yet, the fourfold repetition of the entire sentence emphasizes the idea that poetic inspiration is a force which cannot be controlled. It responds without control, as we are told in the second stanza:

La Pensée! La Pensée! Qui, drôle
Est ce drôle d'engin qui répond sans contrôle
Quand il devrait se taire, et ne peut que déplaire
A des grands qui bâillonnent, et voudraient défaire,

Déchirer, décomposer - détruire, en un mot -
Chaque mot composé, compressé sous le flot
D'une pensée.

These lines contain a veiled reference to the poet's own experience in monastic life as regards writing poetry, not so much at La Trappe, but rather at the charterhouse in Sélignac. This idea is supported by the fact that he was asked for to compose this very poem (cf. letter, 30.12.1990).

In the third stanza Alun Idris calls the muse "Ce tout, tout petit esprit, cet ange, ce vent / Qui peut venir, revenir une heure, un moment, / Et peut partir à jamais;" The inconsistency of its nature is its very essence. The images chosen to describe the muse are conventional. Then, however, the poet continues to address her directly:

[...] Sais-tu,
Mon amie, mon amante, ce qu'un jour j'ai su
En t'écoutant? J'ai su, mon amie, ma traîtresse,
Que la drogue qui calmait ma longue tristesse
Solitaire - l'extase si douce en ton sein -
Allait un jour me rompre, corrompre ... - Enfin
Tu as gagné.

This passage beautifully describes the poet's relationship to the muse: "Mon amie, mon amante", which is striking in its melodiousness, as opposed to "mon amie, ma traîtresse". The muse is his friend, his lover, but also his traitoress, which has particular force when bearing in mind that the writing of poetry was an important reason why Alun Idris did not stay in the charterhouse. The muse was the one who calmed his "longue tristesse / Solitaire", - her healing function is explicitly mentioned here and even reinforced by "l'extase si douce en ton sein". One day it was more than he could bear, one day she was going to break him and, at last, she won. He was unable to resist her any longer, - he was bound to start to write.

As is indicated in the subtitle, the poem was written to celebrate Père Emmanuel's feast day, which means that the poem was intended to be read out aloud; in that respect it differs from all the others. Bearing this in mind, the honesty the poet uses to describe the importance of poetry and the muse's inspiration to him is arresting, given the possible risk he was running. It lay within the realm of possibility that the Trappists, just like the Carthusians, might not be particularly favourable towards his poetic activities, and that is what, unfortunately, happened in the end.

The fourth stanza is the only one which is repeated entirely at the conclusion, without any modification. In part, this stanza is an adaptation of the second one: the first two lines of stanza two are repeated exactly in the fourth stanza, the third and fourth line are slightly modified.

La Pensée! La Pensée! Oui, drôle
Est ce drôle d'engin qui répond sans contrôle
Quand il devrait se taire, et ne veut pas le faire,
Quand il devrait se taire, et ne peut que déplaire
A des grands qui bâillonnent, des grands qui talonnent
Ton passage trop bref, tes éclairs qui sillonnent

> Pour un instant mon ciel - notre ciel, douce amie,
> Car ton sein me consola, fidèle ennemie,
> Et tu gagnas.

The strange, gentle friend, yet faithful enemy won; the contradictory terms hint at her ambiguous nature: faithful as the muse is, in the charterhouse she has become his "fidèle ennemie". How close he feels to her is indicated by "mon ciel - notre ciel, douce amie", - they form a unity.

In the seventh stanza the poet projects a climax, which finally leads to naming his strange friend in the eighth, i.e. last but one stanza:

> Ton nom, mon amie,
> Confidente imprudente, impudent ennemie,
> Tu le connais trop bien, et tu t'en amuses,
> Amusée d'abuser de tous ceux qui refusent
> De te nommer.
>
> Ton nom, mon amie, oui, c'est MUSE,
> Ton domaine, ma belle, est MUSIQUE; ta ruse, [corr.]
> C'est de briser le sceau du secret du grand coeur
> Du trop grand seul-à-seul des trop peu connus pleurs
> De l'inconnu.

Her contradictory nature is again implied by the word play "confidente imprudente, impudent ennemie". The muse breaks the seal of the heart, - she offers a means to release the tension. The term "muse" has the same linguistic origin as "music", - there is a firm connection between the two: the domain of the muse is music, which suggests the melodious flow of words and sounds. To Alun Idris the connection of poetry and music is vital: as has already been pointed out, a great number of his poems can be chanted. They are even meant to be sung, as music acts as an additional means to reinforce the affective component of verse, thereby making it all the more powerful.

Alun Idris' views on the nature of poetry and the qualities which constitute a good poem differ from those of most contemporary poets. In "Reading a modern" (*World*, 48) Alun Idris takes the micky out of modern poets, who exercise poetic licence without restraint:[142] "Ignoring Thesis, Arsis and the voix / Of beaten Discipline". "The point is that in all history of poetry, discipline and movement and regularity has always been there. When you take all these away - you are free if you want to - you must put something pretty good in its place" (letter, 8.4.1990). He shares these conservative views with many other Welsh people, as Welsh poetry used to be fairly traditional as regards rhyme and metre. But, of course, there are other trends as well in Wales, in particular in contemporary Anglo-Welsh literature. Alun Idris closes his sonnet with the following, rather biting lines, which leave no doubt about his view on such modern trends:

---

[142] Here, in particular, Alun Idris had a contemporary Welsh poet-priest in mind, whose literary fame has spread over the whole of Europe.

```
                              "[...] What
    Could I have writ, save
                      'It
            takes
To                        sweat
            write like
                              Tha-
    T'?"
```

In "23.iii.67" (*World*, 53) Alun Idris meditates on the power of the word, - how much words have influenced and formed his life. The date given in the title refers to the day of his evangelical conversion when he was a schoolboy: it was just "a murmur" of a friend which was bound to "call me to my Lord". This was the beginning of his life dedicated to the Lord, and there were more important events to come, which were provoked or influenced by a powerful, though "frail, stray word":

> Who knows the pow'r hid in one frail, stray word?
> 'Twas on this day in childhood that a friend
> Did by a murmur call me to my Lord;
> 'Twas by a word that Thou the Word didst send
> To stifle henceforth every word and be
> A being made of Quiet; 'twas a sound
> That passed between the silence that can see
> Behind two eyes that meet, that Life rebound.
> A word again had bid these penned words cease
> And they had ceased; and in their ceasing yelled
> To be let out, till doctors bade release.
> Released again, a word had them withheld ...
> Till one breath one sound gave ... And had it not,
> Would some hour breathed for twain have lain forgot?

Words have changed his life, which becomes apparent in this sonnet bathed in allusions to the poet's own biography. The rhythmical pattern of the opening line, the initial spondee, the inverted third foot, followed by two more spondaic feet, firmly emphasize the value and power radiating from words. The anaphora in ll.2 and 4 underlines the idea of enumeration, stressing the manifold occasions when a word was of decisive influence for him. The capitalized "Word" in l.4 refers to the living Word of God, which was imparted to him through the word of a preacher. It eventually had the effect of making him a "being made of Quiet" (l.6), a monk in a contemplative monastery. In ll.7 and 8 there is a reference to the possibility of letting a friendship develop ("two eyes that meet"), therefore of creating life ("that Life rebound"), which was stopped by a word as well. He ceased writing poems ("these penned words cease") at Sélignac, yet the pain which the suppression of his creative impulse caused was hardly bearable: "in their ceasing yelled / To be let out". The spondaic "let out" emphasizes the inner tension caused by the suppression of the poetic vein. It was not the solitude which was causing the major problem, it was his suppressed creativity. Although allowed to write again at first, the novice master's remark at La Trappe arrested the flow once more, till at last, at Roscrea, he was encouraged to resume writing. The closing couplet is striking because of its rhythmical irregularity: the accumulation of stresses (the spondees in the second and third foot of each line) in 1.13 underline once more the power of the word, which made him write again, while in 1.14 it is emphasized that by writing poetry the poet is able to share his experience with others, with those reading his poems. Writing poetry is a way of preserving precious hours, in order to share them with someone who might come across the poem in the future, "some hour breathed for twain".[143]

The very image of the "frail, stray word" hints how quickly it is launched, too quickly perhaps at times, as is suggested in the opening lines of "Falling" (*World*, 59), where we read: "We do make many promises in heat / And many break in cooling." - a line which reflects a truth known to us all. Powerful as a word can be, we sometimes tend to forget what we have said before, ignoring the possible consequences involved. The nature of a sensible utterance is described rather meticulously as:

> [...] when com*ple*te
> Were all the circui*t*s of wire*d t*hough*t*, re-*set*
> *F*or ac*t*ing on reac*t*ing nerves, ea*ch*, all [corr.]
> A*twitch at* each *s*ent me*ss*age, all, I *s*ay,
> In their *t*ens*ed* armoury, the very *c*all
> Of Order e'en *f*ore*st*alling in array [...] [corr.]

Following such instructions, not one single nonsensical utterance would ever cross one's lips; the massive presence of hissing sounds and sharp plosives (as is indicated in italics) underlines the attempted scientific explanation of the procedure on the part of the author. However, how quickly an ill-considered word is uttered ("so feeble and so small"), is implied as the sonnet continues. The consequences of such an utterance can be painful, not only for the person addressed, but also for the one who uttered it, firmly regretting the slip of the tongue: the line "e'en now w*r*ings ou*t* my hear*t's roots*' *sp*leen", with the accumulation of voiceless t's and s's conveys the pain caused by the faux pas.

"As letters are reaching destination" (*World*, 55) is another meditation on the power of the written word. The relationship which is built up between the author and the reader is described as follows:

> And when a particle, a grain, a trace
> Of this our present thinking thinks again
> In some heart e'en unseen, unknown, whose face
> In its hid weeping may ne'er share its pain
> With him who, passing, shared it with its Past,
> Then doth that mind walk minds in one grain cast.

A written word, be it in the form of a poem or a letter, can be picked up again by an "unseen, unknown" heart whose own life, pain and suffering is not known to the author. And yet, they share "a particle, a grain, a trace": the word can be of help to the reader. Consoling in its effect, it can offer a source of knowledge and joy, - "Then doth that mind walk minds".

---

[143] When this poem was written, it was not then foreseeable that his poetry would ever be published.

A record-player is the image used for an analogy at the beginning of "'I suddenly realise the power of the typewritten word'" (*World*, 33): the record itself has no voice, and yet by being linked to the "machine's great workings" it can make the whole room throb. In the same way the typewriter's silent ribbon transmits sounds which can, through being plugged to the reader's brain, be transmitted to the heart and make it throb:

> Nay, nay, my sister, lifeless things can move
> Two ways, and in their coming back recoil
> With tripled movement from the spinning groove
> That without e'en a voice hath pow'er to toil
> At this machine's great workings where it throbs.
> For I perceive in list'ning to mine eyes
> That they hear more than when their seeing robs
> The silence of its ears, in ill-heaved sighs.

The synesthesia in ll.6-8 underlines that when we see people face to face we "rob the silence of its ears" in that we fill silence with comments ("sighs"), and thus behold the inward person less clearly than when we see merely someone's words. When reading a line, the words are allowed to resonate in the receptive air of solitude, which seems to be less feasible than when meeting someone in person. In that sense it is possible to listen to one's eyes and let the words resonate.

The poet's preference of the written word to the spoken one is continued in "An unopened letter" (*World*, 38), which describes the tremendous joy on receiving a letter. The sonnet powerfully conveys the excitement felt by the poet:

> There are hid things that, gagged, yet find a way
> To mutter to the heart that jumps to see
> The casement of a thought-wave that can say
> In this delayed transmission more than we
> In our unthought heaped output instantly
> Emit from troubled breasts as face scans face.
> We are best seen when we are constantly
> From sight removed, for depths with ink embrace.

The straight-forwardness of these opening two quatrains underlines the message the poet aims to convey. The joy on receiving a letter is immense ("the heart that jumps to see"), experienced all the more powerfully in a Cistercian monastery. Letters seem to tell us more in a sense than personal encounter, as those "hid things" (the spondee reinforces their usual inaccessibility), which perhaps cannot be uttered otherwise ("gagged"), find expression in written form. The choice of "gagged" powerfully conveys the idea that there are things, feelings, thoughts in the human heart which strive to be communicated but cannot be expressed orally. The spondee in the "unthought heaped output" helps to underline the rash, ill-considered nature of many a conversation, "as face scans face". The image used to describe the personal encounter is characterized by an excessive use of hissing fricatives, using voiced /z/ and voiceless /s/ alternatively. A certain discomfort is firmly implied in sound. The image as such equally conveys the idea of a confrontation rather than giving one's time and attention to the other person. Ll.7 and 8 summarize the message of the previous lines when the poet concludes "for depths with ink embrace". And yet, from l.9 onwards, the poet admits in a rather involved manner that the personal encounter has its value as well, concluding that "for but one ray / That eye sent eye tore well this seal away". He sticks to the metaphor of letter writing when describing the encounter: the "seal" which is there when meeting a person is taken away by a sympathetic glance, conveying attention or affection. In a glance there is often incipient comprehension.

As the title indicates, "Swearing" (*World*, 37) deals with the bad custom of using religious words irreverently. "*Till mischief yell/ Its fill of vomit grace from lips o'erblest.*" (ll.7f.) explicitly refers to the fact that people frequently use sacred words when they swear, forgetting how sacred they are, or maybe they act as though they did. The harsh, sharp sounds prevailing underline the feeling of disgust conveyed. The idea of vomitting grace is a powerful image: the lips which receive the sacrament, and therefore grace, are the same lips which "vomit" holy things in the form of swearing. Later on we read: "A tongue can bear the weight of Angel Hosts / And by a stroke itself an angel make." (ll.9f.). The term "Angel Hosts" suggests a double meaning: it refers to the consecrated bread, but also suggests whole "armies" of angels, a concept which provokes various associations. It lies within the power of the tongue of a priest to baptize a child ("Angel Hosts"), whilst a child who dies in innocence is an angel for heaven. Equally, when he pronounces the words of absolution, he can cleanse the soul again. Another association is that a tongue which preaches the gospel can convert a soul, and thus create an angel (cf. letter, 25.8.1991). The closing couplet does not leave any doubts as regards the effects of swearing: "For but a vibrant column moves awhile, / Yet it bears rays that turn marred eons vile." The "vibrant column" is the column of air, the rays suggest the spiritual power of words, for good or for evil. If power is used for evil, "that turn marred eons vile", abusing sacred things, abusing grace, can have terrible consequences that may affect us throughout eternity.

In "Obituaries" (*World*, 41) the poet meditates on what we leave behind when we depart, concluding the poem with the line: " For little things / Can sometimes *linger long* where brief *Song sings*." The alliteration and abundance of /ng/ and /l/ sounds suggests the idea of song. So much is forgotten of what has gone before. A "brief Song", however, like a poem, can make such "little things", which need not necessarily be so insignificant after all, "linger long".

Alun Idris' belief in the power of the written word was certainly nourished by his life in silent orders. To him the poetic and the religious inspiration, the "divine madness and divine truth" (Fairchild 1939, 129) are closely akin. A contemplative monk experiences the nature of words differently, more powerfully than outside the monastery. The written word has gained special importance for the poet: he considers poems an outlet for accumulations of feelings which cannot be canalised in their flow. It is a natural process as soon as the muse starts working on one's mind. There is no escape from it. Stopping the flow wilfully is bound to harm the soul, as an important part of one's personality is thereby neglected. Suppressing the creative vein, in particular in a contemplative order, can provoke problematical, even unbearable situations.

3.2.2.4. PROVIDENCE

Faith in providence is an attitude of mind, which in Alun Idris' case is of great importance, as could already be observed in his Carthusian period.[144] This belief in providence underlies many a poem of his Trappist period as well.

"Before re-taking the habit" (*World*, 43) was written after having left La Trappe, just before joining the community at Roscrea. This step made the poet reflect about providence and how it had all been arranged in advance:

> Had I known yesterday what this day held,
> Could I have faced the promise of its dawn?
> Thy ways, O Providence, were they beheld
> By th'infant at the hour his hours are born,
> Would they curtail its crying, or it feed?
> And when the agèd sinner sins his last
> And lies down half-willed Destiny to heed,
> Doth he then feel thy great chains clinging fast?
> O Ancient Vision, dost thou see and let,
> Or let and see till we ourselves have seen
> How little we can see of this vast net
> We tie with years and rays that nothing mean,
> Unless it be to ratify that Yea
> That nodded at eternal folly's way?

The poem meditates on the nature of providence, in particular on the speculative idea of what would happen if we knew beforehand what providence has arranged for us. The frequent use of choriambi characterizes the first two quatrains, which underlines the notion of uncertainty concerning the future. The rhythmical pattern of l.1 in particular attracts attention: the initial choriambus is followed by a pyrrhic, while the closing two feet are spondees; l.2 starts with a choriambus as well. These opening lines meditate on the idea of looking into the future for just one day, not any further, to know in advance "what this day held"; yet the poet doubts whether he would be able to face the "promise of its dawn". He is more courageous as the poem proceeds: supposing that the infant knows from the very first moment onwards what providence has arranged for him or her, would these hours "curtail its crying, or it feed?". The poet then jumps from childhood to old age when he asks whether an old person is, at last, willing to give in and accept that his or her destiny has been pre-arranged. The image of "thy great chains clinging fast" vividly suggests that one cannot escape the powers and the influence of providence. The third quatrain is addressed to providence itself, asking how it really works,

---

[144] See chapter 3.1.2.1., pp.98-102.

whether every little step has been pre-arranged for us, or whether providence changes according to our acts, - "dost thou see and let / Or let and see", both of which resulting in our ways having been predestined. This idea is firmly implied in the closing couplet. The spondees in the first and last foot of l.11, "How little" and "vast net", emphasize human ignorance, how little of our future path we can know beforehand.

In the monastery at Roscrea it was noticed that Alun Idris found it very hard to settle, which is implied in a poem called "'Ο Πνευμάτικος", which means "The spiritual man/father" (*World*, 49f.). The title echoes the idea that in Eastern spirituality the monk is formed by personal contact with a holy man, spiritual paternity being of paramount importance. The poem, which consists of two sonnets, starts with a reference to two monks in the monastery who advised him as spiritual fathers: "'Tis strange, good Lord, that two should say one thing, / And stranger when the two should be Thy twain". The "two", who are "Thy twain", refer to these two fathers, whom Alun Idris had talked to, who saw the suffering he was enduring: they realized that he was not able to fully adapt, being so much used to total silence; however, to live in complete and utter silence was exactly what Alun Idris had hoped for, as is expressed in the second quatrain:

> Good Master, I had heard Thy silent pull
> And thought perhaps that it would lead to peace
> In some recluded solitude, not full
> Of Effort to bid broken silence cease.
> 'Tis good, good Lord, to be yet young, for, old,
> When the last chapter hath been read, no more
> Illusion can there be. As now unfold
> The pages of th'Adventure yet in store,
> I thank Thee for this sealed tome yet to know,
> Thought, penned, read, marked, recorded long ago.

In l.7 we find a direct reference to the yearning for reclusion, "In some recluded solitude, not full / Of Effort": the spondaic "not full" suggests the amount of activity necessary at the moment. Apparently, living in solitude to the extent he had hoped for was not possible. Nevertheless, despite the suffering he experienced, he clung to his belief in providence, as is expressed in the closing lines. The future was still waiting to be revealed. He had not yet lost hope that the Lord was leading him to something positive; in that sense the plan He had was enticing ("The pages of th'Adventure yet in store"). The factual enumeration in the final line of this first sonnet underlines how providence has arranged his whole life. The second sonnet, which forms the second stanza of this poem, closes with the hope of fulfilling his dream:

> Yet Master, if the strangeness of this word
> In Thy name uttered, from Thy counsel came,
> If this deep sigh within without be heard,
> Then let this stored, hid seed grow, find a name
> And be, for only once shall I walk by,
> And 'twould be sleep, a dream re-seen on high.

He longs to let that "seed grow". He is desperately longing for solitude, as he has only this one life at his disposal. The closing couplet is rather obscure, yet it implies that the foundation he has dreamt of could now be seen materialized. It could have already been the dream of someone else who, looking down on earth from heaven, then might see his "dream re-seen on high", i.e. materialized on earth.

In "News from the Mediterranean" (*World*, 29) an item of news, a surprising, perhaps even shocking one, provokes a meditation on the nature of providence:

> Shall we perhaps yet meet upon a day
> Not planned or scheduled by my wearied flesh,
> But seen by ages old, far, far away
> On foresight's screen, ere trapped in this great mesh
> Of happenings successive Night was caught?
> We whim awhile our times and are hard pressed
> Ere they in time be giv'n. For whims are fraught
> With Waste, the thief of hours too richly blest.
> Hot willed, yet marionetted - Ah! the thought [corr.]
> That one great lucid Forethought thought it all,
> And could sit back and watch as th'eons fought
> Their thuds into a mighty tale t'enthrall
> Dreamt angels ere were worlds, or even thoughts,
> But only Sight, so bright that naught it thwarts.

The use of alliteration, assonance and consonance (as is indicated in italics) is striking. The first four lines are united by the long vowel /iː/, which can be found in each line. While l.3 and the first part of l.4 suggest a notion of eternal wisdom and peace by the dominance of long vowels and diphthongs, l.2 and the second part of l.4 (after the pause) are dominated by harsh violent consonants, "Not planned or scheduled by my wearied flesh," "ere trapped in this great mesh", which suggests the narrowness of human plans and knowledge. The sound symbolism of "We whim awhile our times and are hard pressed / Ere they in time be giv'n." is striking: the /w/ and the long diphthong /aɪ/ indicate a certain ease concerning how we choose to use our time, which seems to be our personal decision, while the explosive "hard pressed" suggests rather the contrary. The use of the verb "whim" in combination with the imprecise "awhile" is significant and adds a notion of inconsistency. The /w/ is picked up again as the poem progresses, "For whims are fraught / With Waste", where the alliteration evokes the ease of wasting time. The paradox "Waste" - "blest" is emphasized by the consonance employed. The third quatrain starts with the exclamatory "Hot willed, yet marionetted - Ah!", which summarizes the idea of providence basic to the entire poem. L.10 attracts particular attention because of the three stresses in a row ("one great lucid") and also the almost excessive assonance on /ɔː/. The alliteration continues in l.12, where the pattern /θ-t-t-t-t-θ/ is balanced, and is underlined by heavy use of assonance in the closing couplet: "ere were worlds, or even thoughts, / But only sight, so bright that naught it thwarts." - which also abounds in striking consonance. The poet aims to emphasize the absolute unquestionability of God as the origin of all, - "naught it thwarts". The phonetic form of the lines suggests a certain continuity, which cannot be disturbed. We may have our plans about our lives, we are concerned about our future, doubtless we have our will, but nonetheless man is described as "Hot-willed, yet marionetted". We are on the strings of fate.

The problem of fate occurs again in a poem written soon afterwards, "After receiving picture of Grimshaw's painting" (*World*, 30), where he commences "And yet is this truth true, that we are tied / As puppets to eternal chains that pull?". It is only a rhetorical question, emphasizing the impossibility of grasping the nature of providence, not a real doubt, as is indicated by the tautology "is this *truth* true". In this poem the memory of a past decision, his leaving the charterhouse, reappears, as now it seems as though a similar decision has to be made: the poet was not settling at Roscrea, the life there was different from the Trappist ideal he had been formed to at La Trappe.

> And now again I see between the stars
> That omen here and there the unforked way
> That nothing, nothing, save one small thing, mars -
> I see, I say, that that one thing today
> Stands mightily before me, has a name,
> And can, if giv'n to speak, ne'er act the same.

The decision about his future has not been made yet, - there is still "the unforked way" lying before him. The accumulation of stresses in "save one small thing mars", after the repetition of "nothing", emphasizes this mysterious "thing" which mars and which now "stands mightily before me": firmly implied but not named, it is man's free will, which gives him the power to decide his future. The future does indeed lie in one's hands, although this somehow clashes with the idea of our "marionetted" fate, guided and foreseen by God, that was propounded in the previous poem.

The idea of providence is interspersed in many other poems, though such musings as a whole might not exclusively deal with providence as such. The sonnet "'And you do not ever ... But you can't FEEL God.'" (*World*, 31) is a typical example. It was stimulated by the occasion of donating blood, as mentioned in the subtitle. Trivial as it may seem, one has to bear in mind that for the monk living in a cloistered world such an event stands out from the regular pattern. It is a new experience, which is bound to leave a much deeper trace on the monk than it would on a person living in non-monastic surroundings. Surprised about the fact that it was he who was to give blood, he writes: "Is there one / Event in our small happ'nings that some store / Of well-thought stories hath not from aye spun?" The rhythm of the last line quoted underlines his doubt that there may be one: x///xx/x// - starting with an iambic foot, a spondee and a pyrrhic follow, while the line closes with an inverted followed by a spondaic foot. Even such an event as this present one of giving blood seems to have been foreseen from all times, although he cannot understand why: "Why is't that two unguided feet were led, / And not two others, to predestined eyes". Why was it he who was to gaze "Into the blueness of uncloistered skies", - the skies outside seem different, it is a different blue, as it is an entirely different world. And yet, providence seems to have pre-arranged it for him.

The examples given strongly express Alun Idris' belief in providence, - the divine pre-arrangement of all things. Such an attitude must not be confused with lethargy, - rather the contrary, as we do not know what the Lord has pre-arranged for us. The poet reacts actively and immediately to any indication of providence, as can be clearly seen from the various stations of his life.

3.2.2.5. APPARITIONS

A number of poems in *A World Within the World* reflect the poet's amazement at various, scientifically inexplicable incidents. Doubtless the message of such exciting news stirred his poetic vein. The wonder at the mysterious happenings is captured in these musings. Most of them were written at La Trappe.

The subtitle of "Between 6 p.m. and 7 p.m." (*World*, 7), "after beginning the most enthralling book ever begun", explains the origin of the poem, which is full of wonder and excitement:

> Can this be true, my Mother; true? Is't true,
> That at the very instant that I write
> Thou'rt here among us, in a land I knew,
> Thy feet on ground I trod; that now a sight
> Too fair for human eye five humans see
> For human kind, whom they but represent?
> Ah! Mother, now, this very now, I palp for thee,
> I know thee there. I know why thou'rt there sent,
> But will this human kind pay any heed?
> Why try thy utmost, Mother? Why? Is there
> A point? ... Or point in this chance thrown out seed [corr.]
> To barren rocks - yes, thine, that here dost share
> With us these weeping seconds inked in rhyme?
> Our Mother cares. Dost thou? We've *no more Time*.[145]

There is some indication in the poem as to the location of this apparition of the Virgin: those "five humans" who at present have visions of Our Lady, well-known enough to write books about it ("the most enthralling book ever begun"), clearly points to the happenings at Medjugorje. The wonder the poet feels is strongly conveyed: the frequency of inversion and spondees to be found in this poem is striking, which intensifies the atmosphere of excitement. The irregular rhythm of l.1 sets the tone of agitation: "Can this be true, my Mother; true? Is't true." Starting with an inversion, the first, though very short pause occurs before the spondaic apostrophe "my Mother". A longer pause follows, just as after the first repetition of "true?". The metrical variation in combination with the three-fold repetition of "true", underlined by the apostrophe interspersed, vividly portrays the excitement of the poet, as well as a notion of the absolute incredibility of what he is reading. The spondaic "Thou'rt here" conveys the wonder at

---

[145] Poet's italics.

the very thought of Our Lady being present. Ll.3-5 all start with direct reference to the Virgin, which is reinforced by the spondaic opening of each of those lines. L.5 even offers a second spondee in the fourth foot, - "five humans", thereby emphasizing how blessed they are to be chosen. The exclamatory "Ah! Mother" in l.7 indicates a change. The doubts and wonder he expressed so far whether this could really be true, seem to be over. He knows and feels that it is true, at this moment, "this very now", "I know thee there". This short sentence does not leave any doubt at all about the veracity of the apparition, underlined by the spondaic second foot. The medial pause is followed by an accumulation of stressed syllables: "I know why thou'rt there sent", which lends additional emphasis to this statement. More spondees are to be found in l.9 "this hu-man kind" - "pay a-ny heed", which suggests the improbability of such behaviour. The question of why she chose to appear on earth is emphasized by the spondees employed in l.10. Most of the seed she cast seems to have fallen on "barren rocks", apart from those that "here dost share / With us these weeping seconds inked in rhyme". The poet knows that Our Lady cares, the interspersed "Dost thou?" is a rhethorical question rather than expressing real doubt. The final sentence, the italicized "We've *no more Time.*", is a reference to one of the messages received at Medjugorje, as at that moment there was a real danger menacing the world (cf. letter, 10.12.1989). The danger does not seem to have diminished.

The town mentioned in the title "Dozulé" (*World*, 24) is not far from La Trappe. It is the town where a lady was said to have had a vision about an approaching disaster, yet prophesied that a particular place of prayer nearby in France would be preserved. The poem starts with a quote at the very beginning, "'Peace in our time'", which echoes the words of Arthur Neville Chamberlain, the British Prime Minister preceding Churchill, after having arranged an agreement with Hitler (cf. letter, 10.12.1989).

>"'Peace in our time,' said one, as he trod down
>On pastures green, on which in time there lay
>Bright crimson gory rivers. And our own,
>Is it to be more peaceful? In our day
>Shall we see more than e'er before was seen?
>Are we the ones that Chance did aye set forth,
>On History's charts, to be, as 'twere, between
>The Yesterday and Morrow of its wrath? [corr.]

The "pastures green" in l.2 refer to the famous English hymn "Jerusalem", by William Blake.[146] The quote on peace contrasts with those "*B*right *cr*imson *g*ory *r*ivers", a metaphor for all the blood shed in the second World War. The sounds used in that metaphor, voiced plosives in combination with voiced /m/,/n/ and /r/, convey a sinister tone, - the constant flow of unnoticed blood. The question in l.4 concerning our own time, "Is it to be more peaceful?" is apparently full of irony, as those days with which the present is compared were anything but peaceful. If

---

[146] In the opening lines of Blake's hymn we read: "And did those feet in ancient time / Walk upon England's mountains green? / And was the holy Lamb of God / On England's pleasant pastures seen?" (*A Selection from your 100 Best Hymns* 1980, 62).

our time really was more "peaceful" than the period of the World War, what would a war be like today?

The exclamation "O Dozulé! sweet, quiet little town" at the beginning of the third quatrain indicates a certain change in mood, reminding one of a sigh of relief in comparison with the foregoing. "As He trod down / From nimbus heights" (ll.11 and 12) is an original image of the Lord's descending from heaven, in order to appear at this little town. The poem closes with the following lines wondering whether it really was possible that "He said that He would claim / These Norman acres on which we are trapped / As His - e'en if, as't seems, our time in Hell is wrapped?" - "On which we are trapped" is apparently a word play on La Trappe, where the monks are trapped in a sense. The prospects of our future seem far from positive, - "our time in Hell is wrapped".

The following poem called "After hearing about Kibého" (*World*, 24) is another musing dealing with an apparition, this time in the African town Kibého, which is, according to Alun Idris' own words, a kind of "African Medjugorje" (letter, 7.4.1991). There the Virgin expressed her frustration about the fact that people in Europe were very hard-hearted at times, sophisticated and trying to argue her down: "Thy kindly words, once more, in vain did fall / On clever European ears." The criticism on modern man and his stubbornness is obvious. The people in Kibého seem to have acted differently to the sober-minded Europeans: "Thy feet / Depose on more receptive soil". The use of the colloquial form "gossiping with natives in their tongue / - At length" indicates the naturalness of her appearance, chatting with the people for a while, and also the considerable duration of the apparition, underlined, of course, by the explicit mentioning of "at length". The lines "At length, as though to take count of the fact / Of Lengthiness in lands where Time is long" sound rather presumptious and prejudiced but try to express that, traditionally, African cultures have a different attitude towards time than people from Western civilizations (cf. letter, 10.12.1989). Implicit criticism is directed against our civilization, as we do not take time to reflect, it is a hectic society we live in, where there is hardly any time left for God and prayer.

As the title indicates, "Guadalupe" (*World*, 23) deals with the miraculous picture of Guadalupe, recalling almost unbelievable results of the analysis of the picture, as is explained in a note in brackets. The poem takes the form of a hypothetical dialogue between the poet and "little John", i.e. Juan Diego, whose tunic bears the miraculous imprint of Our Lady.

> We know too much about the things of men
> To be so quickly fooled, my little John.
> Thou couldst not read nor write, and yet again
> Thou'ldst have us swallow what was seen of none.
> "Nay, nay 'twas seen," I hear thee say, "'twas seen, [corr.]
> And if thou'lt ope thine eyes, thou too may'st see!"
> Aha! Aha! good lad, this time the screen
> 'Twixt thy Today and mine here placed must be.
> "Nay, nay, but lift it; thy Today hath found
> The means to reinhabit my sweet Dawn." [corr.]
> Good lad, to bed. 'Tis time. No more one sound

> May I from thy sealed lips hear of that morn
> On which thou saidst 'twas seen. For e'en if 'twas,
> A dream would it too dream?
> What say'st?
> It has?

By taking a deliberately sceptical attitude the poet emphasizes the difficult position modern man finds himself in, - how hard it is for the sensible being to simply believe what he or she is told, in particular when there is no scientific explanation whatsoever for a certain incident. A feeling of superiority is noticeable when pointing out that "little John" was illiterate. The very use of the diminutive form suggests superciliousness. Modern man cannot be "so quickly fooled" as those people in ages past were, who apparently knew much less than modern man, - "We know too much about the things of men". It has become difficult to mislead him. "Thou'ldst have us swallow what was seen of none" suggests how ridiculous it seems to even think that this could be believed, - the use of "swallow" in particular underlines the absurdity. In the second quatrain the poet stresses the incompatibility of the two periods, the early 16th century and late 20th century. The world has changed too much. However, "little John" stubbornly insists that what he saw is true, and is still true: he even suggests that modern man has additional means and possibilities to prove the truth, - "lift it; thy Today hath found / The means to reinhabit my sweet Dawn." The imagery used suggests the possibility to believe, "reinhabit my sweet Dawn", to share the joy of that truth. And yet, the poet remains unmoved, which is reinforced by behaving like an adult towards a child, - "Good lad, to bed". His superiority seems unquestioned; however, the ultimate question casts doubt on the superciliousness, whether it really is justified or not.

What the poet aims to convey with this poem is the fact that modern man has been trained to try and find logical explications for every happening. He is convinced that all can be scientifically explained or comprehended. If explanations are lacking, we may be surprised and astonished for a moment, yet tend to think that one day even that "riddle" too will be solved. With the picture of Guadalupe it will be difficult. A note hints at the analysis by modern microscopic photography. It was discovered that the iris of Our Lady reflects a picture of

> an Indian in the process of opening out his mantle before a Franciscan, on whose face can be seen a tear rolling slowly down; a native of the country in his early youth holding his hand to his beard with an air of consternation; an Indian naked from waist upwards, almost in a posture of prayer; a woman with fuzzy hair [...] that is, the same episode as that related in Nahuatl by an anonymous native writer, in the course of the first half of the XVI century and edited in Nahuatl and Spanish by Lasso de La Vega in 1649. [147]

It appears extremely credulous to presume that such an imprint could have been produced by man in the 16th century, as it is still impossible to achieve it in the present century.

---

[147] Jones, Frère David transl. "Our Lady of Guadalupe", 3f.

The very title of the following poem, "After hearing of the latest reports from Turin" (*World*, 28) suggests the context of its origin. In Christian circles it is clear that the synectoche refers to the shroud found in Turin, which is said to be Jesus' shroud.

> What happened on the night that left this mark
> Upon the unmarked columns of a page
> Of shelved, unfiled, locked Science? What strange spark
> That glows beyond dimensions of our age [corr.]
> Did wander from beyond Beyond's own land
> And walk into our Time, what did it do
> In this its ancient mischief? Do we stand
> Beside an imprint of a world but passing through?
> Our wizzards [sic!] say that ultra-allthing Force
> A second split to atoms must have come
> Our sleepy way, that 'twas the intercourse
> Of utmosts in a night that left rags numb [corr.]
> And yet unshredded 'neath the tearing of a pain
> So huge that were it known 'twould worlds explain.

The spondee followed by a pyrrhic at the very beginning of this sonnet places emphasis on the question central to the poem which cannot be answered. "This mark" at the end of l.1, which receives full stress, is used in l.2 for a word play, where the prefix "un-" receives the stress: "unmarked colummns of a page". The tone of the poem changes according to its subject: when talking about the mystery of the shroud, long vowels and diphthongs dominate ("that glows beyond dimensions of our age" - l.4), while when treating the scientific approach towards this inexplicable incident, short and hissing consonants prevail. Particularly striking is the phrase "Of shelved, unfiled, locked Science" (l.3), where the succession of harsh sounds suggests the idea of presenting pure facts. In a previous version, l.4 started with "That stars beyond dimensions", where the verb is highly suggestive of the spark that radiates, having its origin as a star.

The process of Jesus' image being printed on the shroud is beyond the understanding of science. "Our wizzards say that ultra-allthing Force / A second split to atoms must have come / Our sleepy way": the imagery used to describe modern scientists as well as the attempt to account for the inconceivable energies which must have been present, this "ultra-allthing Force", scoffs at the human tendency to name and find explanations for everything, including the inexplicable, even though this might be beyond the frontiers of human reason. "Atom" means that it cannot be split further: Greek *a-tomos*, *tomos* being the word for splitting.[148] Modern technology allows the splitting of atoms which releases great energies. It is a procedure on the fringe between energy and matter: matter is disintegrated, even destroyed and transferred into energy. If we knew what it was that allowed Jesus' image to be printed on the shroud, the nature of the force involved, it would perhaps give us some idea of how the

---

[148] The word was already used by Aristotle and Democritus of particles of matter (the smallest of all), and also by Aristotle of Time: *Physica* 236a6 and 263b27. We also find it in St. Paul, in 1 Cor. 15:52 ("in a moment, in the twinkling of an eye"). The atom was the smallest medieval measure of time, and it corresponded to 15/94 of a second (cf. letter, 13.7.1991).

world came into existence in the first place, what forces and combinations of patterns God used in the process of creation ("'twould worlds explain").

The poems mentioned in this chapter demonstrate the amazement felt when hearing about certain inexplicable, mysterious happenings. By adopting either a pro or a contra-attitude towards the incident in question the poet tries to convey the difficulty for modern man to believe. Living in a contemplative monastery does not mean to be credulous: there might be even more scepticism found there than elsewhere; however, the scepticism is combined with the ability to accept the possibility of divine intervention, if the evidence is convincing.

3.2.3. POETRY OF HIRAETH

3.2.3.1. THE NATURE OF HIRAETH

Virtually untranslatable, hiraeth has often been rendered as "longing" or "homesickness", although these English terms are not entirely adequate. Sometimes the Welsh word is kept in the English translation, and a sense of the term may be grasped though its context. The rich connotations of the word can be conveyed through a variety of examples. Certainly, there is no shortage of material for this purpose. Hiraeth is so complex and powerful an emotion that is has naturally become a major theme in the literature of Wales (cf. Polk 1982, 11).

The fountainhead of the literature of hiraeth lies in the ancient elegies and lamentations of Welsh writers. However, the farther the theme travels from the source, the wider, deeper and stronger the flow becomes and apparently hiraeth has been given poetic expression even more frequently in recent times than the past.

The fact that this "most Welsh of emotions" (Polk 1982, 11) has found increasing expression in English over the past few centuries is not surprising when bearing in mind that basically hiraeth is the emotion of separation. *Gorau Cymro, Cymro oddi cartref* - the best Welshman is the Welshman away from home - says an old proverb, which in itself reflects the essence of hiraeth.

Hiraeth can be found in more or less any context. A few examples will be mentioned below which are of importance to the poetry of Alun Idris.

First of all there is spiritual and religious hiraeth, - a form of forward-looking hiraeth, in which many Welsh people find spiritual edification. It could be compared to a yearning for an ideal homeland beyond this world. In becoming more spiritual, more religious, the hiraeth acquires a deeper intensity.[149] H. Idris Bell describes a good poem of hiraeth as follows:

---

[149] Examples for spiritual hiraeth are to be found in the poetry of William Williams of Pantycelyn, the famous hymn-writer. Such spiritual hiraeth should not be confused with religious experience, much less with hypocrisy or lip service (cf. Polk 1982, 114f.).

When this note of wistfulness is united with the delicacy of conception and the power of bare, direct, seeming-effortless and infinitely significant expression which are other characteristic gifts of Welsh poetry the resulting verses are at times quite heartrendering in their perfect simplicity.[150]

Many hymns of hiraeth were written during the Welsh Methodist Revival, their fervour often reaching apocalyptic intensity.[151]

There has always been a strong bond between poetry and hiraeth. According to Dora Polk, real sufferers of hiraeth will hardly find release through the recovery of beloved places, people, things or conditions which they have lost. A certain relief from the pain can only be achieved through the "catharsis of expression". (Polk 1982, 124) Therefore hiraeth and poetry have always been inextricably linked in the Welsh literary tradition.

Some poets go so far as to suggest that poetry can be equated with hiraeth in its mission of recollection of the lost states of glory, and prevision of a return to the ideal (cf. Polk 1982, 126).

A remembrance of things past is, of course, an important literary category. Among Welsh writers it has been developed over the centuries into a minor art form, and always in lower key. Grief or sadness caused by loss of loved ones is a fundamental right for every individual. In the Welsh context, however, this condition can quickly expand itself into a longing for a lost world, and may develop into an endemic disease (cf. Humphreys 1983, 65). Emyr Humphreys even suggests: "It is in clear parallel with the long-held historic notion of a chosen people being turned out of the earthly paradise and being left with a gnawing yearning to return" (Humphreys 1983, 65).

This peculiar, Celtic form of nostalgia can add much depth to poetic expression as the accurate reflection of the nature of the human condition, although it should be remembered that this observation is certainly not limited only to Welsh people.

When referring to the Welsh explicitly, however, Emyr Humphreys describes this emotion thus: "Hiraeth has become the innocent opium of a people obliged to remain helpless and inert without the capacity or the desire to take control of their own destiny" (Humphreys 1983, 65). It is not for a non-Welsh person to judge the verity of this observation.

In the poetry of Alun Idris a notion of hiraeth can be encountered frequently as a longing for things not available at the moment, memories or events of the past, which cannot ever return. At times, however, his poems reflect the yearning for a future prospect, which could materialize one day. In this case hiraeth seems to be a bitter-sweet experience, a desperate longing on the one hand, a wonderful picturing of the dream on the other.

---

[150] Bell, H. Idris, "The Development of Welsh Poetry", quoted in Polk 1982, 113.
[151] Famous examples are the hymns "Trefaldwyn" and "St. Beuno" by William Williams of Pantycelyn, translated by Gwen Watts Jones (cf. Polk 1982, 116f.).

3.2.3.2. THE HIRAETH FOR RECLUSION

The examples given in chapter 3.2.2.1. have already demonstrated that the yearning to become a recluse was strongly felt by Alun Idris. Several poems of his reflect this hiraeth to live as a hermit in perpetual solitude.

Both "Lines written on Dom Damien's stone" (*World*, 22f.) and "Others written the following morning against a stone of his doorway" (*World*, 23) were composed at Camaldoli, as we are told in a note attached to the former. The two poems express the deep yearning for solitude which was felt by the poet. The abbot of La Trappe had given the poet permission to visit Camaldoli. Dom Damien, whose name was Girolamo (i.e. Jerome) in the Camaldolese Order, wrote a book about his life: he had been well-known as a missionary before he eventually became a Camaldolesian monk (cf. letter, 7.4.1991). The call to replace Dom Damien as a recluse at Camaldoli is expressed strongly in his "Lines written on Dom Damien's stone":

> My father, my dear father, dear, dear friend,
> The paper that here speaks rests on thy rest
> Of deeply buried silence. Here doth end
> What can here, here, begin, if but be blest
> The prayers I, kneeling pray on thee to pray.
> O little word! did e'er seven strokes so hurt
> The heart of sighing man? We pass this way
> To where thou art, but once. This fair white skirt
> That still protects Cistercian peaceful days,
> Will it soon change its form? The time is short.
> It was for thee. One day, one way, thy ways
> For e'er and e'er confined. 'Twas but as nought, [corr.]
> The whim that passed thy head, yet clung and clung
> Ere't passed its way, and left one sweet song sung.

The apostrophes in l.1 indicate the strong affective bond the poet feels he has with Dom Damien: the rhythmical irregularity suggests an idea of beseeching and yearning, underlined by the use of repetition. The three stressed syllables at the end of l.3, "Here doth end" add a tone of solemnity and finality, which is reinforced by the opening inverted first foot of l.4 followed by a spondee; a second inversion occurs in the fourth foot, which emphasizes the yearning. The rhythmical irregularity of l.5, whose pauses place heavy stress on the intermediary word "kneeling", indicate the poet's excitement at the very idea of becoming a hermit. The "seven strokes" in l. 6 presumably refer to the seven letters of "recluse", each of which he now experiences as causing tremendous pain. The emotion conveyed by the imagery stresses the yearning to become a hermit. The pain seems to be doubly sharp as the poet is aware of the fact that there is only one chance given, which he would have to use well, - the time is passing. ("We pass this way / To where thou art, but once.") In the third quatrain the poet envisages himself as a hermit ("This fair white skirt ... Will it soon change its form?"), and underlines once more that time is precious, as it is so short. The closing couplet describes how the call reached Dom Damien, just as it had reached the poet himself: it was but a "whim that passed thy head", a whim which did not disappear into oblivion but "clung and clung". Once the call has reached you, once it has seized hold of you, there is no way of return.

The sonnet with the rather elaborate title "Others written the following morning against a stone of his doorway" (*World*, 23) continues describing the poet's hiraeth for perpetual solitude:

> Did e'er four walls hold such a heavy weight
> Of emptiness? O sacred earth, that bore
> The prints of sacred feet, O yawning gate
> Whose eyelids were so sealed, did ye of yore
> Know aught of what ye sheltered, what ye nailed?
> The sound of isolation laps mine ears
> As it did thine, O Poltergeist here railed
> By one small inch of thickness, from the years
> That could have passed hereby without such pain.

The rhythm of the first line attracts attention: the inverted first foot is followed by two spondees ("four walls hold such"); as they are all monosyllabic words, they require a short pause between them, which adds to the effectiveness of the message. It makes the reader feel the "heavy weight / Of emptiness". The pause in 1.2 places extra stress on "emptiness", thus reinforcing the message. The tone created by means of these poetic devices is one of pain and yearning. The gate, the way to enter Camaldoli, seems to be open now: the apostrophe ("O yawning gate / Whose eyelids were so sealed") is used for emphasis. It also implies, on a very subtle level, the affective attraction the hermitage exerts on the poet. The image of the awakening hermitage powerfully suggests the chance given at this moment, that this might be the day of becoming a recluse and entering the gate of the hermitage before it falls asleep again, with its eyelids being "so sealed", which implies there would not be another chance. How highly the poet estimates the ideal of living as a hermit is implied when he asks, "did ye of yore / Know aught of what ye sheltered, what ye nailed?". The paradox of this line refers to the paradox of living the life of a recluse. Offering a place of shelter, a place of warmth and love on the one hand, the monk is, nevertheless, also nailed to the hermitage on the other, which is therefore bound to be a constant source of pain. The "sound of isolation" is referred to as "Poltergeist": the capitalization implies the divine nature of that pounding, hammering sound which is calling him constantly. The final year in solitude, i.e. the seventh year at Sélignac, was a year of virtual reclusion: the classes stopped. It was a year of pure prayer and spirituality. Alun Idris had already felt that yearning for complete solitude then, but it was not possible to become a recluse at that time.

The yearning is apparent in many of the poems written at La Trappe, - the feeling of having made a mistake and not listened to the call to complete solitude. "What might have been" (*World*, 6) deals with this problem:

> Alone we are together in this place,
> Alone in our shared loneliness, alone
> As though enclosed for e'er, each lonely face,
> 'Neath pointed hoods, not as of linen sewn,

> But walled of brick and boulder, though unseen
> The barring seal that fastens each recluse.
> Reclusion! I had thought of thy vast screen,
> And written for its nailing ... But what use
> The closing in of all except the door
> That ope's all others? For Camaldolese
> Must natter, shrive, direct - crack every law
> Of Silence, to content who'd gape at these
> Caged specimens ... while here, not e'en thou, frère, -
> Frère X, - shalt know, canst know, what Y's locked there.

The first six lines describe the solitary life in a Trappist monastery: it is a "shared loneliness", as is conveyed by the paradoxes in the first two lines. The monks are alone, and yet together, sharing their individual loneliness. The anaphora of "alone" and its repetition at the end of l.2 emphasize the solitary aspect of the Trappist life, which is further explained as the poem progresses. The "pointed hoods" appear to be "Not as of linen sewn / But walled of brick and boulder". They are walls which separate the monks from each other. The image "walled of brick and boulder" is harsh in sound, - it underlines the firm, insurmountable barrier which separates the monks, though, of course, invisibly, "Unseen / The barring seal that fastens each recluse". The seal makes them appear almost as recluses. The tone, which had been one of objective observation so far, changes at the beginning of l.7: the exclamatory "Reclusion!", followed by a pause, has a certain tenderness about it, which is completed by the image of the "vast screen", which suggests the never ending range of possibilities, supported also by the long vowels employed. Even the use of "nailing" loses its frightening connotation, as it merely helps to underline that he had ardently wished to become firmly attached to the hermitage, not leaving it again; of course, an implication of the pain and struggling involved is conveyed as well. The pause after "nailing", as is indicated by the three full stops, is followed by another change in tone, not neutral any longer as it now suggests a touch of deception, even disappointment. In particular, the enumeration of "na*t*ter, *sh*rive, *d*irect, - *crack*" with its harshness in sound, caused by the abundancy of plosives and the hissing /ʃ/ reinforced by the /r/ attached to it, supports this idea. The image of those "caged specimens" is anything but pleasing, either in meaning or in sound, which stresses the fact that is almost impossible to understand how people can live happily under such circumstances. The closing lines return to tenderness in tone, the change being indicated by "while here": there is affection between the monks, despite their silence, despite the fact that each one of them has "locked" his heart.

The following French poem called "After looking at Abbot de Rancé's portrait and hearing his poem" (*World*, 20f.) is bathed in the hiraeth for solitude. It is a touching expression of his love, his yearning for solitude and silence. The honesty behind it is striking. The poet seems to be thinking aloud, letting his heart speak. Numerous exclamations and apostrophes underline this impression. The poem rhymes in couplets and consists of 9 stanzas varying in length. The stanzas are well interwoven with one another, as the closing line of each stanza is actually the first part of l.1 of the following stanza. In the second stanza Alun Idris addresses the abbot:

Mon Père! tu pondais aussi
Et tes vers m'ont trop parlé. Mon Père! est-ce ainsi
Que tu veux me retenir, me tenir un temps
Encor ficelé? Ah! Vieilles cordes d'antan, [corr.]
Vous me perdez encor. Cette trappe, de quoi [corr.]
Est-elle ourdie?
         O! pierres, O! pierres, pourquoi
Me regardez-vous ainsi? De quoi êtes-vous
Ciselées? De nos âmes? Et toi, lac si doux
Qui reflètes sans bruit nos visages muets
Qui te parlent, de quoi, oui, de quoi es-tu fait?
De regard?

The "trappe" mentioned has, of course, a double meaning, apart from referring to a "trap" it suggests "La Trappe" as well. The abbot's poem speaks powerfully to Alun Idris, - his words as well as the ideal he represents: solitude and silence. "Tu pondais aussi" is suggestive of this double meaning, writing verse on the one hand, yet stimulating young brethren to opt for a life in silence on the other. The exclamatory "Ah! Vieilles cordes d'antan" suggests the poet's longing for solitude. The other stanza quoted echoes the setting of the poem: it was written outside, at the edge of the lake of La Trappe, where the poet is addressing the stones he sees, the gentle surface of the lake he beholds. The question "De quoi êtes-vous / Ciselées? De nous âmes?" is striking and provokes different associations. It implies that the souls of the monks seem to have manifested themselves in these stones, they have become a part of them, thereby suggesting continuity and resistance to external influences. Apparently, however, the image of the stones also has negative connotations, pointing to the possibility of hardened souls. The way Alun Idris addresses the lake suggests the numerous, endless meditations and ponderings which have taken place beside the lake, so that now it seems as though it was made "de regard". It appears to consist of the very glances of the monks, so much of their meditations has coalesced with the lake and become a part of it. The fifth stanza again expresses how much the poet is attracted by peace and solitude:

Paix! Oh Paix!
         Comment parler encore
T'ayant connue? Mon corps, tous mes os, tous mes pores
T'ont absorbée. Je suis comme toi, doux étang,
Sans murmure ni ride. Silence! mon sang
A ton rythme s'est rythmé - au rythme du chant
De Toujours.

The silence and peace which radiates from these lines is overwhelming. The rhythm is slow. Many pauses are interspersed, which make the rhythm decrease as well. The alliteration in "*t*ous mes os, *t*ous mes pores / *T*'ont absorbée." underlines the finality of his being completely absorbed by silence. The comparison to the silent lake beautifully suggests the inner calm experienced by the poet, the still surface of the lake symbolising his inner equilibrium.
In the closing stanza he once more addresses this little word, ce "petit mot":

> Petit vœu, petit mot, petit bruit de serrure
> Qui engage ou dégage les portes si dures
> A refermer - car ce petit bruit ouvre tout
> Ou peut tout fermer pour tous les temps. Ah! si doux,
> Oui, si flou ... et pourtant si durable. Ta voix
> Chante encore en enfer - comme au ciel. [...]

The three-fold repetition of "petit" conveys the affective bond felt by the poet towards silence. It is that little word which opens or closes all, - the poet employs a word-play on "engager" which, in the religious sense, refers to the step of commitment involved in vows. How beautiful the very sound of silence is finds expression in the exclamatory, indulging "Ah! si doux, / Oui, si flou ...", which iterates the joy felt at the very thought of silence. The onomatopoetical effect of the internal rhyme on "doux" - "flou" conveys the idea of utmost enjoyment, the sweetness experienced almost melting in the mouth. Despite its sweet delicacy it is yet so lasting, this beautiful sound of silence, which sings still in hell, as well as in heaven: "enfer" refers to those monks who, having made a vow, do not keep it. The poem closes with the firm determination of his will to be faithful to silence: "Facile / Est le bruit, le doux vent, la douceur qui dit 'Oui', / Encore 'Oui', Oui, Oui, Oui; Seigneur, OUI, aujourd'hui / Pour toujours." What sweetness lies in this decision to live in silence forever is firmly pronounced. How much the poet longs to experience it and live in solitude is expressed by the excessive repetition of "Oui". The closing phrase "Pour toujours" is a reminiscence of the formula used at the solemn profession, "promitto in perpetuum" (cf. letter, 10.2.1991). Forever he longs to be faithful to silence.

The longing to live in solitude was preserved as the years passed by. In the Trappist monastery at Roscrea the yearning for reclusion was just as strongly felt by the poet as before in La Trappe. In the sonnet called "St. Benedict's Day" (*World*, 52) Alun Idris remembers on the feast day of this saint the fullness which can be found in solitude:

> The thought that did awake with me this morn,
> Though dormant long, will it grow up to be
> Incarnate vision? All that e'er was born
> Is light from night received, sweet child, like thee.
> And Benedict himself had been alone
> And in his nothingness had something been,
> For emptiness ne'er nourished any one
> And others better see what rests unseen.

The thought, which had been "dormant long", is the possibility of becoming a hermit. The poet meditates on the question whether it will materialize one day, "grow up to be / Incarnate vision". He reinforces the possibility of it becoming true one day by pointing out that anything born "is light from night received", this thought of becoming a hermit as well. The apostrophe "sweet child" indicates the affection the poet feels towards this idea, how much his heart desires to become a hermit. The second quatrain turns to St. Benedict, who is presented as a shining example: it is not emptiness which is found in solitude, but one is, in fact, filled with a great fullness there, "For emptiness ne'er nourished any one". Others detect this fullness, as it happened in the case of St. Benedict, for people came in great numbers to ask him for advice, to share the fullness he experienced, as "others better see what rests unseen".

The rather elaborate title of "After hearing of the appeal for a monastic presence to save the island of Skellig Michael" (*World*, 54) explains the origin of its composition. An announcement had been made that the lighthouse was being automated, therefore removing all human presence from the island. Skellig Michael, an island further west than Ireland, abounds in ancient ruins, - a great number of Celtic beehive cells are still to be found there, where the monks used to live and pray, as well as a ruined church. The idea of going there and become a hermit was tempting:

> Could this yet be, my Lord, my God, my all?
> Coincidence, that we call Chance, is this
> The harbinger of Providence's call?
> The grace that Bardsey in its lonely bliss
> Did in its ancient silence hum to me
> Yet found no means to give, could this blest isle
> That stands alone on this world's farthest sea
> Where Time hath slept, it wake for us awhile?
> O rocks of frozen Penitence, these souls
> That sucked from you their glory, do their eyes
> Recall th'unchanging waves that Age still rolls
> In its unhurried passage 'neath the skies
> Of these forgotten yesterdays, your own,
> That could in my rememb'ring stand alone?

His search for the right mode of addressing the Lord in l.1 "my Lord, my God, my all" conveys an idea of excitement: being informed about the possibility of becoming a hermit on this island awakens a strong sense of hiraeth in him. The news seems to be providential: "is this / The harbinger of Providence's call?". "Bardsey" mentioned in l.3 is another solitary island which had been tempting to the poet as a possible place for living as a hermit ("did in its ancient silence hum to me"). He hopes to see the island "wake for us awhile", as there "Time hath slept", - the island did not change as the years passed by, it is still the same. This idea of continuity is further developed in the third quatrain, where he addresses the isle as those "*rocks of frozen Penitence*": the severity of the life there has not altered, which is underlined by the employment of sharp, hissing sounds. The paradox implied as the line continues, "these souls / That sucked from you their glory", indicates the bliss to be found in the severity of such a solitary life, when the hermit shares his solitude with God only. The image of "Th'unchanging waves" points to the stability of life there, which remains the same forever.

The call to become a hermit is also firmly conveyed in "Haec ultima Thule" (*World*, 30f.), a poem which reflects the hiraeth to live as a hermit on Skellig Michael, that center of monastic life in Celtic times. The title is a reference to Pliny and Tacitus, who talk of furthest Thule, the furthest part of the world.[152] The poem consists of six stanzas of seven lines

---

[152] Possibly a reference to a real place in the extreme north of Europe. Seneca having called it *ultima* ("farthest"), the phrase came to mean any far away, mysterious region.

rhyming ababcdc: iambic pentameter lines alternate with iambic dimeters, the last line being written in iambic trimeter. This structure is kept throughout the entire poem, apart from a few minor deviations like inversion etc.

> There is an isle 'mid lost Atlantic seas
>   That calls on me,
> And in the surgings of its ancient pleas [corr.]
>   Can I rest free
> And in my depth not hear the pull of years
>   Sing, "Come awhile,
>   Shed here thy passing tears"?

The lines convey the idea that he perceives the call and the pull to solitude firmly, as exerting an irresistable attraction to him. The closing line suggests the difficulties involved in leading such a life as a hermit. In stanza two the life as a hermit is described as "Pain's thick gloried Hell", which explicitly refers to the dual nature of such a life: it is a kind of hell the hermits create for themselves by this extreme penance, yet it is a hell which is rich in glory. The "pull of the years" invites the poet to:

> "Come, come, we are alone on this wide land
>   Of oceans blue.
> We have not moved, nay, look how still we stand
>   In mystic hue,
> Unrippled by the waves that washed away
>   Too many hours
>   That had not time to stay.

This third stanza describes the immobility of the life as a hermit. Time seems to stand still in these solitary places, life has not changed there at all, "unrippled by the waves". What is important about it, however, is that "'Beyond the waves / A world is waiting here.'", - an aphorism which has struck all those hermits who have spent their lives there before. The poet feels the pull:

> O little land, thou criest from afar,
>   And many heard.
> Flesh of their flesh, born 'neath this Celtic star,
>   A child is stirred
> By this his elder brother who no more
>   Sees lights of Home
>   On this thine orphaned shore.

Alun Idris addresses the island, which itself cries from afar, and to whose cry a certain number of monks have responded in the past. The dimeter "And many heard." is given additional emphasis as the sentence ends with this line. L.3 bears a reference to their being proper Celts, the Irish just like the Welsh, forming one people. The "elder brother" is the imaginary monk who lived on this island in the Celtic period, and for whom it had been home for many years. The metaphorical "orphaned shore" emphasizes that today it has ceased to be a proper home. In the final stanza the poet addresses an imaginary brother: "If ye in seraph habit can walk near", which indicates that it is no longer a black habit of penance but that by now it will have turned into a glorious habit of radiant light.

The possibility of becoming a hermit is also central to "Electrified correspondence " (*World*, 32), a poem which expresses the tension in the poet about either getting involved with the Charismatic Renewal or becoming a hermit. "To build a loneliness in hallowed stone / And on this farthest Thulé [corr.] so to stand / Above the waves of Rumour": the lines strongly express the hiraeth to become a hermit, yet the poet also hears the "angel voices" of his friends telling him "'Away, away / Away to where it burns; if not, here ends / What here begins and, lit, outglows thy day.'" The lines convey the urge to join them in their work for the Charismatic Renewal, to be active, as the fire is already "lit"; if he does not join them, the work might be endangered. However, the sonnet ends with the following couplet which emphasizes his dominating yearning to become a hermit: "And yet this Solitude sings well, sings well, / And there is Beauty in a hermit's knell." What appears to be morbid at first glance is a way of expressing that the thought of dying as a hermit is very beautiful to him. In this poem hiraeth takes on a different aspect: a decision has to be made for the future, both options are possible and equally tempting; however, one way by its very nature excludes the other, which makes the decision all the more difficult and problematical, - an ideal ground for a poem of hiraeth.

3.2.3.3. OTHER POEMS OF HIRAETH

The longing for things which are not to be obtained anymore, the mournful memory of past events which cannot be repeated and therefore used in a better, more appropriate way, is often to be found in his verse. Mournful memories of the poet's youth occur frequently, as for instance in "Group Mass in which were sung folk hymns of youth" (*World*, 29): the title presents the context of the poem, a group mass in church, which evoked memories of the past:

> *W*hen sometimes *w*e recall *w*hat *o*nce *w*e *w*ere
> And *f*eel again a *f*eeling that we knew,
> When noises of dimmed echoes *s*till bes*t*ir
> The mem'ry-banks that, dozing, wake to view
> The re-clad spectred pageantries of yore,
> And when we call to mind a distant tear
> And pass behind the clock to what no more
> We may i*n* grow*n* ha*n*ds *g*rasp, then, then I fear
> That I have walked too *m*any *m*iles alone
> And thought but of the sorrow in one head.
> For I perceive that many hours ill-known
> Were left unlived and have as phantoms sped   [corr.]
> To where they now e'er lie regretting all
> That came but once, for e'er and e'er to call.

The alliteration in the first line, as is indicated in italics, is striking; both w- and f-alliteration suggest the idea of motion of a light and easy kind, - we move in thought back to our past, "The mem'ry-banks that, dozing, wake to view / The re-clad spectred pageantries of yore": the computer term "mem'ry-bank", although suggestive of the amount of information to be stored therein, clashes in style with the elegance of the other words used; its modernity does, however, imply that the "mem'ry-bank" as such is part of our present life, while all our memories belong to the past. The metaphor "re-clad spectred pageantries of yore" is powerful indeed, evoking a whole array of associations. Past events are still vividly present in one's memory; they can be as elaborate as "pageantries"; "spectred" adds a mysterious aspect: memories come and go, - they appear suddenly, like a flash in the dark, and disappear again into the past. It also hints at the fact that frequently memories echo only brief moments, certain details re-appear, perhaps even distorting the real event. "Re-clad" emphasizes that those memories are clad in bright colours again, - they cease to be grey and pale, as soon as they are awakened by "dimmed echoes". "The re-clad spectred pageantries of yore", which as a phrase is far from smooth in sound, conveys the idea of movement and inner stirring. The feeling is even intensified in "what no more / We may in grown hands grasp", which suggests some kind of discomfort, almost distress at the fact that these past events are gone forever. While the first two quatrains ponder on the nature of memories, how they appear and are experienced, the third quatrain contains a conclusion which surprises: doubts are creeping in. The question arises whether it was really the right way he had opted for: "Then I fear / That I have walked too many miles alone / And thought but of the sorrow in one head." These two lines form an inner unit and act as a couplet, while ll.11-14 possess stanzaic unity. The "couplet" in ll.9f. expresses the fear that his life in the Carthusian monastery was too self-centered, in the sense that he was predominantly confronted with his own problems and sorrows, although, of course, the concern for the rest of mankind was certainly there, as this is part of the Carthusian vocation; however, daily life means daily confrontation with oneself. Thus the "sorrow in one head" is central. The danger of it becoming all too dominating is there, - it is possible to forget that there is more to life than one's own concerns. The last four lines express his becoming aware of other possibilities in life: "that many hours ill-known / Were left unlived". There is a certain feeling of regret present in these lines, as these chances of the past, which he was not aware of at the time, are lost forever, "That came but once". These lines represent a pure form of hiraeth.

A different type of hiraeth is expressed in the following sonnet, where the urge to belong to a monastery, to feel at home again in monastic surroundings was becoming very strong. "Roots" (*World*, 45f.) is centered on the importance of feeling one's roots, of building one's life on firm ground and not moving constantly:

> We live but once and one life can we live,
> Though there be moments that two lives contain.
> One second can at times to all time give
> Another form. Tomorrow, wax and wane
> Shall moons and new-moons o'er our Yea and Nay
> And say to us perhaps, "My twin, had he
> Been let to live, had I, Nay, been born Yea ...?"
> And weep perchance the hour that bid hours be.

Yet there is one thing that I 'gin to feel,
As felt are all the feelings of the heart
That feels out 'twixt the aches of woe and weal
For rays of Home 'mid crumbling homes that part,
And that one thing is that one thing alone
Doth hold awhile th'unmossed, unwanted, stone.

The first quatrain implies that there are important moments in our lives, powerful in their potentiality, with two possible paths: there are two channels lying ahead ("moments that two lives contain"), which will, of course, affect the rest of our existence. Our whole life is made up of such decisions to be taken every day: "*wax and wane* / Shall *moons* and new-*moons* our Yea and *Nay*" - the line reminds one of the the sound of a magic spell with the alliteration and assonance. The inversion of the first foot in l.9 points to a change: "one thing" is fully stressed, and given additional emphasis by the pause which follows: one thing "that feels out 'twixt the aches of woe and weal / For rays of Home 'mid crumbling homes that part" - the yearning to feel a true "Home" again, indicated by the capitalization, is strongly implied. All that seemed to be his home is dissolving, "crumbling homes that part". The closing couplet reflects his awareness of the truth of the proverb: "a rolling stone gathers no moss", - he is that rolling stone who has not found his place yet, but the need to belong is very strong, as well as the fear that he will perhaps never have any roots at all if his life continues to be characterized by so many changes of course as in the past.

The yearning to bring the fire of the spirit back to Ireland is expressed in "Seeing the pictures of Celtic Ireland" (*World*, 61), where we read that "The ardour of left Youth e'en yet can burn, / And flame with flame enflamed more flames can take." The repetition and the presence of all those f's, l's and m's suggests the ever increasing torrent of the flow: the Charismatic Renewal could make it happen once more and turn Ireland again into that place of deep spirituality it used to be. The early Celtic saints had "heard a call sirenic that once sang [...] Of *choicest pain, unpuzzled by its pang*": the plosives and the affricate underline the ferocious penance they felt drawn to. The oxymoron of the "choicest pain" suggests how much they yearned for suffering. The great yearning for austerity is still there, the poet's hiraeth finds effective expression.

Alun Idris' Welsh patriotism is apparent in many a poem, as e.g. in "After receiving a letter-card from St. Davids" (*World*, 25). In the note to that poem we read "St. Anne used Breton at Auray", referring to St. Anne d'Auray, a centre of pilgrimage where St. Anne appeared to a peasant speaking Breton, which is Welsh.

Dewi!
Didst thou once walk these pleasant fields
On which I stood, and long to stand again?
The beauty of the sound that my tongue yields
In singing thy sweet name to that fair strain
Of sacred unchanged language, didst thou too
Once know its quiet magic? And did ears
That heard these ripples form, hear oceans woo
The presence of this sound to distant years

> And distant lands, like this near which I sing
> And whereon sang awhile its gentle tones
> The Mother of the Mother of my King
> As she reclaimed these Breton lands she owns? [corr.]
> For Heaven too this music doth record,
> There where words hold no more a heart outpoured.

Naturally, the mother tongue is of special importance to everyone; however, here in these lines we detect real patriotic feelings for the poet's native language and "its quiet magic": it is more than the usual bond which binds one to one's mother tongue. The poet loves the beauty of the sound of Welsh, this "sacred unchanged language". Here he implies that Welsh has not altered a lot in the course of the centuries, - it has remained resistent against innovations and influences or borrowings from other languages.[153] How much the poet delights in speaking Welsh, in hearing the "beauty of the sound that my tongue yields / In singing thy sweet name" is underlined by the fact that the first foot of l.1 stands apart, "Dewi!" which emphasizes the delight he experiences. Dewi is Welsh for St. David, the patron saint of Wales. The hiraeth he feels to return to Wales is explicitly expressed in l.2, "and long to stand again". He yearns to see the beauty of his country, he longs to listen to the sonority of the Welsh language. "And did ears / That heard these ripples form" is a reference to the gushing forth of St. Non's well in Pembrokeshire at St. David's birth, as is indicated in the note. L.12 implies that Britanny on the West coast of France has remained very Catholic, - it has kept faith, as St. Anne "reclaimed these Breton lands she owns". The closing couplet meditates on the fact that whenever saints appear on earth they use human language to talk to us, "For Heaven too this music doth record", - a line which in particular refers to the Welsh language that St. Anne employed. The final line implies that in heaven there seem to be other means of communication, as words cannot express what is felt there, they cannot embody the contents of the heart; however, it is also a reflection on the force words exert on us here on earth, - our hearts can travel through our words, can be poured out through our words: "Words are living things containing a part of ourselves, containing our inner essence in a way" (letter, 10.12.1989).

The close connection to his mother country, the hiraeth for Wales, is also noticeable in a poem explicitly called "Hiraeth" (*World*, 25). Although it is addressed to St. Dewi, it actually reveals much about the author himself. The connection he feels to his name patron is clearly implied: not only was he a Welshman with a strong love for his country, as Alun Idris is, but St. David was also a monk - a Celtic monk in the sixth century, who lived almost one hundred years. The Carthusian Order did not exist in those days, but his life was not at all dissimilar to the Carthusians' austere mode of existence. The Carthusian Order has a strong link with Eastern spirituality, some of its teachings originate there; similarly, the Celtic monks were strongly influenced by the monks of Egypt and Syria (cf. letter, 10.12.1989).

---

[153] This fact explains why the literary language of Welsh does not differ much from the everyday language used in Wales.

> Dewi!
> Didst thou too know this gentle sound
> And walk these ancient ways? Didst thou once hear
> The song of Peace upon these hills? This ground,
> Didst thou its acres tread? Wast thou once here?
>
> Dewi!
> Didst thou too know the quiet power
> Of Song, and of the beauty of a word?
> Didst thou respire far Eden in a flower,
> And in these singing fields was Heav'n once heard?

The poet's own love for his country and his mother tongue is speaking through these lines with a Celtic, almost pantheistic directness. The hiraeth, his longing to be there, is strongly felt when reading the verse. The importance of the senses is referred to, including the phenomena of odours.[154] The beauty of song and poetry is also touched upon, implying the obligation to use these gifts: "Our role as Christians is to use what God has given us, everything He has given us to give Him praise again from His creation" (letter, 10.12.1989).

The poem consists of five stanzas of iambic pentameters, where the inverted first foot is placed apart as an extra line. This first foot is repeated throughout the entire poem, - it is an apostrophe to St. Dewi. The apostrophe helps to increase the urgency felt by the poet to express his love for Wales: by asking his patron saint whether he, too, felt the same love for Wales the poet implicitly declares his own love for his home country.

The third stanza switches to the present, indicated by the use of "Dost thou" in 1.2, asking St. David about his present feelings concerning his past, while the fourth, just as the first two stanzas, deals with questions concerning the saint's own past as he experienced it then, and not his present feelings about it:

> Dewi!
> Dost thou recall where we once knelt,
> When young, when burning yet with Love's first flame?
> And dost thou sense again the incense smelt
> In Prayer's vast cloud? With Age, was it the same?

The switch to the present reinforces the idea of hiraeth, as the poet thereby implies that St. David's love for Wales, the yearning to see his home country again has not diminished in all these years. Stanza four bears a reference to the old age of the saint when the poet asks him, "With Age, was it the same?". It was in Wales where "Love's first flame" was burning, which makes it all the more special to Alun Idris. In the final stanza the poet switches again to the present:

> Dewi!
> In Heaven too doth hiraeth melt?
> Dost thou recall? Dost thou recall awhile
> The timeless sense of Timelessness we felt?
> And Dewi, if thou dost, look back ... and smile.

---

[154] "Respire far Eden in a flower" refers to the special aromas noticed on the apparition of saints, - the odour of sanctity! In a letter of 10.12.1989 the poet mentions as an example Lydwine of Schiedam, a Dutch lady, who had such an experience.

Life in heaven is different. The question whether hiraeth melts there "too" almost has a sceptical note about it, as there seems to be no cure. The repetitions used in this stanza reinforce the poet's longing to know the answer, which cannot be given.

"After seeing a picture of Aberystwyth" (*World*, 26) describes the poet's feelings after seeing that picture of the town where he used to live as a student. The poem is full of hiraeth:

> When eyes behold what hands no more can touch,
> When something in the heart no more withholds,
> When memories of times, past times, times such
> As come but once as Destiny unfolds,
> Flood once again this little ball we wear,
> And when, as though surprised by something new,
> We see once more a dead hour coming near
> And feel long healed rent hearts wrenched at one view,
> Then, Lord my God, I can but bow my head,
> This little head too heavy 'neath its load,
> And weep upon thine own, for it too shed
> A tear of molten sadness on our road ...
> And yet this little something that I feel,
> Is it from Thee? Doth hiraeth hermits steal?

The three quatrains form one long sentence, which adds to the atmosphere of lament. The anaphora in the first three lines, completed by other repetitions, reinforces the degree of hiraeth. Ll.1-8 describe in detail the experience which arouses the yearning to return to his home country: it is only l.1, however, which refers to the outward stimulus of seeing the picture, - all the other lines describe interior experiences that follow. We realize that little is necessary to provoke a flood of hiraeth. How precious the past in his home country was and still is for him is strongly expressed when he writes "times such / As come but once as Destiny unfolds". It lies in the nature of hiraeth that one longs for something which cannot be grasped again. L.8 culminates in the painful expression "And *feel long healed rent hearts wrenched at* one view": the contrast in sound between the first two feet and the rest of the line is striking. Hiraeth is not only a painful experience but also an indulgence in happy reminiscences, as is implied by the long vowels and the peaceful l-alliteration. The other side of the coin, its painful aspect, is conveyed as the line continues by the excessive use of harsh consonants, in particular /r/ and /t/, and short vowels.

The third quatrain describes the poet's reaction to such memories, - one full of lamentation. The pain is too much to bear, "This little head too heavy 'neath its load", - he can but weep a silent tear. The sonnet closes with a question: in the couplet the poet asks the Lord whether it is possible that this strong feeling of hiraeth is God-sent as well, "Is it from Thee? Doth hiraeth hermits steal?". This final question strongly implies how much hiraeth can dominate one's thinking and one's being, one can even forget - for a while at least - that one is a hermit.

Hiraeth can be called a characteristic feature of Alun Idris' poetry. It is increasingly noticeable from the Trappist period onwards, perhaps as a result of the difficulties he was facing. The notion of hiraeth adds a touch of melancholy to his poetry; certainly, it is a means for the poet to find relief by expressing his yearning. It is, in particular, the longing to become a hermit which triggered off a vast number of poems of hiraeth. The idea of becoming a hermit had always been very tempting to the poet; in his Trappist period the hiraeth to live in a hermitage intensified, which is reflected in his poetry.

3.2.4. HYMNS

"After the hymn of praise they went out to the Hill of Olives." (Mark 14:26). This occasion marks the origin of many Christian traditions, and ever since the hymn has been an "exceedingly important vehicle for the expression and spread of Christian doctrine and devotion" (Ferm 1987, 595).

Basically, a hymn is a song of praise or prayer to God. Practised by the apostles, hymn singing became popular among early Christians and led to the creation of vast treasures of hymnody both in the Greek and Latin churches, though it had been largely restricted to the clergy after 600. The reformers rediscovered the importance and effectiveness of congregational song. Inspired by Luther, Germany was leading in the composition of hymns and melodies. With the extension of the Calvinist influence, hymns tended to be replaced by rhymed versions of the psalms (cf. Ferm 1987, 595).[155]

> In Welsh there can be no question about the place of hymns within the literary heritage of the nation. Their explicitly religious nature is not felt to be an embarrassment even when the particular beliefs they embody may be no longer held. (Allchin 1976, 3)

Arthur M. Allchin does not leave any doubt about the importance of hymns in Welsh literature, nor does Gywn Thomas, professor of Welsh literature at the University of Bangor, who firmly maintains their significance when he writes: "The hymn is, without doubt, the most influential of all literary forms in modern Welsh literature (though this influence is not primarily a literary one)" (Thomas, Gwyn 1986, 58). Given the high status of hymns in Wales (which developed as a result of the Methodist Revival with its emphasis on the gospel of salvation), it is not surprising that Welsh hymnology has been an important influence on Alun Idris.

The two outstanding figures of Welsh hymnology are William Williams of Pantycelyn[156] and Ann Griffiths of Montgomeryshire,[157] whose deep and simple piety gave voice to the

---

[155] In English speaking countries, Ken and Watts (early 18th century) and Charles Wesley were the first in the long line of great hymnists (cf. Ferm 1987, 595). A few examples of outstanding hymns are: the famous Olney Hymns by the melancholy poet William Cowper and John Newton, a clergyman at Olney, published in 1779. James Montgomery can be called one of the best English hymn-poets (cf. Ferm 1987, 353).
[156] William Williams of Pantycelyn (1717-1791) was educated with a view to becoming a doctor, but he underwent a religious conversion when he listened to the Methodist Hywel (Howel) Harris preaching. (The anglicized form of his name is Howel(l) Harris.) Thus he left everything for the sake of the great awakening. He was ordained a deacon of the Church of England and served as a vicar, but was refused ordination as a priest. He joined the Methodists and became one of their most prominent leaders. Williams published several volumes of hymns as well as long poems and prose. In his hymns he often refers to the desolation of a sinful world, and,

thoughts and aspirations of the Welsh people, and who set to music a thoroughly Welsh feeling, having almost as great an influence as the burning words of the famous preachers themselves[158] (cf. Fraser 1952, 97).

The singing of hymns is traditional in Wales, having acquired what Emyr Humphreys even called the "status of a national pastime" (Humphreys 1983, 98). The Welsh celebrate in popular hymns the mysterious nature of divine love and the greatness of the suffering Lord. The hymns live on, as a part of the national heritage.

The number of hymns written by Alun Idris is considerable: they are not only sung in monastic surroundings but have been and still are used in several Welsh churches as well. Many of his poems were set to music by the poet himself, others by Father Laurence Bévenot, his spiritual father, who used his outstanding musical talent to compose the music to words written by Alun Idris.

"Our patronal feast" (*World*, 50f.) is one of these prayer-poems which can be sung: the "Hymn in honour of St.Joseph" (*World*, 51) was composed especially for this poem. The music is an adapation of a Polish carol called "Nuit de lumière", which was used for the whole of Christmas vespers at La Trappe (cf. letter, 10.12.1989). "Our patronal feast" consists of four stanzas, with dactylic tetrameters as the basic metre, though employed with a few slight variations: each line lacks one unstressed syllable in the fourth foot, some syllables receive

---

world, and, equally often, he expresses the ecstasy of the glory of God (cf. Thomas, Gwyn 1986, 59f.). He composed over a thousand hymns as a means of communicating his experience, and many of them are great poetry. He was engaged "in expressing the inexpressible: in translating the language of his understanding of the Godhead into a language that could be grasped by the simplest member of a congregation. The first lines of so many of his hymns have that warm memorability and breathlessness of immediate experience that an English reader finds in the first line of, say, a Shakespeare sonnet. [...] Williams's strange combination of transcendental obsession and idiosyncratic eloquence makes him a solitary figure in the Welsh scene." (Humphreys 1983, 97). According to Emyr Humphreys, to this day, a Welsh rugby football crowd can roar out a verse of Pantycelyn with impressive fervour, though perhaps most of them have long ceased to be chapel-goers. Williams' hymns were the most obvious and audible part of the religious awakening, and they remain what has come to be regarded as a national characteristic (cf. Humphreys 1983, 97f.). Despite his substantial contribution to the sum total of good poetry in Welsh, he had no influence on the general course of poetry in Wales, although thousands of Welshmen have read, sung and learned his hymns (cf. Parry 1963, 286).

[157] Ann Griffiths (1776-1805) lived in Dolwar Fach, a farmhouse in Powys, and was converted whilst listening to a sermon in Llanfyllin, near her home. Many of her hymns have been preserved because her maidservant at Dolwar Fach, Ruth Evans, memorized them and later repeated them to her husband, John Hughes, who transcribed the hymns. Ann Griffiths herself married a local farmer and died in childbirth at the age of twenty-nine (cf. Humphreys 1983, 117).

Ann Griffiths is a revealing symbol as well as a proto-product of Methodism itself: a simple country person who - transformed by the happenings during the Welsh Revival - was able to write some of the most theological hymns in the Welsh language (cf. Rees 1981, 10). Her hymns reverberate with rich scriptural allusions and are characterized by an intensity of emotion that recalls the intensity of some of the great mystics. Indeed, authorities on Christian mysticism compare her to St. Teresa of Avila and Julian of Norwich. The hymns are based on a deep understanding of Calvinist theology and in particular the doctrine of the sovereignity of God and the debt of homage she owes and longs to pay (cf. Humphreys 1983, 117f.). In this respect she has much in common with Alun Idris.

[158] There is a striking difference between Ann Griffiths and Williams. "Williams could consider his experiences and analyse them - meditate on his own religious emotions; that is seen in his hymns, and particularly in his prose writings. But what we see in Ann Griffiths's hymns is the natural excitation bubbling forth, not bridled or fettered by metre or reflection. She is not expounding divinity, not praying, not moralizing. Rather, she is giving herself up to the mystery of the knowledge of God incarnate. She was a mystic [...]." (Parry 1962, 321).

additional stresses. The rhyme scheme is rather irregular, although attempts have been made to let 1.2 and 1.4 of each stanza rhyme. The structure of the poem is characterized by repetition, as will be noticed in the two stanzas quoted:

> Joseph, our father and father of all men,
> Look at this time, look again to thy children
> Whom in adopting thy Lord thou hast fathered, [corr.]
> Whom thou hast gathered to be thine own brethren.
>
> Called by thy name, on thy name we are calling:
> Thy charge we are, see the perils befalling
> This house that shields 'neath the strength of thy wisdom,
> This child that seldom finds help in his falling.

The anaphora and the internal rhyme in ll.3 and 4 is continued throughout the entire poem (except for the absence of anaphora in stanza four), which makes it sound smooth in its flow. The diction used is well-chosen and of a solemn nature, characteristic of Alun Idris, who always exercises great care in the selection of his words, yet still the hymn is straight-forward. The only line which might remain unclear is at the beginning of the second stanza: "Called by thy name" seeks to impart the fact that in Roscrea the community was under St. Joseph's patronage, which normally would not be known.

The tune is gentle in tone and fairly simple, - there should not be any difficulty for the congregation to adopt it easily. The hymn certainly fulfils the conditions given by Hoxie N. Fairchild (Fairchild 1939, 131), who describes a good hymn as follows:

> A good hymn should be singable. It should be not only religious but thoroughly Christian in doctrine and tone. But above all, a good hymn should achieve a balance between two opposing factors: without going beyond the intellectual and emotional range of the congregation, it should possess something of that individuality of thought and style which is essential to poetry.

The same tune can also be used for "Christmas at La Trappe" (*World*, 16), a poem consisting of three quatrains, with the same basic dactylic rhythm as the previous one. As an additional variation several lines (ll.1,2,3 of stanza 1, ll.2,3,4 of stanza 2 and l.2 of stanza 3) start with an extra unstressed syllable at the very beginning; when read out aloud, the rhythm moves regularly, as the second unstressed syllable of each closing foot is missing.

> Sweet darkness of even, fair dimness of heaven,
> Grow darker, grow darker, Tomorrow is given;
> Tomorrow, tomorrow is born in thy dying,
> Helplessly lying till by morn thou be riven.

Here again the poet employs internal rhyme in ll.3 and 4 ("dying" - "lying"); additionally, he makes use of consonance in the first line ("even" - "heaven") and of repetitions, which are found throughout the entire poem. The use of literary words convey a solemn tone. The imagery of this poem is highly suggestive of associations, it is certainly not as straight-forward as the previous one. The first stanza expresses the poet's yearning to let the night pass quickly

("Grow darker, grow darker, Tomorrow is given"). He cannot await the coming of the Lord. The second stanza is fairly obscure, and it is to be doubted whether its meaning can be fully grasped when singing it; however, the internal rhyme employed makes it sound very smooth:

> Night has grown fainter, the thickness of winter
> Has warmed at the passing of one ray more tender
> Once sparked by Another ere kindled was morning
> Or dawning adorning the Void's unlit splendour.
>
> This is the dawn of a morn many mornings
> Awaited, created by Hands now in swaddlings;
> This is the light by these hands once engendered,
> This is Peace rendered more peaceful in all things.

The anaphora in the third stanza underlines the special nature of this day, which the poet has been awaiting impatiently. All these lines start with a stressed syllable, which adds additional force to them.

"Saint Columcille" (*World*, 42) was written as a present for the abbot on his feast-day, as we read in the note attached to the poem. It consists of five quatrains rhyming aaab cccd etc. with the first three lines being written in iambic tetrameters followed by a line in iambic dimeter. Saint Columcille, also called St. Columba, lived in the Scottish monastery of Iona, off the coast of Mull, and founded monasteries from there in Europe (cf. letter, 25.8.1991). The poem was written shortly before Alun Idris left the monastery at Roscrea. It was written to fit to the notation of the French tune "Qui es-tu, Roi d'humilité":

> O Master, who hast trod before
> This ancient path, where trod of yore
> The silent feet of many more,
>   Thou still dost guide us.
>
> And when the tears of many years,
> The secrets kept from mortal ears,
> Are known again where thy word steers,
>   Thou still art list'ning.

The regularity of the rhythm lends the poem very much the character of a prayer, which can easily be sung. The soil referred to is the nurturing ground of ancient spirituality, "this ancient path", be it Scotland or Ireland. The "tears of many years" mentioned in the second stanza emphasize the idea that the tears of the monks today are the same tears as those of who lived here yesterday, in the days of St. Columcille. The pains have not changed. The saint is still engaged, which becomes apparent from the dimeter lines. That his word is present even today, although hardly heard anymore, is implied in the fourth stanza, when we read:

> For thou didst call and, calling, heard
> The distant echo of this word
> Call on and call till nothing stirred
>   In dying wonder.

It seems as though the strict injunctions which he gave are calling from the past, but they have lost their original power; the closing line firmly implies that "all the precepts of these old monastic legislators have no more effect, the wonder of the newness has gone away, it has died" (letter, 25.8.1991). The closing couplet tries to combat these tendencies when the poet lets the "ancient love" whisper: "'Faint not, we conquer.'" It is important not to be discouraged.

> The use of vocal and instrumental harmony in divine worship I shall recommend and justify from this consideration; as such harmonies "contribute extremely to awaken the attention and enliven the devotion of all serious and sincere Christians". (Atterbury, edition of 1880, 553)

The idea expressed here by Francis Atterbury early in the 18th century conforms with Alun Idris' opinion about the usefulness of church music, as music can indeed help to "enliven" the devotion of the congregation. Music enriches the devotion, emphasizing the emotional level of the experience. The following poem-prayer called "Adieu" (*World*, 60f.) was composed to fit the notation of "Abide with me", as is indicated in a note in brackets; the music certainly helps to reinforce the message the author tries to impart. He wishes to render thanks to the Lord. The poem was written just before a delegation of Carmelites left (cf. letter, 27.9.1991). It consists of four iambic quatrains, rhyming in couplets, and is a hymn thanking the Lord for the gift of having met these nuns:

> Lord, for the *gi*ft of every *gi*ven day
> B*orn* in the night of D*awn*'s primaeval ray,
> Br*eathed* and bequ*eathed* to us who by it live,
> *E*re b*ur*ned, to th*ee* ret*ur*ned, w*e* th*ee* thanks give.

The gift of the day is returned to God. The assonance and alliteration (indicated in italics) underline the prevailing peaceful atmosphere. Each day comes from God, is "Born in the night of Dawn's primaeval ray": the image suggests that God ignited the first light, thus permitting the first possibility of day. Therefore the poet uses "primaeval ray". Light is all of one origin it seems, the day just like the dawn: dawn means that the rays of light reach us, the day being also a symbol of our day, our life.

In the third stanza the happy memory of the conference days is referred to: "And of our days we have lived some apart / And mem'ries made that sometimes ne'er depart". These days were special and would stand out in the memory forever, in particular when all one's days are similar to each other. "For days there were that Thou didst dream for us, / That we have shared awhile and gather thus." The lines clearly convey the idea that God has seen our days from all eternity: he happened to "share awhile" his days with these Carmelites. The poem closes with a prospect of the future:

> For many days shall dawn on us again
> 'Neath other dawns and dusks that shall remain
> One in their falling, myriads in their fall
> On these horizons now to which they call.

L.3 implies that the whole of mankind shares the time given by God. The same days and hours will come to us all, however differently they may be employed, - "myriads in their fall": we all have different "horizons", which are beckoning us, different aims.

The examples in this chapter only represent a small selection of hymns written by Alun Idris: there is a great number of poems which can be chanted as well, as the poet feels the vital relation between poetry, prayer and song is unified in hymns. Doubtless, his Welsh background, the deep roots in Welsh hymnology are an important influence. The power of hymns can chiefly be seen in "advancing that most heavenly passion of love, which reigns always in pious breasts, and is the surest and most inseparable mark of true devotion" (Atterbury 1880, 553). This quotation by Francis Atterbury certainly has not lost its legitimacy. It is the affectional aspect of hymns which makes them precious and powerful, as, without love, all our spiritual offerings, our prayers and praises are "insipid and unacceptable" (Atterbury 1880, 553). Hymns enable us to perform prayer with utmost vigour and cheerfulness. They beautify ideas, enrich the already enriched by furnishing it with an additional dimension, that of musical harmony (cf. Ferm 1987, 595). Musical harmony provides the fertile soil for love to grow and celebrate.

3.2.5. FEELING THE UNION WITH GOD: POETRY AS A MEANS OF DECLARATION AND CELEBRATION

The joy of having entered La Trappe provided the fundamental basis for a considerable number of poems, which reveal the poet's personal religious experience. They reflect the firm union felt, a feeling of utter oneness with the Lord: an immense love radiates from the lines, the poet feels he belongs to God alone, is His own. The affection is seemingly boundless.

This joy caused by the feeling of unity with God is powerfully expressed in "Le matin de la prise d'habit (commencé, en pensée, devant le tabernacle)" (*World*, 3). It celebrates the poet's love for God and succeeds in revealing a personal religious experience:

> Ma joie, je t'appartiens. Tu m'enveloppes
> A nouveau aujourd'hui de Nouveauté
> De Vie qui désormais se développe
> En mort ensevelie dans la beauté
> De ce Sourrire inconnu que je sens
> Sans rien sentir, rien ouir, sinon
> Son silence, en cet être qu'il reprend
> Pour l'engloutir au creux de son creux son.
> Ô Pâque! Dans la nuit, la matinée
> De ce matin, aurore de l'Aurore
> Qui brillera désormais, je suis né.
> Sagesse cachée! Je me tais. J'adore.
> Car Tu as vu ce que je vois, avant,
> Proféré cette aurore auparavant.

The first line sets the tone of the entire poem: "Ma joie, je t'appartiens." The short, but precise nature of this statement is striking in its honesty, summarizing that he entirely belongs to God. "Tu m'enveloppes / A nouveau" is ambiguous: literally, it refers to his taking the habit, i.e. the occasion which provoked the composition of this poem. In a figurative sense, however, it also implies that the Lord's presence swathes him anew, absorbing him completely, firmly becoming a part of Him. The paradox conveyed in the "Nouveauté / De Vie qui désormais se développe / En mort ensevelie dans la beauté / De ce Sourrire inconnu" indicates the seemingly paradoxical nature of living such a life in silence: Trappist monks seem to be dead to the world. They do not perceive anything sensual anymore in the sense that they do not receive messages from the outside world, as is implied in l.6, - all is silent. And yet, it is the purest form of Life which surrounds them and which they are bathed in interiorly. The moment of taking the habit means to opt for the sound of silence. The emotional outburst at the beginning of the third quatrain echoes the poet's joy, his unbounded happiness that on that day, that "aurore de l'Aurore / Qui brillera désormais, je suis né". He is born anew, in the presence of God, willing to silently contemplate Him from this day onwards: "Sagesse cachée! Je me tais. J'adore." The succession of these short three sentences underlines the decision made. The sonnet closes with an echo of the poet's belief in providence, expressing his conviction that God has seen this beautiful morning before, "Car Tu as vu ce que je vois, avant".

The decision to offer his voice to God, and never to speak again, is explicitly described in a sextain, rhyming in couplets, simply called "Written on my knees, midday on Good Friday, after much prayer" (*World*, 2): it expresses in a striking, straightforward manner that he aims to give all to the Lord:

> Meurs, meurs, ô Vie; et tue-moi avec Toi:
> En offrande, aujourd'hui j'éteins ma voix.
> Ni phechaf mwy, ni fedraf bechu mwy;
> F'arf bechu, na, 'nhair arf, fe'u cleddais hwy.
> Here for all time I offer my last worth:
> My voice I give. Mere whispers e'er'll come forth.

The Welsh lines mean: "I shall not sin hereafter, I cannot sin hereafter; / My sinning tool, no, my three tools, I have buried them." (*World*, 2). One tongue is not enough, the poet uses three languages to underline that he is determined to cease to speak for the Lord's honour, with the "three tools" apparently referring to those three languages. The contrast at the very beginning of the poem "Meurs, meurs, ô Vie" echoes the paradox touched upon in the previous poem: as a Trappist monk he casts away his former being in order to start anew in the presence of the real life, "Vie", i.e. God.

The joy of having taken the habit at La Trappe is apparent in "Quasi modo geniti ..." (*World*, 3), which was written immediately afterwards, as is indicated in a note.

> O day of days! Who thought I'd see thee rise
> Behind these hills, these sacred hills, that now

Enshroud the paradise of Home? My eyes
Behold at last the unseen whitened flow
Of Time enveloping this little corpse.
For I am dead; and buried. This new state
To which I rise, is pure as snow. Nor warps
Its slender beauty any untamed fate.
For on this day arisen, I now live
The day that will repeat itself till days
Repeat themselves no more. Vast Cîteaux! give
This newly born what this word "Trappist" says
Of those who say no other: here I live
Where Trappists lived before; now dressed as they
- Who came unheard, and unheard went their way.

The rhythm is characterized by a great number of inversions with spondees interspersed, which help to underline the poet's tremendous joy and excitement. The pause in l.1 offers the reader a chance to reflect briefly on the initial image: "O day of days!" The special nature of that day is reinforced by the spondees which follow in both the third and the fifth foot, a device to underline the unlikeliness of such a happening. The accumulation of stressed syllables, separated only by a brief pause in between, in "these hills, these sac-red hills" suggest the poet's wonder at the beauty of La Trappe, which has at last become his "Home", these hills "that now / Enshroud the paradise of Home". The imagery used implies the cosiness experienced, the love he is now bathed in, - all attributes of a real home. The enjambement of l.4 "the unseen whitened flow / Of Time" provokes a pause after "Time", which makes the contrast to the remaining part of l.5 appear all the more intense. The second quatrain introduces the idea of his departure from the world, his death, his body becoming a corpse in the eyes of the world, in his eyes, too: the rhythm of l.6 underlines this idea with its abundance of stressed syllables, the second, third and fifth foot being spondaic, with pauses after "dead" and "buried". The quick rhythm of "For I am dead; and buried" underlines the finality of the utterance, reinforced by the pause in between. The paradox is continued when he writes "This new state / To which I rise": he is buried in the eyes of the world, yet he rises to new life in the Lord. How much he is filled with excitement is expressed by the spondees which follow in ll.8-13, - "this day", "now live", "no more", "Vast Cîteaux!", "This new-ly", "no o-ther", completed by a number of inverted feet. The third part of this poem consists of five lines, there is one line too many to make it a regular sonnet. This third part celebrates his re-birth, referring to himself as "this newly born". The closing couplet suggests that the poet already starts to feel the bond to all those brethren who went that way before, "now dressed as they / - Who came unheard, and unheard went their way". Their lives remain unnoticed by the world, buried as they are behind the monastery walls.

One of the earliest poems written at La Trappe called "After taking a firm resolution" (*World*, 1) powerfully describes how it all began, when here at La Trappe he first started to feel God's pull. The poem is a declaration of his firm decision to live as a Trappist in La Trappe:

> [...] Here it began:
> Its pull pulled e'er so hard that all this world
> Could not pull back, but only tear in two.
> La Trappe! thy bait had caught me. Is it real,
> This odour smelt again? Is this thing true,
> That thou this day henceforth dost from me steal
> What was hereto my cord umbilical?
> My link with Man is sawn. I have said all.

The closing line has a theatrical touch about it: the two short sentences effectively suggest that the decision has been made and cannot be altered anymore. In particular the closing phrase, "I have said all", with its slow and solemn rhythm, underlined by the stresses employed, does not leave any doubts about the invariability of the decision. His "cord umbilical", a powerful metaphor for his voice, is sawn, - there is no bond left to man anymore. He is determined to lead a life apart in silence. How strong the pull was which La Trappe had exerted on him is graphically suggested: had he not "given in" and responded to the pull, he would have been torn "in two". He is trapped, "thy bait had caught me".

The poem reflects the enormous power exerted by La Trappe, an attraction he was unable to resist. Having only just arrived, he still finds it hard to believe that his return home really should have come true. More than joy, it is a feeling of wonder which predominates. The happiness, however, of finally having returned to La Trappe, is reiterated in "Before the Tabernacle, Sunday morning" (*World*, 4); the title itself suggests the divine presence felt:

> It is a long, long time since last this sound
> That sounds so much like Heaven in the ears
> Did slowly fill the silence all around
> The Altar where I knelt. Once more, two tears
> Of deep, deep Happiness are sucked by chords
> Of deep'ning Harmony re-echoing Thine own,
> From 'neath the resonance th'eternal cords
> Of Tune make to vibrate where they are known. [...]

The lines are charcterized by harmony and balance, conveyed by the dominance of long vowels and diphthongs. The pauses decrease the rhythm as well and make it appear more solemn and peaceful. The peace had been experienced before, when the poet first came to visit La Trappe in the summer of 1976, before he finally entered the charterhouse at Sélignac. How distant this first encounter seems to be is indicated by the repetition in l.1, which also suggests a notion of hiraeth and tender memorizing of this past event. The repetition in ll.5f. provokes the same effect. Experiencing this happiness anew is reinforced by remembering the joy of those days, "a long, long time" ago, which makes the present happiness doubly powerful. He feels truly at home at La Trappe (the use of "sucked" firmly suggests the notion of home), - is filled with "deep'ning Harmony". Hearing this particular music again makes his heart resonate in divine harmony with God.

It is in silence that one can best speak to the Lord, for it is in silence that God listens. The divine presence in silence is implied in various poems, such as in "After the prayer meeting" (*World*, 8), which expresses the poet's joy at knowing that "in the midst / Was Love":

> I have prayed much since last we prayed like this
> On folded knees, about this little flame,
> Each with his thought, his word. We shared the bliss
> Of Presence, known to them that in His name
> Agree on what to ask, for in the midst
> Was Love. I mean Thee, quiet, quiet Lord,
> That listened to our silence, heard, and didst
> What Thou didst not when word on word on word
> Of unthought Worldiness was hourly gushed
> From one Tibetan prayer-machine, alone
> And neck and neck with Schedule. This night, hushed
> Was friends' worst friend, what friendliness supplies
> Lest mouths unfilled give heed to hung'ring eyes.

The poem is a meditation on the divine presence in silent prayer. It is an adaptation of a sonnet, as the third part lacks one line: interestingly, it is l.10, "From one Tibetan prayer-machine, alone", which stands apart. Whether or not the irregularity was intentional is difficult to judge. In any case, the solitary nature of l.10 is highly suggestive. The first seven lines describe the peaceful nature of the prayer meeting, praying in silence, "Each with his thought, his word". In their individual solitude they "shared the bliss / Of Presence", "for in the midst / Was Love". Whenever a group of people gathers in the name of God, Jesus is there among them. The beauty, the thrill of the experience is firmly implied, in particular when the poet addresses Jesus personally: "I mean Thee, quiet, quiet Lord". He realizes that it is only in silent prayer that one can feel the Lord's presence, and "not when word on word on word / Of unthought Wordiness was hourly gu*shed* / From one *Tibe*tan *p*rayer-ma*ch*ine, alone / And ne*ck* and ne*ck* with *Sch*ed*u*le." The repetition of "word" suggests the nature of reeling off prayer, unconscious of what one is really saying, mumbling without thinking. The sound symbolism employed reinforces the idea of rattling off prayers unreflectingly. The image of the "Tibetan prayer-machine" is striking, firmly suggesting the idea of an indispensable regularity of prayer, fully automatized. The negative connotations provoked by the paradoxical combination "prayer-machine" underline the absurdity of such an activity, which ceases to be a real prayer, being dominated by the time table only ("And neck and neck with Schedule"). That night, however, the noise of the "prayer-machine" had ceased, - no loud word was uttered ("hushed / Was friends' worst friend"). Only silence was present. The imagery used in the closing line is highly suggestive: "Lest mouths unfilled give heed to hung'ring eyes." Those "mouths unfilled" refers to mouths unfilled with words, silent mouths. The image as such provokes associations with hunger, which is picked up as the line continues in "hung'ring eyes". Eyes can speak just as mouths can, though on a different level. The hunger expressed in a glance, the yearning to feel the divine presence, can be much stronger than when expressed in words.

In the following sonnet called "Absolution" (*World*, 46), written at Roscrea, the poet talks to God as to a friend, sharing with Him the memory of their first encounter: the grace he experienced then is still strongly felt:

> Give grace, sweet Lord, to keep this sweetest grace
> Intact, for 'tis at present as 'twas then
> When Thou didst show me first Thy smiling Face
> A long, long time ago, one evening when
> Th'angelic, evangelic strains did rise
> To where Thou art, to where Thou didst call up.
> And I recall how 'neath those childhood skies
> Thou didst use one small verse to knock and sup.
> Aha! sweet Lord, this sweetness is the same,
> And 'tis today enwrapped in silent white.
> How could I think of shedding this balmed name
> That hath enshrouded saint and saint from sight?
> And yet 'tis true, Thou knowest, quiet Lord,
> How this thy peace hath plucked another chord. [corr.]

The rhythm of the poem is very slow, additionally reduced in speed by the frequent interspersed pauses. The poet's balance at the moment of writing is strongly felt in this sonnet. He feels God's sweet grace as powerfully as before ("for 'tis at present as 'twas then"). This idea is repeated in 1.9, "Aha! sweet Lord, this sweetness is the same", which adds to the balance of the poem as a whole. "Intact" at the beginning of 1.2 is given additional emphasis by the pause which follows, - the poet strongly desires to continue to be filled with this "sweetest grace". The use of the absolute superlative underlines the wonderful, unique nature of the experience. The second quatrain brings back the memories of his first encounter with God when he was still a child, ("'neath those childhood skies"), where "Th'angelic, evangelic strains did rise / To where Thou art", referring to the students from Moorlands Bible College Guildford, in Surrey, who encouraged the first contact (cf. letter, 26.8.1991). "Thou didst use one small verse to knock and sup" is a reference to verse 20 of the third chapter of the Apocalypse[159] they were discussing, which had a strong impact on the young poet (cf. letter, 26.8.1991). The sweetness felt today is "enwrapped in silent white", apparently referring to the white habit he was wearing, with the "balmed name" echoing the name of the Trappists, of course. And yet, the poet, just as the Lord, his quiet friend, is fully aware of "How this thy peace hath plucked another chord:" a second chord was plucked as well, - the chord of complete solitude, living as a hermit.

What is striking about all the examples given is that most of them were written soon after the poet had become a Trappist monk at La Trappe. There are very few poems written at Roscrea which celebrate his love for God. The problems the poet faced in Ireland seem not to have stimulated such declarations and celebrations. The inner struggle apparently had a too dominating influence as to allow musings about the union felt. His early period at La Trappe,

---

[159] "Here I stand knocking at the door; if anyone hears my voice and opens the door, I will come in and sit down to supper with him and he with me."

however, mirrors the joy at entering this monastery. The peace and calm experienced provided a fertile soil for musings on the union experienced, as the bond he felt to the Lord, as well as to La Trappe, was extremely strong.

3.2.6. (IN-)COMPATIBILITY OF THE TRAPPIST AND THE POETIC VOCATION

As regards their immediate quality, the poems supply glimpses of the silent life in the Trappist Order, mirroring a whole world which usually is firmly closed off from the rest of mankind outside the monastic walls. They offer the possibility of insight into the daily routine of a Trappist monk by reflecting on seemingly trivial, yet often typical situations. The reader is enabled to re-experience such moments as they were experienced by the poet himself, as for instance "Le matin de la prise d'habit" (*World*, 3), where one is bound to feel the poet's joy at this moment: "Ma joie, je t'appartiens. Tu m'enveloppes / A nouveau aujourd'hui de Nouveauté / De Vie [...]". Alun Idris' poems present realistic ideas about the life led by the monks, mirroring joyous as well as woeful situations, the penance done day by day. The numerous poems echoing inner strain, which remind one of a silent cry of despair, reflect the problematical situation of a monk unable to find a home where he can settle. They mirror the stony way to God, as the circumstances never allowed him to settle and do what he most ardently wished to do, namely to live in union with the Lord, to experience Him, to celebrate his love towards Him. The hiraeth to become a hermit was still there, perhaps even stronger than ever; however, it was not possible to live in virtual seclusion, which became another source of pain and frustration. Writing poetry meant finding an outlet for accumulated feelings and thoughts: the monk in solitude experiences feelings far more intensely than other people, for there are no outward stimuli to distract his attention. Using his creative vein also became a means of working problems out, again due to the impossibility of communicating them; i.e. discussing them with others.[160]

Similar to the Carthusian period, we find many meditations on the nature of grace, which offers insight into the poet's own ideas about this divine gift. The poet's belief in grace and providence is unbroken, despite the difficulties he had encountered in the past. Poetic inspiration is a form of divine grace as well, as is clearly reflected in his verse. Despite his previous experience, the poet still does not perceive any contradiction in leading the life of a silent monk and simultaneously writing poetry. On various occasions Alun Idris implicitly conveys his belief in the perfect symbiosis they form: "Where comest thou, sweet Grace divine,

---

[160] For instance, the poem "Lines written in the thirteenth century building on the evening of St. Benedict's Day" (*World*, 10) deals with the question of becoming a recluse after not having fully adapted to La Trappe. "Questions" (*World*, 26) is centered on the same problem: this key poem was written when there seemed to be a realistic possiblity of being accepted as a hermit in Wales - for a discussion of the poem, cf. p.159.

/ And thou, hid muse, from line to line / That dost th'unthought with Thought entwine / In silence?"[161] Echoes of the "divine blowing" (2 Timothy 3:16) become apparent. "Answering the request" (World, 15f.) deals exclusively with the idea of writing and the Muse's central role. Here the poet explicitly refers to the healing function the muse has had in the past, by referring to her as the one who calmed his "longue tristesse / Solitaire". Once the Muse has started to flow and exert her healing effect, it is difficult and most painful to suppress the poetic vein.

Time, death and afterlife continue to be important themes in his poetry, all the more, as the poet happened to be present when several of his brethren passed away, which stimulated an intense meditation on the nature of death, and in consequence the writing of verse.

Apparitions provide a new realm of poetic inspiration: various poems meditate on particular, inexplicable events and incidents, which help to suggest how difficult it is for modern man to believe what he is told. The poet shows great understanding for scepticism, although there cannot be any doubt in his own personal credo.

Following the tradition of Welsh hymnology, Alun Idris writes hymns as well, as they provide an ideal means to combine poetry, prayer and song. Chanting is a means to reinforce the affectional element, typical for a Welshman, whose compatriots are renowned for their love of song. Alun Idris is very Welsh in that respect, and many of his hymns are used to this day in masses and celebrations of the office. Hymns form an essential part of his poetic output, an observation which is valid for the entirety of Alun Idris' poetical work. In his hymns the affective component is of predominant importance. There are other poems as well, however, which reflect the poet's love for God: they clearly demonstrate how he uses poetry as a means to declare and celebrate his love. The union he feels he enjoys with the Lord in these moments, the harmony and inner peace experienced then, is impressively conveyed.

Alun Idris is fully aware of the power of the word, in particular the written one. At the Trappist monastery of Roscrea he realized the possibility of exercising influence on the readers of his poetry, enkindling perhaps new religious fervour through his verse.

As the most outstanding external feature of the poems written as a Trappist monk, the sonnet has developed into Alun Idris' favourite stanza form: more than 85% of all the poems written in Trappist monasteries are Shakespearian sonnets. There are only a few examples where the poet aimed to write a sonnet but failed to to do so by employing one line either too many or too few; at times he adds an additional quatrain.[162] These can be regarded as exceptions, for Alun Idris takes the utmost technical care in the writing of his verse. The poet continues to versify in the tradition of his literary fathers, sticking to the rules and guidelines of traditional forms. How much he opposes trends in modern poetry, which neglect all rules - something which he considers to be vital for poetry -, is reflected in poems like "Reading a modern" (*World*, 48), which clearly demonstrates Alun Idris' attitude towards such

---

[161] "In the cloister garth" (World, 11f.).
[162] In "Photocopying" (*World*, 46) he experiments by employing an additional couplet.

innovations. The stylistic features characteristic of his Carthusian poetry intensify: the use of archaic words and constructions (negation without "did", as in the line "left not life the same"[163]) characterize his verse. These archaic forms underline that we are still in the realm of religious poetry, and help to provide a solemn tone which he considers to be suitable for writing poems to the Lord. The poet continues to use rhythm as a means to suggest and emphasize changes of feeling and agitation. Poems of inner strain gain in number: they are forceful because the poet is able to crystalize his inner struggle and despair in the rhythm of his verse. There is no euphemism at all to be observed but honest mirroring of his deplorable inner state. Doubtless, poetry becomes a means to release this strain.

Due to the novice master's decisive remark he stopped writing completely, which explains the long break of poetry being written at La Trappe. At the Irish house he resumed, when asked to continue writing, for the superiors there considered the writing of poetry primarily as a means to praise and celebrate the Lord rather than seeing possible dangers involved. The accumulation of the poetic flow at this point explains the flood of poetry written at the beginning of his stay at Roscrea, where a seemingly slight occasion prompted the writing of a poem. Thus we find frequent meditations on recent events, trivial as they may appear, which are primarily meant to please the ear and to be appreciated for their values in sound, rather than provoking deep, philosophical meditations. They are light, easy poems in whose freshness the reader might take delight.

The strong element of hiraeth noticeable in the Trappist period, marks Alun Idris as a truly Welsh writer. This typically Celtic notion of longing and homesickness can be called a characteristic feature of his verse. Most of all it is spiritual and religious hiraeth which can be found, in particular the hiraeth for reclusion. The melancholic tone prevailing in such a poem of hiraeth powerfully mirrors the poet's own inner struggling and yearning for something which cannot be grasped at the moment, which perhaps cannot ever be attained: life as a recluse.

---

[163] "After an act of kindness" (*World*, 44f.).

3.3. THE PERIOD OF RESTLESS SEARCH

The period referred to in this chapter covers the time span from Alun Idris' departure from Roscrea in June 1986 until his leaving the Benedictine community of the Subiaco Congregation at Farnborough in the spring of 1988. It is a period of restless search: the yearning to settle in a monastery was the driving force to make the poet visit a number of religious houses in Great Britain; he made retreats at Pluscarden Abbey in Scotland, Prinknash and Ramsgate in England, finally at Ealing near London. His enthusiasm about the possibility of re-establishing monasticism in North Wales is apparent in many of the poems written at that time, just as we find his immersion in the Charismatic Renewal reflected in his verse. The graduate diploma in Primary Eduacation he took in 1986-87 brought the poet "back to the world". He found himself involved in society again, a completely new experience after almost ten years of solitude, which is reflected in his poetry as well. Leaving the monastic world altogether and dedicating himself, for instance, to the spreading of the Charismatic Renewal in the secular world was another option which could have been realized. All these trends echo the inner struggle of finding the right way, a new home, his roots. The dominant yearning to settle made him finally take the decision to enter Farnborough, which was a hurried one, as later events were to show. There, his contemplative formation became so predominant that eventually it was impossible for Alun Idris to continue. His original preference for Prinknash Abbey is implied in "Gŵyl Ddewi" (*World*, 79), but it was not possible to enter the monastery at the time.

This period of intense inner struggle concerning both the poet's past and his future path is not only mirrored in his poetry, but verse also becomes an important vent for his accumulated feelings. The examples discussed below show how important poetry was for him as a release from inner strain.

Despite the difficulty of the situation, Alun Idris never lost his belief in providence, which had envisaged and pre-arranged his life. This firm belief is mirrored in chapter 3.3.1. Naturally the enthusiasm for the Charismatic Renewal in Wales left its mark on the poetry; similarly the hiraeth for solitude, the possibility of re-establishing monasticism in Wales, even becoming a hermit himself, is firmly implied in several poems. His final entry at Farnborough Abbey is accompanied by joy at having found a new home again, which he had longed for so intensely. The happiness felt allowed him to celebrate the union with God in his poetry again, - a joy which had too long been overshadowed by the difficulties he had had to face. There are numerous meditations on different themes both of sacred and profane nature, some of which are discussed below. Naturally recent, unexpected events also act as stimulating force for the writing of poetry, just as the power of memories is reflected in his verse.

3.3.1. PROVIDENCE

Given the difficult and frustrating personal situation the poet found himself at the time, it is all the more striking to see that his belief in the guiding hand leading us through life, his belief in providence was not shattered in the least. Several poems reflect this belief, which helped him to overcome the difficulties he was facing. Providence was to become the anchor which helped him never to lose his footing.

One of the earliest poems written after having left Roscrea was "Back to France" (*World*, 63), a sonnet which is full of wonder at the diversity of events that happened in this short period of time already since his departure from Ireland. The first quatrain implies the monotony of living the life of a contemplative monk:

> Did e'er a week contain so many things
> Or days so bulge with happ'nings so intense?
> What unto changelessness a small change brings
> None knows but who fasts long on void immense.
> Had I foreseen the pow'r beneath a line
> Of silent ink, would I have stretched this wire
> That made these parted yesterdays entwine
> Their unspent charges in this cosmic fire?
> For I perceive that two worlds have passed by
> And yet have stood their course, their mighty course,
> For many things have made far dreams draw nigh
> And in th'encounter some deep guiding force
> At last hath said, "I am and have e'er been
> Behind this drama that ye have not seen."

The imagery used to describe the enormous change he experiences in comparison with his silent years in the monastery is striking: the days "so bulge with happ'nings so intense", - using the word "bulge" is highly suggestive of the quantity of happenings that occurred recently; the repetition adds the idea of wonder. The word "bulge" contrasts with the "void immense" (1.4) he had lived on before, even more, had fasted on it. The "luxury" of the present differs sharply from his past. The second quatrain reflects on the recent past, pondering about the hypothetical question of whether he would have acted as he did, had he known the consequences before. Such hypothetical reflections can often be found in his verse, they mirror the mind of a man who does not take anything for granted, who reflects about his life carefully, considering other possibilities as well. It was "the pow'r beneath a line / Of silent ink" which let him meet this friend, who is not described any further. The power of the written word caused their encounter, "That made these parted yesterdays entwine", - apparently they had know each other before, their "parted yesterdays" are re-united. "Entwine" suggests that their lives not only met but that they felt the bond of friendship very strongly, perhaps even considering walking together on their future paths. The image of the "unspent charges in this cosmic fire" underlines this idea. There was an unspent capacity of energy and power which could be used now. The third quatrain leads up to the message of the closing couplet, pointing to the presence of divine providence, "some deep guiding force", which cannot be clearly defined, as is suggested by the imagery used. Yet it is "Behind this drama that ye have not seen". The image of our mundane drama directed by providence well conveys the influence it has on our lives. As actors playing our roles, we organize our lives to a large extent ourselves, we shape our own performance, and yet we are subject to the instructions of providence.

"Un détour par Tours (et S. Martin)" (*World*, 63) is a French poem firmly centered on the idea of providence as well, on how we seemingly lose our way by our own "égarements", and yet how providence is using these to make us march our ways, continuing on the right path. We are walking on a route which has been planned for us:

> Sur ce chemin d'égarements
> Qui nous amène rarement [corr.]
> Où nous allons, là tu attends
> Depuis des siècles.
>
> Car y a-t-il détournement
> Du jour qui éternellement
> Poursuit son cours fidèlement
> Sans nous attendre?

The basic question is: is there a deflection of the day, can we possibly deflect it? It seems as though our day, our life, was fixed in its direction from all eternity, "qui éternellement / Poursuit son cours", which goes on, uninfluenced by our approval or disapproval ("Sans nous attendre"). Our day seems to follow a course, - nevertheless, the question remains: is a deflection of the eternal purpose possible? The first stanza only suggests that at the end of our way, "là tu attends / Depuis des siècles", the Lord will be there, without any real implication that this way has been pre-arranged beforehand.

> Ancien des jours, tu étais là
> A l'aube que traçait déjà
> L'Amour qui nous entraînera
> Là où il rêva.

"Ancien des jours", "ancient of days" is a scripture reference to the Book of Daniel 7:9+13+22, a quote which appears frequently in Alun Idris' poetry. "L'aube" is a metaphor for the beginning of life as such, while the capitalized "l'Amour" is a symbol for God, who created "l'aube". God seems to have traced our path right at the beginning, the path which leads us to that place He has dreamt for us. "Là où il rêva" is striking for its imagery: the idea of God dreaming the world, dreaming the whole of mankind, suggests the ease with which it happened. Yet also provokes a feeling of uncertainty about how the dream is realized eventually: does the dream correspond to reality? What is the nature of providence? Just a vague frame, a pattern, or a completely pre-arranged path? The following stanza, too contains a scripture reference, notably Exodus 3:14 in l.4 (cf. letter 2.10.1991):

> Car qui es-tu sinon ce qui
> Est sûrement le seul qui suit
> Le sillon de ce grand Je Suis
>   Qui fut prononcé?

The great "I Am" of God, God encompassing all of time, all destiny in Himself in a way: God is He who englobes all destiny, He was there at the beginning, "God is an eternal pronouncement in a sense" (letter, 2.10.1992), as Alun Idris himself described God. It is only in Him that destiny makes sense. The passage as such is not all that clear, yet its mysteriousness has a suggestive function: can God be known and fully grasped? All we realize is that He is at the origin, He is at the end. We are a part of the great destiny, the great utterance being what God said.

The poem closes with the following stanza:

> Tu seras et sauras demain
> La raison de nos changements
> Que déjà dans ton lendemain
>   Tu faisais poindre.

The word-play in l.1, emphasizing the phonetic similarity of "seras" and "sauras", underlines their inherent contradiction: God is tomorrow, God knows tomorrow, He has known it for all eternity. God is the reason of it all, He is the reason behind providence. In providence's ancient tomorrow, before every tomorrow of the past occurred, before all eternity, God was preparing our paths. The use of "poindre" suggests that while creating dawn, God was already directing light towards its return to Him, leading light, as well as man, ultimately back to the original source.

3.3.2. THE CHARISMATIC RENEWAL

The poems below reflect how intensely Alun Idris got caught up by the spirit of the Charismatic Renewal, - how strong its influence was on him. The Charismatic Renewal had started in France, where the poet had become acquainted with it first. He was full of hope that he would be able to continue the work of renewal in some form in Britain, - a renewal which he felt to be urgently necessary.

"Arrival" (*World*, 64) was written while the poet was living in L'Abbey Blanche in Normandy, an old medieval abbey which used to house Cistercian nuns (cf. letter, 7.10.1991). Just as the abbey was the fruit of the great renewal in the Middle Ages, so the new movements like Le Pan de Vie, which emphasizes perpetual adoration, or the community of the Line of Juda, were the fruit of the renewal of Vatican II.

> A newness in antiquity so old
> That it held ancient beauty mellowed o'er
> The years that bade it fade: this song re-told
> By voices young a past age doth restore,

And in these crumbling *stones* a *something stirs*
The passer-by that could have passed by this
And never known how little Time here blurs
The smile of new-born Christendom's first bliss.

The inital image refers to the timeless beauty of the old Cistercian abbey, which has not lost its original power to attract during the course of the centuries, despite a certain outward fading. The attractivity, the "newness" has "mellowed o'er / The y*a*rs that b*a*de it f*a*de", - it seems to have become even stronger, having gained in power. The long diphthongs (as indicated in italics) underline the notion of endless time. Now "this song" is "re-told / By voices young", which implies the youthful splendour of the Charismatic Renewal. The onomatopoetical effect of l.5. is striking, as the sounds not only suggest the constant crumbling of stones, but also how the passer-by is continuously "ensnared" by the attraction the abbey exerts, though in a very gentle, subtle form. That this splendour has not been lost by the abbey is implied in the line "how little Time here blurs / The smile of new-born Christendom's first bliss". Here, the original glow, the first love can still be felt, as it can be felt in the Charismatic Renewal. The exclamatory "O mighty Dove of yore" in l.9 addresses the Holy Spirit, who exerted the same influence in the early church that He still exerts today.

The poet's enthusiasm concerning the Charismatic Renewal is marred only by the difficulties he foresees in Great Britain: having started in France, he feared that the movement would perhaps not be able to implant itself in Britain, "our phlegmatic isle", as we read in "Frightened" (*World*, 64):

And yet there is a violence now too strong
For ancient lands. There are in this old world
Some corners yet untouched by newer song
Whose beauty hath things into orbit hurled.
We are alone on our phlegmatic isle [corr.]
And are not moved at once to alien trance.

The "violence now too strong / For ancient lands" implies that Britain is not yet prepared for the coming of the spirit: the Charismatic Renewal in its forcefulness might frighten the British rather than make them feel enthusiastic about it. The images used to describe the island ("ancient lands", this "our phlegmatic isle") (the French talk about the "flegme anglais") imply criticism on the lack of spontaneity and the ability to be enthusiastic, - the English "are not moved at once to alien trance". This image of the "alien trance" suggests the power radiating from the movement, but also conveys a certain criticism of the reservedness of the English vis-à-vis foreign ideas.

"Ars" (*World*, 66) mirrors how much the poet felt obliged to work in the renewal, having realized its tremendous power: "Here it begins; henceforth but one sole way / Can ever lie before my startled eyes." These opening lines of the sonnet leave no doubt about his firm decision to work in the Charismatic Renewal. The "age / Long buried long ago" refers to the early church, which seemed to be buried, yet the "passing of an age" has nevertheless allowed its ancient power "to linger", - the power was passed on: it was always there, though in a way dormant. Today the very same power is at work. It had been passed on, as the image of the "oft read page" suggests. Saints had worked miracles before, they received words of illumination in ages past, - the Cure d'Ars is a classical example. The poem closes with "A song of myriad eons long unknown, / That have returned and Hist'ry overthrown". Although the splendour of the early church period had been forgotten for so long a time, these eons have returned, they overthrew history in the sense that they made the past relive in the present through renewal.

The following sonnet mirrors the poet's conviction about the future radiation of a certain powerful movement, which is not explicitly mentioned. However, there are several subtle indications which imply that it is the spirit of the Charismatic Renewal he is referring to in "Sailing out of Ouistreham" (*World*, 66):

> Again, again we leave this dearest land,
> And yet there shall be more. More things shall be
> One day here sailing homeward, to withstand
> The ebb of Time e'en after this great sea
> We have at last crossed over to the end.
> The wonders of a wind can travel far
> And 'tis not untaught Hasard that doth send
> My cousin exiles 'neath a roving star
> To where this thing hath happened, happens now
> And labours deep within to happen more
> Where we belong, where like his like doth know;
> For though this force be one, its varied store
> Of unoped throbbing might throbs not the same
> Across these waves that alter every name.

The poem is bathed in metaphorical language: the voyage made by the poet "out of Ouistreham", as is indicated in the title, becomes a metaphor for the spreading of the Charismatic Renewal. France is "this dearest land", which is to multiply, - soon there will be other lands as dear as France, as full of the spirit of the renewal as France is. Ll.2f. emphasize the poet's conviction that the powerful influence will affect Britain as well, "one day". The "great sea" in l.4, apart from its literal reference to the sea he was crossing, is also a symbol of life, the great voyage towards eternity. Bringing the spirit over the sea to the other side, to Britain, means to be able to withstand the "ebb of Time", the spirit will continue working long after our own journey has terminated. "The wonders of a wind can travel far" is not only a literal observation but of highly symbolical implication: the wind is the symbol of the Holy Spirit. The line echoes John 3:8, "The wind blows where it wills; you hear the sound of it, but you do not know where it comes from, or where it is going. So with everyone who is born from spirit". The Greek uses one single word for "wind" and "spirit" with both meanings (cf. *The New English Bible* 1961, Popular Edition, 147). His "cousin exiles" refers to the Welsh who got caught in the spirit of the renewal in France, a foreign country, which explains the use of "exiles". How close the poet feels to his fellow Welshmen is indicated in the very image of "cousin exiles", as well as in ll.10f. expressing his wish "To happen more / Where we belong, where like his like doth know". L.12 suggests that the force of the renewal is the same everywhere, in every country, but the manner in which it finds expression in different languages and cultures varies considerably, - it "throbs not the same / Across these waves that alter every name". The closing line suggests the different languages used on either side of the sea.

This small selection of poems demonstrates Alun Idris' hiraeth to be able to work actively within the renewal. The spirit had seized him to the full. The ardent yearning to bring back the spirit to Britain is almost an obsession. Such fervour appears to be a natural reaction: after almost ten years of living as a contemplative monk, which had been years of intense prayer for the world in silence, the poet is filled with a longing to actively contribute to the renewal, as providence seems to have offered the chance. The poems reflect his hiraeth to spread the spirit of the Charismatic Renewal, and also the hiraeth to work actively for this renewal in Britain, particularly in Wales.

3.3.3. HIRAETH FOR SOLITUDE AND SILENCE, RECLUSION

The hiraeth for solitude and silence, which had been apparent in some of his earlier poetry as well, was becoming stronger. More than just solitude, the idea of re-establishing monasticism in Wales, perhaps becoming a hermit himself, was extremely tempting and attractive to the poet. This longing finds expression in "Benedictine Peace" (*World*, 72f.), a sonnet written at Ealing Abbey, as is indicated in brackets, where the poet was on retreat. The peace and quiet experienced in the presence of the blessed sacrament reminded him of the peace experienced before, which allows the hiraeth to be felt all the more strongly:

> When we are far away from little things
> That smile and cling and make us what we are,
> When in our emptied ears a something rings
> And echoes silent echoes from afar,
> When there is nothing but this something there
> And this again begins once more to be
> What once it was, for that all else seemed ne'er
> To be allowed to roam Eternity,
> Then there is also some small thing within
> That answers to a tune, a tone once known
> And bids an ancient Gladness enter in
> And rest awhile in one place once its own.
> O quiet Gaze, that lookest on and on,
> I did but linger where a stray beam shone.

The use of "thing" in the first two quatrains of the sonnet is striking: the frequent employment of the word in different combinations was apparently used on purpose by the poet, although it can hardly be considered a device adding to the beauty of the poem. The "little things / That smile and cling" reflects the course on teacher training the poet was pursuing at the time (cf. letter, 7.10.1991): remembering the children in the silence of his retreat, these children to whom he feels he has a strong emotional bond, as is implied by the imagery used. In this solitary silence, "in our emptied ears a something rings", - this "something", which seems to be difficult to grasp in words, as is suggested by the vague description "something", "echoes silent echoes from afar": the void experienced in this retreat allowed the poet to hear once more echoes of the void experienced before, silent echoes though. The second quatrain concentrates on the moment of being emptied completely, experiencing the void, the moment when nothing is left anymore but "this something", still not described in any greater detail. All that we are told is that it mysteriously "begins once more to be / What once it was", i.e. it gains in importance once more. The poet is bound to realize that nothing else ever seemed "To be allowed to roam Eternity": how special this "something" is, is firmly implied in this line. It is the absoluteness of the one thing, i.e. contemplation, the presence of God, which crowds out all else when it takes over. The demand of the absolute is so great that everything else seems excluded for all eternity. Alun Idris describes the monk as follows: the monk is the one who gathers all into one, all his being is orientated towards one direction. It is the process of integration, of harmonization, of bringing all into one that makes the monk what he is, a monk. The word "monk" means a solitary one, but it can also be interpreted as meaning the one who makes unity of his life, being a person who is at one with himself, with God, with creation because he has orientated himself in one sole direction (cf. letter, 7.10.1991). The apostrophe in l.13 is addressed to God, referring to the gaze of God one feels when looking at the blessed sacrament. What almost sounds like an excuse in the final line refers to the poet's own recent past, - events which had drawn him away for a while. They were but "stray beams" of God's goodness, originating in God as well.

The following sonnet strongly expresses his longing to become a hermit in Wales: "Caldey" (*World*, 71) was written with reference to Caldey island, an island off the south coast of Wales where there is a small Cistercian community, the only monastery in Wales.

> It would be well to spend a life alone
> With none but Thee to fascinate the eyes,
> And yet these closing doors ope wide Thine own
> Somewhere, somehow, beneath some other skies.

The hiraeth to become a hermit on Caldey is firmly implied in these lines. "These closing doors", which were actually closing only for the time being, refer to the fact that Caldey was willing to take Alun Idris, yet the abbot wanted him to wait nine months (cf. letter, 7.10.1991). The poet knows that new doors will be opened "beneath some other skies" after this period of time has elapsed, which is also implied in the line "And yet we must go on and move away / Ere this old silence may be heard anew". This period of time seems to consist of "slowly-moving hours", which reflect the idea that it seems to be a rather painful experience to have to go back to the world again, not to have that peace immediately which he had known before.

Three poems were written on the occasion of his possible joining the monks on Caldey island, one in Welsh, which was published in *Cri o Gell*, and two in English, the other one being

"Desiderans desideravi" (*World*, 72) (cf. letter, 29.10.1989). The very title of the poem, which is a quotation from Luke 22:5, emphasizes the desire the poet felt to live on Caldey island. The emotional outbreak at the beginning of the third quatrain remains unclear, if the reader does not known about the abbot's suggestion of waiting for nine months, which the poet had in mind here:

> - Ah! one small word so many words hath borne
> And in one breath much breathing hath been stored,
> For by one will another hath been torn
> And in an hour a year hath been outpoured.
> Yet Silence was ne'er heard as well as when
> 'Twas bid not be by words of silent men.

The closing couplet presents a form of pure hiraeth: it suggests that the yearning for that Trappist silence, which was immensely audible at that time, was never felt so strongly before as when he was told that he could not have it, at least for that period.
The monastery on Caldey island was down to less than ten monks then and it was quite uncertain whether it was going to remain open or not.[164]

The fascination of the hermitage also finds expression in "Llaneilian" (*World*, 72), referring to a little church attached to which is the only reclusery still standing in Wales (cf. *World*, 72). Alun Idris employs ironical language to emphasize the greatness of the life of the hermits who will not at all regret the penance of reclusion in heaven, the seclusion from everything but God:

> What suffering was borne within these walls,
> What pains and sorrows were in this place known,
> What depth of Thought once hummed, no thought recalls,
> For here for evermore all is outblown
> By winds of hurried Progress that guide well [corr.]
> From prisons narrow and horizons barred
> That dwelt too long on punishment and Hell
> And knew not how much Pleasure they had marred.
> O Sisters of a passing Pain, these hours
> Stored deep within these walls, do they return
> From time to blissful time, and are your pow'rs
> Of agile Glory made to glow and burn
> A little more where now they are no more
> Confined by what defined all time before?

The first two quatrains elaborately present the life of the recluse in a deliberately negative manner in order to emphasize the greatness of such a life. The third quatrain as well as the closing stanza firmly suggest that self-denial on earth is amply compensated for by the fulness received for all eternity. Far from denigrating the recluses, the poem glorifies their vocation. The capitalized "Progress" refers to the notion of progress which is all englobing. It appears as though we were living in a new, enlightened age, but the poet suggests the contrary is the case: the entire process of being hurried, being progressive and on the way to something greater

---

[164] The community eventually recovered.

which, in fact, means moving away from the center of all. That this "Progress" should guide well, is meant ironically. "Where now they are no more / Confined by what defined all time before" refers to the afterlife. The poet asks whether these monks still recall the memories of the past, the penance, the pain, after they have left this world. The "agile Glory" echoes one of the qualities souls have, namely the quality of agility, being able to move from one place to another, with the speed of thought. "Made to glow and burn / A little more" sugests that these monks, who spent their lives orientated towards God only, were therefore more ready for God when He came.[165]

The eremitical life exerted enormous attraction on Alun Idris over a prolonged period. The following poem with the Greek title "Ἀρκεῖ σοι ἡ χάρις μου" (*World*, 78) reflects this strong appeal. It was written after having been loaned a book on the eremitical life, as is mentioned in a note attached to it [corr.][166]:

> There is but oneness in these many things
> That pull toward a better than the last
> And in their several sirens one voice sings
> The selfsame Song heard often where Thou wast,
> O Beauty of Simplicity, before
> In utter nudity, alone, alone
> With this our naked soul, the bared of yore
> Who had no one but Thee, its gaze made one.
> We look upon too many things below
> The sphere of where Thou art; we know too well
> To be made ignorant enough to know
> Th'unlearning that in utterness doth yell
> For something, but for something, for in this,
> Void's Truth, there is but Hell, there is but Bliss.

"These many things", "their several sirens", these different ways actually all bear one thought only, one aim, - it is but "one voice" that sings, all pointing to "oneness": the call of reclusion. This "selfsame Song" which he now hears again he has heard before many a time, "often where Thou wast". The second quatrain describes the beauty of feeling at one with God when secluded from the rest of the world, "in utter nudity, alone, alone", the solitude shared with Him only. "The bared of yore / Who had no one but Thee": the "naked soul" is emptied of all but God, there is nothing else left which might take away one's attention from Him. In the third quatrain the problem of being involved too much in profane matters is touched upon. These eventually impede our approach to divinity. They are like obstacles standing in between, hindering our direct gaze to God. The word-play in "we know too well / To be made ignorant enough to know / Th'unlearning" emphasizes our ability to alienate ourselves from Him. We

---

[165] The interest in Welsh tradition and its continuation had become stronger by the end of the teacher training course. Alun Idris' awareness of the need to actively work for the preservation of Welsh culture had grown tremendously. On Caldey island, although geographically belonging to Wales, no one speaks Welsh anymore. It has turned into an English part of Wales. This fact lessened his yearning to join the community there, so that eventually he rather preferred the idea of bringing back a small foundation to the Welsh part of Wales, i.e. the north, the west or mid-Wales.

[166] Note in false position in printed text.

manage to become ignorant of the knowledge that only in utter emptiness God can be experienced. "Th'unlearning that in utterness doth yell / For something" powerfully conveys that if we were prepared to listen, we would not miss the "yell" telling us that in reclusion, "in this, / Void's Truth, there is but Hell, there is but Bliss". Both hell and bliss are firmly attached to the idea of reclusion, the poet is fully aware of these two essential aspects of a hermit's life .

The yearning to be able to reintroduce monastic life at Penmon Priory on the Isle of Anglesey, which has lain desolate for centuries (cf. Hogg 1988a, vi), is apparent in "The Penmon bell" (*Threshold*, vi):

> There is an eye that sees through many years,
> A mind that dreamed these things ere minds began
> To *t*urn *t*heir *t*houghts *t*owards a day's *f*ull *f*ears
> Of matters great, that mattered so to man
> That he saw not the Sight that saw it all,
> And would see for himself, lest Sight be not
> As well prepared as he, who details small
> Could for whole days map out and duly plot.
> O unchimed bell that nought doth pull below,
> But yet, 'tis said, art heard upon a shore
> That well records thy sound, thine hour doth know
> (Since gentle boreal light sings as of yore) [corr.]
> And thy hid Ringer sees at His reveil, [corr.]
> Art thou a cry o'erheard from Hypnos' vale?

The yearning to re-establish monasticism in Wales is combined with a strong belief in providence. The first two lines of this sonnet reflect the omnipotence of the creator, the long vowels and diphthongs supply and reinforce the solemn tone conveyed: "There *is* an *eye* that *see*s through many *yea*rs, / A m*i*nd that dr*ea*med th*e*se things". The rhythm changes with "ere minds began", when the poet starts to describe human activity, where short vowels and plosives dominate, as is indicated in italics. The alliteration in "day's full fears" underlines the daily struggle imposed on mankind, implying also the difficult situation the poet found himself in at the time. L.4 is ironical, indicating however overwhelming a problem may appear to man, it is only of a minute scale when considered in relative terms. And yet, man tends to be so obsessed by his problems and posited ways to solve them that he loses the ability and sensitivity to view things on a larger scale: "That mattered so to man / That he saw not the Sight that saw it all", - man forgets that providence has seen, has pre-arranged it all beforehand. Human insignificance is particularly implied in ll.7f., when the poet describes the meticulous preparation and planning necessary to satisfy human needs; the spondaic "whole days" stresses this idea. After having presented his belief in providence quite elaborately, the poet turns to Penmon bell, addressing it affectionately: "O unchimed bell that nought doth pull below" - the spondaic opening reinforces the tone of lament apparent in this line. And yet, the sound of the bell seems to be heard still in Wales, - "upon a shore" the chime is still echoing, it has not completely disappeared. The poet thereby implies that the possibility of re-establishing monasticism in Wales is still there. He strongly feels the need to contribute in some way or another to the re-establishment, for the need is there. "Thy hid Ringer sees at His reveil" refers to God, who seems to still ring the bell at Penmon that people are hearing at 4.30 a.m., as is indicated in a note. The use of the word "reveil" is a French influence, which implies a certain distance, an idea of mystery. The closing line emphasizes the mysterious nature of the sound of the bell. The imagery used beautifully implies the early hour that the chime is said to be heard.

The call to solitude was strongly felt by the poet, he ardently longed to become a hermit. However, the previous chapter demonstrated his hiraeth to work actively within the Charismatic Renewal and help spread its spirit in Britain. These two yearnings are contradictory, as, logically, one excludes the other, although both of them ultimately lead to the same goal. Such an interior struggle is an ideal ground for poetry of hiraeth. The poet is longing for both, as he considers both paths to be of utmost importance, although he is fully aware of the fact that only one can possibly be realized.

3.3.4. BACK TO ENCLOSURE - CELEBRATING THE UNITY WITH GOD

The decision to enter Farnborough Abbey was hurried along by the strong yearning to settle. Joining the community triggered off the joy of being united with God again, which becomes apparent in the poems below, although the sorrowful experience of the past still continued to exercise its baneful effect. Unfortunately, the hopes he had placed in this new "Home" were shattered in the end.

Although the following sonnet aims to reflect the happiness of being back to enclosure, of ultimately having found a new home, "Aurora Virginalis" (*World*, 75) is dominated by the sorrowful memory of the past, which is still vividly present to the poet. The despair he had experienced as a result of his not having been able to settle in any of the monasteries he had lived in so far is apparent in these lines. The joy he now feels originates in the newly risen hope at the present prospect of a final stability, of ultimately having found the proper place to stay, a real home:

> "What 'tis to feel a joy within the heart
> That hath 'neath darkened seasons beaten on,
> To know that there can be a home apart
> From this world's homeless hearth, that Time's frail son
> Can pass the untapped hours that yet abide
> Their turn upon the slipping wheels of Fate,
> Not in a passing frenzy, that can hide
> The echoes of our depths, but in a state
> Of waiting and of list'ning for the next,
> That it might be well used should e'er it come -
> This is to read beyond the sacred text
> Of Fortune's one true story, and to hum
> Our little note within this Symphony
> Of accidents that brought this day to be.

The feeling of joy present in l.1 is overshadowed by the pain expressed in l.2, "the heart / That hath 'neath darkened seasons beaten on": those "darkened seasons" is a metaphor for the problematical period of his life which seems to have come to an end now. At last he realizes that "there can be a home apart / From this world's homeless hearth": the hope that there is still the possibility of finding a home is implied, however homeless his past had been before. "Time's frail son" is a metaphor for the poet himself, with the frailty suggesting the shortness of the periods spent in monasteries, not being able to settle in one place and stay forever. The "passing frenzy" emphasizes this idea of restlessness. He longs for calm and peace, for inner tranquility which will allow him to make the right decisions, enable him to use the chances offered by grace, "That it might be well used should e'er it come". The "Symphony / Of accidents that brought this day to be" reflects the poet's belief in providence: the endless number of accidents, coincidental as they seem, emerge into one great "Symphony", forming a whole, which firmly implies that all has been foreseen by providence.

The following hymn called " Ἅγιος, ἀθάνατος" (World, 76) is part of the *Liturgy of Saint Deiniol* (30), a liturgy including a considerable number of hymns written by the poet himself to be used in church. This hymn has a deeply prayerful character. It was written in the spirit of the joy felt at being united with God again:

>   Holy God, Love is your name:
> You are the Maker and Giver of all;
> Holy and strong, ever the same -
> You called us forth, and again you will call.
>
>   Lord and Christ, Truth is your name:
> You are the Saviour, Redeemer of all;
> Holy and strong, ever the same -
> You called our name, and again you will call.
>
>   Living Breath, Peace is your name:
> You are the Healer, the Mover of all;
> Holy and strong, ever the same -
> You know our name, and this name you now call. [corr.]
>
>   Alleluia, alleluia;
>   Alleluia, alleluia.
>   Alleluia, alleluia -
> Hear us in peace as your name we recall.

The metrical pattern is maintained throughout the first three stanzas of the poem: the common metre is the basic underlying metre, although considerable rhythmical changes are employed. The first line of each stanza could be scanned as a cretic followed by a choriambus, with a medial pause in between. In l.2 both the first and the fourth foot are inverted, while the third foot is a pyrrhic. The balance achieved in l.3 as a result of the two choriambi employed is striking. It is given all the more emphasis by its repetition in each stanza. L.4 also has a medial pause: the solemn rhythm of the first half achieved by the initial spondee contrasts with the second half of the line, where a pyrrhic introduces the closing choriambus, which suggests a feeling of urgency. The poem is characterized by repetition: apart from l.3, which is repeated without any alterations, the poem contains considerable parallelism, viz. in ll.1 and 3 of each stanza. God is the union of Love, Truth and Peace, He is the moving force behind the world. L.4 employs a kind of incremental refrain: after being called forth, the Lord "called our name", calling us personally, until in stanza three we read "You know our name, and this name you now call", stressing the immediacy of the call. "This name" is the only rhythmical variation when compared with the other stanzas, given additional emphasis by the spondee employed. The fourth stanza obviously differs from the other three, leading to an elaborate praise bestowed on the Lord. The inversion at the beginning of the final line adds urgency to the plea.

The taking of the habit inspired the writing of the following poem, which reveals the love Alun Idris felt at that moment. A note in brackets informs the reader that the poem was written on the day of "reprise d'habit" (which happened to be the feast of a Benedictine martyr, St. John Roberts).[167] The use of French indicates his burning love: frequently the poet switches to French, unconsciously perhaps, when referring to something with which he feels he has a strong affectional bond. The title of the poem is French, too: "Effacé" (*Beyond*, 98), although the sonnet itself is written in English.

> To be, now to be nothing but to be
> A being that is part of all that is
> Is all that here remains, for herein we
> In lying in the Isness that is His
> Are made as He had made us, not alone
> A glory to an hour that waited not
> Upon our act, but mightily struck down
> To be a spark of glory here forgot.
> ᾽Ω Μοναχέ! to be this very thing
> Wherewith thou'rt named - to be a oned of soul
> That looks upon a Gazing, speaks to sing
> And moves within the rhythm of the whole
> Of cosmic Dance - this is this night to live
> Within the ecstasy that two can give.

The poem meditates on his being a monk again. In the first two quatrains, which form one sentence and are dominated by a slow, solemn rhythm, the poet describes the nature of a monk by using different forms of "to be", at times unusual ones, such as the noun "Isness" for instance. Such elaborate use of "to be" points to the very essence of life as a monk: "A being that is part of all that is" (1.2) suggests various meanings. On the one hand it refers to the fact of how much monks are absorbed by God, becoming one with him. "In lying in the Isness that is His" (1.4) reinforces this idea. On the other hand it also underlines their important role for mankind, forming an essential part of the world.

"To be [...] Is all that here remains" indicates that the monk's life and being is all that is left for him while here on earth, to be immersed in God is his only aim, "a spark of glory here forgot".

---

[167] At Farnborough, Alun Idris took the religious name of "John", - the only time he was not called "David", as there were already a Father David and a Brother David in the community; another reason for taking the name "John" was the close connection the poet feels he has with St. John Roberts (cf. letter, 7.1.1990). John Roberts was a Benedictine monk, priest and martyr, born at Trawsynydd (Merioneth, now Gwynedd), who was hanged and quartered at Tyburn on 10 December 1610 (cf. Farmer 1979, 345f.).

Seemingly forgotten by the world (the title of the poem points to this idea of obliteration as an individual), as today hardly anyone pays heed to monks living in monasteries, the monks are, nevertheless, sparks of God's glory. The third quatrain, starting with the sigh uttered in Greek, suggests the fulness of what it means to be a monk. It expresses the poet's wonder and stupefaction at the very thought that he himself should be one of those, "to be a oned of soul", a line which attracts attention because of its unusual use of "oned". This term reinforces the original idea of the monk, the meaning of the word as such: the monk goes back to the One, back to union, back to the whole, integrity. It is a singular view: just looking in one direction, drawing together everything into one. He is a monk now himself, one "That looks upon a Gazing": the nature of contemplation is implied here. In the act of contemplation one is in harmony with the whole of creation: "And moves within the rhythm of the whole / Of cosmic Dance". The monk is at one with the rhythm of the whole, at one with the rhythm of creation, with God, which is even more implicit when we read "this is this night to live / Within the ecstasy that two can give". It reminds one of the dark night of the soul depicted by St. John of the Cross, with the loving soul climbing up the ladder to be united with the beloved, with God. Such "Brautmystik" is not unusual among mystics: the idea of considering Jesus as one's bridegroom seems logical when bearing in mind that it is above all love which unites the mystic with God.[168] The night of having taken the habit again means to the poet living within this ecstasy caused by the love-relationship between God and man, which powerfully conveys the love he feels for God.

The nature of monasticism, the firm union the poet feels with God, is also implied in a poem written shortly afterwards called "A virgin new year" (*Beyond*, 99). Here we also find implications of the importance of using well the grace given to the monk, not abusing it:

> My heart has its own secret, and a song
> Known only to one soul, the one that here
> Unseen, unknown would flee the busy throng
> Of uncontainèd spirits that ill steer
> The energies within that could return
> To their first point, the spot whence all rays starred,
> The spark of being's glowing, - could they burn
> But less in burning out such forces marred.

The use of spondees in "own secret", "Known only", "one soul", "Unseen" and "unknown" reinforces the idea conveyed, pointing to the root of the word "monk", being one in God. The assonance in "Known only to one soul" implies even more strongly the idea of oneness. "The busy throng / Of uncontainèd spirits" refers to the people outside the monastery, possibly inside as well, rushing around, talking, their spirits bustling. The second quatrain leads back to the theme of monasticism, the unity which the monk achieves, bringing all together to one, making the One the object of his life, with all his attention being drawn into One, into God: "To their first point, the spot whence all rays starred, / The spark of being's glowing" - all these

---

[168] "Brautmystik" was already used by Hildegard of Bingen, for instance, a mystic of the twelfth century.

descriptions refer to the One, the origin of all. Using "starred" as a verb reminds one of God's command, "Be!". The "spark of being's glowing" not only suggests God as the source of all life but also implies our coming back to this source. L.8 refers to the abuse of energies given by God to the contemplative, misusing the power of word, thought and prayer for other things. It implies the enormity of words wasted in life. How many actions have no rapport with eternity! The closing line of the poem contains an effective image when Alun Idris describes the heart that "fondles with a pulsing of traced word". Literally the line refers to letters written with affection, yet the image also suggests that the word is pulsing just like the heart, being very much alive. The living word seems to be a part of his "song", which brings us back to the very beginning of the poem, - the importance of the written word, be it a letter or a poem.

The poet's return to enclosure inspired the composition of various poems meditating on the nature of being a monk, which emphasize the idea of being one with God, forming a firm union with Him. The poems express the joy of having entered a community again, as the poet hopes to find therein a new home, where he can fulfil his task as a monk, lead a life in and for God alone.

3.3.5. PRAYERFUL MEDITATIONS

Many poems written in this period of searching can be described as prayerful meditations, dealing exclusively with religious themes. They mirror how central God and things divine are in his life, be it while living in a monastery, be it while living in the secular world. The meditations echo central aspects of the religious life. They invite the reader to share the experience with the author.

The healing effects of fasting are forcefully described in a sonnet called "The Fast" (*World*, 65), where the poet meditates on the fruits of fasting.

>There is an emptiness within that fills the soul
>With many things that fulness cannot hold.
>The weakness of the part opes wide the whole
>To quiet sounds that energies withhold
>From entering within where they are fed.
>We are *t*oo busy in sa*t*ie*t*y
>*T*o be made *litt*le and *t*o *l*eave unsaid
>The many noises of variety.
>The *h*ollowness of void doth echo well
>The *h*ole *w*e are and *w*e are *w*ell *w*hen not
>As full of *w*aste as are the years of Hell,
>*F*or o*ft* we *f*eed the *f*ood of very rot
>When all that enters draws out more and more
>Of what, unfed, feeds on things stored before.

The first two lines of this sonnet summarize the central message of the poem as a whole, which is further developed as the sonnet progresses. The paradox of these lines arises as a result of the mingling of the literal and the figurative levels: the physical emptiness experienced when fasting feeds the soul on a spiritual level, thereby filling it "With many things that fulness cannot hold". Here the literal meaning of "fulness" is referred to. More contrasts follow ("weakness" - "energies", "part" - whole"), which emphasize the paradoxical nature of fasting, its filling through emptying. "The weakness of the part opes w*i*de the wh*o*le / To qu*i*et s*ou*nds" is beautifully gentle in sound. In particular, the long diphthongs employed point to the vast scale of fulness reached through fasting, which contrast in sound to the "wea*k*ness of the *part*", where short plosives are dominant.

"Too busy in satiety" in l.6 refers to both our need to eat, achieving a state of physical satiety, as well as out need to talk and communicate, thereby reaching a state of satiety and satisfaction as well. Our striving for satiety is underlined by the t's and l's which appear with remarkable frequency. "The hollowness of void doth echo well / The hole we are" suggests a number of meanings. It implies that fasting ("the hollowness of void") helps to realize our capacity for being filled with the divine spirit, pointing to the vast range of possibilities. It seems as though we were made to be filled with divine grace, although the filling as such depends on ourselves to a large degree, - whether we are open to grace or not. However, the "hole" also implies how little we have stored already, suggesting our spiritual emptiness. We seem not to have made much use of divine grace so far. On another level, the "hole" suggests human smallness and unimportance, - man is made up of only a hole.

The alliteration in l.12 reinforces the foolishness of feeding things which "draw out more and more / Of what, unfed, feeds on things stored before". Alun Idris' predilection for word plays is noticeable in this closing line (as well as in ll.10f., which is reinforced by the use of alliteration). Inner strength can be gained by fasting ("unfed"), the strength "feeds on things stored before", i.e. it receives its spiritual nourishment from the grace given before.

The following poem reflects the strong impact of Byzantine Vespers on the poet: "The laying on of hands (after the word of knowledge)" (*World*, 65f.) describes the nature of the word of knowledge:

> There is a force and beauty in this place
> That is not of this world. There is a tongue
> Unknown of him that sings, that beareth grace
> And order in this orchestrated song
> That none on earth e'er wrote. There is a light
> That sees the unseen regions of the heart
> And, known within by means yet unknown quite, [corr.]
> Sends forth a beam that makes the touched soul start;
> For there is more in this place than mere men
> And though man be full man, a thing divine
> Hath travelled through this perfume. For e'en then
> When man made most, he made not this. 'Tis Thine
> To know what Thou dost know alone, to be
> Where Thou didst say Thou'ldst be with two or three.

The parallelism employed in the first two quatrains emphasizes the special nature of the event. Only in l.1 we find "There is" placed at the very beginning of the line, the two repetitions in ll.2 and 5 are placed in the fourth foot, being preceded by a pause. This technique serves to unify the two opening quatrains, which thereby very forcefully depict the beauty of this moment, its otherness, not being of this world: the "tongue / Unknown of him that sings" refers to the word of knowledge given by the Lord, "That none on earth e'er wrote". The inversion of the first foot in 1.9 indicates the change: the reason is given why all these things are present, as they were mentioned before, "For there is more in this place than mere man". Not only the first, but also the fourth foot is inverted, while the last one is spondaic. L.10 starts with two inverted feet, followed by a spondee: "And though man be full man"; then the rhythm continues regularly: "a thing divine / Hath travelled through this perfume." The "perfume" is a metaphor for the incense used during the vespers, which provokes beautiful, enchanting associations. The incense was used to convey the divine message, and though only heard by one, the divine presence was noticeable to the remaining congregation as well, through this special odour. The alliteration in 1.13 aims to emphasize how great an effort people make to create a beautiful liturgy. However, with all this endeavour, it can never reach the beauty achieved through the intercession of the Holy Spirit. The closing couplet is a reference to Matthew 18:20, "For where two or three have met together in my name, I am there among them."

In "Témoignages" (*World*, 64) the poet meditates about the nature of miracles, prompted by a film about some apparently inexplicable incident. The first line of the sonnet suggests a possible definition of a miracle:

> A miracle is but a broken law,
> And yet in *juggling thus with these Thy* toys,
> Thou do*st* some*times s*ome puzzle *s*et before
> Our troubled eyes. No work Thy work destroys, [...]

The dominance of voiced consonants in 1.2 conveys the notion of a roguish prank: to Him who is "juggling thus with these Thy toys" it does not matter whether a law, though God-made itself, is broken due to His own intercession; however, the poor human soul who is unable to find any logical explanation, is at a loss. L.3 conveys our puzzlement, underlined by the presence of both voiced and voiceless fricatives. "No work Thy work destroys" implies that there is nothing at all which could threaten the majesty of God's creation as such, the truth of His having created our world.[169]

The memory of a departed beloved person is a sorrowful experience. In particular on days like All Saints' Day and All Souls' Day the pain is doubly felt. This sorrow is conveyed in a sonnet called "All Saints" (*World*, 77) where the author writes in the first two quatrains:

> And shall again this song be heard to move
> The hills from which we're hewn - the very ones
> That feel the hollows of a parted love
> And know the scar of Absence where now runs

---

[169] "The discovery" (*World*, 65) concerns a miracle as well, the vision of the fire and the lamb a nun had in the sacristy of L'Abbaye Blanche years ago, receiving the message: "Un jour sortira de ce lieu un grand rayonnement." (*World*, 65). Such "rayonnement" was apparent while the poet was at the White Abbey, - the spirit of the Charismatic Renewal was spreading.

The scurrying of teeming emptiness
Where Peace filled all before - the peace that here
Wells up and would return this land to bless
With what it knows, it knows to be here near.

The "song" mentioned in l.1 refers to the vigil of All Saints' Day, which has a conventual mass sung in Latin (cf. letter 7.4.1991). The metaphor in l.2, the "hills from which we're hewn" powerfully conveys the importance of roots to the poet: we are like trees growing on the hills of our mother country, being deeply rooted there, until the day of felling comes for us as well, and "we're hewn". The death of a beloved person creates a void in those still living which cannot be filled again. It is "the scar of Absence", an image which powerfully conveys the indelibility of the pain experienced, - nothing can compensate the loss. Former peace is replaced by "The scurrying of teeming emptiness", an image which reinforces the feeling of bursting void. Ll.6f. imply how the pain wells up again on these days in November, when we remember the departed. The lines convey the pain experienced and show deep understanding and sympathy.

The following meditation reflects his entry at St. Michael's Abbey. "Enclosed" (*World*, 79), the last but one poem of the entire volume, meditates on the nature of being enclosed:

There is a world within the world that spins
That turns less quickly on an axis known
But unto them that know where earth begins
To be no more. This little land we own,
Whereon henceforth the hours shall run us through,
Hems in the Paradise or Hell we choose
To make for our heart's dwelling. [...]

L.1 contains the title which was eventually given to the entire collection of poems, for indeed it is "a world within the world that spins": the life in a monastery is another world with its own rules. It "turns less quickly" than the rest of the world, time seems to stand still to some extent, as there life has not changed much during the course of the years. For the monks in enclosure the "earth begins / To be no more", - profane things lose their importance, the monks concentrate all their life and being on God only. L.6 echoes the dual nature of life in an order, for it is "Paradise or Hell we choose", - both are potentially contained therein. The enormous power of the "small / Yet resonating echo of a word" (ll.11f.), the consequences of being enclosed, are firmly implied in the closing couplet, when he writes about this word "That came again this night from where Thou art / Knows now somehow that two vast worlds here part". Enclosure means the final separation of the sacred and the profane world.

The following sonnet called "Reading" (*Beyond*, 100), is a form of meditation in itself:

The force of Word is in its rebound call,
The silence wherein echoes all it holds.
A syllable of Sense, if let to fall
Upon a cushioned rest, no more withholds
Its germ of life. There are but rarely times
When Time may not be staggered in its flow

> And made to hear its murmuring betimes
> Ere it pull on and on whither we go.
> We hear the sound of thumping in our ears,
> For Noise holds well its audience as it makes
> Each itch well-scratched; yet feel not fall the tears
> Of little things, sweet things shed for our sakes
> But small unhurried angels that see all
> We miss as on we press without recall.

The beauty of meditating on a line, feeling the "force of Word", is emphasized at the beginning of this sonnet. The capitalization indicates a line of scripture which is meditated upon, lectio divina, whereby the monks ruminate on the Word, reading very slowly in the scriptures, letting the Word speak to the soul in meditation. "The silence wherein echoes all it holds" (1.2) implies the necessity to be silent, in order to make the spirit receptive, which is also suggested by "if let to fall / Upon a cushioned rest": one has to empty one's soul's faculties to be able to take in the sense, to be able to listen. Given that one is resting inwardly when reading and meditating, being captured by "A syllable of Sense", then the word "no more withholds / Its germ of life". The poet firmly stresses that the word is living, - a powerful, vital instrument. The second quatrain meditates on the fact that while reading time seems to stand still. Reading halts the flow of time for a while, "Ere it pull on and whither we go". In the third quatrain the idea is introduced that, as a result of our constant living in the midst of "Noise", representing noise in the general sense of activity, excitements, pleasure etc., we tend to lose the ability to perceive silent things, - "we feel not fall the tears / Of little things". The idea of noise is graphically conveyed in the line "Ea*ch itch* well *scratch*ed", where the accumulation of harsh sounds adds to the feeling of disquiet. The "small unhurried angels" in 1.13 suggests the idea of angels gazing, observing unhurriedly. They see more than we do. Another possible meaning involves the use of these "angels" as a metaphor for writers, poets themselves: "angel" means "messenger", a person seeing the truth, passing it on as a message from the realm of what is lasting. He observes and transmits to others, interpreting creation similarly to the poet. Apparently the poet implies a link between the arts, beauty and God. Arts are directly inspired by God: by writing, composing, by creating the artist passes on eternal truth. He freezes it in print or some other form for someone else to pick up. The artist assumes what can be called an angelic role in his intermediary function of passing on the message from the realm of the everlasting to the present world. Apparently Alun Idris does not see any contradiction between his role as a poet and his role as a man of the Church. He attributes to poets the ability to see more, similar to angels, though on a different level, of course; the poet acts as a kind of prophet, informing other people about truths he has already been able to perceive. The final phrase "without recall" suggests that very often we do not allow the echo to come back, even in ordinary conversation we are frequently unable to listen properly. Especially when reading it is important to do so with a receptive mind, in the spirit of complete openness and reclining on the "cushioned rest", in order to allow the word to resonate interiorly.

Having exercised the function of acolyte already in France, Alun Idris assisted with communion at Farnborough as well, in particular at High Mass on Sundays, where the faithful not only receive the host but the chalice as well (cf. letter, 7.1.1991). "Communio" (*Beyond*, 103) meditates on his giving both communion and the chalice to the congregation:

> There is a presence o'er the Presence that I bear:
> 'Twixt lip and lip an inward world untold,
> In breast on beating breast a thought all bare
> To Him who enters - all that lives can hold
> Is held within a corpulet so fine,
> So fair, less fair, nay, ever fairly made
> By Hands that bid my hand hand on Love's wine
> To each new hand-caress - here, here 'tis laid:
> Within the tent of flesh that Flesh and Blood
> Encounters in a drop, within the veil
> Of every hidden secret, there is good
> And evil - in a little thing so frail
> That it must needs return from worlds apart
> And in this whisper have in One a part.

The first two quatrains describe the process of giving communion: "The Presence that I bear" refers to the real Presence in the poet's hand when giving communion. Apart from the divine presence, there is another presence as well, - the presence of people, the two presences are meeting whilst receiving communion. L.2 implies giving the chalice to the people, each of them having a world of their own, unrevealed by the lips now receiving the Lord; however, their world is not unknown to God: "A thought all bare / To Him who enters". The image of the "corpulet so fine" (l.5) refers to the body of all those who are approaching to receive communion, - bodies which vary considerably, and yet all are made by God, "fairly made / By Hands that bid my hand hand on Love's wine". Alun Idris' predilection for word-play is apparent in these lines. "Love's wine" refers, of course, to the passing of the precious blood, the chalice given to "each new hand-caress": the imagery used to describe the holding of the chalice suggests the presence of love, embracing the Lord by holding the chalice. "Within the tent of flesh that Flesh and Blood / Encounters in a drop" refers to the Old Testament, where the tent of meeting was the tabernacle. The line suggests that we are a tabernacle as well, all the more so when we receive the Lord's Body and Blood, as then He is really present in us: it is this "tent of flesh" that the Lord enters.[170] Even though this our body is "a little thing so frail", "a corpulet so fine", it contains a world of its own: the mystical tabernacle, which is our flesh, contains a world of good or evil, a whole universe, despite its frailty. The closing couplet suggests the central role of communion, i.e. it forms the center in which all have a part: when receiving communion the people come together, each from his own world, from separate orbits, "worlds apart", but they come back to their center, uniting around the chalice. It is a real sharing of this one central strength, the power that comes from the eucharist. "And in this whisper have in One a part": when receiving the Lord they have a part in God, in the One. The

---

[170] The verses 1-5 of 2 Cor 5 contain the notion of this tabernacle, body and flesh, also 2 Cor 5:6-10.

language of love is gentle, it is a whisper, referring to the people's answer when receiving the Body of Christ.

The title "'Quid clamabo? Omnis caro foenum ...' (As new bells are being cast)" (*Beyond*, 104) echoes the inscription on a bell in Sélignac, as is indicated in a note. The inscription is taken from the prophet Isaiah 40:6, where we read, "Vox dicentis: 'Clama!' Et dixi. 'Quid clamabo?' Omnis caro fenum, et omnis gloria eius quasi flos agri."[171] The poem was inspired by the occasion of casting new bells, as we read in the subtitle, which took place in London, White Chapel: "That moment, when I was writing it, was the 'molten moment of eternity' in a sense" (letter, 7.1.1990).

> A molten moment of Eternity
> At this repeating hour herein is cast
> In lambent heat whose cooled serenity
> Will shape the frigid hours slow-trickling past
> These windows that look down upon a world
> Oft called, recalled by brazen muezzin sound
> From its own noisy clamour, ever whirled
> Back-forth, back-forth till hushed by rushed Fate's bound ...
> O passing of a whimper wherein Earth
> Re-echoes her sons' cry, thou seemest all
> To all that hear thy pain or bring thee mirth,
> Yet these new souls inanimate will call
> Each dusk and dawn across a din too full,
> There is time yet one gap from Time to pull.

"A molten moment of Eternity", though it recalls the moment of casting the bell, is in itself a most proper and beautiful image for a bell. The alliteration and assonance employed suggest a solemn atmosphere, which makes this very moment of casting the bell appear all the more special and full of grandeur. Equally, to describe those newly cast bells as "new souls inanimate" (l.12) is most striking and stresses the fact that bells in a monastery are much more than merely objects made of bronze or cast iron: although not an animate, living creature, a bell, nevertheless, has its own soul. While the first quatrain concentrates on the actual casting of the bell, the second presents the bell in its essential role as the "organizing principle" in a monastic order: it almost appears as a means to reign over the body. It regulates the passing of the hours in a monastery, - an idea, which has been touched upon, even criticized, before.

The bell "will shape the frigid hours slow-trickling past / These windows": the imagery evokes negative associations, suggesting the slow passing of time, filled with sorrows, when times seems to pass "trickling", not floating by as usual. The image of the "brazen muezzin sound" reflects the essential role of the bell as the muezzin calling the community to prayer: similar to Islam countries, the same pattern of being "called, recalled" exists in Western countries as well, when the world is called to prayer by the bell. "Ever whirled / Back-forth, back-forth till hushed by rushed Fate's bound ...": the bell is going backwards and forwards all the time, in a

---

[171] At the charterhouse in Sélignac they are four bells: one for the church, the other three connected with the clock (cf. letter, 7.1.1990).

way suggesting a parallel to the ever restless moving world; eventually, however, all the rushing ceases: it is hushed, having reached its limit, till its chime finally fades away. The imagery implies the busy noise of life, all the bustling, going backwards and forwards.[172] The exclamatory "O passing of a whimper wherein Earth / Re-echoes her sons' cry" (ll.9f.) suggests human insignificance, the sounds we make are but a whimper, yet we live in a world where sadness and sorrow are constantly growing: "re-echoing" suggests the ever increasing problems and difficulties threatening the world.

The closing line implies that the chime of the bell tells us that the time is not yet ripe for us to pass on to eternity, more time has still to pass. The bell is calling us to detach ourselves and to pray on behalf of the world. The use of "pull" in l.14 suggests a double meaning: on the literal level it refers to the act of pulling the rope, in order to ring the bell; in a figurative sense it also implies pulling the people to church, i.e. making the people give time to God.

The examples given show that prayerful meditative poems occur frequently. They cover a wide range of subjects, although exclusively religious ones. They demonstrate how much the poet still feels he is a monk, despite the fact that some of the poems were written outside monastic walls. In spirit, he remained a monk all the time.

3.3.6. MEMORIES

Memories do not cease to act as a source of inspiration to Alun Idris, despite the relative abundance of inspiring forces at that time, as a result of his return to the secular world. The power radiating from memories, their importance in difficult situations, is implied in a number of his poems where he meditates on happy memories of the past. In that sense memories offer a source of consolation in periods of strain.

The following lines of "Tintern - Prinknash" (*World*, 68) reflect the happy memory of having been there many years before:

> O wonder of all wonders, Master Time,
> In thy great stillness thou dost move the world.
> As here once more these distant mem'ries climb
> Within the mind that by thy game is hurled [...]

Tintern Abbey is a ruined Cistercian monastery not far from Prinknash. The first line of the poem reminds one of the initial lines of Wordsworth's famous poem written at Tintern Abbey, "Five years have past; five summers, with the length / Of five long winters!" (Hutchinson 1932, 205). In the past Alun Idris had gone there a couple of times with a friend of his Paul Thomas, an Anglican priest, and these memories welled up again when returning there many years later (cf. letter, 29.10.1989). Re-living the experience of his youth made him also remember the

---

[172] Incidentally, Farnborough is on the commuter-line, - many people travel up to work in London (cf. letter, 7.1.1990).

Abbey of Prinknash, which had been an important part of his life, - the poet almost entered this strict Benedictine community straight from school.

The nature of memories, which have always been of special importance to the poet, is described in the first quatrain of a sonnet called "'Goodbye, perhaps for ever.'" (*World*, 73) which was written after having spent a week-end at his friend's vicarage, as is indicated in a note in brackets.

> There is a substance in our yesterdays,
> For ere they were they ne'er had pow'r to be
> The stage on which each spectred image plays
> E'ermore the one sole script of Memory.

Memory preserves our yesterdays: "each spectred image" suggests the variety of memories which appear all of a sudden, from nowhere as it seems. The departure from his friend's vicarage made him realize that "this day's bliss will be our morrow's pain". The happiness of their meeting will cause future pain of mournful memory, when the encounter will be memorized only. "Yet there is sweetness in our suffering / And we behold with wonder what is not - / That it could once have been", as we read in the third quatrain. The pain experienced when memorizing happy moments of the past is mingled with a "sweetness", too, as well as with a feeling of wonder that such happiness ever occurred.

The memory of those happy days spent at Prinknash (cf. letter, 9.12.1990) radiates from the following sonnet called "Gŵyl Ddewi" (*World*, 79), which means "St. David's Day". It is the last poem in the volume *A World Within the World*, echoing memories of his youth:

> When 'neath the blows of many hardened sounds
> We lie alone until their echoes die
> And grasp awhile a tone wherein abounds
> A resonance once heard when passing by
> This Siren that dies not, long, long ago
> When first the whiteness of this Vestal robe
> Became too dazzling in e'en sparked Youth's glow
> To let another flame its entrails probe -
> When now again a face that shone before,
> A hand that, unbid, traced a line of life
> From some unsummoned corner, on this shore
> Of sheer Despair and utterness of strife,
> Appears between the clouds and beckons, "Come",
> I know the warmth within the sound of Home.

The imagery used to describe the monks of Prinknash Abbey radiates warmth and tenderness. This calm affection clashes with the imagery used at the beginning of the sonnet, when the poet refers to the present, "'neath the blows of many hardened sounds", which conveys the idea of roughness, the lack of peace and tranquility. The pain experienced is reinforced in 1.2, where the poet indicates the slow fading of the echoes of those "hardened sounds", being left all alone in such a painful and difficult situation. The third line introduces the memory of happy days which creep in, and which cause a mighty "resonance" within. "This siren", which never stops calling, refers to his own call to live in a monastery and devote his life to God, possibly the hiraeth to enter Prinknash. The second quatrain glances at the memory of those happy days in his youth, when he was fascinated by "the whiteness of this Vestal robe" for the first time, referring to the white habit the monks wear at Prinknash.[173] The splendour, however, became "too dazzling", underlined by the spondee employed, "to let another flame its entrails probe". The imagery describing his possible return to Prinknash suggests that such a return would have been more than just to superficially sample the life there, for then he would have probed "its entrails". However, the "whiteness [...] became too dazzling". He did not return. L.9 switches to the present, "When now again a face that shone before", apparently referring to one of the monks at Prinknash who contacted the poet in some way. Using the synectoche "a face that shone" powerfully conveys the love present in the meeting, how close the poet still feels to these monks. A second synectoche appears in 1.10, pointing to the fact that it was this monk who had searched for the poet, who had "traced a line of life / From some unsummoned corner", of his own accord. The imagery also echoes the tracing of a line of life on one's hand, inspecting the past and predicting the future. L.12 returns to the present state of the poet, "this shore / Of sheer Despair and utterness of strife", which is self-explanatory. In the middle of this difficult period, this darkened sky, "appears between the clouds" a voice well-known in the past, inviting him to "Come". It is the voice of home the poet hears, for it was Prinknash where he first felt at home.

3.3.7. RECENT EVENTS

As could be observed before, recent unexpected events represent a powerful source of inspiration for poetry. The poems reflect events of that period and are of both sacred and profane nature, with religious ones prevailing. Most of them represent a vent for the accumulation of feelings, of oppressive despair, which becomes apparent in the poetry.

"The day it happened" (*World*, 67) marks the beginning of a series of poems[174] centered on an unexpected event. Alun Idris had only recently decided to spend a year at the Normal College, Bangor, which meant that he was back to the world again; this new contact, and his being involved with other people, is reflected in the sequence.

> A word is but a word, save when an ear
> Hath held for evermore its sound within.
> O little noise, ere thou wast made, so clear
> And calm was th'air in its hummed sleeping din.

---

[173] At Farnborough black habits are used, although the community is a daughter house of Prinknash, where the white habit was retained, which the founder, Dom Aelred Carlyle, introduced in Anglican days, before the community was converted to Catholicism quasi en bloc.

[174] Other poems belonging to the sequence are: "After seeing a priest" (*World*, 67), "In retreat" (*World*, 68), "The first morning" (*World*, 68), "The last morning" (*World*, 69), "Paroxysm" (*World*, 70), "A week apart, for prayer" (*World*, 70), "A year today" (*World*, 74).

> But thou wast heard, and unheard ne'er shalt be,
> Nor shalt thou now return to whence this came.
> Thou now shalt live and in thy living see
> The names of names e'er echoed in thy name.

Some mysterious "word" fell on fertile soil, it seems. The first seven lines elaborately describe the experience. How profound it was is firmly implied, when we, for example, read "Hath held for evermore its sound within" or "unheard ne'er shalt be", "Thou now shalt live". Before the word touched his ear, before "it happened", the air was calm "in its hummed sleeping din", "so clear" and now it is stirred. "The names of names e'er echoed in thy name" implicitly points at the nature of the experience, the encounter with love. The unrest on the author's part caused by this experience is obvious in the closing lines of the following sonnet, "After seeing a priest" (*World*, 67):

> We have been made for love and we love well,
> And in our meltedness when we give all
> There is a knowing that of Thee doth tell,
> For e'en in this dark chasm Thou dost call.
> And yet I know not how to know Thy thought.
> This night, great Knowledge, Thou hast left me nought.

"This dark chasm" refers to the difficulty of the situation. The poet is riven by the question of how to continue, which path to take. He is aware that man was "made for love", and yet he is aware of God's calling him as well, "Thou dost call". God calls for love, too. The poet is at a complete loss, not knowing how to continue, "This night, great Knowledge, Thou hast left me nought".

A certain release of the pressure is to be noticed in the next poem of the sequence, "In retreat" (*World*, 68) a release due to the poet's firm belief in the guiding hand of the Lord: although "There is a myst'ry in our morrow still" the poet is consoled, "And in our mind's own union we were three, / For in our battle One too with us fought" [corr.]. The retreat was held at Father Barnabas' little monastery, a hermitage in mid-Wales inhabited by a Welsh-speaking Eastern orthodox monk (cf. letter, 29.10.1989).

The uncertain, unknown future is still present in the following poems, as in "Sending the letter" (*World*, 69): "O mystery of human Destiny, I know thee not, and yet I'll yield to thee." The lines express absolute trust in his destiny, his faith in providence. How much he longs for guidance is also implied in the closing couplet of "A chance meeting" (*World*, 69), where we read: "O ancient Thought, if Thou hadst thought of this, / Let fall a word, and we'll return Thy bliss." He longs to receive a sign which will point towards the right direction.

"The last morning" (*World*, 69) reflects the writing of a letter to the bishop on that morning (cf. letter, 7.10.1991), as is implied in the first line: "There is yet pow'r within this envelope / And force to do a mighty, mighty thing." The lines echo his vocation to priesthood which was deeply rooted in the poet. He closes the sonnet:

O little sheet of meaning, canst enclose
The voyage of a soul to the Beyond?
What mark or order will thy marks disclose
To th'eons where shall lie two now so fond?
O rending of a soul! I am not well:
There are two roads, but each bears th'other's knell.

"What mark or order" refers to the character engraved upon a soul when one receives a sacrament of order. There are three sacraments which place a character upon a soul, viz. baptism, confirmation and the sacrament of order. This character, which is imprinted on a soul, is still imprinted in the world to come, indelibly engraved forever (cf. letter, 7.10.1991). "Th'eons" point to the finality of such an imprint. The closing couplet mirrors the poet's painful struggle, as is implied by the imagery used. The two options naturally exclude each other, he does not seem to know yet which direction his future path would take.

The decision, however, was soon taken, for the divine pull was strongly felt by the poet. His happiness to hear this "sweetest voice" is conveyed in " Ὁ διδάσκαλος πάρεστιν καὶ φωνεῖ σε." (*World*, 71):

Thou callest, sweetest voice; I know thy sound,
For 'tis the echo of a sound within:
A resonance when note its note hath found,
A tingle ling'ring from a passing din.
O Peace! come, come again to this tossed soul
And ne'er more share thy temple with a throng
Descend and in thy falling here make whole
These torn and shredded wounds left gaping long.
O Master, call, I'd hear this sound again,
For it recalls a calling long ago,
That called but once and with a sudden pain
Tore every strand that could this bliss not know.
O deeper Love, I'd follow Thee alone;
Mark now the way, for 'tis from hence Thine own.

The two pauses in l.1 decrease its rhythm enormously, leading to the solemn "I know thy sound". The movement conveys that peace has entered his soul again, for he now feels once more this sweetest of all voices. The divine call is not unknown to him, as he had felt it before, this "t*i*ngle l*i*ng'r*i*ng from a pass*i*ng d*i*n": the dominance of light i's in this line, completed by massive consonance, suggests the vividness of the sound heard, fascinating in its nature, almost reminding one of a spell which one cannot escape. The honest outbreak in l.5, however, points to the fact that his soul is not yet completely filled with peace. The inner strains experienced before are not yet completely forgotten. L.6 refers to the New Testament episode in the temple described by John 2:13-17, depicting Jesus driving out the dealers from His Father's house. The fundamental thought behind this is the image of the soul as the temple of the Lord, which should be at peace through reverence to the spirit. "One can be a contemplative in all circumstances if this inner temple is in order" (letter, 29.10.1989). The important point is to let the Lord be the Lord in one's heart, which can be achieved in non-monastic surroundings just as well. The second quatrain reflects the poet's beseeching for peace to come and fill his heart, "make whole / These torn and shredded wounds left gaping long". The imagery used vividly suggests the vastness of the pain experienced before, underlining his yearning for peace. In the third quatrain he asks the Lord to call again, reassuring Him "I'd hear this sound again", for he has known the call before. He had experienced it with all its tremendous force, "with sudden pain". A notion of insecurity has entered the lines. The former clarity about the call he felt in the first quatrain is not so strongly implied anymore: he is willed to follow Him alone, but he desperately longs for another sign, which is revealed in the closing couplet. "O deeper Love, I'd follow Thee alone" - the comparative implies that human love is apparently of lesser strength and depth than divine Love. In that sense the sonnet becomes a vent for the accumulation of his feelings; however, the poem also reflects on the power of the word. The title is a quotation from scripture (John 11:28), when the Lord is visiting his friends Lazarus, Mary and Martha: the Lord is there, he is calling - "Magister adest et vocat te". This Latin verse was written on the altar cloth of a chapel at Aberystwyth, which to the poet was like a word directly coming from the Lord. "To see that word there speaking quietly [...]; the Lord has strange ways of talking really, He used to talk to me through that verse" (letter, 29.10.1989).

During this period of restless search the poet visited several religious houses in Britain. While he was staying at Belmont, the nearest religious house to Caernarvon, he was reflecting on the decision he had to make, knowing that the community at Ealing was willing to take him (cf. letter, 7.4.1991). "Décider" (*World*, 74) describes the difficult situation:

> What pow'r is held within a passing thought
> O'er things that shall not pass ere thinking cease ...
> Eternity was by a moment wrought
> Too often in its heat, when wiser Peace
> Gave not its frigid counsel, nor knew how
> To stay the flow of minutes that did press
> With all the presence of a forcing Now
> For room in th'annals of Fact's utterness.
> We hold as yet the pen within our hands
> And this clean page we are yet free to mark,
> Yet on the first etched sentence all else stands
> And eon after eon shall e'er hark
> The noise that one small syllable did make
> Within the brain that did its leisure take.

The poem reflects the difficulty of "décider" about important matters which affect the future course of one's life. "What pow'r is held within a passing thought" suggests the idea that the very thought of a possible future way, the plan as such, is full of power in its potentiality to change our life. The initial spondee underlines the tremendous force contained therein. How much moments can affect our life, or rather how much our life as such is made up of moments and decisions made then is implied in l.3, "Eternity was by a moment wrought / Too often in its heat": the spondaic opening and the medial pause in l.4 suggest how often decisions are made unwisely, without having been given careful consideration. Emotions and feelings are too frequently given priority, which is not to be disapproved of on principle, as it is lack of reason which essentially causes the problem. "When wiser Peace / Gave not its frigid counsel", - "frigid counsel" suggests the opposed nature of reason and feelings, while "wiser Peace" refers to reason, possibly to a union of reason and feeling, as is implied by "Peace". The second quatrain adds another problematical aspect: the factor of time. "The flow of minutes that did *press* / With all the *pres*ence of a *forc*ing Now" can increase the tension and provoke a precipitate decision, apparently previsaging the poet's own hurried decision to enter Farnborough. The onomatopoetical effect of the lines increases the notion of force. In the closing quatrain the poet seems to calm down again, reassuring himself that, after all, it is one's personal decision what to do, "We hold as yet the pen within our hands": it is we who write in the book of life, we decide how to fill the pages. However, ll.11f. are full of doubts and fears again, as the poet knows that, despite our free will to decide, the decision, which will be made at last, will affect the rest of our life. It will be indelibly written in the book of our life, marking our future. Here again, the sound symbolism used by the poet underlines the difficulty of the problem, when he refers to the "*first etched sentence*", abounding in harsh sounds. The consequences of any decision are enormous: "eon after eon shall e'er hark / The noise that one small syllable did make". It is the decision of a moment which affects the whole of our life.

After a long struggle about his future path the decision was finally made that the poet would join the Benedictine community at Ealing. The title of "'Mae'n ddiwrnod mawr iti heddiw.'" [corr.] (*World*, 75) echoes the words of a friend before the train set off to Ealing, as we are told in a note in brackets. "It's a big day for you today" is the English translation of the Welsh title of the sonnet; and a big day it was indeed, as he decided to become again a member of a monastic community, although at first only as a guest of the house (cf. letter, 4.7.1991). The poem meditates on the unknown future which lies before him.

> What does this Silence hold within its walls?
> What morrow waits in peace to be born here?
> The quiet yesterdays that this recalls
> Are heard again and, in their coming near,
> A closer yesterday moves far away,
> And what this morn was held and pressed to heart
> This eventide can no word softly say
> Across the clattering miles that e'er depart.

The uncertainty as regards the future is present from the very first line onwards: the inverted first foot in l.1 is followed by a spondaic second foot, which suggests a notion of impatience and curiosity to know what lies ahead. L.2 continues this notion by starting with a spondaic first foot. The rhythm appears regular afterwards, implying the regularity and calm of those "quiet yesterdays" he now recalls. The memory of the past makes "A closer yesterday" move far away. Those recent happenings of the past are fading away, constantly losing in importance, as now a much more powerful memory fills his heart again. Ll.6-8 echo the strong feeling of separation experienced by the poet as a result of his departure: the words of this friend, the warm-hearted fare-well can be remembered afterwards, but the presence of the friend will never be experienced again. "Across the clattering miles that e'er depart", - the image of the "clattering miles" evokes the situation of travelling by train, sitting in a railway compartment crowded with passengers.

In a period of sorrow and despair, an unexpected positive surprise, however slight it may be, can offer much consolation to the disheartened soul. Such an event apparently provoked the meditation called "Little things" (*World*, 76f.), where the poet describes the healing effect of such a little gesture of care:

> There are but moments in a thousand years,
> Yet one of these can make a thousand more.
> A moment wipes another moment's tears
> And tames the rage of hours that went before [corr.]
> Without a thought for what their course did bear
> Of unsensed Sweetness that hard, harnessed Haste
> Paused not to prove or thank, for coming ne'er
> Within the hour's Utility, 'twas Waste.
> And yet there is a gaspillage that saves
> A day from utter ageing with the rest:
> A blast whose prodigality behaves
> With that strange madness that with sense is blest.
> For we walk on in this our hurried fate,
> And pass th'appointed time lest we be late.

The first two lines mirror the idea that time is but made up of moments. The quality of these moments moulds the quality of the time. It lies within the power of a moment to "make a thousand more": a happy moment is able to feed the soul with numerous other happy moments, each time when it is remembered again. The same applies, of course, to unpleasant happenings. Yet here it is a happy moment we are dealing with, for it is a moment that "wipes another moment's *t*ears / And *ta*mes the *ra*ge of hours that went before": the alliteration and assonance employed reinforce the idea of sorrow which characterizes the past. The second quatrain describes the soul accustomed to being filled with sorrow, not expecting happy moments any more ("Without a thought"), as a result of the pains and disillusionment experienced. L.6 abounds in alliteration and consonance, "Of un*s*en*sed S*weetne*ss* that *h*ard, *h*arne*ssed H*a*s*te / Paused not to prove or thank": "hard, harnessed" is given additional emphasis because of the spondee employed. It seems as though "unsensed Sweetness" was hardly ever experienced, stressed by "unsensed", with his own soul always being in a hurry, not at peace. The third quatrain explicitly mentions the healing effect of such moments of care, as they contain a "gaspillage that saves / A day from utter ageing with the rest": the lines mirror that ten years living in France did not pass over the poet without leaving traces. Using the French "gaspillage", however, emphasizes this implication, as it indicates a certain exclusiveness and splendour. Such a moment abounds in beauty and will be remembered forever, always sparkling in one's memory. It is "a blast" even, tremendously powerful in effect, although one perhaps does not even know why it occurred. It "behaves / With that strange madness that with sense is blest". Coming out of the blue, without a visible motive, it has an important function of brightening for a moment the soul not used to experiencing such happy moments any more. The closing couplet echoes the idea of how little time we take to pause a while, and be more receptive to such "little things", which can yet be so tremendously powerful in effect.

The following poem can undoubtedly be considered a fruit of pain. The very title "'You do not fit in.'" (*Beyond*, 105) explains some of the circumstances under which it was written. The sonnet, which is striking in its shocking honesty, mirrors the lamentable happenings at Farnborough, which eventually led to his leaving the order. Disillusionment, deep sorrow and endless pain, which characterize this poem, are bound to find an echo in the reader:

> I know not whence this comes, save that the word
> Bears some familiar sound, heard in these parts
> At this same season - yes, this pain was heard
> Before upon this road. These little hearts
> That throb awhile and draw to passing dreams
> Till they can throb no more, hold many things
> In their unheard soft patter, and it seems
> That they were made for breaking, for the wings
> Of youthful passion can be clipped too oft,
> And there is fear in loving when the bliss
> On agony is spent.
>   ... Yet e'en this soft
> And muffled groan that groans amiss
> Far form a listening ear, can it yet know
> A joy in this great Void whither we go?

The first quatrain presents his personal acquaintance with disillusionment, telling us that the pain "bears some familiar sound": using "familiar" in this context reinforces the sorrow, as the word provokes positive connotations. However, having become used to that "word" of pain so as to make it familiar firmly implies the utter disillusionment the poet experiences. It was a word, as is indicated in the title, for "this pain was heard / Before upon this road". In the second and third quatrain the poet leads on from his personal experience to more general ideas and reflections about the pain we are to suffer in our lives, the lines being full of melancholy. The imagery speaks a very clear language: it seems as though these little hearts "were made for breaking"; the "wings of youthful passion" have been "clipped too oft". This time was one too many, - he is unable to fly anymore, suffers an irrepairable loss. These are all hints of the experience of past years, when, too often, his enthusiasm, his "youthful passion" was utterly destroyed; the agony expressed leads to the climax of it all in the first part of l.11, for "there is fear in loving when the bliss / On agony is spent". The message of this line is reinforced by its abrupt ending, being continued only in the next line. The reader is given a chance to reflect on the vastness of the pain experienced. Although the following "yet" implies a certain change, the pessimistic mood is still dominant, - the loneliness is almost too much to bear. He wonders whether "this soft / And muffled groan" will ever know some form of joy again. The use of the synectoche underlines how much his being is filled with sorrow and despair. Nobody knows of the tragedy taking place, - he "groans amiss / Far from a listening ear". The "great Void" mentioned in l.14 is not a denial of God: it implies that there is a great uncertainty in our future, which no one knows. Touching rock bottom is where the Lord can meet us, in this complete emptiness, the void within.

The poems discussed in this chapter mirror the poet's restless search in an impressive way. It was a period characterized by diverse pulls in opposing directions. He had wanted to remain a monk, and interiorly remained one, as the numerous religious meditations demonstrate. He had originally intended not to abandon the monastic world at all when he left the Trappist monastery at Roscrea. Providential as it seems now, it was impossible at the time to enter Prinknash Abbey, which he would have loved to do, nor was it possible to become a hermit in Wales, another pull he felt strongly, as is apparent in the poetry. The work of the Charismatic Renewal, however, had been equally tempting, and the yearning to actively contribute to the spiritual renewal was doubtless there. The decision to either stay in the secular world, perhaps even to marry, or to remain a religious, possibly heading for ordination, was basic to this period. After having finished the teacher training course, the decision was made to enter Farnborough Abbey, a hurried one, though, caused by the poet's wish to settle and find a home where he could live and celebrate the union with God. The poems written after his entry reflect a certain joy at the final re-union with God, living in monastic surroundings again. However, it was not possible for him to settle, as the ultimate poem mentioned clearly demonstrates.

Doubtless, his poetry at this period served as a vent to release inner strain, which was considerable at the time. Despite the sorrow experienced, however, the poet never lost his faith in providence.

3.4. INTERIM PERIOD OUTSIDE MONASTIC QUARTERS

The period in question covers the time span from Alun Idris' departure from Farnborough Abbey in spring 1989 until his return to enclosure in autumn 1991, when he joined the Norbertine Canons at Kilnacrott Abbey, Ireland, where he is still pursuing his monastic vocation. His work written during this period mingles religious and secular poetry in various proportions, though doubtless religious poetry prevails. The work differs from preceding periods in so far as a new dimension is added to his verse, a new source of inspiration was found, which turned out to be extremely fruitful, as will be indicated later.

During the first months after having left Farnborough Abbey, Alun Idris translated texts of the Fathers of the early church from Latin and Greek into modern English, many of which are included in *The Promise of Good Things: The Apostolic Fathers* (1992), published by Oliver Davies. Internal problems at Prinknash Abbey prevented the poet from entering the community there, which he would have preferred to do. He spent some time at Talacre Abbey with Dom Basil Robinson, the former prior of Farnborough. His return to Wales inspired a great number of poems written in Welsh (cf. letter, 1.2.1990), which, unfortunately, cannot be discussed here. In October 1989 Alun Idris resumed university studies, when he started to study theology at the University College, Bangor, to take a Bachelor of Divinity course whilst reflecting on the future. During that period he was actively involved with different groups of the Charismatic Renewal, which is echoed in his poetry. At the end of summer term in 1991 he was able to finish his studies. Shortly afterwards it was decided that he would join the Norbertine Canons at Kilnacrott. The poetic output of this period is very rich and offers great variety. The poet not only celebrates the love he feels for God, but also human love.

3.4.1. ACCUMULATED FEELINGS OF INNER STRAIN: POETRY AS AN OUTLET

Just as in the preceding periods, poetry serves as an outlet for accumulated feelings, it is a means to release pressure from the poet's soul. In many of the poems the tense atmosphere which caused the verse to be written is still to be felt while reading, - it has been transformed into the poetry.

One of the first poems written in this interim period is '"Home, where the music's playing ..."' (*Beyond*, 106), which is an outcry really, the fruit of despair and endless pain. It continues the mood already prevailing towards the end of his stay at Farnborough:

'Tis not Despair that hurts, but only Hope,
For when there is no more, no further ill
Can here be feared. 'Tis e'en a joy to grope
For light 'mid th'ash of life. But when yet still
A shimmer of a something lingers on
And on and on, not giving Hell its prize,
The fractured soul begins to leave undone
Its own titanic work, and sits and sighs [...]

The poem was written on 27 February 1989, the day he left Farnborough Abbey. These first two quatrains convey a feeling of disillusionment, although a slight "shimmer" of hope seems to be still on the horizon. Anyone who reads the lines in ignorance of the circumstances (as most readers probably do read them) would realize that some great sorrow had come to the poet, but s/he would not know what it was, and would not need to, in order to understand the poem's structure. What the poet has learned, clearly, is the reality of suffering. The lines honestly reflect their author's personal experience. He realizes that it is hope, and not despair which hurts, for as long as there is hope, there is still something left to linger on, which can eventually be destroyed. Apparently, there was still some trust left as regards being able to continue to be a Benedictine. It is only when all hope is gone that "no further ill / Can here be feared". The line "'Tis e'en a joy to grope / For light 'mid th'ash of life." is arresting, for it implies that the poet utters a truth he knows from his own personal experience.

A little hope leaves the soul "fractured", unable to progress anymore. In the closing lines of this sonnet Alun Idris refers to a "well-marked journey pre-arranged / By faultless thinking armed with calcule dense / And something out of Nothing that hath Sense". This "well-marked journey pre-arranged" suggests the attempt to combine divine providence and human interference; the closing couplet expresses his hope to return to Wales to make a foundation. The capitalized "Nothing" refers to the actual tragedy which he had experienced shortly before. It looked like a void, a nothing, an absurd situation, and yet the capitalization suggests that God was present there as well, - the "Nothing" was part of divine providence. The title of the poem, a line taken from the song "Homeward Bound" by Paul Simon and Art Garfunkel, underlines the poet's coming back to Wales, the "land of song".

"'You'll have to saw me in two.'" (*Beyond*, 107) is a poem which was written while still with Dom Basil, the ex-prior of Farnborough, at Talacre Abbey, at a time when it was still not clear whether Brother John alias Alun Irdis was going to be transferred to Prinknash or not. At first glance the sonnet seems to be different in mood from the previous one, simply because of the presence of children, as indicated in the subtitle. Apparently, playing with these two children was a melting experience, although their presence could not really mitigate the all too powerful atmosphere of pain still prevailing:

> There is within the sh*ining* of a ch*i*ld
> A ti*ngling* that the frozen heart doth melt,
> And *i*n the clamber of a clamour wild
> With purest joy, a something yet is felt
> That this heart felt before [...]

The assonance in l.1 and the consonance in ll.1f., as is indicated in italics, underline the softness, the tenderness of this experience, which made his "frozen heart" melt. "The clamber of a clamour wild" implies that the children did not hesitate to clamber all over him in their spontaneity: "a something yet is felt" at the presence of such innocent sweetness, which leaves the impression as though it had almost become difficult for the poet to feel anything positive any more. "We call and call / At our meridian as at our dawn's smile" (ll.7f.): the line implies that we cry out for love, for attention, for affection both at "our meridian", i.e. in the prime of our lives, as well as when we are children, "at our dawn's smile", "dawn" being a word-play on the name of one of the two girls, "Dawn".

"Ange" (*Beyond*, 108) still bears the heavy mark of disillusionment, sorrow and pain, although it shows that there was still a glimmer of hope left even in this period of despair:

> Le vide qui attend attend si bien
> Qu'un rien de rien du tout peut tout refaire,
> Peut lui complaire, car combler un rien
> N'est pas si dur, si difficile à faire.
> O! pauvreté, O! dernier abîme,
> Qui montres mon visage à qui le porte,
> J'ai su, ici j'ai su ce mot intime
> Que seul ton grand écho ici rapporte.
> O Jésus, je t'ai cherché, je t'ai pris
> Entre mes mains à l'heure de l'extase
> En jouet, petit jouet mal compris,
> Mal aimé, car de ce grand jeu la base
> Est aujourd'hui rencontrée, montrée, vue,
> Et ce soir sachant rien enfin j'ai su.

L.1 indicates the poet's complete emptiness at the time. He was waiting and praying. This emptiness is implied in images like "le vide" (l.1), "un rien" (l.2), "la pauvreté" (l.5), "dernièr abîme" (l.6). "O! pauvreté, O! dernier abîme, / Qui montres mon visage à qui le porte": the void he experiences shows him who he is. His prayers seem to have been answered, as is implied in l.2.[175]

In the third quatrain he addresses Jesus whom he had searched for, "O Jésus, je t'ai cherché, je t'ai pris / Entre mes mains à l'heure de l'extase / En jouet": the mournful apostrophe underlines the poet's loss, - it reminds one of a sigh uttered to a friend who seeks understanding and support. When he was young, just after having started his life in God, he was in ecstasy, making the decisions himself, controlling the Lord in a way; even more, he was toying with the Lord, using Him as his toy to give him spiritual satisfaction. He was using God to realize his own plans, "En jouet". The feeling of utter failure is strongly implied, and yet "ce soir sachant rien enfin j'ai su.": at the moment of utter nakedness, utter emptiness and inner void hope has returned, - God seems to be at work again by sending this "Ange". The poem shows that a glimmer of hope is nevertheless still left.

The high degree of authenticity present in "Regret" (*Beyond*, 114) makes it is a very powerful, moving poem. Alun Idris' own personal experience is implicit from the very beginning. *This* pain of the heart can only be known to the one who has experienced it:

---

[175] The subtitle, "a mysterious telephone invitation" throws additional light on what happened: a friend of the poet's, Oliver Davies, had phoned and offered some work, a translation of the Fathers into modern English, which was highly welcome (cf. letter, 1.2.1990; the translations were published in 1992).

> There is a pain of heart the heart knows not
> How well to hold, withhold, lest it be known.
> There is a secret that no pen will jot,
> For rarely was a night by markings shown.
> There is a yearning for what never can
> Be giv'n again, for this one thing bears all
> Away in its one coming. For to man
> A moment is the place whence hours e'er call.
> There is within the history of Time
> Another that is writ in ink so fine
> That aeons pass it by and onward chime
> As if no eye could read or see the shine
> Of little things that mattered once a lot,
> For matter of small weight was soon forgot.

The descriptive tone in the enumerations of the first two quatrains reinforces the degree of disillusionment, of pain. The honesty in the very first sentence is striking: its plain, direct nature makes it all the more impressive. The poem presents the dichotomy between the (objective) history common to the whole of mankind, and the world of the individual that no one else will see, the interior world, the most personal intimate sphere that will never find verbal or poetic expression, as it will always and can only exist within one's inner self ("There is a secret that no pen will jot / For rarely was a night by markings shown"). The great time machine marches on relentlessly, the outward history is recorded, while inner suffering is not seen by others, - it is private. Apparently it was this experience of overflowing pain which brought the poem into existence, as is implied in ll.1f. The second quatrain abounds in hiraeth, "There is a yearning for what never can / Be giv'n again": having missed a chance ("a moment is the place whence hours e'er call") means that it is lost forever, - it does not come again ("for this one thing bears all / Away in its one coming"). The poet implies that it is important to use chances well, to get crucial decisions right. The personal, individual history "writ in ink so fine" tells of "little things that mattered once a lot, / For matter of small weight was soon forgot". The final line is to be taken ironically, as in fact these things are of great weight for us, although they seem to be but petty in relation to eternity and for other people. The most important thing in a person's life is unimportant for the rest of creation: an event which means everything in one person's life passes by without any trace on the history book, - "Matter of small weight was soon forgot".

The following poem, written much later, echoes the pain present at the time. It conveys the idea that music is the language which best expresses pain: "Music is love in search of a word" (*Beyond*, 209). He starts the sonnet with the following lines: "When there is but the sound of pain within / And in the air nought but the stillness full / Of knowing that sweet moments did begin / Once to be known;". These lines echo the presence of pain, the use of the past tense "did begin once to be known" firmly implies that the sweetness once experienced is gone forever. It ceased soon after it had begun to be felt. The few hints at the past sweetness ("starlit seconds", "one cherub smile") underline the sorrow at having lost it. In such moments of intense pain, it is hard to find language to express the sorrow:

> Then there is but one language that can hold
> The heavy weight of void, there is but one
> Last grammar that may yet enfold
> The meaning of a sigh, and when 'tis done,
> The pause that hid us may perhaps be found
> Still lingering hard by some broken sound.

The closing line contains a word-play on "broken": a sound is broken just as a person can be broken, echoes linger there. The importance of music is firmly indicated (although it is never mentioned again throughout the entire poem, apart from the title). Just like poetry, it offers a means to release inner strain, to give voice to one's feelings.

The death of Dom Laurence Bévenot, one of Alun Idris' most important spiritual guides, was a painful loss.[176] On the commemorative card for the requiem mass we read: "Outstanding among his many gifts was his musical ability, especially as a choirmaster and composer of music for liturgical use." Doubtless his musical ability was of importance and influence also as regards Alun Idris: he set to music a great number of Alun Idris' poems. The sorrow caused by his passing away is implied in "LB" (*Beyond*, 182):

> There is a little lamp that will not burn
> Again upon our shore, there is a source
> From which no more can flow, nor shall return
> Another page charged with semantic force
> Across the skies that ne'er could hold apart
> A father from his child. [...]

The initials of Laurence Bévenot "LB" appear again in the first line in the imagery used to suggest his passing away. The "source / From which no more can flow" records his musical talent, which enabled him to compose a great number of hymns and songs. The first quatrain implies how much the poet mourns for him: he will miss his company and advice, as is implied by the metaphor of the lamp. He laments the drying up of the "source" which caused many a tune to rise, and he will also miss the force radiating from his letters, those pages "charged with semantic force", as his advice had always been of special importance. How close the poet feels to him is suggested in l.6, where we read that nothing could hold apart "A father from his child". It is, in a way, a father he loses.

Although Alun Idris in general makes much use of enjambement in his poetry, the run-on lines in this poem suggest the idea of an abrupt ending, the line has stopped but something is still missing: the sentence continues in the following line, life goes one, despite the lamentable loss. This pattern is repeated, which can be interpreted as an allusion to the continuation of the daily round, but not in the smooth habitual way. In the third quatrain we find further imagery alluding to his musical talent, though at the same time strikingly suggesting death as well:

---

[176] Dom Laurence Bévenot (1902-1990) became a Benedictine monk at Ampleforth in 1920 and was ordained priest in 1928. He devoted the last 26 years of his life to the parish of St. Mary's and he was so committed to his duties that he would not accept retirement, and remained active in pastoral work until illness made it impossible for him to continue.

"There are but decomposings in the land / That holds the gentle head that made of Song / The paradise of ears". The use of "decomposings", apart from its literal meaning, also implies the end of his time as a composer of music. Laurence Bévenot was able to create "The paradise of ears", his musical talent was pre-eminent.

International political developments are to be found among the sources of inspiration as well. The date given for the composition of "Daeth bachgen un ôl i'r ysgol i ddweud 'Ffarwél!'" (*Beyond*, 198), 15-16 January 1991, indicates the connection with Saddam Hussein's invasion of Kuwait. The poem was written at the outbreak of war, when the Allied Forces opened fire on the Iraqi army. The Welsh title of the poem means "A boy came back to school to say 'Goodbye'", referring to the departure of a young Welsh soldier to the Persian Gulf. The poem closes with the following lines, mirroring the terror and anxiety the poet is filled with:

> The bell that counts this midnight counts the blood
> That in young veins still flows, still flows, still flows
> A little closer to the stagnant flood
> Of piercéd Pain, that its blest dream bestows.
> For many wait upon that lotus shore
> Who hurried their eternity before.

The bells recall of death tolls, which indeed they were for numerous young people. The three-fold repetition of "still flows" evokes the idea of a bell chiming, apart from suggesting the regularity of the heart beat, and also reminds one of the ticking of a clock, which ticks on mercilessly, demanding its tribute. The seductive tone in "A little closer" terminates abruptly with "*t*o the *st*agnant *fl*ood / Of *p*iercéd *P*ain": the alliteration and the use of sharp hissing sounds serve as a means of emphasis, underlining the abhorrent nature of war. Furthermore, the capitalization suggests the idea of the inmeasurability of that suffering, apart from reminding one of the passion of Christ, whose heart was likewise pierced. The oxymoron "stagnant flood" is another means to emphasize the idea of pain. The alliteration on the voiced counterpart of /p/ in "*b*lest dream *b*estows", a phrase dominated by voiced consonants, produces another change of tone, however. The metaphor in the closing couplet surprises at first sight. The lotus flower has always been a symbol of love, the white lotus as the symbol for giving love, the pink one for receiving love. In tarot the lotos flower usually appears in connection with cups, i.e. cards referring to the element of water. Thus the lotos flower perfectly fits in with the other "liquid" imagery presented before, like blood flowing in veins or the "stagnant flood". The final line implies that the "lotus shore" refers to the shore of the beyond, but it also suggests a reference to the shore of life, - that is life on the brink of death, facing death, as when soldiers report for front line duty. Using this symbol of love and life serves as a means to underline the innocence of their wasted young lives, the hopes they had for the future.

The examples given demonstrate the important role of poetry to release inner strain: the strain ranges from deep interior struggling and despair, utter disillusionment, to the sorrow experienced on different occasions, such as the death of his dear friend Laurence Bévenot.

3.4.2. RELIGIOUS MEDITATIONS

This period outside monastic walls abounds in religious meditations, a fact which in itself suggests the firm bond he feels with the religious world, how much it is a part of himself, despite his dwelling in the secular world.

It appears as though the strict separation of the religious and the secular was not experienced so rigorously anymore. The poet started to entertain the idea that the two worlds, as both were made by God, cannot be segregated in such a strict manner. This concept is firmly implied in "Printemps" (*Beyond*, 110), written "au bord des eaux", as we are told in the subtitle.

> La voie qui nous amène en ce grand lieu
> Qu'un jour d'antan on appelait le Monde
> M'a été trancée par un ciel si vieux
> Qu'un monde ou deux vus dans l'idée profonde
> De sa Pensée, ne semblaient pas, je pense,
> Si loin de ce fin centre qui les tient.
> Ce vide où je me trouve sans défense
> Contient peut-être un Etre d'où il vient.
> Je pense à ta Pensée, Ancien des Jours,
> - A son vieux coin qui vit ce coin du temps:
> Le vit, le revit, le revoit toujours
> Posé à l'horizon d'un seul printemps ...
> Je marche seul en ce lent, lointain rêve,
> N'en voyant que l'ampleur d'une heure brève.

"Le Monde" (1.2) implies that the poet is back to the world again, the secular world that is, having only just landed there, for until that time he had been a monk still with Father Basil (cf. letter, 1.2.1990). The strict dichotomy, the separation of the sacred and profane is no longer stressed as was the case in earlier poems. L.3 refers to the idea of divine providence, including also a juxtaposition of "ciel" and "monde", sacred heaven placed up against the world. The whole passage has a metaphysical touch: the road on which the poet was walking had been traced by a heaven so old and ancient, "Qu'un monde ou deux vus dans l'idée profonde / De sa Pensée". The question implied here is whether there are one or two worlds in the eyes of heaven, whether there are two domains, that of the cloister and that of the world. What the poet is trying to convey is that in eternal thought the two worlds are not separated: God is the centre of the monastic world just as He is the centre of this world. His presence is everywhere: "It is this focussing on Him as the centre of the soul, that is the crux of the matter, the essence of monastic life anyway" (letter, 1.2.1990). One cannot separate the two worlds. It is all the world of God's order, His creation, under His guiding hand. "Je me trouve sans défense" (1.7) refers to the fact that the poet had no more "défense", i.e. no more walls around him any more. He felt God's presence there, being close to creation on the edge of the water, alone with God. "Ce vide où je me trouve sans défense / Contient peut-être un Etre d'où il vient": God as the author of the void is contained therein. In the void one finds God. Using "peut-être" does not so much intend expressing the poet's doubts but is rather a word-play on "être". "Le vit, le revit, le revoit toujours" (l.11) refers to "ta Pensée, Ancien des Jours", stressing the eternity of God, which the poet powerfully experienced on that day in spring. L.10 implies that somewhere in the corner of eternal thought there was this little moment of time he lives and experiences now, a minuscule unimportant iota of time which does not really matter. The imagery used in l.12 suggests that God was watching from one great spring, to which we are all returning eventually, to the ultimate resurrection, which is the crowning spring itself. Additionally, "printemps" conveys the idea that the poet himself was experiencing a new spring, - a new period of his life was about to start. The closing couplet stresses his personal solitude and loneliness. He seems to be all alone on the highway of life: "Je marche seul en ce lent, lointain rêve / N'en voyant que l'ampleur d'une heure brève"; "lointain rêve" implies the dream of divine providence, the dream God had in mind. "Lointain" stresses the length of that dream, reminding one of the long period of time previously spent in monasteries, which were all a part of His dream. However, we cannot ever observe the dream as a whole, we merely behold and perceive the length of one small hour, whereas eternity can see it all. The poem meditates on how insignificant we are in comparison with the vastness of providence.

The "Great Divide" into the secular world and the religious world is also central to "'Mary and Martha alas have parted.'" (*Beyond*, 206), a sonnet inspired by the "Lament for Farnborough" sent to Alun Idris by Fr. Alban from Prinknash. Although apparently referring to the misery of the present situation at Farnborough Abbey, the poem can equally be read outside that particular context, as the truth contained therein is of much more general application.

> What is the essence of the Great Divide
> 'Tween life within and life abundantly
> In overflowing spilt? Who e'er did hide
> The depth that was not there when constantly
> The inward was without? And who saw not
> The vast terrain within when but a word,
> A look, a gesture, did unveil the spot
> Where echoes of some Harmony were heard?

The first two quatrains pose the question of the great division between active and contemplative life. The two sisters Mary and Martha have always been taken as representing the two aspects of life: the active and the contemplative. They appear frequently in religious literature as representing these two conceptions. While Martha is trying very hard to care for Jesus' bodily welfare, Mary is sitting there and listening with her heart and soul to the Lord's words (cf. Luke 10:38-42).

In the early days of monasticism, such a division had not existed: the monks and nuns lived in the local community, devoting themselves to works of mercy.[177] In the Western Church these two separate categories of contemplative and active life were firmly ensconced from the high Middle Ages onwards. In a more general context, the "Great Divide" is the big chasm between

---

[177] "Virgines subintroductae" is the technical term for these nuns (cf. letter, 13.6.1991).

inner life (inward truth and reality, the real being) and outward appearance. It seems as though there was no concordance between these two aspects as regards Farnborough. Apparently, the community split in two at that time, the more contemplative half, and the more pastoral half, though separating amicably by means of a Chapter vote (cf. letter, 13.6.1991).

The "echoes of some Harmony" refers to the fact that even if people are actively engaged, this does not hinder them from living in interior harmony. They are integrated, in tune with God. "God is not a God of disorder but of harmony" says St. Paul in 1 Cor 14:33.[178]

Dom Basil looked after Talacre Abbey until it was sold: the community had left for Chester, where they now live (cf. letter, 1.2.1990). The Benedictines were leaving Wales, closing this abbey that represented the last contemplative Benedictine presence in Wales. "Beginnings have an ending here on earth", - the first line of "Last night at Talacre" (*Beyond*, 109) echoes the passing of the Benedictine presence. Today the monastery is no longer church property. The "ending" also implies, of course, the end of the poet's life as a Benedictine monk. The closing couplet is addressed to Providence, the eternal weaving of plan, - "O thing! O thing, contrived not upon earth, / Thou hast a name, where ancient notes have birth." The "ancient notes" refer to the previously mentioned "beauty of thy song": it is as though there was a stupendous song in eternity. It all fits into this great orchestration, the symphony of providence, the great tune which has been played from all eternity. We cannot see it in its entirety, nor hear the whole melody. We only hear our part which fits into the rest. The use of the word "thing" here is not very poetic; however, as the poet himself pointed out in a letter, even Shakespeare makes use of it[179] (cf. letter, 28.2.1990), which apparently Alun Idris considers as the poetic justification to employ it in a repeated apostrophe as well, despite its rather displeasing nature and lack of poetic appeal.

The nature of providence is central to "'God's got a present for you'" (*Beyond*, 210), the title being a quotation from "a word of knowledge given through someone involved in the Renewal just before we met", as is indicated in a note.

> There is an eye that saw the whole of Time,
> And several times, ere it a measure had.
> There is a pupil that watched aeons climb
> From chasmèd void to bliss when one thought bad
> The story be: there is a brain that knew
> The lengthy moment and the rapid age
> Ere e'er the well-read future, coming new
> To hominides' pale gaze, could mark this page.
> And there is something, sister, in this earth
> That bent the blind trajectories of hours
> And in a plaintive song placed notes of mirth
> To be perceived but once by carnal pow'rs.
> And yet a grain of bliss can be twice bliss
> When ere it pass a warning comes of this.

---

[178] Phillips Modern English Bible.
[179] For example, Shakespeare uses it for the ghost in *Hamlet*: "What! has this thing appear'd again to-night?", uttered by Marcellus (*Hamlet* I, 1:21).

The sonnet is a meditation on time and providence, how it all has been planned before and written down in the Book of Life, whose pages are slowly turned. The metaphors used to describe God's pre-knowledge are all taken from anatomy, which reinforces the idea of proximity between God and human beings; at the same time, however, His eternal wisdom contrasts sharply with the ignorance of human creatures. Oxymorons like "lengthy moment" or "rapid age" suggest human limitations, our ignorance, the failing capability to understand the course of our lives. When confronted with His almightiness, we appear with "hominides' pale gaze", an image emphasizing our insignificance. In the third quatrain, the poet mentions his addressee, "sister". In the original version he employed "seraph", which would have been even more powerful and suggestive. The "blind trajectories of hours" is a striking metaphor for their courses of history, i.e. the poet's own course of life and his "sister's" course of life. The image itself powerfully suggests the idea of providence, - we cannot do much about it: "blind", not seeing where we go, the "trajectories" are pre-arranged, well-planned. There is a cosmic power which guides all. This was also the doctrine of Julian of Norwich: providence is guiding us, "underneath are the everlasting arms", as we read in Deuteronomy 34:27. The closing couplet of this sonnet hints at the idea that in the renewal, when the gifts of the spirit are at work, the rules of time are broken and the providence of God crashes into our time. We are enabled to enter His time, to jump time, - prophesy is possible. The ability to know things beforehand through God's intervention is prominent in the Charismatic Renewal. "This word of knowledge was given, the warning was a nice warning" (letter, 13.6.1991). "Twice bliss" refers to the happiness of the occasion when it comes and also to the joy of looking forward to it. The poem can be sung as well, - Alun Idris composed a tune for it, which well reflects the message of the sonnet.

Being involved with the Charismatic Renewal and filled with its glowing spirit is central to "'The one with the tie'" (*Beyond*, 212), which was written "after being called out specially in a charismatic meeting". The note places the poem in its original context, but even without the knowledge of the specific occasion, the enthusiasm conveyed in these lines is immediately felt:

> The light of Ars can burn across the years
> And without stole or surplice shrive the heart
> That basks in these old rays, for as it nears
> The ancient shining many fears depart,
> And limbs and sounds set free can tell a tale
> That saints and hermits told with but the mind,
> For well the walls of prayer hid from this Gale
> The practised soul full formed to grind and grind.

The Curé of Ars is said to have had piercing eyes: he could see into people, and this "light of Ars" can still burn, as is implied in the opening line. The image also refers to the poet's own personal experience of feeling the spirit in the Charismatic Renewal. The image of his heart basking "in these old rays" is highly suggestive, spreading the idea of calor, happiness, security, almost nurturing his heart with warmth and love. The renewal is carried by the Holy Spirit, "this Gale", with whose help people involved are able to utter words of knowledge. The alliteration and repetition in "practised soul full formed to grind and grind" suggests the mechanical repetition of prayer, habitual prayer, where the real power has evaporated. The line is a side-swipe at what might happen in professional religion, especially in Catholicism, where one is formed to say prayers, to "grind and grind", but where the original power, the first excitement and enthusiasm can, unfortunately, be sadly missing. Ironically, it seems as though the walls of enclosure were excluding this power, concentrating completely on the grinding. The "sadness of it all" mentioned in the final line of the sonnet indicates that although the gifts are there, people are not accepting them. There are still far too few people involved in the Charismatic Renewal.

3.4.3. HYMNS

Alun Idris' return to Wales is most of all noticeable in the number of hymns composed in this period, several of which are dedicated to Welsh saints. Back to the land of song, where hymnology still forms an important part of Welsh life, he was inspired to write many hymns, which can be and still are used in the mass. The prayerful character of the verse, complemented by a plain tune that can be rapidly grasped by the congregation, turns these poems into real hymns.

"Dewi Sant" (*Beyond*, 145f.) is a hymn composed for St. David's day, and was sung at a students' mass on his feast day, the first of March, as we are told in the subtitle. The simple music and plain words make it very suitable for the occasion, but it is also an homage to Wales itself.

<blockquote>
Dewi
Pray for this our land,
Place on us you hand,
And be near.

Dewi
Pray that we may see,
Pray that we may be
Truly be.
</blockquote>

Each of the five stanzas starts by addressing the saint, i.e. a monometer line, which is followed by two rhyming trimeter lines and a closing cretic. The hymn has a deeply prayerful character, as is obvious from the first two stanzas quoted. It is interesting to note that Alun Idris does not use the old form "thou" to address the saint, a form he normally employs in his poetry. In the third stanza the poet mentions "Gwalia lân", which means "pure, holy Wales", demonstrating the poet's love for his country.

The following hymn called "The wind, the wind!" (*Beyond*, 147f.) was written on St. David's Day itself and is also dedicated to the patron saint of Wales. The tune is an adaptation of "Qui es-tu, Roi d'humilité?", a hymn composed by a French priest. The poem presents itself as a dialogue between the poet and the saint, though only the poet speaks, i.e. asks the saint questions:

> And did you, Dewi, hear these seas?
> Did you once listen to this breeze
> And see one hour what this hour sees
>   On this horizon?

Here again the poet sticks to "you", instead of using the old-fashioned form of address "thou". The pattern of each of the five stanzas is the same, repeating "horizon" in each closing line, though utilising different prepositions. This closing line can be called an incremental refrain. Three lines of rhyming iambic tetrameters are followed by an iambic dimeter line, each of which has an additional unstressed syllable attached to it.

> Did you, too, Dewi, know the pain
> Of seeing glory one day wane,
> Of wanting days to come again
>   O'er this horizon?

The "too" in l.1 suggests that waning glory is all that can be observed in Wales today. Addressing the saint in such a direct way illustates the close relation the poet feels he has with St. David. The tune has a very solemn character. It is plain and easy to remember, suitable for use at mass. The closing line is repeated when chanting the hymn.

The following hymn written in honour of "St. John Roberts" (*Beyond*, 214), to whom Alun Idris is very devoted, fits an adaptation of the tune "Finlandia" by J. Sibelius. It is an English version of the Welsh poem which was published as "Sant John Roberts" in *Seren Cymru* (March 3, 1989, 8).

> Child of our land, chaste father of a throng,
> Dost thou this night recall to whom belong
> These parts of earth that once to heav'n were wed,
> These silent quires where once thy feet did tread?
> Dost thou still hear the echo of this pause
> In ancient song that long flowed 'tween the pores
> Of heavy stone where buried lies awhile
> A patient spring, an old familiar smile?

"A patient spring" refers to the longed for springtime of the Spirit, who desires nothing more than to bring light, truth and grace to Wales. The poem, which consists of eight lines of iambic pentameters rhyming in couplets, is full of allusions to St. John Roberts and "his" church at Gellilydan: the "quires" refer to those of Cymer Abbey, a ruined Cistercian foundation, which had fascinated the young John Roberts. After his conversion to Roman Catholicism he wanted to bring his faith back to Wales, but was martyred at Tyburn, having been arrested in the act of celebrating a mass (cf. letter, 13.6.1991).

The inversion at the beginning of the poem, reinforced by the medial pause, emphasizes the Welsh origin of St. John Roberts. The spondee in the third foot, followed by a pyrrhic, stresses that his life had been dedicated entirely to the Lord. L.3 powerfully suggests the heyday of Catholicism in the Middle Ages, when we read about "These parts of earth that once to heav'n were wed", the insertion of "once" implying that these times have long passed. The "ancient song that long flowed 'tween the pores / Of heavy stone" suggests how much the church was bathed in prayer and song, even filling the "pores" of stone. By addressing the saint in such a personal way, we receive the impression as though he was sharing memories with him, a good old friend. Such an intimate atmosphere underlines the close connection the poet feels he has with St. John Roberts.

Another favourite saint of Alun Idris' is the Curé d'Ars, who, like John Roberts, has appeared in his poetry previously. "Pauvre malheureux prêtre" (*Beyond*, 223) is entirely dedicated to him, completed by a tune, simply called "A tune for the Curé d'Ars", which is of a very slow and solemn nature. The title of the poem, which consists of two sonnets (one in English, one in French), is taken from the Curé's own writings, who used to sign his letters thus.[180] Such a mode of address does not imply that he was unhappy, - it only refers to his material poverty, for he was rich spiritually.

> O Saint of God, whose eyes saw as His saw,
> Thou wast not made for earth, yet didst it shake,
> For Ars meant nought to any heart before,
> Yet nations did by storm this village take
> And lay thee under siege for but a word,
> A sound whereon to found the coming years -
> A word, O Father, but a word once heard
> From the Beyond whereon thou hadst strange ears.
> O! mystery of Choice that dost descend
> To crannies of this globe, 'twould seem each age
> Traps somewhere some stray rays that Thou dost send
> To dullard brains when aiming at the sage.
> O Père! though now thou'rt o'er the Stygian sea,
> On this day canst thou find some sound for me?

The first two quatrains reflect the similarity between the Curé d'Ars and the desert fathers, as both the desert fathers and the Curé were called on by many people and asked for counsel: "nations did by storm this village take / And lay thee under siege for but a word."[181] The truth of his word could not be doubted, - it was taken as a guiding light for the future, "A sound whereon to found the coming years". Ll.7f. imply the special nature of his ability, the link he had to the Beyond, direct contact with God. The third quatrain switches to the present, implying that such sources of divine knowledge are to be found in our time as well, for "ea*ch* a*ge* / *Tr*a*ps s*omewhere some stray rays that Thou dost send": the accumulation of plosives and hissing sounds suggests the difficult access such "stray rays" find to "dullard brains". The synectoche not only implies our ignorance but also reinforces the idea that such "stray rays" cannot be grasped intellectually by reason. The apostrophe in l.13 reminds one of a sigh, which reinforces the immediacy of the wish expressed in the closing line.

---

[180] The director of the present thesis signed himself as a Carthusian "indignus frater" until the prior forbade it on the grounds that it was undesirable to draw attention to what was so obvious!
[181] He was able to prophesy the future, being fully cognizant of the will of God. He is also said to have been able to see people's past, telling them their sins (cf. letter, 17.8.1991).

Alun Idris was devoted to the Curé d'Ars in his youth, this "Saint de Dieu, ami de mon enfance" as we read in the French sonnet. He drew the poet close to grace in adolescence, when the call to be like the Curé was strongly felt. This call has guided him over the years. As a young Christian the call to a life of preaching was dominant, which was, in a way, his first call, "leur premier sort". The link with the Curé d'Ars is a double one: he felt the call to preach, and yet, like St. John Roberts, he also felt the call to be enclosed, - the yearning for a silent life was also manifest.[182] Both the pull of intense prayer and the pull of preaching in Wales were felt (cf. letter, 17.8.1991).

St. Winefride, also called "Wenefred" or "Gwenfrewi" (cf. Farmer 1979, 408), is a very popular saint in Wales. Alun Idris dedicated "Saint Winefride"[183] (*Beyond*, 220) to her, a poem consisting of one Welsh and one English stanza, completed by a tune composed for it.[184]

> O gentle maid, white virgin of a day
>   That marked all days to come,
> Thou too didst know the treading of a way
>   Found hard at times by some.
> Thou too didst know, know well, what 'tis to burn,
>   But couldst not be aglow
> By halves, by quarters - that can this fire turn
>   On more than one - or show
> What 'twas to love ere thou Love hadst become.

The poem reflects the story of St. Winefride, who was martyred. Not being given a chance to "be aglow / By halves, by quarters", refers to the brutal way in which she was killed. The day of her death "marked all days to come" by the presence of the spring which welled up on the spot where her head had fallen. By dying for the Lord, she became "Love" herself, implying that she became a part of God.

The poem has an interesting stanza form, identical with the Welsh stanza: it consists of nine lines, iambic pentameter lines, alternating with iambic trimeter lines, with the rhyme scheme ababcdcdb.

There cannot be any doubt about Alun Idris' deep roots in Welsh hymnology, as becomes obvious in his own attempts to contribute to the corpus of Welsh hymns. The poet's musical talents support his yearning to crystalize a verse of prayer in the form of a hymn, thereby increasing the latent emotional power. The title of a poem mentioned before (cf. pp.272f.), "Music is love in search of a word" (*Beyond*, 209), beautifully suggests this idea: what cannot be uttered verbally is expressed in the music which accompanies the verse.

---

[182] The Curé escaped twice from his parish, trying to enter a monastery, but was struck down. St. John Roberts joined a very strict community in Spain, where he took a vow of enclosure. However, it was decided that he should come back to Britain, as the need was very great there, while remaining a member of the Benedictine order.
[183] Also published under the title "Gwenfrewi" in *Seren Cymru*, August 16, 1991, 3 and in *Y Tyst*, August 15, 1991, 3 (with notation).
[184] An unpublished note attached to the tune explains the origin of the healing water of St. Winefride's well: "[...] and after the hede of the Vyrgyne was cut of and touchyd the ground, as we afore have said, sprang up a welle of spryngyng water largely enduryng unto this day, which heleth al langours and sekenesses as well in men as in bestes, which welle is named after the name of the Vyrgyne and is called St. Wenefrede's Welle [...]".

3.4.4. HIRAETH

Hiraeth enters his poetry on different levels. One important form of hiraeth concerns Alun Idris' yearning to bring back the monastic presence to Wales. The hope still burning within his heart finds expression in "Letter from America" (*Beyond*, 112), with the note in brackets explaining part of its contents: "Pecos' hope for a house in Wales".[185]

> Could this yet be? In this our little land,
> In this our land, our own, our only home,
> Could there again one day a something stand
> Through this great storm, borne on these winds whence come
> The rushing sounds that were heard here before?
> Could this the land that knew it know again
> The fire of Egryn that moved here of yore
> And see steel hearts remolten 'neath its pain?
> O Wales, wilt thou again sing what thy youth
> Knew well, knew very well how well to sing,
> And will the sound of preaching bear old truth
> Through electronic ears and mouths, to bring
> A little of the Hope that here returns
> From whence it comes, where still, I think, it burns?

The first two lines powerfully imply the poet's love for his home country. The repetition in l.2 and the diminutive "our little land" are devices used to underline the strong love he feels for Wales. The excitement sensed at the very thought of re-introducing the monastic presence in Wales is again firmly conveyed. The "rushing sounds" were heard here before, as "The fire of Egryn" suggests: it refers to the phenomoneon of numerous fiery lights linked with the renewal, reported and seen in many places in 1904-5, as is indicated in a note. "Egryn" is short for "Llanegryn", where moving balls of light are attested to have been observed, although this supernatural phenomon was witnessed in many other places in Wales as well. "The whole of Wales was put on fire by the Holy Spirit" (letter, 1.2.1990). The phrase "fire of Egryn" is taken from a poem by T.H. Parry-Williams, one of the finest Welsh poets.[186] He did not possess formal Christian faith but he harboured a certain belief. His poems about the 1904 revival mirror his scepticism, but he mentions the lights, "golau Egryn", the fire of Egryn: "Cariadon Crist a glewion yr Ysbyd Glân / Yn gweled yng 'ngolau Egryn' eu Duw yn dân;" ("Christ's lovers and the Holy Spirit's stalwarts / Seeing in 'the light of Egryn' their God all fire;") ("1904", Parry-Williams 1972, 108).

In Alun Idris' poem the "fire of Egryn" is used as a synectoche for all the fiery lights observed at the time. The poet wonders whether it might be possible to see again "steel hearts remolten

---

[185] "Pecos" refers to the Pecos Benedictine Monastery in New Mexico, which is fully charismatic (cf. letter, 1.2.1990).
[186] Parry-Williams died in Aberystwyth in 1975, at the time when Alun Idris was studying for his degree there. The poet had some impact on Alun Idris. One of his greatest, most famous poems is "Dychwelyd" ("Returning") (Parry-Williams 1972, 39), which ends with the famous line "Ni wnawn, wrth ffoi am byth o'n ffwdan ffôl, / Ond llithro i'r llonyddwch mawr yn ôl." ("We do not, as we flee forever from our mad rush but slip back into the great stillness again.").

'neath its pain" (l.8): the use of "remolten" suggests that those hearts have been molten before, at the time of the renewal. The exclamatory sigh, "O Wales" underlines the firm bond he feels towards his home country. "O Wales, wilt thou again sing what thy youth / Knew well, knew very well how well to sing": the repetition and the word-play stress the art of singing and preaching perfectly mastered at the time. The poet wonders whether this art can be mastered again in our time, so different from the past, "Through electronic ears and mouths", where technical progress allows us to use different means of spreading the message. On the one hand, these means enable us to reach more people, yet on the other the imagery used implies that it happens on a less personal level. The closing line suggests that the fire, the first flame is still burning in Wales. At least the poet is cautiously optimistic, as is implied by "I think". The poem expresses Alun Idris' yearning for a charismatic foundation in Wales, which could work for the spiritual renewal of the country.

"The prophet" (*Beyond*, 190) was written after hearing a "word of knowledge" concerning Wales, as we are told in a note in brackets. The poem reflects Alun Idris' hiraeth to see the Holy Spirit kindle hearts again in his home country: "Will there be light again upon this land / That heard the rushing Wind come o'er its hills". The "rushing Wind" refers to the sound heard by the apostles at Pentecost (Acts 2:2). The Holy Spirit had already been active in Wales several times, in the periods of renewal: "This little flame that glows / Upon this planet's shore has glowed before, / For 'tis the Egryn fire that others saw." The fire of Egryn appears again as clear evidence of the Spirit at work in Wales, which had been observed by many.

The following sonnet mirrors a different kind of hiraeth strongly felt by the poet, - his love for La Trappe, which is still ardently burning in his heart. The poem shows that there was a glimmer of hope left for him to return, although it was scarcely probable that it would be fulfilled. It lies within the nature of hiraeth, however, to yearn for something which can scarcely or improbably be attained. "Attrapé" (*Beyond*, 113) was written after seeing brochures of La Trappe and writing to the Abbot, as is indicated in a note in brackets. It is a love poem to the monastery. The title of the poem is a word play on La Trappe and the verb "attraper", which powerfully suggests that the poet is still "trapped" by the glamour of this monastery, his love has not diminished:

> Visage d'autrefois qui restes jeune
> Et me regardes comme en d'autres jours
> Tu le faisais, ce goût de paix, de jeûne
> Que tu rappelles, me porte à toi toujours,
> Sans me quitter. Je sais ce que tu fus,
> Ce que tu es, et peux redevenir.
> Ces petits mots qu'ici, tout seul, j'ai lus
> M'ont rendu à mes frères. Revenir,
> Oui, revenir à l'endroit où le tout
> A été joué, où l'amour a su
> Qu'il était aimé - revenir à vous,
> Mes frères, mes jumeaux, que j'aurais pu
> Aimer de tout l'amour de mal aimé -
> O joie! - Pourtant l'amour sait essaimer ...

This sonnet not only mirrors his hiraeth to return, it is a celebration of the longing he feels for La Trappe and the love he experienced there. The brochures he had seen reminded him of the past, - La Trappe had not changed at all, "Visage d'autrefois qui restes jeune": it has not lost is youthful glamour. Seeing the pictures evokes sensual memories as well, "ce goût de paix, de jeûne", that "me porte à toi toujours". L.6 explicitly expresses the possibility of returning: "Je sais ce que tu fus, / Ce que tu es, et peux redevenir." The line suggests that in La Trappe the past, the present and the future are all united, the monastery does not change. In the third quatrain the hiraeth to return is firmly present: "Revenir, / Oui, revenir à l'endroit où le tout / A été joué, où l'amour a su / Qu'il était aimé". The repetition of "revenir", a word which is repeated for a third time in l.11, underlines the yearning to return to that place so full of love. The use of "jumeaux" in l.12 suggests how close he still feels to the monks there, the bond between them has not been broken. "Jumeaux" is also a veiled reference to one of his brethren who started his postulancy the very same day as Alun Idris started his, which made them twins in the eyes of God, being "re-born" for God on the same day (cf. letter, 28.2.1990). All the hiraeth expressed so far leads us to the emotional climax in the final lines: the exclamatory "O joie!" refers to the joy of going back to La Trappe, to the possibility of joining the community there again. However, the final phrase "Pourtant l'amour sait essaimer ..." implies some scepticism as to whether this dream could ever be realized. Nevertheless, the line also expresses his happiness about the fact that, despite all the depressing and sorrowful events that happened, he still knows how to be enthusiastic, how to swarm for something, how to love. The fact of having preserved this happy memory is a sign of the deeply rooted affection he feels towards La Trappe as well as a sign of growing maturity.

"Aberystwyth" (*Beyond*, 111) is a most touching poem full of nostalgia: from each line radiates deep feeling, the strong personal link the poet feels to that place abounding in happy memories of his youth:

> This is the place where many loves were strong,
> Where dreams were bright, and clear as daylight's sight.
> This was the corner where our nightly song
> Rose in an ancient tongue in careless flight.
> This was the sea that lapped our coursing years
> And heard us listen to the sages' shave.
> This is the door that witnessed thy soft tears,
> Forgotten truth, that stopped not at a wave.
> This is the land where many, many things
> Have come and gone - and yet, and yet, remain;
> For even in deep sorrow some joy clings
> To where it was, to where the sweetest pain
> Of wanting and of waiting was first known,
> Ere e'er Time's massive gaspillage was shown.

The anaphora employed in this sonnet underlines the special nature of this place. In particular the first two quatrains are full of tender references to Aberystwyth, which convey the idea of how happy the period of his life spent there was. "This is the place where many loves were strong, / Where dreams were br*ight*, and cle*ar* as dayl*ight*'s s*ight*." The use of assonance and interior rhyme is quite effective, just as in ll.3f. ("song" - "tongue"). Ll.3f. bear a reference to a biographical detail: in his first and third year the poet was staying with the Carmelites, where at compline the "nightly song" was sung in Latin, "in an ancient tongue in careless flight", which implies the rapture of being young, the carelessness of youth (cf. letter, 1.2.1990). Aberystwyth, a town situated on the sea coast, was the place of his studies, as is implied in ll.5f.: "This was the sea that lapped our coursing years / And heard us listen to the sages' shave." The footnote explaining "shave" as "French: rasoir" sheds light on the passage and represents a rather biting comment on the fact that studying was not always the most enthralling and exciting thing to do. The third quatrain returns to the present, - we read that, despite all the events that happened in the meantime, all the pain he had to endure ever since, he still treasures for this place an extremely positive and beautiful memory, with the notion of hiraeth expressing itself strongly: "For even in deep sorrow some joy clings / To where it was"; the following medial pause underlines the discrepancy of the past and the present. "To where it was" implies that here and now, in the present, the joy felt then can only be recollected again, but not re-experienced. Most of all Aberystwyth was the place where "the sweetest pain / Of wanting and of waiting was first known": while he studied at the university, he was waiting to be allowed to enter Prinknash Abbey, although he eventually joined the Carthusians at Sélignac. The imagery used to describe the period of waiting, this "sweetest pain" implies the massive yearning to enter the monastery. The final line is very effective, and forms a sharp contrast in mood to the tenderness present at the beginning of the poem: "Ere e'er Time's massive gaspillage was shown." The line refers to the years spent in different orders, searching for that place, that community, where he would feel truly at home, which would be his home forever. However, the image "massive gaspillage" indicates the disillusionment and frustration felt when he experienced that the finding of a home can be a lengthy, interminable process. The use of the French word "gaspillage"[187] aims to emphasize the length of time that has passed, the long years of unsuccessful search.

    The poems of hiraeth mentioned mark Alun Idris as a truly Welsh poet: this typically Celtic yearning, which has been noticeable from the Trappist period onwards, echoes the poet's longing to find his roots and settle. He is filled with hiraeth to bring the monastic presence back to Wales, though at the same time his heart still burns with the yearning to work actively within the Charismatic Renewal. The memories of his past equally provoke poems of hiraeth, which reflect the love he felt at various stages of his life.

---

[187] The word also appears in "Little things" (World, 76f.).

3.4.5. MEDITATIONS ON TIME

In a monastery the progress of time is experienced more consciously than in the secular world. Having been accustomed to the dogma of using time well and not wasting it, the nature of time is of great importance to the poet and the source of many a meditation. The phenomenon of time still fascinates him, particularly the future.

"'We're making a Yesterday ...'" (*Beyond*, 140) consists of five seven-line stanzas of iambic pentameters alternating with iambic dimeters, except for the final line, which is written in iambic trimeter.[188]

> When on and on the ancient sea still roars,
> Where will we be?
> When o'er this hill, this isle, the Ruah soars,
> What destiny
> Will then have swept us off, will then have been
> Our part, our lot,
> When we are no more seen?

This first stanza is exclusively oriented towards the future, pondering about the idea of "¿Qué será?". Ruah is the Hebrew spirit of God that was hovering over the face of the deep in the first chapter of Genesis.[189] The note in brackets referring to Penmon, situated at the tip of Anglesey,[190] sheds light on the use of "the Ruah" in this context: Anglesey is very windy, at any rate in winter. The timelessness of the "ancient sea", the wind and this Welsh island contrast with the finite nature of man. The second stanza turns from more general considerations about the flow of time to the poet's personal situation:

> When there are waves and waves again to roll
> O'er this our isle,
> Will there be other feet this way to stroll
> Where once a smile,
> That lit the universe beneath its beam,
> Shone all alone
> Where two shared one same gleam?

"Our isle" in l.2 is the first indication of the special situation he is referring to, which becomes all the more clear as the poem progresses, until there is no doubt left anymore in l.7. The stanza combines ponderings about the future with the beauty of the present moment: will there be "other feet" that tread the same isle in the future, when they "are no more seen"? The imagery used in ll.4f. powerfully suggests the happiness of that moment. The third stanza concentrates on what remains of such a happy moment:

---

[188] Alun Idris uses this structure in other poems as well, e.g. in "Ensuite?" (*Beyond*, 115).
[189] "When God began to form the universe, the world was void and vacant, darkness lay over the abyss; but the Spirit of God was hovering over the waters" (Genesis 1:2).
[190] "The situation of Penmon is one of the sweetest and most peaceful that can well be imagined. The land rises steeply to the north, and the spurs of hill enfold a little basin in which trees grow luxuriantly, and the sun loves to linger, where flowers bloom early and the bees hum." (Baring Gould and Fisher 1990, 177).

> When there are winds that travel on their way
>   Into the past,
> Will there be something of this yesterday
>   In th'hours that last
> Within the tingling of the air that held
>   A molten bliss
> That hours to hours did weld?

The imagery used to describe the moment of happiness is striking: it is a "molten bliss / That hours to hours did weld", a moment of utmost love and happiness. In the fourth stanza the poet describes the day as "The fullest Now", reinforcing the happiness experienced. The steady passage of time is implied in ll.1f., when we read about the winds that travel into the past. In the final stanza he mentions "this path we trod one winter wild / As we came home / To this our long-forgotten part of us": "home" refers to Alun Idris' coming back to Wales, after having lived abroad for many years. It also suggests "home" in the sense of love, a feeling he had denied for so long, "our long-forgotten part of us".

A similar meditation on what the future will be like "when we are gone" is presented in the poem "'I want to be buried here'" (*Beyond*, 183f.). It also was written with reference to Penmon, as is indicated in a note in brackets. The poem consists of six stanzas of three iambic tetrameter lines followed by an iambic dimeter line; the four lines of each stanza rhyme. The poem can be sung as well: Alun Idris composed a tune for it, which is of a gentle and solemn nature and perfectly reflects the message of the poem.

> When we are gone, when we are gone,
> What sound will linger gently on,
> What will be found when work is done,
>   And we are gone?
>
> When days have passed, when days have passed,
> What hours of these our hours will last,
> When we ourselves have anchor cast,
>   And days have passed?

The pattern used throughout the poem becomes apparent in these first two quoted stanzas. The repetition in l.1 is taken up again in l.4, where it is employed as an additional means of emphasis. This repetition reinforces the poet's glance at the future. While the first stanza is held in a rather general tone concerning what the future will be like, the second stanza meditates on the question of what will remain of us in the future, what will remain as a part of ourselves. The pattern of the closing stanza differs slightly in the final line:

> When nothing more, when nothing more
> Of this our ripple laps the shore
> Of Penmon, will what went before
>   Do nothing more?

"Do nothing more" implies exercising active influence on the future: can it be that we leave something behind us which will be of lasting character? The imagery used in l.2, "this our ripple" suggests human insignificance and frailty, and yet is it possible that "this our ripple", which "went before", is of lasting effect? Are there ways and means to let parts of oneself live on, "when we are gone"?

Penmon Priory was founded by St. Seiriol in the 6th century. St. Seiriol's Island, also called Ynys Seiriol or Puffin Island (from the puffins which abound in it), is not far from Bangor, - it is the place where St. Seiriol lived as a hermit: "To this island the saint was wont to retire for solitary meditation, and it was seemingly much regarded as a happy resting-place, for the soil, when turned over by rabbits, exposes human bones" (Baring Gould and Fisher 1990, 178).[191] Penmon places its visitors in contact with the past, as we read in "'Deus, in adiutorium ...'" (*Beyond*, 127), a sonnet written at Penmon:

> There are upon this little orb we tread
> Some spots that have not moved. Their yesterday
> To this, Time's latest child, by some strange thread
> Is linked. Their morrow too is here today,
> For there is Someone there who saw it all.

The ancient priory of Penmon triggers off ponderings on the nature of time. Here it seems as though time has not progressed, it is one of these "spots that have not moved". Here each day is firmly linked to the others, the days are woven into one another, forming a whole. Even "their morrow is here today", for providence has seen it long before. The divine presence is firmly felt on this island, as 1.5 implies. "Time's latest child" is a fine image for "today", indicating that it is bound to grow until it too will turn into another yesterday.

The time which follows our brief séjour on earth is of special interest to the poet, as we have already observed in a number of poems previously mentioned . "'I'll have you fluffing up my halo'" (*Beyond*, 227) equally deals with the passage of time, as is already indicated by the very title of the sonnet. The imagery used to describe the future in the first two quatrains is striking, as it conveys an idea of the present as well:

> When aeons have rolled on and here below
> We are but letters chiselled in a stone,
> When waves of time have lapped the lands we know
> And hushed to sleep each nursed and rested bone
> That now is stroked and fondled; when the days
> That gulp the moments shared and rack those not,
> Have in Oblivion dropped from mem'ry's gaze,
> And ages have in trickling all forgot;

The imagery employed in 1.2 firmly points to our death, suggesting in a rather direct manner what will be left of us once we are gone. The sea is used as the symbol of time when the poet talks of the aeons that have "rolled on", the "waves of time" that have lapped our lands. The alliteration and assonance employed in 1.3 indicate the continuous flow of time, whose rhythm

---

[191] Giraldus Cambrensis wrote that the island was called Enis Lannach, i.e. the Ecclesiastical Island, because many bodies of saints are buried there, and also because of the hermits living on the island (cf. Baring Gould and Fisher 1990, 178).

does not change, floating on steadily. L.4 powerfully conveys an idea of the happiness of the present moment, where the image of "each nursed and rested bone" suggests how happy and well-cared for he feels; however, "bone" is ambivalent, also affording a link with the gravestone alluded to in 1.2. The great "Oblivion" will "gulp the moments shared": the imagery implies human insignificance, - our lives are but short moments when compared to eternity. These happy moments will one day have "dropped from mem'ry's gaze", which beautifully echoes the process of memorizing a happy event. With our departing, memory too will disappear.

Beautiful imagery characterizes "'We don't feel time when we're together'" (*Beyond*, 155), in particular the first quatrain of the sonnet. The poem is a meditation on the nature of time and its smallest units, moments:

> What is a drop of Time in this great sea
> Of ebbing moments that come ne'er again?
> What is the measure of Eternity
> Where stars forget to turn and moons to wane?
> What is the length of moments here below
> Where little ticks can tap out such great things
> And 'tween two beats ne'er one same rhythm show
> As one heart groans and one heart softly sings?

The sea is used as a symbol of time, "a drop of Time" being one short moment. The "sea / Of ebbing moments" suggests the constant flow of moments which characterizes our time here on earth: it is a steady coming and going of moments, until the last one comes. This sea "Of ebbing moments that come ne'er again" therefore refers not to our time on earth but to eternity, as is explicitly mentioned in 1.3, "What is the measure of Eternity". The imagery used in 1.4, "where stars forget to turn and moons to wane", well expresses the nature of Eternity, where movement has become superfluous. The question underlying this first stanza is: how can eternity be measured if it is not measured in moments? What is a "drop of Time" in eternity? The title of the poem, however, suggests a connection between the measure of time in eternity and the fact that the progress of time is not noticed by those who are happy. The second quatrain concentrates on our time on earth, implying that a moment of bliss can be extremely powerful and lasting, "little ticks can tap out such great things". In the closing couplet, Alun Idris unifies the question of time measured in eternity and time "here below": "And is Eternity so very long / When untraced hours ill hold but one brief song?"

The nature of time on earth is central to "'The future doesn't exist'" (*Beyond*, 157), a poem where we again find philosphical ideas about time. "Tomorrow never trod upon this earth / And Now was only Then at its own death, / Which never happened, for there is but birth / Of virgin seconds": Alun Idris' predilection for word plays is reflected in these lines. In the third quatrain and the closing couplet of the sonnet we read:

> The aeons that have been and that will be
> Were all by moments held, and we hold all
> In this hard squeezing of Eternity,

> For though the time draws on and us doth call,
> There is a little corner in this hour
> In which to shelter from the moment's pow'r.

Time is but made up of single moments, aeons "Were all by moments held". "This hard squeezing of Eternity" implies the grasping of eternity on earth, taking hold of an intense moment, with the pressure of time constantly present: the idea might be frightening to those who are unable to accept the vanity of mundane things. Time is cruel in passing on mercilessly, "the time draws on and us doth call", yet "There is a little corner in this hour / In which to shelter from the moment's pow'r". In the presence of love time ceases to exist, it loses its importance in our restless society, dominated by time-tables and engagement-diaries. A moment in the presence of love contains all eternity. By concentrating on an overwhelming moment, living it to the full, the future ceases to exist.

The meditations on time in this chapter reflect the poet's own intense search for his future path in that period: while studying theology at the University of Bangor, he had the opportunity to reflect upon his future. Naturally, such a situation provokes meditations on the nature of time itself, as is reflected in the poems: we find meditations on the very essence of time, on how to use it while still on earth, on what will finally remain of us, once we have left the world, once we have exhausted our share of temporal time.

3.4.6. CELEBRATING FRIENDSHIP AND LOVE

There is a whole series of poems starting with "Tu" (*Beyond*, 124), which reflect the development of a friendship which began to blossom at that period. How precious these moments of sharing were, is mirrored in the poems. The quantity itself reflects the intensity of his feelings, as within a rather short space a great number of poems were written. These poems open up a new field in his poetry, add a new dimension. The subtlety in them is striking. The tone is generally very gentle and smooth, and yet they are at the same time tremendously powerful. They are bathed in the atmosphere of friendship and love, just as they are bathed in the spirit of prayer. These poems are the testimony of an important period of his life, hence they form an essential part of his poetry as a whole. Honesty and sincerity on the part of the author is ever present in his poems, yet here in particular the honesty apparent makes them all the more powerful and touching.

"Tu" (*Beyond*, 124) is the first sonnet of the series, characterized by a soft and gentle tone. The feeling of wonder about "the magic of a name" is present in this poem, the amazement at how powerful its sound can be:

> There is within the magic of a name
> A force made not of letters. There is more
> Within two notes than sound that came
> Across a ringing sky. How oft before

> Were echoes made to echo in the deep
> That lies 'neath th'emptied breast, by one or two
> Stray utterings? Therein the hid child's sleep
> Was roused by something old he somehow knew.
> There is a road within whereon hath trod
> The author of a sound. There is a place
> Where eye and I can meet. Here stood unshod
> The one giv'n once the Name, but ne'er the Face.
> For there is all our wanting; there is all
> Our waiting to be wanted by a call.

The idea expressed in the first sentence is taken up again in the second one, emphasized by the different rhythm used: the spondaic fifth foot in 1.2 and the spondee in the second foot of 1.3 underline how much more there is "Within two notes than sound", that it is indeed "A force made not of letters". L.3 consists of four feet only, yet the spondee employed makes up for the missing foot, the line eventually has five stressed syllables. It is not entirely clear whether the observation of the "magic of a name" was made as regards the hearing and uttering the name of his beloved or of hearing his own name being called by her, for both possibilities are valid. There are some indications, however, pointing at the latter, in particular the second quatrain suggests that it is his being called by her: "How oft before / Were echoes made to echo in the deep / That lies 'neath th'emptied breast". Hearing her call his name is bound to cause echoes within, beneath an "emptied breast", which suggests the void he was experiencing. As a result of his being called, "the hid child's sleep / Was roused", the child referring to love, which suggests the love which was awakening in him, and also points at the fact that he never felt such love towards a woman before, his love being new, innocent as a "child". "Something old he somehow knew" implies that he had known love before, but it was only a vague idea he had grasped then, as is suggested by the repeated "some-", and cannot in the least be compared to the experience of love he feels now. The third quatrain beautifully suggests that, although he knew that love existed, he did not know it would exist for him as well: "giv'n once the Name, but ne'er the Face." Alun Idris' predilection for word play is evident in 1.11, "Where eye and I can meet": listening to this poem being read out aloud supports the implication of alternative meanings. The closing couplet stresses the poet's desire to be "wanted by a call", to be needed and loved.

Many indications of places and Welsh references are integrated into this series of poems. We find numerous allusions to the Welsh countryside, to beautiful places in Wales. "'Thankyou, Father, for the sea'" (*Beyond*, 126) was written with reference to Ynys Llanddwyn, as is indicated in the subtitle. Llanddwyn is attatched to Anglesey, but becomes an island when the sea is in.[192] The mood of the poem is set in the very first sentence: "Upon the edge of this *wide world we* stood / Alone with all that mattered." Alliteration and consonance is used to reinforce the mood. The long vowels suggest a certain solemnity about standing there,

---

[192] "Dwyn" is the name of a Welsh saint and means "blessed", "llan" means "church of": the Welsh genetive is formed by putting the two words next to each other. Anglesey is a very peaceful island. The past is ever present there. Many ancient celtic sites date back to prehistoric times.

at the very end of the world. The moment seems to have been all the more precious because of the presence of his beloved, "Alone with all that mattered".

"'Will we be in a grave like this?'" (*Beyond*, 129) was written on Ynys Tysilio, another small island near Anglesey, named after a Welsh saint, S. Tyssilio, half way between Anglesey and the mainland. It is an island, despite the footpath across the isthmus, an isolated place which has been used as a cemetery. The graves still to be found there explain the title of the sonnet. The solitary nature of the island inspired this poem, meditating on solitude and loneliness, which the poet had experienced for many years, but which seem to have come to an end now:

> Within, within there is a lonely soul
> That ponders 'tween the frontiers of a mind
> And heart that, though unknowing, knows the whole
> Of what is known to lonely human kind.
> Without there is a world that moves and moves
> And pauses not to meet the man within.
> The sound of many thinking voices proves
> The thought that is not there when there is din.
> Yet in the holding of two molten hearts
> Within a ring of need, within a sound
> Of wanting but a whole where there are parts,
> A world within an empty world was found
> Where one small soul meant some small thing to one
> Who knew what many years alone had done.

The first two quatrains concentrate on solitude and loneliness, which seem to characterize our world: in the first quatrain the poet ponders about the solitude within, confined to "the frontiers of a mind / And heart", interior solitude. It is a loneliness known to all who have experienced it. Our restless society does not "pause to meet the man within". There is no time left to dedicate to others. People do not take interest in the interior lives of strangers. The repetition of "Within, within" in l.1 and "moves and moves" in l.5 emphasizes that the loneliness is nurtured both from within and without. And yet, "The sound of many thinking voices proves / The thought that is not there when there is din": thought and care can only be experienced when there is silence, such as pervades Ynys Tysilio. The third quatrain beautifully describes the event which utterly changed the loneliness felt before. The imagery used in l.9 shows how strong the love is which he feels, expressed not only by the holding of two hands, but of "two molten hearts / Within a ring of need". The ring as the symbol of perfection suggests the harmony experienced. As the symbol of infinity it implies that this love will never cease, - there is no escape from it. By this encounter "A world within an empty world was found". The poet discoverd a new world, - huge, gigantic, within a world which had been empty: the realm of love. The diminutive used in the closing couplet emphasizes the preciousness of this experience, so new to someone who "knew what many years alone had done".

More than four years after permission was refused to be allowed to live as a hermit on Ynys Enlli, i.e. Bardsey Island, Alun Idris saw the island again for the first time.[193] "Ynys Enlli" (*Beyond*, 130) reflects the experience of visiting that place. In the closing lines the poet addresses his love:

> O fair, fair creature, mirage of the sand
> Where burnt the desert hours, that thou shouldst come
> Unbid from the unknown and, radiant, stand
> Upon the tip of Earth, above the home
> That th'eremite ne'er had, and say this word -
> Is this part of a song that aeons heard?

The poet sticks to old forms like "thou" or "shouldst" to address her. The situation seems strange, almost unbelievable: he returns with this "fair, fair creature" to this island, where he had longed to live as a hermit, but had been refused permission to do so. "Mirage of the sand / Where burnt the desert hours" powerfully implies how unreal the situation seems, how inexplicable it is to see her beside him, "unbid from the unknown". The image also suggests a connection to life as a hermit, which is life in a desert to some extent. This strange situation makes him ask the question in the closing line whether this coincidence is "part of a song that aeons heard". The question is a rhethorical one, for the poet firmly believes in providence. He knows that it is "part of a song".

The subtitle in "'NEVER AGAIN, never again will you be alone.' (Eglwys Cwyfan)" (*Beyond*, 132) refers to the church of an old Celtic saint, Cwyfan (Kevin), situated on a rocky island called Ynys Gwyfan in Carnarvon Bay, which is completely cut off when the sea is in (cf. Baring Gould and Fisher 1990, 201).

> There is an isle beyond a lonely shore
> Where two were one a while beyond the world.
> There was a prayer to one who walked before
> Between the waves that yesteryear had hurled
> Their voice at Love's mad building.[194] [...]

The first two lines set the tone of the poem, expressing the harmony experienced in the solitude of this tiny island. Apparently, this ancient church, Eglwys Cwyfan, is used as a place of prayer, which it was for so many years, as is implied by the imagery. The poem is characterized by the peace felt on this isle, in the middle of "this world's chill, for flames did meet" (l.8). The image of "this world's chill" contrasts sharply with the heat of the love felt, when their "flames did meet". The innocence, the purity of their love, is implied in the closing lines, when we read that there was no "fear / Of being watched above, for for a while / Two hearts alone, alone, felt heaven smile". The repetition of the word "alone" at the end of the poem goes right back to a poem written at the end of his Carthusian period, "After Reverend

---

[193] Cf. "Questions (After seeing the Bishop and Bardsey Island)" (*World*, 26).
[194] The prayer was prayed in St. Cwyfan's church, to St. Cwyfan, who had out of love built a church in the most inaccessible place, so as to be alone with the One he loved.

Father's refusal" (*Threshold*, 90), as is indicated by a note, where we read: "O thick Unknown! I walk alone, alone / From what I know so well that 'twas not known." The difference in significance of the repetition "alone, alone" in the two poems is clear.

The following sonnet, too, bears reference to a poem written earlier (cf. letter, 1.2.1990): "Ynys Cariad (St. Dwynwen, 25/1)" (*Beyond*, 135), which means "Island of Love". It was written on the feast day of St. Dwynwen.[195] The presence of love characterizes the poem:

> O night of nights, who thought I'd see thy stars
> Look down from yesteryear upon an hour
> Allowed to be by One whose law debars
> The coming of weak virgins 'neath the pow'r
> Of something far too great? The day has been
> That in its setting was not as its rise,
> And those soft-winking witnesses have seen
> An unmeant moment shatter Time's calm skies.
> O little thing, that dost hold all there is
> Within my wanting world, who gave thee wings
> To flutter from a past that had known His,
> His kiss alone, where His own Life-blood clings?
> O cup of loving, we held twice this night
> The pow'r that makes or mars our future quite.

The first line echoes 1.1 of "Quasi modo geniti ..." (*World*, 3), a poem written on the day of taking the habit in La Trappe, which starts with the line: "O day of days! Who thought I'd see thee rise". The parallel is obvious. Both events had seemed to be totally unlikely, yet they occurred. The first two quatrains express the present excitement. The poet is captivated by the feeling of love. The improbability of the event is implied in the first line, yet God "Allowed to be" the seemingly impossible. They feel the power of love, "Of something far too great". This day does not leave any doubt about the love they feel, as is firmly implied in 1.8, "*An unmeant moment shatter Time's calm skies*". The onomatopoetical effect of this line is arresting: the melodious nature of "an unmeant moment", caused by the abundance of nasals, creates an illusion of singing, which implies the special nature of that beautiful moment, but was, however, of lasting consequences unseen and unexpected before. The plosives and hissing sounds in "*shatter Time's calm skies*" suggest these effects of movements the love provokes, although at the same time, the long vowels and the soft m's indicate the peace and calm present before. The third quatrain is an open declaration of love: "O little thing, that dost hold all there is / Within my wanting world, who gave thee wings". Her presence has become most precious to him. The accumulation of light i's and the alliteration of /w/ suggest wind and wings, a light motion; his wonder at her appearance and entry into his life is expressed by the very question of "who gave thee wings / To flutter from a past that had known His, / His kiss alone, where His own Life-blood clings?" The enjambement used in 1.11 is effective, as it suggests a double

---

[195] Dwyn or Dwynwen is the Welsh patroness of true lovers. Her name is retained in Llanddwyn and Porthddwyn, her "church" and "port" in Anglesey (cf. Baring Gould and Fisher 1990, 387f.).

meaning: reading the line implies that the poet's past had known God alone, "His", i.e. God's life, but there is actually more implied than just knowing, as we read on: "that had known His / His kiss alone". The poet's past was dominated by the love felt for God, the love given by God. The "cup of loving" in the closing couplet is a reference to the chalice which both had received that day (cf. letter, 1.2.1990). It also implies that the pull from the altar, the pull to dedicate both of their lives to God only, is present as well.

How much this friendship is bathed in prayer is powerfully suggested in "'I prayed that you would be a priest, if God wanted'" (*Beyond*, 137), which mirrors their receptiveness to God's pull. Feeling the call to dedicate one's life entirely to the Lord is of prime importance and given priority over personal feelings:

> When love seeks not its own but loves beyond
> The will to have for one, the will to own
> Alone that half of which a halved is fond;
> When hearts can burn, yet burn before the Throne
> That bid all burning be; when two hands join
> And leave two others spread forth to the sky; [...]

The word play in l.3 firmly suggests how close they feel: "a halved" refers to one of them who is but a half of the one they form together. And yet ll.4f. imply that the love which made their hearts burn is God's love, who "bid all burning be". Their hearts "burn before the Throne" as well. Both of them show deep love for God. Ll.5f. suggest the prayerful spirit their relation is bathed in, always letting God participate: "when two hands join / And leave two others spread forth to the sky".

"There is a madness in the wayward heart / That only fondness knows." This is the initial line of a sonnet called "A sketch that utters volumes" (*Beyond*, 138), referring to the afflictions of people in love. After enumerating a number of incidents and contradictions inherent in that kind of situation, the tone changes at the beginning of the third quatrain, as less happy memories of the past crowd in and are mingled with the present:

> But in the aching aeons there are whiles
> That stop the Void's long yawn, that ease the groan
> Of calculated Failure. Unthought smiles
> That shone a moment on this path of stone
> Have had more meaning than vast well-meant hours
> That in the name of Love drained all love's pow'rs.

These lines refer to his arduous and persevering spiritual quest. However, it was a "calculated failure" in the end, a phrase which not only powerfully expresses his feeling of personal failure in not being able to settle during his monastic past, but also stresses his firm belief in providence. How painful the experience had been, and still is, is implied by images like "aching aeons", or "the Void's long yawn", which underlines the dimension of the pain experienced. The poet realizes that "Unthought smiles", despite their shortness, "Have had more meaning than vast well-meant hours / That in the name of Love drained all love's pow'rs". These lines suggest that little things can teach a lot more about love, and therefore about God, than many hours of automaticized spirituality and prayer. The capitalized "Love" refers to love in the theological sense, meaning the pure love of God, whereas "love" spelt with a small letter refers to human love. Such "vast well-meant hours" can drain "all love's pow'rs". The imagery used to describe the possible loss of love in a monastery is deeply disturbing, for there love is most essential.

Frequently the poems can be sung. "St. Valentine's day on Llanddwyn" (*Beyond*, 142), which was written to fit the notation of "Amazing Grace", is a good example. It is a tender love poem, whose mood is set in the very first line:

> How empty would the world have been,
>   Had one soul not been there!
> What hours no day would ne'er have seen,
>   Had paths collided ne'er!

The poem consists of four stanzas written in common metre. The spondee employed at the beginning of l.1 emphasizes the utter void the poet would experience, had his beloved not been there. The entire poem meditates on the theoretical possibility of what the world would be like, had their paths "collided ne'er", which is an implicit expression of his love. The presence of love is already implied in the very title, as both the date and the place, the isle of love, suggest the idea of love. In the closing stanza we read:

> And had the two that now were one
>   Glimpsed this day from afar,
> Would halves that were entire still shun
>   The pull of this strange star?

This stanza is different from the others in so far as it does not ponder about the idea of what would have been, had they not met, but rather what would have happened, had they known beforehand about "The pull of this strange star", the pull of love. The pantheistic touch at the end implies that the force of love originates in God as well: all belongs to God, there is no division into a secular and a divine world. Whatever the spark of love is, it comes from Him. How close the poet feels to his beloved is implied by the imagery used, "the two that now were one".

The following sonnet, "'Having your voice, I needed your touch'" (*Beyond*, 151) is characterized by almost excessive use of alliteration, assonance and consonance, as is indicated in italics:

> When parts of us can travel through the air
> And leave the rest behind; *w*hen *w*hat *w*e say
> Can through *th*ese cogs and *wh*ee*l*s yet *l*inger *th*ere
> Whi*le* Sound'*s* own organ*s* wa*n*der far away;
> *W*hen *w*e *c*an *s*ing a *s*o*ng*, *an*d hear a *s*igh
> Lo*ng* hours bey*on*d its e*n*di*ng*; *wh*e*n w*e *kn*ow
> That our heart's tears another *eye* wi*ll* cry
> And that burnt days can on this band sti*ll* g*l*ow,

> Then we do well to think what trace we leave
> On this our staggered present, we do well
> To see the parting hours one hour can cleave
> And think how heav'n ungrasped is deeper hell.
> And yet when there will be no more to hold,
> Will there be no use for a spark so old?

The first two quatrains are fairly straightforward, describing the recording of one's words on tape, which makes "parts of us" "travel through the air". The synectoche used in "cogs and wheels" apparently refers to the tape recorder. Ll.7f. imply that a written poem, just like a recorded voice, enables the reader or listener to re-experience the contents of the message and the feeling conveyed, "our heart's tears another eye will cry / And that burnt days can on this band still glow". In the third quatrain the poet reflects on what has been said before and makes the reader, just like himself, aware of the consequences involved, aware of what must not be forgotten: it is important to think of the "trace we leave" (l.9), i.e. we have to be aware of our actions and the consequences resulting from them. When writing down a poem, a letter even, the author leaves an indelible trace, his presence can be made long lasting. The idea of "verba volant, scripta manent" is implied. The power of the written word is imminent.

The pattern of alliteration used becomes more complex as the thought becomes more subtle, "how heav'n ungrasped is deeper hell" (l.12): this line has alliteration and consonance on five different consonants, with a clear pattern, /h-h-n-n-s-p-d-s-p-d-h/. The line contains a dense message and provokes elaborate meditations. When regarded in the context of the origin of the poem, it suggests that there can be great craving for the absent beloved person, which involves much suffering as well. In a more general sense, however, the line can be applied to religion, to one's belief: using all the chances which bring us closer to God, i.e. the beloved, logically draws us nearer to heaven. A missed chance makes us stagnate in our present state of belief, hence a "deeper hell" is involved. In terms of eschatology, all this likewise holds true, hence the abuse of grace has eternal consequences. The line also contains an anology between human and divine love: the idea of Christ as the beloved of the human soul can be visualized by comparing the love felt towards Him to the love between human beings. The important point here is that there is a communication of a living contact, - whether it is love felt towards a human being or love for God, "a spark so old" -, it is a power of loving which can regerminate, which can be sparked off again, as is implied in the closing lines of the poem. The power of freezing intense moments in some form and being able to pass the intensity on in time, not to lose it, is suggested. As Alun Idris points out in a letter, it is the same with mystics, "one can feel the fire of love reading these old mystics again long after they are gone, whether it is human or divine love. The fact is that we can freeze time, make it spark again long after we are gone" (letter, 6.5.1990). Both spiritual love and human love originate from the same flame, displaying the same power of loving. Writing about that love can endow the lines with eternal youth: when reading about the past love of people who have gone before us, we are able to experience their youth again, - in that sense time is rejuvenating itself (cf. letter, 6.5.1990).[196]

The title of the following poem called "Among the hiphils" (*Beyond*, 153) is clear only to those who master Hebrew: a hiphil is a Hebrew verb in the causative form. The poem, which is apparently placed in the context of studying, can be sung as well.[197] It consists of three stanzas written in iambic trimeters, with the rhyme scheme abbacddc. The outer lines of each embracing rhyme have masculine endings, the inner lines employ feminine endings. The first stanza meditates on the nature of quietly working together, a stanza which radiates much calm. The second one, though slightly uneven in rhythm, continues the meditation ("There are some little things / That are best said when silence / Can make heard its own eloquence"), and leads us to the closing stanza:

> And when there is no sense
> But only pulse of feeling
> And moments of long healing
> That carry long years hence,
> There is a passing stream
> Of knowing in soft holding,
> Of hearing in beholding
> The rays of Love's fair beam.

The lines are very gentle. The poet emphasizes the meaning conveyed by the sounds he uses, the music of the words. It reminds one of a gentle love song, vividly visualizing the situation which triggered off its composition. The poem fully incorporates a particular situation, - the whole atmosphere of a moment and all its connotations are captured therein. It enables the reader to re-live and re-experience that very moment as it was experienced by its author. In particular the lines with the feminine ending have a contemplative touch about them, describing these "moments of long healing" as they were experienced, these moments where there is "only pulse of feeling", contemplating them. The synesthesia employed in ll.6f. reinforces the atmosphere of harmony.

The consequences of an important decision are central to a sonnet called "A question" (*Beyond*, 158), as is apparent in the opening lines: "When but a sound can change a life or two / And one unuttered word can utter all". While this poem reflects the uncertainty as regards the outcome of a particular situation, "An answer" (*Beyond*, 160) suggests that now there is no doubt left, a decision has been made, as the very title implies. The poem is characterized by massive use of alliteration, assonance and consonance, particularly in the first two quatrains and the closing couplet, which emphasizes the idea of providence, the underlying pattern which has been made and pre-arranged before:

---

[196] Alun Idris explained that when reading those poems written in the monastery, he is filled with a strong yearning to be a novice again there, where he experienced that happy young love: it is still the same heart which beats, all the same love (cf. letter, 6.5.1990).
[197] The tune is an adapation of a French melody, as is indicated in a note.

> *W*hen in the dark *w*e *w*alk *w*ithout a *l*ight
> *S*ave one *s*mall *l*amp of *fai*th; when one *fai*nt cry
> Bears *up* the *p*rayer of *tw*o in*t*o the Height
> Of unseen Vision; when the ancient *sk*y
> Loo*ks* down with it*s* own *s*ilence on the land
> *W*here *m*ortals *l*ive and *l*ove *w*hile *l*augh they *m*ay;
> *W*hen on the edge of *W*anting *t*wo *s*ouls *st*and
> A*w*aiting but a *w*ord that *w*ould all say,
> Then there are many years within the folds
> Of one *s*mall envelope that one day *s*ent,
> And in the messages that dumb ink holds
> The earth to Heav'n a voice hath somehow lent.
> For though *w*e *w*ere al*one*, *w*e *w*ere *w*ell kn*own*,
> And could not give *w*hat *w*e did never *own*.

The difficulty of the situation is implied in the very first line, "When in the dark we walk without a light"; however, there is one light guiding them, "Save one small lamp of faith". This suggestion implies that the decision was placed in the Lord's hands, which is indicated by several other lines as well, as e.g. ll.3f. "the prayer of two into the Height / Of unseen Vision", "two souls stand / Awaiting but a word that would all say" (ll.7f.). God seemed to have provided the answer, as is firmly indicated in the closing couplet. It seemed as though they were alone, free to choose their future path, and yet "we were well known", the Lord was always present, He knew their need well. The final line implies that both of them had given themselves to the Lord. In a sense they were therefore not their own property and thus "could not give what we did never own". The alliteration and interior rhyme suggest the pre-arranged pattern, God as the guiding and leading hand behind the scene. The "envelope" mentioned in l.10 apparently contained a letter, whose message seemed like an answer to the question. Ll.11f. indicate that the letter was a sign from God, "in the messages that dumb ink holds / The earth To Heav'n a voice hath somehow lent".

The rhythmical pattern at the beginning of "'One day it will stop beating'" (*Beyond*, 165) is striking: we find a threefold repetition in the first two lines, "A beat, a beat, another beat of love, / Unheard, unnoticed, yet unwearied still". In the first line, "beat" is repeated, while in the second line, the negative prefix appears three times, which suggests the steady pounding of our heart that is not consciously noticed. The repetition is taken up again in l.12: "But one, but one, but one beat coming still ..." The exact repetition emphasizes the regular nature of the heartbeat. The closing couplet, slightly removed from the preceding three quatrains, is an honest declaration of love, directly related to the title of the poem: "Should one sound no more come, would anything / Again in this Creation ever sing?" Her loss would be most painful, as is firmly conveyed in these lines: the world would lose all its beauty. This idea can be found in several further sonnets as well, e.g. "'You're not letting me go'" (*Beyond*, 172). Here the decision has already been made, the Lord appears to want them for Himself, which is obviously causing inner strain and struggle:

> O angel, shall not we behold the light
> Of molten love that flowed from breast to breast?

Will the unknown yet now escape the sight
Of our awakened eyes, and shall here rest
The dreams of all our yesterdays unshared?
Do many morrows lie 'neath eastern seas
Of nought but wantings made? Are we ensnared
By what stray hours have found 'mid yearns like these?
O heart of Man, vast cosmos of a soul,
What pow'rs of pain lie 'tween thy pulsing walls!
These little valves that tap the ages' toll
Feel too each aching second as it falls
Upon the senses of the great abyss
Within this inward hell of wanted bliss.

The pain experienced by the poet is firmly implied, - the rhythm used underlines the inner suffering. The use of questions suggest the idea of unrest which characterizes the situation. The first two quatrains reflect the cause of the inner strain: can it be that their "awakened eyes", the first experience of "molten love that flowed from breast to breast" is to cease again, after so short a time? Can it be that they shall not "behold the light / Of molten love", an image which emphasizes the love experienced. The imagery stresses how great his love is, suggesting at the same time how immense the suffering therefore must be. The exclamation in ll.9f. is an outcry of pain: "O heart of Man, vast cosmos of a soul / What pow'rs of pain lie 'tween thy pulsing walls!" Here again the vastness of the soul by implication underlines the degree of despair and pain currently experienced. He himself seems to be amazed at the "pow'rs of pain" his heart is capable of enduring. The closing lines summarize the cause of this pain, when we read about the "great abyss / Within this inward hell of wanted bliss". This oxymoron emphasizes the degree of his pain. The poem echoes the tremendous suffering, pain and struggling experienced by the poet when he started to realize that God wanted the two of them for Himself, as every single line hints at the poet's love for her.

Sufferings involved through love, the pain felt when the beloved person is absent, are central to "Help" (*Beyond*, 190), a poem whose title already indicates the abject need for assistance. Towards the end of the sonnet, the poet addresses the human heart in an emotional outburst, which touchingly reveals how close love and sorrow are:

O little, little thing, O human heart,
Wast thou made big enough to hold the strain
Of cosmic Hurt, and was there ever art
To lessen for an hour the oldest pain?
O Craftsman of the years, thy *sen*t*inels
Were *sent* in *t*ime *t*o hold *s*ome bla*st* that *s*wells.

The use of the conventional term "oldest pain" and the original expression "cosmic Hurt" is an effective combination which reinforces the intensity of the pain felt, caused by love. The repetition of "little, little" in the apostrophe emphasizes the frailty of the human heart, how hard it is to imagine that it is capable of containing this tremendous pain, "the strain / Of cosmic Hurt". The imagery of the closing couplet is striking: the "sentinels" is an effective metaphor for help supplied by the Lord, the "Craftsman of the years". The accumulation of s's and t's is a means to emphasize, almost suspiciously in view of the massive accumulation, how dangerous the situation was: "to hold some blast that swells". It seems as though the inner pain was growing rapidly, - the pressure produced was almost too much to bear.

The following lines to be quoted here speak for themselves. Their honesty, their sweetness, yet their sober nature are bound to elicit an echo in the reader. The poem meditates on "What in a sound can lie, what in a name" (l.1), as is suggested by the very title of the poem, her name. In the closing lines we read:

> O meeting of all meanings in a word!
> Could I have known the resonance of sound,
> Would I upon a day have calmly heard
> Two notes that now a symphony have found
> That will play on until the beating heart
> Can cope no more with harmonies that part?[198]

The long vowel /iː/ which appears twice in the first line echoes her name, which is dominated by the very same vowel, just as the "two notes" refer to the two syllables of her name. The exclamatory "O meeting of all meanings in a word!" leaves no doubt about how much she means to him. These "Two notes that now a symphony have found" suggest the tremendous echo her name produces within him, arousing a whole symphony of sounds within. Using the term "symphony" in this context underlines the harmony experienced when she is present. This "symphony" will play on "until the beating heart / Can cope no more with harmonies that part?" - a graphic image despicting the state of his heart. Singing a song in harmony suggests the unity of the song; however, "harmonies that part" implies that the song will not be sung together anymore, their ways are to part literally. The pain caused by the separation is firmly suggested by the imagery used in the closing lines.

There are several poems which contemplate the love he feels in a most touching way. "Un ange inconnu" (*Beyond*, 186), written on the feast of the Immaculate Conception, is one of these beautiful lyrical love poems offering insight into the poet's emotional world:

> There is a little angel that the world
> Knows nothing of, that fluttered from beyond
> Imagination's hope, and swiftly whirled
> Away to whence it came. Some magic wand
> Did tap the fairest soul that could have been
> And bid it be, and gave it form to hold
> The wonder of a being never seen
> Within this lonely vale of tears untold.
> It will be said that this is blasphemy,
> That one in Sion was the fairest maid,
> And yet there was but one that was for me
> From Beauty moulded and for my soul made.
> And I perceive that I am bound to be
> A part of what I was ere I felt thee.

---

[198] *Beyond*, 180.

The first two quatrains contemplate the "wonder of a being never seen / Within this lonely vale of tears untold": his wonder and amazement at the very existence of this "little angel", who "fluttered from beyond / Imagination's hope", is powerfully implied. The "vale of tears" is an echo of the hymn "Salve Regina", where we find the expression "in hac lacrimarum valle" (Hellinghaus 1921, 65), "in this valley of tears". This reference underlines the connection to Our Lady, who appears in the third quatrain. To the poet this "ange inconnu" is "the fairest soul that could have been", a suggestion which is justified in ll.9f.: "Filia Sion" is used as an expression for Our Lady. Of course, the poet does not deny that Our Lady "was the fairest maid, / And yet there was but one that was for me / From Beauty *moulde*d and for *my soul made*". The musical, harmonious effect in this line is arresting, the imagery used powerfully conveying how much he feels he belongs to her. There cannot be any doubt about his incompleteness without her.

The following sonnet, "'One day you'll do as did Ronsard's friend'" (*Beyond*, 196), is another example of utmost tenderness towards his beloved, each single line expressing the poet's love:

> When gold to silver has with ageing turned
> And these same eyes look out upon a world
> That has grown older too; when days have burned
> The fuel of their first yearning, wherein whirled
> Ecstatic minds in love, will these two lips
> Their impish smile still make; will this same face
> Through wearied skin still shine as slowly slips
> The radiance of thy morn apace, apace?
> Can angels age with aeons; can there be
> Less warmth within the heart made all of care?
> And when the years have cut their lines in thee,
> These features that mean all, will they be there?
> And will that cherub-look look back awhile
> At old fond words, and, looking, give a smile?

The dominance of long vowels and diphthongs radiates peace and affection, which is central to the poem. Assonance is to be noticed frequently, suggesting tender progression, - also a progression in age. It is only when the poet refers to his beloved's present state, her youth and beauty, that short vowels and explosive sounds are used, as in "ecstatic", "impish" or "cherub-look". The rhymes are all monosyllabic full rhymes (except for the closing couplet and the rhyme "face" - "apace" in the second quatrain), which lighten the poem and make it sound fresh and vivid.

The very first line beautifully suggests the progress of time, "When gold to silver has with ageing turned", changing her golden hair into silver. The imagery used to describe her mirrors his love: "The radiance of thy morn" (l.8), "the heart made all of care" (l.10), "these features that mean all" (l.12); words like these do not ask for explanation, - they are carefully chosen to express his feelings. "The radiance of thy morn" is a most beautiful and tender image to describe the beloved, radiant and shining, full of light and warmth as the sun. The metaphorical question "Can angels age with aeons" (1.9) includes his beloved, as well as the love he feels towards her, a timeless being, an angel, who will not age through the years, any more than "aeons": an ideal love is presented.

The onomatopoetical effect of the lines below, quoted from "Waiting in the Library" (*Beyond*, 189), is highly effective: despite its sober title, the sonnet is another striking example of overflowing feelings. In the closing lines we read:

> The world is full of feet that walk and walk,
> Yet one sole patter ends the roving yearn
> That hears not sound in song nor truth in talk
> For that it did in gazing this once learn,
> That of all faces one alone would shine,
> That but one could e'er utter, "You are mine."

The first line moves at a rather rapid pace, thereby suggesting the stepping of feet, which is particularly noticeable in libraries. The accumulation of plosives and the use of short vowels underline the echoing of quick steps. However, the speed is abruptly reduced at the beginning of 1.2, with the two initial spondees as well as the long vowels and diphthongs. The spondees place heavy emphasis on these words, suggesting that there is one patter only which "ends the roving yearn". The assonance in "sole" and "roving" additionally underlines the close link felt between this "one sole patter" and the poet's yearning. The poem becomes more and more tender in tone towards the end, as the poet exclusively concentrates on his beloved. "Of all faces one alone would shine" beautifully mirrors the love he feels for her.

Another example of a love lyric, which seems to surge directly from the heart, is "'O lili wen fach, o ble daethost ti?'" (*Beyond*, 203), written on St. Valentine's Day. The title of the poem refers to a popular Welsh song to the snowdrop, "O little white lily, whence didst thou come?", the snowdrop, the white lily being, of course, a metaphor for his beloved:

> I cannot be without a part of me
> That is by hurting there when far away.
> The hours that could have been no more may be,
> For what was left unstirred could p'haps obey
> The frozen will, the chill of chosen peace
> From all that need intrude - but this strange thing,
> The knowing that a being may not cease
> To be half of the world, to Time shall cling.
> O angel, had thy wings not spread their spell
> Upon these little cells that chanced to hide
> Beneath thine unsought flight, 'twould have been well,
> Th'untroubled walk of strangers side by side.
> But I have known thee, I have shown thee all,
> And my unknowing may no more recall.

From the very first line onwards we feel the presence of love. The paradox in 1.2 suggests how much the poet suffers from the absence of his beloved, this "part of me / That is by hurting there when far away". The melodious nature of the first quatrain describing his beloved suggests a tone of longing mingled with melancholy. The hissing sounds in 1.5, however, already commencing at the end of l.4, indicate a change: "could p'haps obey / The frozen will, the chill of chosen peace". The internal rhyme in "will" - "chill" and the alliteration in "chill" and "chosen" make the line appear uneven and scarcely harmonious, thereby suggesting how forced and unnatural the situation without his love would be. The image of the "frozen will" completes the idea of the brutality of a separation, which seems insufferable to him. Equally, the "chill of chosen peace" powerfully suggests that, although a separation would bring peace to his tossed soul, it would be a freezing peace, a decision made by cold reason alone. However, even a separation could not alter the fact that "a being may not cease / To be half of the world", as we read in ll.7f. She will remain part of him, even a half of him forever. The third quatrain starts with a mournful, melancholic apostrophe: "O angel, had thy wings not spread their spell / Upon these little cells that chanced to hide / Beneath thine unsought flight, 'twould have been well". The imagery used to describe the magic power of love is striking. Angels do not cast a spell, thus the poet suggests that it was her wings which "spread the spell", which adds a much more gentle touch than the use of "cast" would have done. Yet it implies that there is no way back. Under the spell of her wings he "chanced to hide", thereby implying the harmony and shelter experienced in her presence. However, in the closing couplet the poet is bound to realize that these are all merely hypothetical speculations of what might have happened, had he not met her: "But I have known thee, I have shown thee all, / And my unknowing may no more recall." Their encounter cannot be reversed; even more, he cannot even remember what it was like before they met.

The following poem called "Just one" (*Beyond*, 231) is written in common metre and consists of seven stanzas. The poet has composed a tune for it as well, which increases its force as a love lyric. There is a certain lament noticeable throughout the entire poem. It has a melancholic touch about it, caused by the omnipresent feeling of loneliness. It is a loneliness the poet has apparently known before.

> The world is less a lonely place
>   When there is one, but one
> To whom the features of one face
>   Are where a world has shone.
>
> The world is less a lonely place
>   When there are but two eyes
> Whose gaze bears some old healing grace
>   To one who was unwise.

The first two stanzas reveal the structure employed throughout the entire poem. The first line is used as a kind of refrain, being repeated in every stanza, while in l.2 the poet employs a parallel structure. The refrain emphasizes how much he has suffered from loneliness before. He seems to be telling us of his own personal experience. The image of "healing grace" in l.3 of the second stanza hints at the suffering which was his lot. "To one who was unwise" (l.4) suggests that as a result of (perhaps) unwise decisions he was bound to suffer a great deal. The first two stanzas firmly imply how much this "face", these "two eyes" mean to him. In her face

"a world has shone", a world as bright and warm as the sun. The stanzas are very smooth in sound, long vowels and diphthongs predominate and create a peaceful atmosphere. In addition, the l's of the refrain augment the atmosphere of tranquillity and peace. The line "To *o*ne who *w*as un*w*ise" is particularly smooth in sound as a result of the dominating /w/.
The senses are the organising principle behind this poem. Each of the seven stanzas concentrates on one of the senses, except the last one: the first two stanzas seem to suggest the visual, while the following four imply the sense of touch, of hearing, of smell and of taste.

>The world is less a lonely place
>   When there is *bu*t a *t*ouch
>Tha*t b*id*s* the hear*t* bea*t* on a*p*ace
>   'Neath *p*ulsings *f*el*t* as such.
>
>The world is less a lonely place
>   When there is but a sound
>That smooths the lines that worries trace
>   On temples that oft frowned.

The third stanza is quicker in rhythm, underlined by the use of shorter vowels and plosives (as is indicated in italics). The change in rhythm corresponds to the acceleration of the heart beat, which seems to be quicker when seeing her face.
The fourth stanza returns to his sad experiences in the past: by memorizing the pain felt then the poet emphasizes how great the healing is which is taking place now.
The closing stanza summarizes what has been implied before: her presence, which he apparently experiences as being very powerful, is most precious to him. The time she spends with him is very special. The poem is a celebration of his love.

>The world is less a lonely place
>   When there is but a friend
>Who in the hurry of this race
>   Had moments yet to spend.

People are endowed with value by being wanted on earth, either by other persons or by God Himself. How important it is to be needed is implied in "'He departed without being desired'" (*Beyond*, 202), a poem reflecting on the death of a person who died without a friend present. The poem is characterized by plays on words and sounds, and the use of long, elaborate sentences. Through trying to find the best expression for an idea, striving for perfection in the imagery used, the verse lacks vividness at times on account of all too elaborate sentence structures.

>To *k*now that we *k*now *n*o*t* wha*t* sha*ll* befa*ll*
>Our unmarked tracks, to *l*ie in *l*imbo *l*ong
>*W*ithout a *w*ord, with nothing hea*r*d at all,
>Is to love much yet to *no*ne to belo*n*g,
>To want what may not be and yet may be,
>To cling *h*ard to a *h*ope not fully snapped
>And be for one more day at liberty
>To be by someone, Someone, sometime trapped.

> To be but wanted is to have a soul
> That sparkled in the aeons just an hour -
> The hour that was its own - for moments stroll
> In aimless amble on when none would pour
> A soothing sound upon th'un-needed one
> That grew and wilted 'neath a hurried sun.

The poem is maintained on an impersonal note throughout. The infinitives and pronouns, like "none", "one", "someone", strongly convey the idea of impersonality. There is no personal bond whatsoever, which perfectly corresponds to the title of the poem. The rhetorical parallelism, almost excessively used in this sonnet, is a device to emphasize this idea. The poem contains a number of contradictions, which add to the mood of unease created: "To know that we know not" (l.1), "To want what may not be and yet may be" (l.5), "liberty" (l.7) - "trapped" (l.8). The use of the word "trapped" is ironical, as in this context it is to be seen positively only: "To be by someone, Someone, sometime trapped" refers to the call of a person or of God Himself ("Someone"), the significant point being to be *wanted* by someone. The first two stanzas aim to suggest the "limbo" of a person who is not wanted, not desired by others. L.6 in particular presents this idea: "To cling hard to a hope not fully snapped" perfectly conveying a notion of insecurity and impermanence. The third quatrain introduces the idea of how important it is to be needed: "To be but wanted is to have a soul / That sparkled in the aeons just an hour / - The hour that was its own -". One is given a value by being wanted while on earth. There is a contrast implied between such a person who has been given value in this way and one for whom time strolls on in "aimless amble". The imagery used in the line "when none would pour / A soothing sound upon th'un-needed one" powerfully suggests the solitary, lonely nature of someone not wanted. For him "moments stroll / In aimless amble on", - there does not seem a proper aim, a destiny for him, which makes him end "wilted 'neath a hurried sun".

In autumn 1991, the decision crystallized that Alun Idris would join the Norbertine Canons in Kilnacrott. The sonnet "Accepted" (*Beyond*, 242) reminds one of a farewell to his "little angel", whom he even addresses as "archangel" in this poem. The first two quatrains reflect the poet's happiness at being able to join the community, although mingled with melancholy when remembering the difficulties of the past. These quatrains can equally be read outside that specific context in a more general sense: they reflect the reception of a message one has desperately longed for after so many failures and disappointments.

> What in a word resides, what in a sound,
> None knows save one who waited for it long.
> What peace can bathe a track, a small path found,
> None sees save one who did to night belong.
> There is yet hope, for we grope not alone,
> But hold the Hand that placed a mark or two,
> Enough that we might tread from stone to stone
> Along an ancient footpath that it knew.
> Farewell, archangel that from Heaven came;
> Complain no more of strokings too well felt.

> Shine on in thy fond smiling still the same,
> For 'tis the gaze that did my winter melt.
> Move on to cherub heights, and there abide,
> And if I reach there first, I'll for thee hide.

The parallelism employed in the first quatrain underlines how much it means to him to be accepted: only the one who just like him "waited for it long" and "did to night belong", only such a person is able to fully grasp and understand what it means to him to have received this answer. The second quatrain mirrors the poet's belief in providence. He knows that he does not walk alone on this path: "But hold the Hand that placed a mark or two, / Enough that we might tread from stone to stone / Along an ancient footpath that it knew." The capitalized synectoche "Hand" refers, of course, to the Lord and His guiding us safely. The image of treading "from stone to stone" (1.7) powerfully suggests the roughness of the path: it seems as though we did not see more than just the next stone, although the footpath is "ancient", - it was conceived for us long ago. The third quatrain and the closing couplet are exclusively dedicated to his love, whom he - for the first time - addresses as "archangel that from Heaven came": the metaphor used for her not only suggests his feelings for her, but also how much he considers her to have been sent from God in a period of strain, - "the gaze that did my winter melt". The still strong affective bond between them is apparent in the imagery used in this quatrain. The closing couplet takes up the metaphor employed before, "Move on to cherub heights", which also reflects her intention to enter Carmel.

This selection of poems mirrors the intensity of love and friendship he experienced: unbounded bliss as well as deep sorrow at the beloved's absence are reflected in the verse. The honesty radiating from the poems, mostly sonnets, allows Alun Idris to frequently capture the atmosphere of a particular moment, encorporating the rapture into his musings. The considerable number of poems written to celebrate this relationship underlines the intensity of the love he experienced. The poems are bathed in the spirit of prayer: both of the partners feel God's pull and seriously consider joining a religious community, as is apparent in the texts, - a pull which they finally submitted to. The poems are also deeply rooted in the Welsh countryside: the beauty of many a Welsh island finds an echo in the verse, which lends them an additional distinctive quality.

3.4.7. THE DIVINE PULL: CELEBRATING THE LOVE OF GOD

The poems included in this chapter mirror the tremendous force of the divine pull felt by the poet. The poems were written at a time when great uncertainty still prevailed as regards Alun Idris' future. It was unclear which path he would opt for, whether entering a contemplative monastery again, being ordained as a priest, which he longed for, living as a hermit or remaining in the secular world. The poems clearly demonstrate the enormous force the divine exerted on the poet. We find many beautiful declarations and celebrations of his love for God. The affective bond with his Creator has not diminished at all, but is becoming steadily stronger. Frequently, by comparing the two loves he feels so powerfully within himself, the love for God and the love for the "little angel", as was demonstrated in the previous chapter, the poet not only indicates that human love is an aspect of divine love, but also that he is bound to realize that God's pull is stronger in the end: both the poet and his beloved experienced that their pull towards God is stronger, an insight which is reflected in the poems considered below.

The love towards his "angel" is tremendous, as is apparent in numerous poems. By describing this love he feels for her, but at the same time indicating that there is another love, which is even stronger and more powerful than the unbounded passion he feels for her, the poet firmly suggests that his love for God stands above all: nothing compares to the love he entertains for the Lord. In the first two quatrains of "Little mother" (*Beyond*, 173) Alun Idris meditates on the nature of trust, implying the idea of how difficult it is to find someone whom one can trust: "there are some / Who ne'er shall trust, for never was trust there." In the third quatrain, however, he addresses his beloved, whom he trusts entirely:

> O angel, I had trusted, I had felt
> The feeling of a meeting never met
> Within the wait of years, yet as we knelt
> Together 'neath the Cross, some feeling yet
> Was somehow left unfelt, for there was more
> That we both knew, for we had loved before.

The love he feels towards his "angel" has never been experienced before, as is firmly implied, - "The feeling of a meeting never met". The alliteration in "*W*ithin the *w*ait of years" underlines the uniqueness of this experience never felt before. However, the consonance in this third quatrain on -t suggests a limitation of some kind, which cannot be traced in the closing lines, dominated by voiced consonants implying peace: "for there was *m*ore / *w*e *b*oth *kn*ew, for *w*e had *l*oved *b*efore." The rhyme on the long vowel /ɔː/ in "more", "for", "before" adds to the feeling of peace, as do the long vowels and diphthongs. However, long vowels are used in the third quatrain too, in particular when addressing and talking about her: "angel", "feeling of a meeting". The rhythmical change in "yet as we knelt / Together 'neath the Cross", which is of a much quicker rhythm than the aforegoing, indicates the change: there is something even stronger than that feeling of trust he had never felt before. Kneeling in front of the Cross together made both of them aware that "there was more": both of them "had loved before", both of them had known God's love previously. They realize that nothing compares with this love, "some feeling yet / Was somehow left unfelt". The love they feel towards each other is great, and yet there is something missing, as is implied in these lines. Having known God's love, having loved before, they are bound to realize that His pull is stronger.

In the following sonnet called "There" (*Beyond*, 205) the poet meditates on how the divine presence can be felt on earth, how the presence of the Lord is experienced. This experience of the divine differs from experiencing the presence of human love:

> When Thou art there, sweet Lord, there is no sound,
> But only Presence felt, and every word
> That from the Godhead comes, to flesh is bound,
> In that in the event the Truth is heard
> And every act bespeaks the fact to be
> Reread for ever on the charts of years
> That mark the turns that steered Eternity,
> For 'tis in looking well that the heart hears.
> When thou art there, sweet maid, at times there are
> In sounds that fill the air some meanings sent,
> But there are presences that can be far
> From frightened breasts that know not what is meant.
> For there are meanings that no sound can hold,
> And there are stories that but One was told.

The first part of this poem, notably the first two quatrains, deals with the nature of divine Presence, which is felt rather than heard or sensed otherwise: "there is no sound, / But only Presence felt". However, a word sent by God reaches us via other persons, "to flesh is bound, / In that in the event the Truth is heard": God's word can be perceived by the senses, while His presence can only be felt. In the second quatrain the idea of listening to His word present in "every act" is emphasized: "every act bespeaks the fact to be / Reread for ever on the charts of years". The assonance in "bespeaks" and "be" reinforces the link between the "act" visible on earth and the divine origin and message behind, the act which "bespeaks the fact to be". The divine word is implied in these acts, it speaks through these acts, tells us the truth. The Lord is present in other people, the Truth is experienced in events. The "fact to be / Reread for ever on the charts of years / That mark the turns that steered Eternity" implies the action of providence, whose course and ways frequently cannot be understood by the human soul, an idea which is reinforced by 1.8, "For 'tis in looking well that the heart hears". The synesthesia effectively suggests listening to the divine word experienced in events through contemplation, "looking well": it is important to look with the eye of faith, to be open to grace, as such "looking well" enables the heart to hear God's words. The Lord is silent, He speaks to us through events. Therefore we have to have our souls, our hearts attuned to that silent voice. The line receives special emphasis through the pyrrhic followed by the spondee at the very end ("that the *h*eart *h*ears"), assisted by alliteration. The following passage by Henry Chadwick might throw additional light on these lines:

> Even to a writer as early as the author of Acts (probably c. 80 A.D.), the expansion of the Church seemed an extraordinary chain of improbablilities. Nothing could have been less likely to succeed by any ordinary standard of expectation. It appeared as a long story of strange coincidence in which human intentions played a subordinate role and where the eye of faith was entitled to discern the tranquil operation of a wiser providence. (Chadwick 1990, 54)

All eternity is the eternity of one unique history, "the charts of years" (1.6). There is no way one can change history once it is written.

The secular counterpart of the first line "When Thou art there, sweet Lord" is to be found in 1.9: "When thou art there, sweet maid, at times there are / In sounds that fill the air some meaning sent". "At times" indicates that these meanings are not always present, which differentiates them from the firm and stable "every word" in 1.2, referring to the Godhead. In the presence of the "sweet maid", his love, "there are presences that can be *far / From frightened* breasts that know *not what* is *meant*" (ll.11f.): the oxymoron of the far presences indicates that the communication between the soul and God is much more direct than it is between human beings. The alliteration used in "*far / From frightened*" indicates a certain disharmony, underlined by the consonance used towards the end of l.12.

The presence of a beloved person reminds one of the divine Presence, as both of them have in common the presence of love. However, the difference between these loving presences is summarized in the closing couplet: "For there are meanings that no sound can hold, / And there are stories that but One was told". The difficulty with human presence and communication is that not everything can be expressed with words, as there are things which can only be felt, feelings, which happen to be the Lord's language ("But only Presence felt" (1.2)); what the poet seeks to imply is that, although the word of God reaches us through events, through other persons, His presence can only be felt: "there are meanings that no sound can hold." Words are not capable of expressing all. They can be complemented by feeling vis-à-vis experiencing the Lord; however, a gap remains as regards human communication, as "there are stories that but One was told", which only God knows.

If one feels the divine pull, there is no escape from it: this message is implied in "Rhiw Goch and Carmel" (*Beyond*, 222). Rhiw Goch is the birthplace of St. John Roberts, as we are told in a note. The sonnet reflects the visit to this place and praying in the Welsh Carmel, as the title indicates. The poet's beloved felt God's pull strongly as well, - she was seriously considering the possibility of entering the Order of the Carmelites. The sonnet reflects the mighty attraction felt by both of them to dedicate their lives to God:

> Beneath this veil there hides an utter force
> That utters nought but matters much to some
> That passing by have once here fixed the course
> Of lengthy vacant hours thenceforth to come.
> Beneath this tent is rent the pulling heart
> That could see what is seen, that could love well,
> And yet, strange unseen Love, here where Thou art
> Can no more think with what is seen to dwell.
> There is a fire that burns the very soul,
> And scorched e'en is the land where some have trod,
> And, sister, we perhaps unwisely stroll
> In regions densely mingled with our God.
> For there are some who come not back again
> From this excruciating Bliss of pain.

The poem is dedicated entirely to describing the force of the divine pull. The first two quatrains differ in rhythm, but they are united by the anaphora employed ("Beneath this veil", "Beneath this tent"). The regular rhythm of the first quatrain provides an atmosphere of peace and tranquility, which is experienced in the Carmelite Order. The force of their silence in God is expressed in the first two lines: "Beneath this veil there hides an *utter* force / That *utters* nought but *matters m*uch to some". The word-play on "utter", the consonance and alliteration, help to underline the tremendous power that hides "Beneath this veil", the dynamic drive which is manifest in these nuns, the presence of divine love. The radiating force is so strong that many a passer-by "fixed the course / Of lengthy vacant hours thenceforth to come". The force ensnared them, and made them join the order, where many hours are spent in adoration of the Eucharist, the Blessed Sacrament, as is implied in 1.4. The second quatrain alludes to the power of human love, which does not in the least bear comparison with the love felt towards God. Realizing this tremendous power of God, feeling again the presence of Love, of Christ "Beneath this tent", is implied in this quatrain, marked by a change in rhythm: many spondees are to be found in this quatrain, which suggests the poet's excitement at experiencing the divine Presence. The spondaic "this tent" (1.5) emphasizes the power radiating from the tabernacle. The stresses in 1.6, "could see what", "could love well" echo memories of the past, suggesting the fascination of human love they had experienced. "And yet" at the beginning of 1.7 indicates that the force of such love cannot, however, be compared to divine love: again the accumulation of stresses, the spondees in the second and fifth foot, the inversion in the fourth point to the power of the love of God. The rhythm returns to regularity in the third quatrain, back to the peace and tranquillity felt at Carmel, despite the "fire that burns the very soul": the yearning to be burning there before the Blessed Sacrament. In ll.12f. the poet ironically suggests that it is dangerous ground on which they are treading. They are in "danger" of being caught by the monastic spirit: "For there are some who come not back again / From this excruciating Bliss of pain." The paradox of the final line expresses the paradox of living in a monastery: it is a mingling of feelings, full of bliss on the one hand, but also of painful experiences at times on the other.

The Dominican ideal is to contemplate and to hand on the fruits of contemplation to others. St. Thomas Aquinas and also St. Norbert felt drawn to such an ideal. When Alun Idris was in retreat at Kilnacrott Abbey for the very first time, he read about the life of St. Norbert, as we are told in a note attached to "Contemplare, et contemplata aliis tradere" (*Beyond*, 235). St. Norbert had lived as a hermit for a time, before he was called to share his experience: his ideal was not to work just for his own sanctification, but to bring others to sanctification through the liturgy and the eucharist in particular. Thus St. Norbert became the apostle of the eucharist (cf. letter, 26.8.1991).[199]

> O Master of the vineyard, what are these
> White robes that are yet offered to a soul
> That could again be plunged in grace, which sees
> The small, the great, the greater, and the whole

---

[199] "His character was not inclined towards the restful, contemplative life. He was a man of fiery temperament and engaging word, a man driven by the needs of his time, not a withdrawn ascetic but much more a man of deed." (Hurk 1984, 73)

> Within a moment's vision, when the sight
> Of what is seen and studied is seen less
> Than things not yet beheld in regions bright
> That open at the stroke of limbs that bless?
> O world beyond the world, can words beget
> New angel bands to walk toward thy shore,
> And is there use for thought more fruitful yet
> Than inward thinking, that packed well its store?
> Is there a way, good Lord, that we can walk
> Together thought in thought, and of this talk?

The encounter with St. Norbert, reading about his life, had a considerable impact on the poet, as is apparent in this sonnet. The wonder and excitement at the possiblity of joining the Norbertine Canons at Kilnacrott is firmly outlined in the first quatrain, which starts by addressing Christ. He knows that his soul "could again be plunged in grace", a beautiful image suggesting the bliss and happiness felt when dedicating one's life entirely to the Lord. Ll.4f. underline the contemplative aspect of the order, allowing the soul to see "The small, the great, the greater, and the whole / Within a moment's vision": the enumeration conveys an idea of steady progression, the art of contemplation has to be practised as well. The fruits of meditation constantly grow, until at last "the whole" is seen "within a moment's vision". The second quatrain introduces the idea of transmitting this experience to others, letting them partake the bliss felt. It had been this balance that St. Norbert had tried to strike between the active and contemplative life. He felt that his call was to make God available to others, which is implied in these lines. Those "regions bright", experiencing the Lord, "open at the stroke of limbs that bless": the imagery used powerfully suggests the presence of Love which is central to this order. By touching those "limbs that bless", by getting into contact with those who have experienced the divine, it is possible to open new "regions bright" for them as well. This call to share one's sanctification with others is not new to Alun Idris: the writing of poetry has, in a way, been an attempt to share his experience of the Lord with others. Although for a long time he did not know that his verse would be published one day, the hope was, nevertheless, there that eventually his poems would reach other souls, and be of help to them.

The third quatrain exclusively meditates on the idea of spreading the faith by combining the active and contemplative life: "can words beget / New angel bands to walk toward thy shore". The rhetorical question is used as a means to emphasize that it is possible to create "new angel bands" by spreading God's words, by not restricting oneself to a contemplative's life only, as is suggested in ll.11f. The closing couplet summarizes what has been said before, advocating the combination of the active and contemplative life.[200]

---

[200] "There are in Norbert's life many divergent directions [...]. If one wants to see in Norbert an example for our times one should look at him as a patron against all despondency and the saint of ever new beginnings." (Hurk 1984, 73). St. Norbert remains an engaging figure: the voice of this great charismatic personality has not been stilled by the centuries. This is another reason why he is a fascinating figure for Alun Idris.

"I am here. Why look any further?" (*Beyond*, 236) is a sonnet which refers to a long period of time spent before the monstrance, as we are told in a note in brackets. The poem radiates the love felt for God while contemplating the Blessed Sacrament:

> O little ring of glory made of love,
> Look on and on and on and melt the all.
> Small particle of essence from above,
> In dead of night without a sound a call
> From depth of Presence dense removes the earth
> From many orbits' centre, and these rays
> With which Man's art would point t'ward Godhead's worth
> Would seem to point to where must point my days.

The lines reflect the poet's meditation in front of the Eucharist, - they visualize the situation of contemplating the Lord. The "little ring" refers to the Body of Christ enclosed in the monstrance: as the symbol of harmony, the ring suggests the perpetual peace and love present in the Blessed Sacrament, but also hints at the deep devotion he feels he has for the Body of Christ. The repetition in l.2 suggests the nature of contemplating and being contemplated: the Host radiates with power and the heat of love, it can "melt the all". The beauty of contemplating the Host in silence, "in dead of night without a sound", is presented in ll.3ff. L.5 in particular affirms the poet's unreserved belief in the supreme vehicle of grace, in the Holy Eucharist, the "Presence dense". "These rays / With which Man's art would point t'ward Godhead's worth" refers to the monstrance itself, whose rays start from the centre, where the Body of Christ is conserved. Contemplating the rays of the monstrance make the poet realize that they point "to where must point my days": to a life dedicated entirely to the Lord.

"Λέγει αὐτῷ, Ἀκολούθει μοι" (*Beyond*, 238) was written for a clothing at Carmel, as is indicated in a note. The Greek title means "He said/says to him: follow me". On reading the poem one feels that the clothing of this nun is a harbinger of the poet's own entry at Kilnacrott. The tone is gentle and peaceful, and yet the rhythm conveys a certain expectation, reflecting the happiness of the occasion. The poem consists of four quatrains written in iambic pentameter, rhyming in couplets. Most of lines have an inverted first foot, which conveys the sense of excitement. The first three stanzas are dedicated to the newly clothed nun. They constitute a prayer written for her, although one might view the whole as a hymn, for the poem was written to fit the notation of "Abide with me":

> O gentle voice, whose noise is seldom heard,
> Voice of my Lord, speak on without a word,
> Bid silence heed the echo of a sound
> Hid from all ears save hers whom Thou hast found.
>
> Master, speak on: Thy servant listens here
> Where Thou art present, where Thy touch is near.
> Words are true words when all is left unsaid,
> For 'tis in silence that e'en angels tread.

The young lady has heard that "gentle voice", a silent voice only rarely heard, and has responded to it. The accumulated use of voiced /z/ and voiceless /s/ in l.1 and also in l.4, as is indicated in italics, suggests the whispering voice the nun has heard: it was the "Voice of my Lord". The poet prays that the voice might continue speaking to her in silence, "speak on without a word", for God can only be perceived in silence. The urgency of his message is emphasized by the inversion of the first foot in l.2 and the medial break which follows. The spondaic first foot in l.3 reinforces the urgency. A closer look at the sounds used in the first stanza shows the balance of the pattern: the diphthong /ɔɪ/ unites the first couplet, while the pattern of vowels in "Bid" - "heed" is repeated in "Hid - "ears" in the second couplet. The consonance employed in l.4 ("ears" - "hers") adds to the symmetry.

The second stanza picks up the idea of the importance of silence already implied in the first stanza: "Words are true words when all is left unsaid" firmly suggests the fulness contained in silence, - the Lord's silent voice can only be heard in silence.

While the first three stanzas are dedicated to the clothing at Carmel, the poet continues with his own hope of hearing the call again in the fourth stanza:

> Call, call again; I'd follow where here trod
> Virgins who felt the treading of their God.
> Master, I'd come; I'd come and follow Thee;
> Bid words of silence be enough for me.

The short exclamatory sentences stress the urge, the pauses reinforce his excitement. Both the first and the last line start with a spondaic foot, while ll.2 and 3 begin with inversion, devices which emphasize the yearning to be called. The poet is determined to follow the voice of God. All he asks for is His call: the poet's longing to dedicate his life to God only is omnipresent.

Alun Idris' happiness at entering the Norbertine Canons, the joy of dedicating his life to the Lord, is apparent in his poems. In some musings of farewell, however, the joy is mingled with a melancholic tone, as the affective bond between the poet and this most dear friend of his is still very strong, as we realize in "Waving" (*Beyond*, 246):

> Farewell, sweet phantom, ne'er imagined, ne'er
> E'er thought to be a possible of time.
> Wave on, wave on and on into the air
> Of faint receding years that now must climb
> Into the ancient past where once we trod
> Together in the wind of mighty things
> That were too strong for us, for they were God
> O'ershadowing lost fledglings with strange wings.

How unreal this love had been is implied by the imagery used: "sweet phantom", "a possible of time" suggest how miraculous her appearance had been to him. However immense this friendship and love was, God's pull was stronger, - both had felt the divine pull before: "the ancient past where once we trod / Together in the wind of mighty things". Together they had experienced the divine calling, these "mighty things / That were too strong for us, for they were God / O'ershadowing lost fledglings with strange wings". The image of "lost fledglings" beautifully suggests the awakening love in them, but also points to the fact that they were lost. God apparently had other plans for them. The power of divine providence was "too strong for us", God's pull irresistible.

The yearning to be filled with God, to be overshadowed by Him, is strongly implied in "'And there was evening ...; the first day'" (*Beyond*, 3). The title apparently echoes Genesis 1:5. The poet celebrates his being alone with God, but he feels bound to cry out in the third quatrain:

> O Master, I let go of all not gone
> From fondness' grip; I'd have a grasp of things
> Not made of what we are, for though there shone
> A gentle light that of a greater sings,
> I know of some strange God-shaped void within
> That will not cease to ache till I walk in.

The melancholy felt as a result of the separation from his dear friend is still apparent; however, he is determined to look to God only. He is already thrilled with the idea of being able to feel God again: the divine pull is strongly experienced, - it is so strong that it hurts. Being fully aware that the pain "will not cease to ache till I walk in", the poet is bound to surrender.

Having been received as a postulant at Holy Trinity Abbey at Kilnacrott at the beginning of the academic year, he was voted for acceptance and clothing on the Feast of the Immaculate Conception 1991, that year the ninth of December. Alun Idris reverted to his religious name of David. The happiness of his return to religious life is powerfully implied in "'Your Order is gloriously eucharistic and eucharistically glorious' (Words of a pope)" (*Beyond*, 13), written in retreat on 24th November 1991. The poem radiates with tender love for God:

> 'Tis good, 'tis good to be for ever thine,
> To gaze upon thy throne, and in thy home
> To have my little dwelling, even mine,
> Hard by thy tent, where Thou dost whisper, "Come,
> Come often, come e'en closer, come and stay
> A lengthy moment here where men come not
> For converse with their God upon their way
> To regions where much action is forgot."
> O sun whence rays of love now warm this road
> That henceforth lies ahead, I would Thee feel,
> Thee fondle, handle, and this small abode
> E'er with my loving shelter and oft kneel
> Where angels are, where matters of great weight
> Can for an unknown matter stand and wait.

3.4.8. THE TWO VOCATIONS: COMPLEMENTARY FACETS OF ONE PERSON?

The meditations written during the period outside monastic quarters, as well as already during Alun Idris' restless search, mirror the poet's development from regarding the religious and the secular world as separated entities to a view of unification. During the silent years in contemplative monasteries he experienced the difference between the two worlds as firmly existing, an attitude, which was to change after leaving La Trappe. The poems reflect the idea of assuming that there is no such distinction, that it is man-made, for, after all, the whole of creation was made by God alone. As is implied in the poems, one can find the Lord in non-monastic surroundings as well, which Alun Idris most intensely experienced in the Charismatic Renewal, where the first love for God, the sparkling yearning for God, was powerfully experienced. His firm belief in the power and necessity of the spiritual renewal in Wales is reflected in the verse.

The poet keeps trusting the guiding hands of providence, his faith in God never leaves him, despite difficult moments of utmost despair. The poems echo his personal way to purification: on the stony path to God, when seemingly all is shattered, a tiny glimmer of hope is always left.

The yearning for solitude and reclusion was still strongly felt by the poet: his verse echoes the bliss as well as the hell experienced in the solitary life of a recluse. He does not shrink from describing its difficult, disillusioning sides, nor does he negate the beauty and ecstasy contained therein. The joy of being enclosed again, of feeling the union with God, is firmly conveyed. While the poems written at his entry at Farnborough Abbey are still dominated by a melancholic mood caused by the difficulties experienced before, the poems written after the decision to enter the Norbertine Canons radiate the love of their author. The experience of human love had let the poet mature in personality, its beauty made him realize not only that all human love originates in God, but also made him aware of how much stronger divine love is. And it was so strong that he was bound to give in, happily, and be united with God again. The spiritual journey laden with numerous hurdles and sheer invincible difficulties, is honestly described in his poetry: it reflects the inner struggle of a man who has to decide about his future path. He does not negate his love towards his beloved "angel": this openness enabled him to experience divine love all the more. Comparing the two loves so powerfully felt within his heart allowed him to judge in the end and decide where his future lies, where his days point: "t'ward Godhead's worth".[201]

The majority of the poems are sonnets: the sonnet has now become the preferred form, best suited for his verse. Alun Idris takes particular care in metrical regularity, only rarely are such deviations to be found as were common in previous periods. The sonnets are characterized by the employment of long sentences and run-on lines. Despite the fact that he

---

[201] "I am here. Why look any further? (At night, before the monstrance)" (*Beyond*, 236).

employs Shakespearian sonnets only, there is a trend to a change of thought after the second quatrain, taking a different point of view or representing the answer to a question exposed in the previous two quatrains. The closing couplet is often integrated into the third quatrain, which suggests a development of thought typical of the Italian form. However, the special role of the closing couplet cannot be negated, for in many a poem it still functions as an epigrammatic close.

The poet takes great care in the choice of his imagery, which often provokes manifold associations and rich connotations. The style is archaic as it was before; there are only very few exceptions to that rule. It is deliberately used to supply a solemn tone, which provides the ground for his mainly religious meditations. Thus the archaic forms are effectively employed. The rhythm of his verse changes according to the development of the thought. The poet also makes frequent use of alliteration, assonance and consonance, sound and sense being skilfully integrated. This characteristic feature marks him as a truly Welsh poet firmly believing in the tradition of verse, opposed to modern trends now current in Wales. His traditional way of writing is nourished by his Welsh background. In Welsh literature, tradition and the preservation of literary forms have always been of utmost importance, as is clearly demonstrated at the Eisteddfod, the national Welsh festival, where the bards are crowned to this day. Welsh literature has kept the tradition, a fact which Alun Idris applies to his English verse as well.

The poet feels a strong link between the arts, beauty and God, often implying that arts are directly inspired by God. He lets his poetic vein flow in the belief that by creating beauty he is able to pass on eternal truth. In this sense he attributes to poets an intermediary function of transmitting truth to their readers, suggesting thereby the role of poets as prophets. The reader with a receptive mind will allow the word to resonate interiorly.

4. CONCLUSION

The foundation of life in a strictly contemplative monastery is love. Without love no such existence is possible. The contemplative monk, burning with his love for God and shining in His presence, searches for ways and means to declare his love, to celebrate it. Love for God made the poetic vein in Alun Idris start to flow, stimulated the urge to write manifestations of beauty in His honour. This love is fundamental to the poetry of Alun Idris.

The Carthusians lead a life of almost total solitude and perpetual prayer. However, literary activities are not excluded, in order to provide a balance and comply with the intellectual needs of the monks. The list of Carthusians who have written poetry in Latin is considerable. Occasional poetic composition certainly does not endanger the monastic vocation, it rather helps the contemplative monk to satisfy his need for creativity. Serious problems arise, however, when the Carthusian monk has a truly poetic vocation. To the vocational poet-monk, the poetic vein is the ideal tool to express and celebrate his experience of the aspired union with God, his poetry becomes a form of contemplation, of prayer even. This concept of a seemingly perfect symbiosis contains, however, a latent source of danger. The poet-monk might commence to regard his poetic output, which was doubtless written for God only and to please Him alone, as a potential spiritual fountain for other souls also in search of God. His own personal experience with the divine, which he managed to capture in his verse, might be of help to others: a perfectly justifiable motivation to publish the verse, as publication means to reach a great number of souls. Alun Idris regards his poetry as a work for God, - he does not in the least aspire towards literary renown. This is evidenced by the fact that when his work was finally published, it was printed anonymously, although he was no longer a member of the Carthusian Order. He considers the writing of poetry as a form of "crystalizing truth, giving God to others in a different form" (letter, 28.2.1990). However, the Carthusian Order, which shuns publicity on principle and which does not wish to attract any attention at all, was firmly opposed to his literary pursuits, above all to his desire to publish his poetry, which clashes with the Order's principles; the awareness of not being allowed to publish his verse the poet himself describes as "one of the frustrations of the Carthusian regime" (letter, 19.11.1989). From the literary as well as the pastoral point of view Alun Idris' Carthusian poetry represents the perfect symbiosis of the poetic vein and strict monasticism: the lyrical musings and meditations are of a depth of thought and mastery of poetic form rarely to be found in an age like ours. His verse reflects the austere life in a Carthusian cell. The firmness of his belief, assailed nevertheless by spiritual struggles, utmost despair as opposed to ecstatic happiness, the fruits of silence contrasted by desperate loneliness, represent an immensely fruitful source for his poetry, a feeling he often succeeds in poignantly conveying. Enhanced by the skilful use of traditional verse forms, his musings merge into a poetry not only of high spiritual value but also offer great aesthetic pleasure. However, it must not be forgotten that the Carthusian Order is not a teaching Order. It has never been reformed (cf. Zadnikar 1983,

52), and one has to respect its principles. Thus from the Carthusian point of view, the Carthusian vocation is irreconcilable with the truly poetic vein.

Similar to the Carthusians, the Trappist monks lead a silent life in the presence of God, although the community element is much more strongly stressed. They follow a strict rule of silence. The famous example of the Trappist monk Thomas Merton shows that the union of the monastic and the poetic vocation is possible. Merton writes about the nature of solitude:

> True solitude is a participation in the solitariness of God - Who is in all things. His solitude is not a local absence, but a metaphysical transcendence. His solitude is His Being [...]. For us solitude means withdrawal from an artificial and fictional level of being which men, divided by original sin, have fabricated in order to keep peace with concupiscence and death. But by that very fact the solitary finds himself on the level of a more perfect spiritual society - the city of those who have become real enough to confess and glorify God (that is: life), in the teeth of death. (Merton 1956, 262)

It is a long way to true solitude: overwhelming moments of pure experience, of complete isolation and total silence, which makes real contemplation possible. Such experience is essentially incommunicable to others, yet it can be captured in the form of poetry. Merton was aware of his duty: "Coming to the monastery has been for me exactly the right kind of withdrawal. It has given me perspective. It has taught me how to live. And now I owe everyone else in the world a share in that life." (Merton 1956, 313).

Similarly, Alun Idris feels that he has to fulfil a duty to his fellow-men. Like many contemplatives, he craves for silence, which is the "voice of God". Only in the midst of silence can he really experience the freedom of God's presence. He feels compelled to try to translate the "wordless" into words, to convey some sense of the holy silence, which lies beneath those words, to help others reflect upon the role of silence in their own lives. Having taken a vow of silence himself, he knows how misleading words can be. Used in the right way, however, they can lead others to greater self-knowledge. Many of the poems written as a Trappist monk prove that to the young novice spiritual experience, the encounter with God, is an existential reality, a matter of actual being. This awareness, complemented by the presence of true feeling, gives strength to his poetry.

The greatest solitaries have written with their fellow men in mind, in order that they might come to a more complete understanding of themselves in the course of reading about such an experience, and acquire a deeper understanding of God in the process: Augustine and other fathers of the Church, Montaigne, Kierkegaard, Thoreau and Merton, for example. It is the fruit of their solitude to be able to share their experience with others while still remaining themselves, alone, mysterious, and inaccessible to the end. This great gift demands enormous emotional and spiritual resources in practice (cf. Hopkins 1976, 99). Poetry as the fruit of the contemplative's solitude coincides with the following definition of the value and function of poetry in general:

> [Poems] exist to bring us a sense and a perception of life, to widen and sharpen our contacts with existence. Their concern is with experience. We all have an inner need to live more deeply and fully and with greater awareness, to know the experience of others and to know better our own experience. [...] Literature [...] can be used as a gear for stepping up the intensity and increasing range of our experience, and as a glass for clarifying it. (Perrine 1963, 4)

In the case of Thomas Merton, who was constantly aware of the apparent dichotomy between his aims as a monk and those as a writer (cf. Woodcock 1978, 39), the superiors at Gethsemani realized the importance and value of his literary output and virtually ordered him to continue. At La Grande Trappe, however, the superiors view such creativity from a different angle, branding Alun Idris' writing of poetry as "tout à fait anti-cistercien" (*World*, 42). The difficulties the novice monk faced at La Trappe fostered the poet's burning desire to become a hermit, where he could unify both vocations: his experience in contemplative monasteries in France had proved that he was doubtless capable of leading a solitary life with and for God alone. However, the equally indelible urge to write and be creative had impeded him from persevering in the various contemplative monasteries, for he always perceived the poetic gift as a divine grace, which can, or rather should be used in return to praise God. It was only the Trappist monastery at Roscrea, Ireland, that shared this view with the poet: the importance of poetry was realized and he was encouraged to resume.

In the Premonstratensian Order at Kilnacrott Abbey the superiors experience the monastic and poetic vocation as perfectly reconcilable. At last, the creative vein in an ardent breast, full of love for God, seems to have found rest and is now able to flow all the more powerfully, although some of the inner tension from which the poems in earlier periods were generated is lacking. To date most of Alun Idris' poems have been published, mainly in ecclesiastical literary magazines, which realize and appreciate the religious value of his work. However, the combination of religious, theological and literary value has also been noticed in a number of publishing houses outside Wales which detect in the poetry of Alun Idris a combination only rarely to be found in present times, a poetry for which, nevertheless, there is a reading public. Form and contents blend into a powerful unity, which is of value not only to the Christian reader but also to the non-Christian lover of poetry.

APPENDIX I:

TIMETABLES OF A DAY IN THE LIFE OF STRICTLY CONTEMPLATIVE MONKS

1. THE CARTHUSIANS[202]

Although there may be slight variations in times in different countries, the following sets out a typical day for a choir monk in a charterhouse.

23.30 - 23.40	Rise.
23.45	Little Office of Our Lady.
0.15	Office of Matins and Lauds (in church), sometimes followed by Lauds of the dead; Psalms are chanted fairly slowly. No organ or other form of instrument is used.
2.45	Little Office of Our Lady. Sleep (in cell).
6.30	Rise.
6.45	Little Office of Our Lady. Prime (in cell).
7.15	Spiritual exercises (in cell).
7.45	Conventual Mass (in church).
8.30	Spiritual exercises (in cell).
9.45	Terce. Study and work.
11.45	Sext (in cell).
12.00	Dinner (in cell). (Hour varies according to the season and if it is a festival day or not). Except on Sundays and great feast days, meals are taken in the cells. Food is brought to each cell by a lay brother and deposited in a hatch. Meat is strictly forbidden.
12.45	Relaxation. Cleaning of cell, mending etc. (in cell).
13.45	Little Office of Our Lady. Nones (in cell).
14.00	Study and work.
16.00	Spritual exercises (in cell); also, perhaps, some gardening, sawing firewood etc.
17.00	Little Office of Our Lady (in cell).
17.15	Vespers (in church). Each monk as he enters the church gives a pull at the bell-rope and hands it to the monk who follows. Sometimes Vespers and Matins of the Dead are also recited.
17.45	Collation.
18.15	Spiritual exercises (in cell).
18.45	Angelus and Compline (in cell).
19.30	Sleep (in cell).

---

[202] Cf. Anson 1949, 64-66 and Lockhart 1985, 141f. Additional corrections have been inserted by Alun Idris.

Spiritual exercise is an all-embracing expression of the interior life equivalent to private contemplation, and covers all forms of prayer, lectio divina, religious study etc. In practice, the Carthusian life of contemplative prayer approximates to that of the Desert Fathers. Monastic meditation, prayer and contemplation, study and lectio divina all involve the whole man. Proceeding from his heart, they embrace his entire being at every level. (Lockhart 1985, 142)

On Sundays and solemn feast days, such as Christmas, Easter Monday and All Saints' Day, there is concelebrated Mass in the church at 9.00, and the offices of Terce and Sext are also sung in church. On these days Fathers and Brothers have their midday meal in the refectory - in strict silence except for the reading of a passage from the Scriptures or from the writings of the Fathers of the Church. On these days, also, all the monks assemble in the chapter house during the afternoon before Vespers for a reading from the Scriptures, from the Statutes or, perhaps once a month, for a sermon by the Prior or by someone delegated by him (cf. Lockhart 1985, 142).

The habit worn by the choir monks is made of heavy white wool, the scapular of the professed monks being joined by bands at the sides. Choir novices wear black cloaks in church. Their scapulars are shorter and without bands. Laybrothers wear brown or white habits according to their status. Except that the scapular is shorter and has rounded corners, the shape of the habit resembles that of the choir monks.

The brothers lead a less solitary existence. They only inhabit single rooms, or cells, but not separate houses.

2. THE TRAPPISTS[203]

Weekdays:

3.30	Rise.
3.45	Vigils until 4.45, followed by Lectio Divina.
6.30	Conventual Mass and Lauds.
8.00 - 11.30	Work.
11.45	Sext.
12.00	Dinner.
12.45 - 14.00	Relaxation.
14.00	None.
14.30 - 17.00	Work.
17.15	Vespers - contemplation.
18.00	Supper (known as "Collation"), followed by a time for relaxation.
19.20	Reading before Compline (only for the convent).

---

[203] Fr. Marianus of the Trappist monastery at Engelhartszell was so kind as to supply the information.

19.30 Compline.
20.00 Monks retire to rest.

The day ends with the solemn singing of the Salve Regina (cf. Anson 1949, 79).

Sundays:
3.30 Rise.
3.45 Vigils, followed by Lectio Divina.
7.00 Lauds.
10.40 Terce - Conventual Mass (11.00).
12.00 Dinner.
14.00 None.
17.15 Vespers - contemplation.
18.00 Supper.
19.20 Reading before Compline (only for the convent).
19.30 Compline.
20.00 Monks retire to rest.

Breakfast[204] is taken individually, there is not particular time reserved for it.

In a Trappist monastery one has the sense of great activity going on amid absolute silence. The Trappists lead a life of solitude in community: they lack individual solitude, practically everything is done in common, both prayer and work. Thus it is diametrically opposite to the life of the Carthusians, which might be defined as "community in solitude" (cf. Anson 1949, 77). All day long, except for the offices in choir, the Carthusian is alone with God.

In English and Irish Cistercian monasteries teaching in schools or colleges is not engaged in, except for the two Irish communities of Mount Melleray and Roscrea.

3. THE CAMALDOLESE (Monte Rua / Congregation of Monte Corona)[205]

3.30 Rise.
3.45 - 7.00 Vigils (in church). Lectio Divina (in cell). Lauds (in church). Meditations on the Scriptures (in cell); mass is celebrated in community.
7.30 Breakfast, followed by work; reading possible (in cell).
11.45 Sext, followed by dinner. Relaxation until 14.00.
14.00 None, followed by reading (in cell) or some useful work, either of personal or common utility.

---

[204] The frugal breakfast is called "the mixt" (cf. Anson 1949, 79).
[205] From the Guide Book to Monte Rua, compiled by Fra. Winfried Leopold E.C. (currently General Prior of the Order), 45f.

17.00	Vespers, followed by meditation and Lectio Divina. Supper.
19.00	Compline as the last common activity. The monks return to their cells to pray or read.

When retiring to bed, the monks can say, echoing the Psalms: "In peace I go to bed and fall asleep immediately; for You, the only true Lord, let me rest."

Alimentary regulations:
1. The monks receive three plain but nourishing meals every day. Meat must never be eaten. Fish is allowed during certain periods of the year. Wine is not forbidden.
   From Holy Cross Day (14 September) until Easter the monks fast: only vegetables are served for supper. The refectory is only used on feast days.
2. According to ancient monastic custom there are two lents: the first lasts from the feast of St. Martin (11 November) until Christmas, the second, before Easter, is practised by the entire church. In these two periods the monks abstain from milk, milk products and eggs. Fridays are days of partial fasting.
3. Sick and elderly monks are exempted from the rules above. They receive all they need. The monastic duty to care for others has to be observed as regards their nourishment as well as all their other needs: above all the monk has to care for his sick brethren and serve them, just as Jesus Christ in person (cf. Rule of St. Benedict, chapter 36).

APPENDIX II:

PHOTOS OF VARIOUS CONTEMPLATIVE MONASTERIES

Copyright:

1	Cl. Sélignac (cf. p.33)
2	Ruyant Production, Paris (cf. p.142)
3	Cl. Sélignac
4-20	Huw Jones
21-24	Brother David Jones

3 Church courtyard and church façade at Sélignac

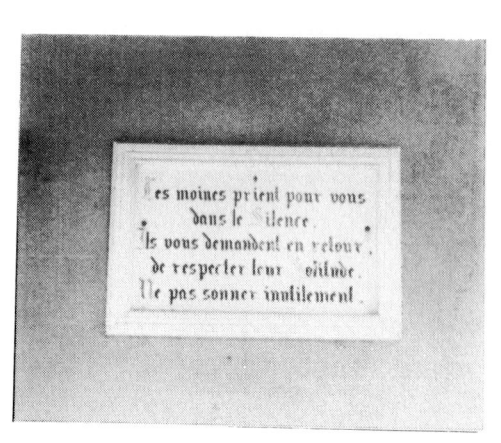

4 Request to the visitors

5 Entrance

6 Great Cloister

7 Great Cloister

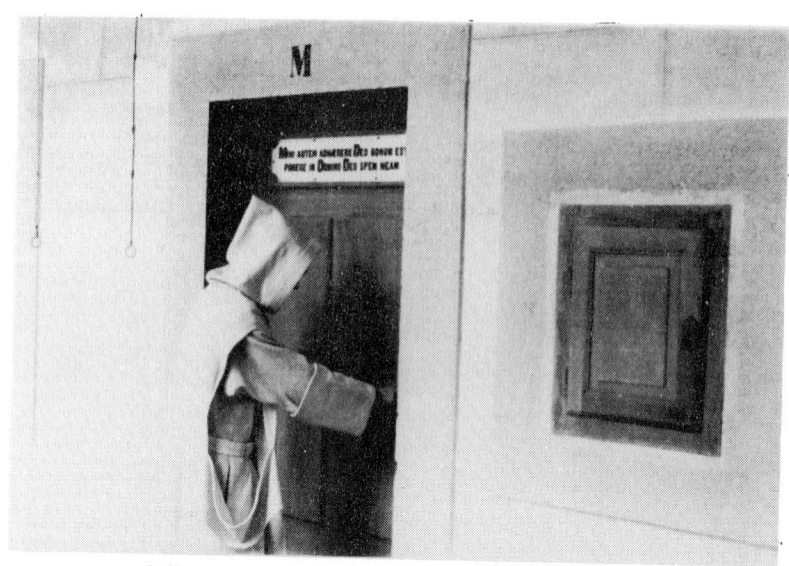

8 Entrance to monk's cell (each cell starts with a letter)

9 Carthusian cell

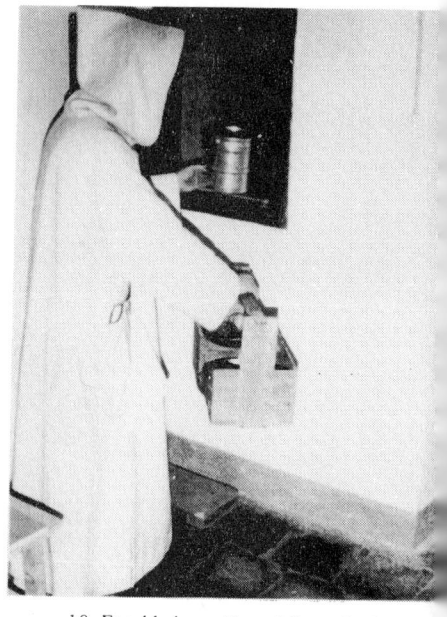

10 Food being collected from the hatch

11 Reciting the divine office in the cell

12 Practising the chant

13 Antiphonary

14 Carthusian monk at work - book binding

15 Writing in the garden

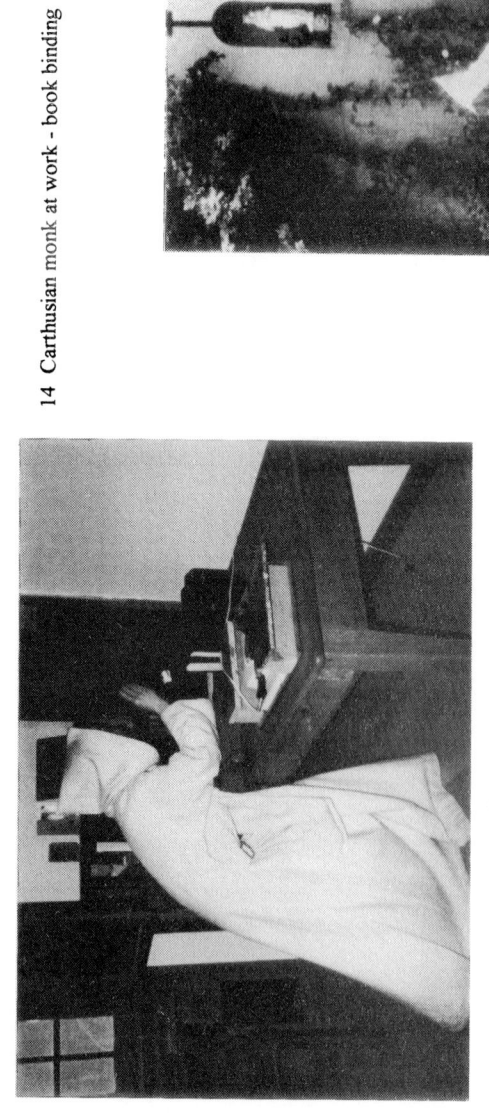

16 Carthusian monk at work - gardening

17 Celebrating mass

18 Carthusian monk in the cemetery
(nameless wooden crosses)

19 In the library

20 Lectio Divina

21 Poet as a novice at La Grande Trappe

22 Poet in working overall at La Grande Trappe

23 Mount Saint Joseph's Abbey, Roscrea, Ireland

24 Blessed Sacrament Chapel at Kilnacrott Abbey, Ireland

APPENDIX III:

A SELECTION OF UNPUBLISHED POEMS

The Sacred Head

O Sacred Head, that held the Godhead's mind,
    And thought of us,
While bearing here the weight of human kind
    And gazing thus
Upon the aeons thus to come and go,
    Look here awhile,
And bid us thy thought know.

O little Head, that read the thoughts of Earth
    Without a word,
Place here thy pain, and while the world's dark mirth
    On high is heard,
Rest, rest a little while thy piercèd brow
    Upon our own,
That we thy thought may know.

O tiny ball, whose call the spheres had heard,
    And come to be,
Hold all the thought of thinking in a word,
    And quietly
Perceive the grieving of the soul too slow
    To pause, to pause,
Thy thought awhile to know.

O mind of Christ, the kindness of all care
    E'er shed on Earth,
Beam into us a knowing of what there
    Is of true worth,
Ere in our haste we marvel as we grow,
    At many things,
And fail thy thought to know.

Mary

From thorns a drop of honey forth did run;
From darkest cloud the morn-star beamed as sun,
And yet of thorns the drop bore not a taste,
And cloudedness the star knew not - 'twas chased:
For drop and star, of such strange origin,
Such gentle and sweet rising, Virgin-bright,
Were but a light to figure what would be.

(The ancient Latin original runs as follws:

Mellis stilla de spinis exiit,
Maris stella de nube prodiit - tenebrosa,
Sed spinosum nil stilla sapuit,
Sed nubosum nil stella habuit - radiosa:
Stilla, stella talis origine
Dulcis ortus et clarae Virginis - sunt figurae.)

The following setting is new:

The picture in the Bible

There was an odour which would fill the world
With memories of hoping: there was bliss
Within a second wherein hours were hurled
From days of hurting ecstasy - for this,
My dream, was all of you in mystic form,
And in two nostrils particles of pow'r
Could jerk the nerves within till they did storm
The dormant depths of Memory's lost hour.
O! wanted one, that wanted to be one
An hour or two with all the time to be
Engraved in cervic banks, a work is done
That undone ne'er shall be - for though I see
But papered smiles, there is awhile within
A fondness in a paradise so thin.

"Unless you change, you will not be received for Solemn Vows."

(Abbot's words regarding solitariness)

To be alone beyond the world of sense,
Or to be sensed by all that sense can own;
To be upon a lonely shore all dense
With absence vast and Presence only known,
Or to be held and felt, to feel a hold
Of old familiar fondling - to be owned
And warmed in one small corner of the cold
And frightened cosmos - or to be yet crowned
With hurting martyr's pricks - for these words come
Not from a hearth whence we can not be lost -
This is the choice, for now the voice of Home
Is long since never heard; for though 'tis crossed,
The Rubicon still flows, and knows the way
To bring us back again to yesterday.

(A lonely shore: at Mt. Tabor Hermitage, Co. Mayo, whose foundress had urged me to think of it.)

News

The power of ink can bend the heavy years
And draw a smile from Reason - e'en the sight
Of carvèd sounds can stroke the hurting fears
Of knowing not the outcome of the night.
Nay, I perceive that strokes can stoke our all,
That there is here, within vibrating lines,
A flow of something mighty e'er so small
That it can touch the untouched part that pines.
I knew not what would come, I knew not well
The world that lay beyond the homely wall
Of solitude's soft pain - I loved the hell
Of wanting and of yearning for the all
That had been left behind, and here I find
The hours of hurting trapped in th'ages' mind.

("By the time you receive this letter it will be published.")

Lines written near the tombs of Keats and Shelley

To leave a word that will be heard awhile
When we have ceased to be - to be beyond
The shore of this wide world, and yet beguile
The thieving æons and the fatal wand
That struck ere pen had gleaned the teeming brain:
To stand, stand very still where stillness stands
Against the rush of passing, and again
Be heard without a voice, but only hands -
This is to halt a second in its course
And bid it hold a cosmos: 'tis to call
The unknown passer by to intercourse
Of soul with lying soul that has said all.
This is, my friend, to hold on to the end
Of Youth and Beauty that no time can mend.

Gregorian

There is a beauty in the heav'ns that here
The earth has ever heard whene'er this came
From something in its soul, for ancient fear
At all the weight of Being e'er the same
Was felt, is felt and will be felt with this
The sound of human sadness, and the years
That travel on these lines that hold the bliss
Of melody all sensate stroke the ears -
Not of a tympan's tremble, but of all
That moves at something fair there where we are
Within, within, awakened by a call
Sent by a fellow-pilgrim from afar.
For he cries out across æonic sound
Of some deep, deeper realm of music found.

Flicker

To stand before the Altar and to call
Not sounds, but Him the Word - to stand and bow
Before a Godhead e'er so very small
That He might fain be missed, for all the how
Of Heav'n's mighty move at this strange sound
Was by no engine traced, and mystery
Is best in silence drawn, for more is found
In incense dense than in philosophy.
O! wonderment of Pulling all unseen!
What is it thus that magically moves
The deepest depths of Man from 'neath this screen
Of Shekinah all veiled? Nay, what are loves,
When Love itself in gentle glow doth say,
"Wilt thou, my friend, my friend, too go away?"

5. BIBLIOGRAPHY

5.1. PRIMARY LITERATURE IN ENGLISH

5.1.1. POETRY (with list of short titles; in chronological order)

Anon. "The Threshold of Paradise: The Poetic Journal of a Welsh Novice Monk in France." *The Threshold of Paradise - Dom Edmund Gurdon. A Memoir by James Hogg.* Analecta Cartusiana 129. Salzburg 1988, 1-90. [= *Threshold*]

Anon. *A World Within the World. The Poetic Journal of a Welsh Novice Monk.* Salzburg Studies in English Literature, Poetic Drama & Poetic Theory 68:2. Salzburg 1988. [= *World*]

Anon. "Poems Sacred and Profane. A Welsh Novice Monk." *Poems Sacred and Profane. A Welsh Novice Monk - D.M. de Silva - Hartwig A. Vogelsberger - With Three Essays by William Oxley.* Salzburg Studies in English Literature, Poetic Drama & Poetic Theory 68:3. Salzburg 1988, 5-45.

Idris, Alun. "A Costly Word". In: *New City* (November 1989), 8.

Idris, Alun. "Gwenfrewi". In: *Seren Cymru*, August 16, 1991, 3. Also published in: *Y Tyst*, August 15, 1991, 3. (with notation)

Brother David. "Late evening at Kilnacrott". In: *The Irish Democrat*, August 30, 1992, 7.

Brother David. "Jesus!". In: *The Irish Democrat*, September 13, 1992, 7.

Jones, Brother David O.Praem. "Hymn to St. Norbert". *The Communicator* 10/2 (December 1992), 5.

Brother David. "Tridentine Mass". *The Irish Democrat*, May 16, 1993, 7.

Jones, Brother David O.Praem. "The Divine Mercy". *The Communicator* 11/1 (June 1993), 5.

Jones, Brother David O.Praem. "St. Augustine". *The Communicator* 11/1 (June 1993), 29.

Jones, Brother David O.Praem. "Wayfarer", *Horizons* (Summer 1993), 43.

Anon. *A World Beyond the World. A Welsh Novice Monk.* Analecta Cartusiana 129:3. Salzburg 1993. [= *Beyond*]

5.1.2. PROSE

Idris Jones, Alun. "Review of: Allchin, Canon A.M. *Songs To Her God. Spirituality of Ann Griffiths.* Cambridge, Mass., Cowley Publications 1987." In: *The Downside Review* 106/365 (October 1988), 301-304.

Jones, Brother David. "Adoration". *The Irish Democrat*, June 12, 1993, 9.

5.1.3. TRANSLATIONS (in chronological order)

Idris Jones, Alun transl. *The Purgatory Manuscript. Le Manuscrit du Purgatoire. The Relations of a Nun with a Soul in Purgatory.* Studies in Women and Religion 29. Lewiston, N.Y., Edwin Mellen Press 1990.

Jones, Frère David transl. "Our Lady of Guadalupe". Unpublished manuscript.

Davies, Oliver ed. *Promise of Good Things. The Apostolic Fathers.* Translations by Alun Idris Jones and Oliver Davies. London, New City 1992.

Anon. *The Hell Manuscript.* Translated by a monk. Middletown, Ave Maria Publications 1993.

5.1.4. UNPUBLISHED ENGLISH AND FRENCH POEMS
(in chronological order)

"Guardians" ("Rita-my angel", "Paul-my angel", "Catherine-my angel", "John-mon ange")
"The Sacred Head"
"Mary"
"Resta con noi"
"The picture in the Bible"
"'Unless you change, you will not be received for Solemn Vows.'"
"Unattended moments"
"Vacans"
"A true nun"
"Lines written near the tombs of Keats and Shelley"
"'I liked the feeling.'"
"קֹהֶלֶת" (Qoheleth = Caller, Assembler, Preacher)
"A night"
"News"
"Gregorian"
"Maggio"
"Flicker"
"Here"
"Noise"
"Fiat"
"Pourquoi"
"Hier ruht in Gott ..."

5.2. SECONDARY LITERATURE IN ENGLISH

5.2.1. RELIGION AND POETRY

Ackerman, John. "Man and Nature in the Poetry of R.S. Thomas". In: *Poetry Wales* 7/4 (1972), 15-26.

Adams, Sam. "A Note on Four Poems". In: *Poetry Wales* 7/4 (1972), 75-81.

Allchin, A[rthur] M. *Ann Griffiths*. Cardiff, University of Wales Press 1976.

Anon. "Poet's Experience in the Monasteries". *Caernarfon Herald*, March 31, 1989, 27.

Anon. "Y Brawd Dewi (Jones)". In: *VIP Wales 1992*. Llandysul, Firstspace 1992, 302.

Anson, Peter F. *The Call of the Cloister. Religious Communities and Kindred Bodies in the Anglican Communion*. London, S.P.C.K. 1964.

Anson, Peter F. *The Religious Orders and Congregations of Great Britain and Ireland*. Worcester, Stanbrook Abbey Press 1949.

Atterbury, Francis. "Usefulness of Church-Music". In: Chambers, Robert ed. *Chambers's Cyclopaedia of English Literature*. Vol.1. London, Chambers 1880, 553f.

Baring Gould, R.S. and John Fisher. *Lives of the British Saints*. Llanerch, Felinfech Publishers 1990.

Binns, Alison. *Dedications of Monastic Houses in England and Wales, 1066-1216.* Woodbridge, Boydell 1989.

Blüm, Hubertus Maria. "Einführung in die Spiritualität der Kartäuser". In: Zadnikar and Wienand 1983, 15-19. [Blüm 1983a]

Blüm, Hubertus Maria. "Wie lebt der Kartäuser?" In: Zadnikar and Wienand 1983, 29-49. [Blüm 1983b]

Bösen, Willibald. *Auf geheimer Straße zu Gott. Das Geheimnis der Kartäuser.* Freiburg, Herder 1988.

Boulger, James D. *Coleridge as Religious Thinker.* New Haven, Yale University Press 1961.

Broakenhielm, Carl Reinhold. *Problems of Religious Experience.* Uppsala, [Uppsala Universitet] 1985.

Brooke, Stopford A. *Theology in the English Poets.* London, Dent 1910.

Buckley, Vincent. *Poetry and the Sacred.* London, Chatto & Windus 1968.

Burr, Nelson. *A Critical Bibliography of Religion in America.* Vol. IV. Princeton, N.J., Princeton University Press 1961.

Burton, Archimandrite Barnabas. *Strange Pilgrimage.* Welshpool, Powys, Stylite Publishing 1985.

Carter, Manfred A. "Poetry Using Ministers". In: *Religion in Life. A Christian Quarterly of Opinion and Discussion* 22/2 (Spring 1953), 243-250.

Cecil, David. "Introduction". In: Cecil, David ed. *The Oxford Book of Christian Verse.* Oxford, Clarendon Press 1951, xi-xxxiii.

Chadwick, Henry. *The Early Church.* Harmondsworth, Penguin 1990.

Curtis, G.W.S. ed. *Dom Maurice Chauncy: The Passion and Martyrdom of the Holy English Carthusian Fathers. The Short Narration.* London, S.P.C.K. 1935.

Davis, Charles. *English Spiritual Writers.* New York, Sheed and Ward 1961.

Doyon, Jacques. *La Recluse.* Paris, Editions Robert Laffont 1984.

Eliot, T[homas] S[tearns]. "Religion and Literature". In: Eliot, T.S. *Selected Essays.* London, Faber and Faber 1966, 388-401.

Every, George S.S.M. "The Two Vocations". In: *Poetry London* 5/18 (May 1950), 22-24.

Fairchild, Hoxie Neale. *Religious Trends in English Poetry.* Vol.I: *1700-1740. Protestantism and the Cult of Sentiment.* New York, Columbia University Press 1939.

Fairchild, Hoxie Neale. *Religious Trends in English Poetry.* Vol.III: 1780-1830. *Romantic Faith.* New York, Columbia University Press 1949.

Fairchild, Hoxie Neale. *Religious Trends in English Poetry.* Vol.IV: 1830-1880. *Christianity and Romanticism in the Victorian Era.* New York, Columbia University Press 1957.

Fairchild, Hoxie Neale. *Religious Trends in English Poetry.* Vol.VI: 1920-1965. *Valley of Dry Bones.* New York, Columbia University Press 1968.

Farmer, David Hugh. *The Oxford Dictionary of Saints.* Oxford, Clarendon Press 1979.

Ferm, Vergilius ed. *The Encyclopedia of Religion.* [Secaucus, N.J.], Poplar Books [1987].

Gaddy, Holly C. "The Poet as Monk". In: *MSE* 9/4 (1984), 1-12.

Gardner, Helen ed. *The Faber Book of Religious Verse.* London, Faber 1979.

Gilbert, Dom H(ugh). "Sonnets from Salzburg". *Pluscarden Benedictines* 81 (March 1989), 9f.

Guillerand, A. *Im Angesicht Gottes. Gebetserfahrungen eines Kartäusermönches.* Würzburg 1989.

Hastings, Adrian. *A History of English Christianity 1920-1985.* London, Collins 1986.

Hauck, Albert D. ed. *Realencyklopädie für protestantische Theologie und Kirche.* Vol. 16. Graz, Akademische Druck- und Verlagsanstalt 1971.

Heim, Bruno Archbishop. "Foreword". In: Lockhart 1985, xi-xii.

Heimbucher, Max. *Die Orden und Kongregationen der katholischen Kirche.* Paderborn, Schöningh 1933.

Hellinghaus, D. ed. *Hundert lateinische Marienhymnen mit den Nachbildungen deutscher Dichter, einer Einleitung und kurzen Anmerkungen.* M.Gladbach, Volksverein-Verlag 1921.

Hill, John Spencer. *Milton. Poet, Priest and Prophet. A Study of Divine Vocation in Milton's Poetry and Prose.* London, Macmillan 1979.

Hogg, James. *Die ältesten Consuetudines der Kartäuser.* Analecta Cartusiana 1. Salzburg 1973.

Hogg, James. *Die Ausbreitung der Kartäuser. - La Chartreuse de Lugny 1172-1789 par Leon Landel.* Analecta Cartusiana 89. Salzburg 1987.

Hogg, James ed. *Los Cartujos Hoy. Una Vida para la Vida de la Iglesia.* Analecta Cartusiana 81. Salzburg 1980.

Hogg, James. "Introduction". In: *Beyond* 1993, xiii-xviii.

Hogg, James. "Kartäuser". In: *Theologische Realenzyklopädie* XVII. Berlin 1988, 666-673.

Hogg, James. "Preface". In: *Threshold* 1988, v-vii. [Hogg 1988a]

Hogg, James. "Presentation". In: *World* 1988, x-xi. [Hogg 1988b]

Hooper, Walter ed. *C.S. Lewis: Christian Reflections.* London, Geoffrey Bles 1967.

Hopkins, Brooke. "Thomas Merton. Language and Silence". *New Orleans Review* 5 (1976), 99-106.

Hurk, A.W. van den, O.Praem. *Norbert of Gennep and His Order.* Transl. from the Dutch by W.J. Smeets and R. Pasensie O.Praem. Averbode, Altiora 1984.

Jasper, David. *Coleridge as Poet and Religious Thinker. Inspiration and Revelation.* London, Macmillan 1985.

Jennings, Elizabeth. "Introduction". In: Jennings, Elizabeth ed. *The Batsford Book of Religious Verse.* London, B.T. Batsford 1981, 9f.

John Paul II. "Message to the Carthusians on their 900th Anniversary, 24 May 1984." In: Lockhart 1985, 137-140.

Jones, Elwyn producer. "Dyn yw Dyn" ("Man is man"). Programme broadcast on Radio Cymru on 22nd November, 1981. Transl. into English by Idris Jones. Unpublished manuscript.

Julian of Norwich. *Revelations of Divine Love.* Transl. into Modern English and with an Introduction by Clifton Wolters. Harmondsworth, Penguin 1976.

Kleineidam, Erich. "Die Spiritualität der Kartäuser im Spiegel der Erfurter Kartäuserbibliothek." In: Zadnikar and Wienand 1983, 185-202.

Knowles, David. *Christian Monasticism.* London, Weidenfeld & Nicolson 1969.

Knowles, David. *The English Mystical Tradition.* New York, Harper & Row 1981.

Krailsheimer, Alban John. *Armand-Jean de Rancé, Abbot of La Trappe. His Influence in the Cloister and the World.* Oxford, Clarendon Press 1974.

Kranz, Gisbert. *Lexikon der christlichen Weltliteratur*. Freiburg, Herder 1978.

Lapati, Americo D. *John Henry Newman*. New York, Twayne Publishers 1972.

Leclercq, Jean O.S.B. *The Love of Learning and Desire for God. A Study of Monastic Culture*. Transl. by Catharine Misrahi. New York, Fordham University Press 1982.

Leigh-Fermor, Patrick. *Eine Zeit der Stille*. Frankfurt am Main, Heinrich Scheffler 1961.

Lentfoehr, Sister Thérèse. *Words and Silence. On the Poetry of Thomas Merton*. New York, New Directions 1979.

Levi, Peter. "Introduction". In: Levi, Peter ed. *The Penguin Book of English Christian Verse*. Harmondsworth, Penguin 1988, 19-31.

Lissner, Will. "Toast of the Avant-Garde. A Trappist Poet". In: *The Catholic World* 166/995 (Feb. 1948), 424-432.

Little, Bryan. *Abbeys and Priories in England and Wales*. New York, Holmes & Meier Publishers 1979.

Lockhart, Robin Bruce. *Halfway to Heaven. The Hidden Life of the Sublime Carthusians*. With a Foreword by Archbishop Bruno Heim. London, Methuen 1985.

Maritain, Jacques. *Art and Scholasticism*. With Other Essays. Transl. by J.F. Scanlan. London, Sheed & Ward 1943.

Martin, F. David. *Art and the Religious Experience. The Language of the Sacred*. Lewisburg, Bucknell University Press 1972.

Mathias, Roland. "Philosophy and Religion in the Poetry of R.S. Thomas." In: *Poetry Wales* 7/4 (1972), 27-45.

Mayled, Jon. *Religious Art*. Hove, Wayland 1987.

Merton, Thomas. *Contemplation in a World of Action*. Introduced by Jean Leclercq. London, Unwin Paperbacks 1980.

Merton, Thomas. *Meditationen eines Einsiedlers. Über den Sinn von Meditation und Einsamkeit*. Zürich, Benzinger Verlag 1976.

Merton, Thomas. *The Sign of Jonas*. New York, Garden City 1956.

Merton, Thomas. *Wie der Mond stirbt. Das letzte Tagebuch des Thomas Merton*. Wuppertal, Peter Hammer Verlag 1976.

Mörwald, Eva. "Poetry in the Order. A Welsh Novice Monk." In: Hogg, James, Hubmayer, Karl and Dorothea Steiner. *English Language and Literature. Positions and Dispositions*. Festschrift zum 25jährigen Bestehen des Instituts für Anglistik und Amerikanistik der Universität Salzburg. Salzburger Studien zur Anglistik und Amerikanistik 16 (1990), 73-82.

Moffatt, James. *A New Translation of the Bible. Containing the Old and New Testaments*. London, Hodder & Stoughton 1934.

The New English Bible. Popular Edition. OUP and CUP 1961.

The New Testament in Four Versions. King James, Revised Standard, Phillips Modern English, New English Bible. London, Collins' Clear Type Press 1967.

Nova Vulgata Bibliorum Sacrorum Editio. Rome, Libreria Editrice Vaticana 1986.

Ormond, John. "R.S. Thomas: Priest and Poet. A Transcript of John Ormond's Film for B.B.C. Television, broadcast on April 2nd, 1972. Introduced by Sam Adams." In: *Poetry Wales* 7/4 (1972), 49-57.

Plessix Gray, Francine du. "Thomas Merton. Man and Monk". In: *The New Republic*, May 26, 1979, 23-30.

Posada, G. *Der hl. Bruno. Vater der Kartäuser*. Köln 1987.

Pouchin Mould, Daphne D.C. *The Monasteries of Ireland. An Introduction*. London, B.T. Batsford 1976.

Reynolds, Anna Maria ed. *A Showing of God's Love. The Shorter Version of 16 Revelations of Divine Love*. London, Longman & Green 1958.

Reynolds, E.E. *The Roman Catholic Church in England and Wales. A Short History*. Wheathampstead, Anthony Clarke Books 1973.

Ryan, John. *Irish Monasticism. Origins and Development*. Dublin, Irish Academic Press 1986.

Ryan, Robert M. *Keats. The Religious Sense*. Princeton, New Jersey, Princeton University Press 1976.

Schwaiger, Georg. *Mönchtum, Orden, Kloster. Von den Anfängen bis zur Gegenwart*. München, Beck 1993.

Seidle, P. Basilius ed. *Die Benediktus-Regel. Lateinisch-deutsch*. Beuron, Beuroner Kunstverlag 1978.

A Selection from your 100 Best Hymns. London, Macdonald 1980.

Sommerfeldt, John R. ed. *Cistercian Ideals and Reality*. Kalamazoo, Michigan, Cistercian Publications 1978.

Spurgeon, Caroline F. *Mysticism in English Literature*. Cambridge, CUP 1913.

Thielen, James A. "Thomas Merton. Poet of the Contemplative Life". In: *The Catholic World* 169 (1949), 85-90.

Thomas, George Finger. *Poetry, Religion and the Spiritual Life*. Houston, 1951.

Thomas, Hywel. "Gerard Manley Hopkins and John Duns Scotus." In: *Religious Studies* 24 (1988), 337-364.

Thompson, E. Margaret. *The Carthusian Order in England*. London, S.P.C.K. 1930.

Veuillot, Louis. *Les Pélerinages en Suisse*. Tours, 1877.

Wakefield, Gordon S. *Kindly Light. Meditations on Newman's Poems*. London, Epworth Press 1984.

Walhout, Donald. *Send My Roots Rain. A Study of Religious Experience in the Poetry of G.M. Hopkins*. Athens London, Ohio University Press 1981.

Weatherby, Harold L. *The Keen Delight. The Christian Poet in the Modern World*. Athens, The University of Georgia Press 1975.

Weber, Sarah Appleton. *Theology and Poetry in the Middle English Lyric. A Study of Sacred History and Aesthetic Form*. [Columbus], Ohio State University Press 1969.

Wolters, Clifton. "Introduction". In: Julian of Norwich. *Revelations of Divine Love*. Transl. into Modern English by Clifton Wolters. Harmondsworth, Penguin 1976, 11-46.

Woodcock, George. *Thomas Merton. Monk and Poet. A Critical Study*. Edinburgh, Canongate 1978.

Zadnikar, Marijan. "Die frühe Baukunst der Kartäuser." In: Zadnikar and Wienand 1983, 51-137.

Zadnikar, Marijan and Adam Wienand eds. *Die Kartäuser. Der Orden der schweigenden Mönche*. Köln, Wienand Verlag 1983.

5.2.2. WALES

Abse, Dannie. "Introduction". In: Abse, Dannie ed. *Wales in Verse*. London, Secker & Warburg 1983, xi-xiii.

Adams, Sam ed. *Ten Anglo-Welsh Poets. An Anthology of Poems by Gwyn Williams, Glyn Jones, Roland Mathias, Harri Webb, Leslie Norris, John Ormond, Raymond Garlick, John Tripp, Gillian Clarke & John Pook*. Cheadle Hulme, Cheadle, Carcanet Press 1974.

Anon. "Salute to a Poet. Review of D. Thomas's Collected Poems 1934-52, published by Dent." In: *Times Literary Supplement*, November 28, 1952.

Archard, Cary. "Editorial". In: *Poetry Wales* 21/1 (1985), 5f.

Bromwich, Rachel. "Introduction". In: Bromwich, Rachel ed. *The Beginnings of Welsh Poetry. Studies by Sir Ifor Williams*. Cardiff, University of Wales Press, 1972, vii-xv.

Cohen, Joseph ed. *The Poetry of Dannie Abse. Critical Essays and Reminiscences*. London, Robson Books 1983.

Conran, Anthony ed. *The Penguin Book of Welsh Verse*. Harmondsworth, Penguin 1967.

Fraser, Maxwell. *Wales*. Vol. 1: *The Background*. London, Robert Hale 1952.

Garlick, Raymond. "Introduction". In: Williams, John Stuart and Meic Stephens eds. *The Lilting House*. London, Dent 1969, xix-xxi.

Garlick, Raymond and Roland Mathias. *Anglo-Welsh Poetry 1480-1980*. Bridgend, Poetry Wales Press 1980.

Humphreys, Emyr. *The Taliesin Tradition. A Quest for the Welsh Identity*. London, Black Raven Press 1983.

Jarman, A.O.H. *Aneirin. Y Gododdin, Britain's Oldest Heroic Poem*. Llandysul, Gomer Press 1988.

Jenkins, Mike. "Editorial". In: *Poetry Wales* 22/1 (1987), 5f.

Jenkins, Mike. "Editorial". In: *Poetry Wales* 24/1 (1988), 2.

Jones, Bobi and Gwyn Thomas. *The Dragon's Pen. A Brief History of Welsh Literature*. Llandysul, Gomer Press 1986.

Jones, Glyn. *The Dragon Has Two Tongues. Essays on Anglo-Welsh Writers and Writing*. London, Dent 1968.

Jones, Gwyn ed. *The Oxford Book of Welsh Verse in English*. Oxford, OUP 1977.

Lloyd, D.M. and E.M. Lloyd eds. *A Book of Wales*. London, Collins 1953.

Mathias, Roland. *Anglo-Welsh Literature. An Illustrated History*. Bridgend, Poetry Wales Press 1987.

Mathias, Roland. "Literature in English." In: Stephens 1979, 207-238.

Morris, Jan ed. *My Favourite Stories of Wales*. Guildford, Lutterworth 1980.

Parry, Thomas. *A History of Welsh Literature*. Transl. from the Welsh by H. Idris Bell. Oxford, Clarendon Press 1962.

Parry, Thomas. *The Oxford Book of Welsh Verse*. Oxford, OUP 1983.

Parry-Williams, T.H. *Detholiad o Gerddi T.H. Parry-Williams. (A Selection of the Poems of T.H. Parry-Williams.)* Llandysul, Gwasg Gomer 1972.

Polk, Dora. *A Book Called Hiraeth. Longing for Wales*. Port Talbot, Alun Books 1982.

Rees, Ben. *Wales. The Cultural Heritage*. Ormskirk, Hesketh 1981.

Rodgers, William Robert. "Dylan Thomas. W.R. Rodgers gives a personal appreciation". In: *The Listener*, May 27, 1954, 913.

Rowlands, John. "Literature in Welsh". In: Stephens 1979, 167-206.

Stephens, Meic. "Preface." In: Stephens, Meic ed. *The Oxford Companion to the Literature of Wales*. Oxford, OUP 1986, v-x.

Stephens, Meic ed. *The Arts in Wales 1950-75*. Cardiff, Welsh Arts Council 1979.

Stephens, Meic ed. *A Book of Wales*. London, Dent 1987.

Thomas, Gwyn. "Welsh Literature after the Act of Union". In: Jones and Thomas 1986, 48-98.

Williams, Raymond. "Introduction". In: Stephens 1979, 1-4.

Williams Parry, R. *'Yr Hav' A Cherddi Eraill*. (*'Summer' and Other Poems*.) Denbigh, Gwasg Gee 1978.

5.2.3. GENERAL REFERENCE BOOKS CITED IN THE PRESENT STUDY

Böhler, Reinhard. *Die Funktion der Dichtung in der Theorie Sir Philip Sidneys*. Inaugural-Dissertation der Philosophischen Fakultät der Friedrich-Alexander-Universität Erlangen. Nürnberg 1971.

Boulton, Marjorie. *The Anatomy of Poetry*. London, Routledge & Kegan Paul 1972.

Carlyle, Thomas. *On Heroes, Hero-Worship and the Heroic in History*. London, Chapman and Hall [1840].

Dante, Alighieri. *La Divina Commedia. A Cura di Natalino Sapegno*. Milano, Riccardo Ricciardi Editore [1957].

Ellis, John, M. *The Theory of Literary Criticism. A Logical Analysis*. Berkeley: University of California Press 1974.

Feuillerat, Albert ed. *The Prose Works of Sir Philip Sidney*. Vol. III: *The Defence of Poesie. Political Discourses, Correspondence, Translation*. Cambridge, CUP 1968.

Gautier, Théophile. "A Zurbaran". In: Jasinski, René ed. *Poésies complètes de Théophile Gautier*. Vol.2. Paris, Nizet 1970, 309-311.

Hamer, Enid. *The Metres of English Poetry*. London, Methuen 1966.

Homer. *Odyssee und Homerische Epen*. München, DTV/Artemis 1990.

Hutchinson, Thomas ed. *The Poetical Works of Wordsworth*. London, OUP 1932.

Lilly, William Samuel. "The Mission of Tennyson". In: Lilly, William Samuel. *Studies in Religion and Literature*. London, Chapman & Hall 1904, 31-52.

Perrine, Laurence. *Sound and Sense. An Introduction to Poetry*. New York, Harcourt 1963.

Roberts, Michael. "Introduction to the First Edition". In: Roberts, Michael ed. *The Faber Book of Modern Verse*. Revised by Peter Porter. London, Faber and Faber 1982, 21-47.

Selincourt, Ernest de ed. *William Wordsworth. The Prelude or Growth of a Poet's Mind*. Oxford, Clarendon Press 1959.

Spender, Stephen and Donald Hall eds. *The Concise Encyclopedia of English and American Poets and Poetry*. London, Hutchinson 1963.

Stallworthy, Jon. "Introduction". In: Stallworthy, Jon ed. *The Penguin Book of Love Poetry*. Harmondsworth, Penguin 1973, 19-28.

Willcock, Gladys Doidge and Alice Walker eds. *The Arte of English Poesie by George Puttenham*. Cambridge, CUP 1936.

5.3. PRIMARY LITERATURE IN WELSH

5.3.1. POETRY (with English translation of the titles in brackets; in chronological order)

"Capel cildwrn". In: *Seren Cymru*, November 11, 1988, 5.

"La Somme". In: *Seren Cymru*, November 11, 1988, 5.

"Ἅγιος, ἀθάνατος" ("Holy, immortal One"). In: *Y Tyst*, February 23, 1989, 3. [Published under 'Y Brawd John'.]. Also published in: *Seren Cymru*, February 24, 1989, 3.

"Dewi" ("David"). In: *Seren Cymru*, March 3, 1989, 4. [Published under 'Y Brawd John'.]

"Dychwelyd i'r Distawrwydd" ("Returning into silence"). In: *Seren Cymru*, March 3, 1989, 8. (Published under 'Y Brawd John'.)

"Sant John Roberts". In: *Seren Cymru*, March 3, 1989, 8. [Published under 'Y Brawd John'.]

Cri o Gell (*Cry From a Cell*). Llanrwst, Gwasg Carreg Gwalch 1989.

"Gair" ("A word"). In: *Seren Cymru*, October 6, 1989, 7. Also published in: *Y Tyst*, October 5, 1989, 7.

"Bwrlwm byw (Hunangofiant Ewyrth Ithel)" ("The bustle of living. About Uncle Ithel's autobiography"). In: *Y Faner*, October 13, 1989, 9.

"Yn ôl i Bendref" ("Back to Bendref"). In: *Cristion* (March/April 1990), 21. Also published in: *Seren Cymru*, May 18, 1990, 4.

"Y Gosber ar Ynys Tysilio" ("Vespers/Evensong on the Isle of St Tysilio"). In: *Seren Cymru*, May 18, 1990, 4.

"Yr hen blant" ("The dear old children"). In: *Seren Cymru*, May 18, 1990, 4.

"Victoire! Tu règneras! O croix tu nous sauveras". In: *Seren Cymru*, May 25, 1990, 7. Also published in: *Y Tyst*, May 24, 1990, 7.

"Ar lan y Fenai" ("On the shore of the Menai"). In: *Cristion* (November/December 1990), 22.

"Rhodri". In: *Y Faner*, March 1, 1991, 16.

"Gwener y Groglith" ("Good Friday"). In: *Y Tyst*, March 28, 1991, 2.

"Nos y Pasg" ("Easter Night"). In: *Y Tyst*, March 28, 1991, 2. [Printed with music.]

"Nos y dyrchafael" ("Night of Ascension (Day)"). In: *Seren Cymru*, May 17, 1991, 3. Also published in: *Y Tyst*, May 16, 1991, 3.

"Gwenfrewi" ("Winefride"). In: *Seren Cymru*, August 16, 1991, 3. Also published in: *Y Tyst*, August 15, 1991, 3.

"Bambino". Christmas Supplement of *Y Seren*, December 20, 1991, 3. [Words and original music.]

"Bethlehem". Christmas Supplement of *Y Seren*, December 20, 1991, 3.

"Nos y Nadolig" ("Christmas Night"). In: *Y Seren*, December 20, 1991, 3. [Printed with Dom Laurence Bévenot's music.]

"Ar ôl y Cymun" ("After communion"). In: *Seren Cymru*, January 10, 1992, 8. [Tôn: St. Catherine (Tune: St. Catherine).]

"Deigryn (ar ôl gweld llun Raymond Williams)" ("A tear - after seeing picture of Raymond Williams"). In: *Seren Cymru*, January 10, 1992, 8.

"Dyma babell y cyfarfod" ("Here is the tent of meeting"). In: *Seren Cymru*, January 10, 1992, 8.

"Gwawr" ("Dawn"). In: *Seren Cymru*, January 10, 1992, 8. [Tôn: Down Ampney (Tune: Down Ampney).]

"Machlud" ("Sunset"). In: *Seren Cymru*, January 10, 1992, 8. [Tôn: Sandon (Tune: Sandon).]

"Gŵyl Ddewi". In: *Seren Cymru*, March 13, 1992, 3. [Published with Olwen Jones' tune, the poet's mother.]

"Te Deum". In: *Seren Cymru*, July 31, 1992, 8. [Words and music.]

"Trugaredd" ("Mercy"). In: *Seren Cymru*, September 25, 1992, 8. [Printed with music, harmonized by Olwen Jones.]

"Gwely Ysbyty" ("Hospital Bed"). In: *Seren Cymru*, August 20, 1993, 8. [Published under Br. Dewi.][206]

"Wedi mynd" ("Gone"). In: *Seren Cymru*, August 20, 1993, 8. [Published under Br. Dewi.]

"Purdan" ("Purgatory"). In: *Cristion* (November/December 1993), 4.

"Resta con noi". In: Seren Cymru, July 7, 1994, 7. [Italian hymn and Welsh poem, published under Y Br. Dewi.]

5.3.2. PROSE

"Digwyddiad" ("Occurrence"). In: *Seren Cymru*, July 23, 1993, 8.

"Ynys y Saint" ("Island of Saints"). In: *Cristion* (November/December 1993), 4.

"Tragwyddoldeb Trwy Lygaid y Canrifoedd" ("Eternity through the eyes of the centuries"). In: *Cristion* (May/June 94), 9f.

5.3.3. TRANSLATIONS INTO WELSH

Allchin, A.M. *Enlli, Cyrchfa i Bererinion. Bardsey, a Place of Pilgrimage*. Transl. into Welsh by Alun Idris. Denbigh, Gwasg Gee 1991.

Anon. "Sain Taizé" ("The sound of Taize"). Transl. of Taize chants. In: *Seren Cymru*, October 18, 1991, 2.

5.3.4. PUBLISHED MUSIC

Yr Offeren ar Gân. Penygroes, Argraffdy Arfon (Arfon Printers) 1987. [Welsh liturgy, published under Alun Idris Jones, 'Y Brawd Dewi'.]

Liturgy of St. Deiniol. Bangor, Y Coleg Normal 1988.

"Kyrie". In: *Y Tyst*, April 13, 1989, 7. [With organ accompaniment by Arwel Hughes.]

Music for a poem by H. Garrison Williams entitled "Ar Ddechrau oedfa" ("For the beginning of a service"). In: *Seren Cymru*, December 22, 1989, 8.

"Vexilla Regis prodeunt" - "Exsultet caelum laudibus" - "Iam lucis orto sidere". In: *Y Tyst*, March 28, 1991, 2. [Three tunes 'transposed' from Gregorian to modern notation, published under 'Alun Idris'.]

"Et Verbum Caro factum est". In: *Seren Cymru*, December 17, 1993, 8. [Hymn and poem.]

---

[206] The Rev. T.R. Jones, who won an award at the Eisteddfod once, gives a literary appreciation of the two sonnets "Gwely Ysbyty" and "Wedi mynd", thanking Br. David for "two very skilfull sonnets from one who understands the requirements of the measure. The beats and the change between the eight-line section and the six-line section show that clearly.Two profound and memorable sonnets to the experience of losing his father ..." (*Seren Cymru*, August 20, 1993, 8).

5.3.5. INTERVIEWS WITH THE POET

Williams, Rev. Robin, for "Bwrw Golwg" ("Casting a glance"). *BBC Radio Cymru*, spring 1976.

Jones, Huw. "Y brawd a'r Brodyr" ("The brother and the brethren"). In: *Radio Times*, November 21-27, 1981, 23. Reprinted in: *Dinesydd* 85 (March/April 1982), 11.

Jones, Huw. "Y mynach - y golled a'r ennill" ("The monk - the loss and the gain"). In: Erfyl, Gwyn ed. *Radio Cymru. Detholiad o raglenni Cymraeg - Y B.B.C. - 1934-1989 (A selection of Welsh programmes - 1934-1989)*. Llandysul, Gwasg Gomer 1989, 114.

Morgan, Dafydd Densil. "Gwrando ar y gri". In: *Barn* 322 (November 1989), 6-10.

Davies, Rev. Olaf, for "Bwrw Golwg" (on vocation and experiences in France). *BBC Radio Cymru*, autum-winter 1989.

Jones, Rhodri Prys, for "Bwrw Golwg". *BBC Radio Cymru*, broadcast 31 December 1989.

Davies, Huw Llywelyn, for "Cadw'r blaidd o'r drws" ("Keeping the wolf from the door"). *BBC Radio Cymru*, broadcast 5 and 9 September 1993.

5.3.6. UNPUBLISHED WELSH POEMS (in chronological order)

The Carthusian Period:

"Noson o Dachwedd" (7/11/81). ("A November night")

"Toriad Gwawr, bore fy mhen blwydd" (16/11/81). ("Break of dawn, on morning of my birthday")

"Gŵyl Crist Frenin". ("Feast of Christ the King")

"Nos Galan '81/'82, wrth iddi dari deuddeg". ("New Year's Night, as it strikes midnight")

"Yr ail o Chwefror". ("The 2nd of February")

"Ar ôl damwain fel EXCITATEUR" (1982). ("After an accident as excitateur")

"Noson" (1982). ("A night")

"Diwrnod ympryd ar ganol gaeaf" (1982). ("A fast day in mid-winter")

"Noswyl San Ffolant" (1982). ("The Eve of St Valentine")

"Benedicite" (1982)

"Grâces"

"Dydd Mercher y Lludw". ("Ash Wednesday")

"Y Grawys". ("Lent")

"Benedicite (Ar doriad gwawr Sul yn y Grawys)". ("At daybreak on first Sunday of Lent")

"Grâces"

"Benedicite"

"Grâces"

"Benedicite (min nos)". ("Evening")

"Grâces"

"Dechrau'r enciliad". ("Beginning of the retreat")

"En retraite"

"En retraite: Lectio Divina"

"Y pumed ar hugain o Fawrth" (1982). ("25th of March")
"Y pumed ar hugain o Fawrth, 3.45 a.m." (1982)
"Y Llyfr Gweddi". ("The Prayer Book")
"Sul y Blodau". ("Palm Sunday")
"Hawl i gyffwrdd". ("Permission to touch")
"Noson y Pasg, 3.45 a.m." (1982). ("The holy night/Easter Eve")
"Stat crux dum volvitur orbis (Llun y Pasg, 3.00 a.m.)"
"Ar ôl gweld llythyr Mrs James". ("After seeing Mrs James's letter")
"Ar ôl debyn llythyr y Tad Laurence". ("After receiving F. Laurence's letter")
"Cyn dechrau cyfieithu". ("Before beginning the translation")
"Sul y Pasg Bach (cyn gwisgo o dringo at yr Allor)". ("The Sunday in Albis, before resting and ascending to the altar")
"Camera"
"Y Cwfaint". ("The convent")
"Noson glir (Ar ôl y Plygain)". ("A clear night after matins")
"Wrth fynd yn ôl i gysgu". ("Going back to sleep")
"Llythyr". ("A letter")
"Y pedwerydd o Fai". ("The 4th of May")
"'Wrth gwrs y cei di weld Glyn y Groes'". ("'Of course you can see Valle Crucis'")
"Chapitre des Coulpes. (Ar ôl camddefnyddio caniatâd i ofyn cwestiwn.)". ("After misusing a permission to speak")
"Y ddihangfa". ("The escape")
"Cofiwch werthfawrogi'ch braint". ("Remember to value your privilege")
"'Custos, quid de nocte? Custos, quid de nocte?'". ("'Watchman, what of the night?'")
"Femur Sancti Benedicti ... Dens S Polycarpi ...". ("St Benedict's thigh bone ... St Polycarp's tooth")
"Trwyn". ("Nose")
"On ne doit jamais voir les mains"
"Nos y Dyrchafael (4 o'r gloch y bore)". ("The night of the Ascension - 4 a.m.")
"Faim est meilleure sauce" (1982)
"Homo est animal risibilis" (1982)
"Ar ôl i'r newyddion ffeindio'u ffordd i'r Gell". ("After the news found its way into the cell")
"Noswyl y Pentecost". ("Vigil of Pentecost")
"Noswyl Sul y Drindod". ("Trinity Sunday")
"Y Galon Ddwyfol". ("The Sacred Heart")
"Gŵyl Sant Iago". ("Feast of St James")
"Y Pumed o Awst (hanner awr wedi saith yr hwyr)". ("5th of August - Transfiguration. 7.30 p.m.")
"Y pymthegfed o Awst". ("15th of August")

"Wrth ymbaratoi at y Cymun (bore Sul)" (1982). ("Preparing for communion - Sunday morning")

"Yr wythfed o Fedi". ("8th of September")

"Gŵyl San Mihangel a'r Holl Angylion". ("St Michael and all angels")

"Y pedwerydd ar ddeg o Fedi, Gŵyl y Grog". ("14th of September, Holy Cross Day")

"Y Pumed o Hydref (chwarter wedi saith yr hwyr)". ("5th of October - 7.15 p.m.")

Poems written at La Trappe (starting 1984):

"Ar ôl yr wythnos gyntaf gyfan (Diwedd Mawrth, 1984)". ("After the first complete week, end of March, 1984")

"Ar y ffordd i Notre-Dame da la Confiance". ("On the way to Notre-Dame de la Confiance")

"Dydd Sadwrn: le Samedi Saint". ("Saturday: le Samedi Saint")

"Ar ôl dechrau llyfr René Laurentin". ("After starting René Laurentin's book")

"Rhoi'r cudyn gwallt yn yr amlen". ("Putting the lock of hair in the envelope")

"Yn y fynwent (ar doriad gwawr Gŵyl San Bernard)". ("In the cemetery - at daybreak of the Feast of St Bernard")

"Ar ôl pererindod y Tremblay o'r Amerig i La Trappe" (1984). ("After the Tremblay pilgrimage from America to La Trappe")

"Dozulé" (4/7/85)

"Ar ôl offeren gyntaf un o'r Brodyr" (14/7/85). ("After one of the brethren's mass")

"Clywed am Kibého". ("Hearing of Kibého")

"Dogfennau Guadalupe" (21/7/85). ("Guadalupe documents")

"Ar ôl derbyn llythyr a lluniau o Dyddewi" (15/8/85). ("After receiving a letter and pictures from St David's")

Poems from 1986 onwards:

"Fy Nghymru" (22/6/86). ("My Wales")

"Yr Offeren Gymraeg". ("The Welsh mass")

"Ar ôl gwrando ar 'Adlais'". ("After listening to 'Adlais', i.e. echo")

"Ailgychwyn" (29-30/6/86). ("Setting off again")

"Dychwelyd". ("Returning")

"Y Beibl Cymraeg". ("The Welsh Bible")

"Ar ôl hir, hir weddïo (Y diwrnod olaf cyn mynd i Ars)". ("After long, long prayer - the last day before going to Ars")

"Gwenan (Wrth groesi ar y llong)". ("Gwenan - during the sea voyage")

"Y 'Lonely Tree' (yng nghwmni Gwenan)". ("The 'Lonely Tree' - in Gwenan's company")

"Dysgu achau". ("Learning genealogy")

"Y 'Missa de Angelis' yn y Capel (a diwedd gwasanaeth anghydffurfiol cyn iddi ddechrau)". ("The 'Missa de Angelis' in chapel - and beginning of a non-conformist service before it started")

"Trafod cynlluniau". ("Discussing plans")

"Pentre Ifan". (A placename)

"Croes Sant Brynach (ac ailddechreuad y Cylch Catholig)". ("St Brynach's cross - and restarting the Welsh Catholic circle")

"Yr allor gyfarwydd" ("The familiar altar")

"12 a.m., 12-13/8/86"

"Yn nyfnder yr enciliad". ("In the depth of retreat")

"Llanllugan" (18/8/86)

"Ar ôl cyrraedd Prinknash". ("After reaching Prinknash")

"Danfon y llythyr (a derbyn y neges ffôn yn union wedyn)" (21/8/86). ("Sending the letter - and receiving the telephone call immediately after")

"Yr Offeren Fawr (a'r amser tawel wedyn yn eglwys Llandwrog)" (24/8/86). ("Solemn Mass - and a quiet time afterwards in Llandwrog Church")

"Eiliad yr eiliadau" (16/9/86). ("The second of seconds")

"Ffarwél, fy ffrindiau bach" (25/9/86). ("Goodbye my little friends")

"Dewis rhwng grasurau" (4/10/86). ("Choosing between graces")

"Agor y Gair ar yr un adnod â thithau" (13/10/86). ("Opening the Word at the same verse as you")

"Garthewin a Gwytherin" (19/10/86). (2 places)

"I Ddosbarth Saith" (3/12/86). ("For class 7")

"Awn ati eto, blant" (5/12/86). ("Let's try again, children")

"Gweddi". ("A prayer")

"Flavigny" (6/4/87). (A placename)

"Y Llyfr Offeren (Gŵyl y Santes Wenfrewi, 3/11/87)". ("The Welsh missal - Feastday of St Winifred")

"X" ("4/11/87")

"Rhiw Goch" (16/4/89). ("Birthplace of St John Roberts")

"Prinknash (13/5/89, yn gynnar noswyl y Sulgwyn)". ("Early on vigil of Pentecost")

"Gwreichion" (13/8/89). ("Sparks")

"Ymwelydd Neifion". ("Neptune's visitor")

"Cân ryngwladol y Ffocolare" (8/9/89). ("The international song of Focolare movement")

"Tanwydd" (12/11/89 - Rhoi gwersi Ffrangeg i Tania). ("Firewood - giving French lessons to Tania")

"Absennol" (3/8/90 - Eglwys Cwyfan). ("Absent - Church of Cwyfan")

"Pelydrau" (4/8/90). ("Rays")

"'Sbwriel?'" (28/10/90 - wrth ddarllen barddoniaeth Elisabeth fach). ("Rubbish? - Reading little Elisabeth's poetry")

"Gwahoddiad (gan yr Esgob)" (5/12/90). ("Invitation - from the Bishop")

"Ffrind" (19/6/92)

"'Mae 'na lawer o gariad ynof i.'" (4/3/93). ("There is a lot of love in me")

"Hwylio" (25/4/93). ("Sailing")
"Llythyr" (28/5/93). ("Letter")

5.4. SECONDARY LITERATURE IN WELSH

Davies, Nest. "Difyr yw bod efo'r beirdd". In: *Plu'r Gweunydd* (April 1989), 6.

Evans, Glyn. "Gwewyr mynach" ("Pangs of a monk"). In: *Y Cymro*, November 15, 1989, 14.

Jones, Harri Pritchard. "Y grym sy mewn gras" ("The strength which is in grace"). In: *Y Faner*, February 15, 1982, 2. [Review of Alun Idris's poem "Yn ystod distawrwydd (mawr) y Grawys" ("During the (great) silence of Lent").]

Jones, Harri Pritchard. "Cri o Gell". In: *Cristion* (September/October 1989), 22.

Jones, Rev. Haydn. "Desg y Golygydd" ("Editor's Desk"). In: *Y Llan*, 26/24 (March 1989), 2.

Jones, Rev. T.R. "Introductory note to 'Trugaredd' by Alun Idris". In: *Seren Cymru*, September 25, 1992, 8.

Jones, Rev. T.R. "Introductory note to various poems by Alun Idris Jones". In: *Seren Cymru*, January 10, 1991, 8.

Morgan, Dafydd Densil. "Canu'r Gell" ("Singing of the cell"). In: *Barn* 320 (September 1989), 44.

Morgan, Dafydd Densil. "Dwy Gerdd am Dduw'n Ymguddio" ("Two Poems about God's absence"). In: *Taliesin* 44 (July 1982), 18-25. [Review of Brawd Dewi's poem "Yn ystod distawrydd y gawys".]

Nicholas, James. "O'r wasg" ("From the press"). In: *Seren Cymru*, October 13, 1989, 7. Also published in: *Y Tyst*, October 12, 1989, 7. [Review of *Cri o Gell*.]

W.J. "O'r Byd a'r Betws." ("From the World and the Church"). In: *Corwen Times*, March 2, 1989, 6.